ENGLAND
IN THE REIGN OF
CHARLES II

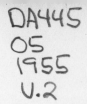

ENGLAND
IN THE REIGN OF
CHARLES II

By

DAVID OGG

SECOND EDITION

VOLUME II

OXFORD
AT THE CLARENDON PRESS

Oxford University Press, Amen House, London E.C.4

GLASGOW NEW YORK TORONTO MELBOURNE WELLINGTON
BOMBAY CALCUTTA MADRAS KARACHI LAHORE DACCA
CAPE TOWN SALISBURY NAIROBI IBADAN ACCRA
KUALA LUMPUR HONG KONG

FIRST PUBLISHED 1934
SECOND EDITION 1956
REPRINTED LITHOGRAPHICALLY IN GREAT BRITAIN
BY D. R. HILLMAN & SONS, LTD.; FROME
FROM CORRECTED SHEETS OF THE SECOND EDITION
1956, 1962

CONTENTS

VOLUME II

privateering: Newfoundland: Virginia: Maryland: the Carolinas: New York and New Jersey: Pennsylvania: the New England colonies: conclusion: the legislative and fiscal relationship between England and the colonies.

SCOTLAND AND IRELAND, 1661–79

By the conclusion of the Third Dutch War England had achieved a standard of material well-being and an acuteness of political consciousness such as could not be matched elsewhere in Europe. In these achievements neither Scotland nor Ireland had taken part. They were nominally sister-kingdoms, but really alien dependencies, their religions, culture, and economic interests being all considered foreign or even antagonistic to those of Englishmen. In the years after 1674 there was this change in the relationship, that English kinship with a majority of the Scottish nation was coming to be realized, while racial contrast with the native Irish was more sharply accentuated. The Popish Plot and the reaction which followed helped ultimately to make possible the union of England with her northern neighbour, for common danger brought about a realization of common interest; equally the same crisis helped to confirm those antipathies which have always separated the Saxon and Protestant Englishman from the Irish Celt.

There were two reasons why Ireland in this period was more fortunate than Scotland, namely, Charles was in sympathy with the Irish Roman Catholics, and the Irish had the good fortune to possess a statesman of integrity and wisdom in the duke of Ormonde. James Butler, twelfth earl and first duke of Ormonde, was one of the most notable of those Anglo-Irishmen who promoted the interests of their country by methods of conciliation and compromise, and his services to the Stuart cause were comparable with those of Clarendon, whom he equalled in prestige and excelled in humanity and vision. He lost more than he gained by his devotion to the Stuarts, and so great was his natural dignity that, when out of office, it was difficult to say whether the duke was out of favour with the king or the king out of favour with the duke. 'Had he been dressed like a ploughman he would still have appeared a man of quality';[1] 'a man of great expense, decent even in his vices'[2]—these two tributes from different

---

[1] Carte, in *Ormonde*, iv. 692.   [2] *Burnet*, i. 170.

quarters agree at least in attesting the gracefulness and nobility of his deportment. Of the other Irish administrators appointed by Charles none descended to the level of the Stuart agents in Scotland. Robartes, who was lord lieutenant for two short periods, at the Restoration and in 1669–70, was hard and grasping; he was also hated as a Presbyterian, but he was just. His successor John, first baron Berkeley of Stratton, was neither just nor austere, but he was not vindictive, and as soldier and friend of Roman Catholics he was popular with many Irishmen. After two years of office he was succeeded (1672) by Arthur Capel, earl of Essex. Though possessed of neither the finesse nor the personal attractiveness requisite for Irish viceregal success, Essex applied himself with zeal and diligence to the accomplishment of his duties, and by mingling moderation with firmness succeeded in conciliating both Papist and Ulsterman; he was also tolerant, in spite of pressure from the zealots, and in his five years of office (1672–7) proved himself one of the ablest and most conscientious of Irish viceroys. On the whole, therefore, Ireland was fortunate in her governors. Ormonde had already acted as lord lieutenant in 1644–5; his second viceroyalty was from November 1661 to March 1669; and his third was in the years 1677–84.

Ireland was a fruitful country, containing some of the best pasture in Europe. Woods had diminished with the coming of the English, but mines were being developed, notably the iron-mines of lord Cork in Munster, and the lead-mines of Antrim and Tipperary. Peat was abundant; freestone, marble, slate, and coal were quarried.[1] The Navigation Acts did not seriously affect Irish prosperity, since Irish provisions could be shipped to the plantations,[2] and in these commodities there was an extensive trade, notably to the West Indies; but a more serious restriction was that of the import of Irish cattle into England,[3] one of many measures intended to keep up English rents. As Irish cattle were assessed at £2 10s. each in the Book of Rates, the crown had to make a considerable sacrifice in its Customs receipts. In Ireland there was complaint and dislocation[4] at first; but in the end, the em-

---

[1] G. Boate, *Ireland's Natural History* (1652), 85, 87, 125.

[2] *Supra*, i. 245. [3] 18–19 Car. II, cap. ii.

[4] e.g. lord Orrery, who had extensive lands in Munster, complained that, in consequence of the prohibition, his estate had fallen in value from £4,000

bargo led to the development of other enterprises, for cattle were thenceforth killed and exported as provisions, and as sheep were pastured in greater numbers, a new wool trade grew up. Hitherto the majority of Irish exports had been to England; thereafter, the majority was to foreign ports, a fact not without influence on the political sympathies of Irishmen. For a time there were restraints on the export of both wool and cloth, but special licences were frequently granted, except to Holland,[1] and there was also profit to be had by smuggling wool to France. That wool continued to be smuggled abroad may be inferred from the complaint of the English clothiers in 1676 that their continental trade was being ruined by the large quantities of Irish material exported to Europe.[2]

The public revenue was derived from two sources—the crown rents payable by prescription or custom, and the duties granted to the crown, including Customs, Hearth Money, and the Excise. During Charles's reign the average amount of the hereditary revenue was £250,000, made up of £70,000 from quit rents, £135,000 from Customs and Excise, £25,000 from Chimney Money, and the remainder from miscellaneous or casual sources.[3] In 1669 these dues were farmed for £219,000; but, after 1683, when the method of farming was abandoned, the revenue was collected by commissioners, and was supplemented by subsidies granted by the Irish legislature, some of them payable in wheat or oatmeal. These figures suggest that Ireland was heavily taxed in proportion to her wealth; but, on the other hand, this was a period of comparative prosperity, as evidenced by the fact that in 1670, 1680, and 1683 there was a surplus of yield over expenditure, the expenditure being accounted for by the Irish Civil List, the military expenses, and the pensions.[4] It became the practice of the later Stuarts to saddle the Irish revenues with claims having

to £500 per annum. (*Cal. S.P. Ire., 1666–9*, 282.) For Petty's estimate of the economic consequences of the prohibition see *Political Anatomy of Ireland*, ch. x.

[1] G. A. T. O'Brien, *Economic history of Ireland in the seventeenth century*, 176–7. For such wool licences see *H.M.C. Rep. Ormonde MSS.*, new series, iv.

[2] *Cal. S.P. Dom.*, *1676–7*, 219, quoted by O'Brien, op. cit. 181.

[3] For details see O'Brien, op. cit. 200 sqq.

[4] In 1676 the expenses on these three heads respectively were £45,906; £146,260; £10,400 (*P.C. Reg.* 65, March 10, 1675/6).

no connexion with either the administration or the interests of the sister kingdom.

Estimates of the population vary between the half million at which it was reckoned in 1659[1] and the conjecture of 1,100,000 made by Petty[2] in 1672. Petty thought that the population was made up of 800,000 Papists, 200,000 English, and 100,000 Scots. Among notes prepared for a parliamentary debate of February 1674[3] are these estimates: number of parishes, 2,278; of priests, 4,000; wealth of Ireland, a fifteenth part of that of England, and its revenue a sixth part. In a memorandum of 1679 the number of families was reckoned at 225,000, of which families only 15,000 lived in houses having more than one chimney; of these latter families, 8,000 were said to be Protestants.[4] Scarce a tenth of the 210,000 cottages were in Protestant possession. Roman Catholic man-power was placed at 150,000, mostly governed by priests; while the few rich Papist families were said to be influenced by their lawyers and by those of their number who had been in foreign parts. Irish shipping amounted to only 10,000 tons, and there were reported to be only about 1,000 seamen.

In accordance with the policy of saving the Irish from themselves, attempts were made to encourage the settlement of desirable foreigners in Ireland; and, as neither the Scots of Ulster nor the Cromwellian soldiers and adventurers were considered desirable, an invitation was extended in 1662 to foreign Protestants;[5] so also, during the Third Dutch War, it was thought that the Hollander might be induced to migrate to Ireland.[6] Sir William Petty, one of the few contemporary Englishmen who expressed a sympathetic view of Irish character,[7] favoured a state-aided scheme whereby Irishmen were to go to England, and Englishmen to Ireland;[8] while other proposals for dealing with the problem

---

[1] For the first of these estimates see *Transactions of the Royal Irish Academy*, XXIV. iii. 319, and O'Brien, op. cit. 122.

[2] Petty, *The Political Anatomy of Ireland*.

[3] *Cal. S.P. Dom., 1673–5*, 157–63. Some of the information was probably derived from Petty.   [4] Ibid., *1679–80*, 353.

[5] e.g. the printed proclamation in French in *Carte MS.* 32, f. 169, where foreign Protestant settlers are accorded the same privileges as Irishmen, and allowed to have six apprentices.   [6] *Supra*, i. 372.

[7] Fitzmaurice, *Life of sir William Petty*, 145–8. For Petty's scheme of union with Ireland see ibid. 277.   [8] Ibid. 148.

of the Celt were these: expelling from the country the small band
of lawyers, clergy, and merchants who acted as advisers to the
rich families; disarming the Roman Catholics and depriving
them of horses; demolishing the thousands of wretched cabins
standing in 'uncouth' places and rebuilding them in the way of
tithings, that is close together; compelling Papists to attend the
parish church; bringing 25,000 unmarried and marriageable
Papist women to England and sending the like number of
Protestant women to Ireland; and, lastly, by forming the
20,000–24,000 able Protestants into a militia.[1] That the native
Irish were a menace to English security was more clearly realized
as French power increased, especially as the threat of French
intervention in Ireland was present throughout the Second
Dutch War, and was repeated in later years when Louis XIV
found that he was being fooled by Charles.[2] Had James II retained the military abilities of his earlier manhood he might have
succeeded in setting up in Ireland a kingdom tributary to France.

More conciliatory was the proposal to secure Ireland by a
legislative union. Such a scheme was put forward by a number
of officers and other persons of English extraction residing in
Ireland, who contended that, in the absence of union, English
people in Ireland were considered foreigners; that descendants
of English settlers became Irish and resisted improvements, and
that many judges were not agreed whether laws made in England
were binding in Ireland. A consequence of this ambiguity was
that embezzling, erasure, and forgery of records were more often
practised than elsewhere.[3] The truth of this last allegation is
shown by the fact that, during the Popish Plot, boat-loads of
perjurers were obtainable from Ireland, providing good material
for the tuition of Shaftesbury and Oates.[4] It may be added that
other legal reforms might have been expected to follow from a
union of the parliaments. Thus, it was not so much poverty as

[1] Cal. S.P. Dom., 1679–80, 353 sqq.

[2] Thus, in August 1682 Louis was reported to have formed the intention
of freeing himself altogether from Charles and possessing Ireland: (lord
Preston to secretary Jenkins, Aug. 12, 1682, in H.M.C. Rep. VII, app. 334.)
See also Cal. S.P. Dom., 1683, 62: information of Capt. Roger Tilly.

[3] Miscellanea Aulica, ed. T. Brown (1702), 203.

[4] See infra, 596. For an instance of 29 witnesses each perjuring himself
in one case see Cal. S.P. Ire., 1666–9, 487–8.

insecure tenure that caused the prevalence of 'nasty, smoaky cabins', occupied by men who held from May to May. Even the chieftains held their estates only for lives, and might be succeeded not by the eldest sons, but by tanists, who were elective; moreover the inferior tenancies were frequently divided among the males of the sept, in a manner not unlike that known in England as gavelkind. The result was that no incentive was provided for improvement; at times indeed human life seemed almost as precarious as in Turkey, and it was said to be not uncommon for restless Irishmen to convey their lands to feoffees in trust, reserving to themselves a life tenure, so that on judgement for treason their estates would not be forfeited.[1] These evils were intensified by the increasing number of absentee landlords, and so Ireland was dominated by three main classes who had nothing but hatred for each other—the native Celt, the Cromwellian soldier-farmer, and the courtier landlord living in London.

Until 1782 the relations between the crown and the Irish parliament were nominally controlled by the institution known as Poyning's Law, whereby the powers of the Irish legislature were limited to the acceptance or rejection of measures submitted by the lord lieutenant and the English privy council. But, long before 1782, the system had been considerably modified; for by 1692 the Irish House of Commons definitely acquired a part in the initiation of legislation, and this privilege appears to have been exercised at times in Charles's reign, through the initiative occasionally entrusted to drafting committees of the Irish Commons.[2] Generally, however, the parliaments of Ireland were as easily controlled as those of Scotland; indeed, except for their sessions in the first six years of the reign, when their aid was necessary for the granting of subsidies and the settlement of the land problem, there was little parliamentary activity in this period; but it may be doubted whether the country suffered much in consequence. From the point of view of the crown, the steady increase of Irish revenues made recourse to parliament less necessary.

Ormonde was appointed to succeed Robartes in November

---

[1] *The present state of Ireland* (1673).

[2] Porritt, *Unreformed House of Commons*, ii. 428 sqq. For the actual procedure see *P.C. Reg.* 59, June 6, 1666.

1661, but before he left England he made his personal conditions with the privy council. These were[1] (1) that no Irish suit for reward or pension should be considered until the ordinary Irish revenue was sufficient to sustain the charges of the crown; (2) that an express *caveat* be directed to the principal secretaries of state and the custodians of the Signet, the Great Seal, and the Privy Seal that no grant concerning Ireland be approved until the lord lieutenant was acquainted therewith; (3) that only fit persons be appointed bishops and judges; (4) that no complaint be received until the lord lieutenant had been informed; and (5) that no new offices be created in Ireland without the lord lieutenant's cognizance. These conditions illustrate the main difficulties confronting Irish administration, and give some colour to the contention that, for a conscientious viceroy, the English Court was a more serious problem than the Irish Celt. His conditions having been approved, Ormonde proceeded to Ireland, where he was soon occupied in the land settlement[2] and in securing the grant of a Hearth Tax by the Irish parliament. His rule was acquiesced in as much by Papist as by Presbyterian. It is true that the moderate Roman Catholics were inclined to expect overmuch from his commiseration, but at least they were encouraged to combine their religion with loyalty,[3] and in their Protestant lord lieutenant they had a statesman prepared to uphold Irish interests, as evidenced by his opposition to the Bill of 1666–7 prohibiting the import of Irish cattle into England. He also did much to develop a native linen industry, and promoted a Bill[4] which was passed by the Irish legislature in 1665–6 whereby it was provided that, after May 1, 1666, no one should let a cottage or cabin outside a corporate town to any one not possessing at least an acre of land, on one-eighth part of which the tenant was required to sow hemp or flax. This measure was supplemented by Ormonde's personal encouragement. Families of skilled workers were introduced from Flanders, the west of France, and Jersey; but the industry, centred at first in Charle-

[1] *P.C. Reg.* 55, June 9, 1662. [2] See *supra*, i. 170–3.

[3] For the convocation of loyal Catholic clergy in Dublin in June 1666 see *Cal. S.P. Ire., 1666–9*, xx and xxx. Ormonde's scheme of separating the moderates from the zealots failed.

[4] *Statutes at large passed in the parliaments held in Ireland* (1786), ii. 157.

ville and Chapelizod, was afterwards developed mainly by Irish and Scots in Ulster.[1]

The only notable incident arising from the discontent occasioned by the land settlement was the plot of March 1663 for the seizure of Dublin Castle and the person of the lord lieutenant. As one of the confederates turned informer, the design was suppressed; but its leader, colonel Blood, after being concealed by the native Irish and Cromwellians, succeeded in escaping to Holland, afterwards to England, where he allied with the surviving Fifth-Monarchy Men, and in 1670 repeated his attempt (this time in St. James's Street) to kidnap Ormonde.[2] Otherwise the duke's administration was comparatively peaceful, and the country remained loyal during the Second Dutch War, when his son Ossory acted as deputy. There was a threat to this security when, in April 1666, a French man-of-war anchored in Kenmare Bay, and in July 1667 sir Jeremy Smith had to hold Kinsale against a possible attack from the Dutch; indeed English loss of prestige in this war might well have been followed by disastrous consequences in Ireland, because the links joining the two countries were as precarious as those uniting India to the British Empire to-day.[3]

The death of Southampton and the downfall of Clarendon in 1667 removed the only statesmen who could in any sense be considered his colleagues; and, as the most eminent of Clarendonians, Ormonde necessarily incurred the enmity of Buckingham and Arlington. His recall from Ireland in February 1668 was therefore not unexpected. He was succeeded in 1669 by lord Robartes, who had already enjoyed a short tenure of office as deputy *in absentia*,[4] and was now to administer Ireland for only a few months. Scrupulous but indiscreet, he encouraged private soldiers to present concerted demands on their officers for arrears of pay,[5] and he upbraided the officers in the presence of their men. A rebuke from the king on this score led to his resignation in May 1670. His successor, lord Berkeley of Stratton, was as dissolute

[1] O'Brien, op. cit. 187.

[2] For good accounts of Blood see *D.N.B.*, and W. C. Abbot, *Colonel Thomas Blood, Crown-Stealer.*

[3] For instances of disaffection see *Cal. S.P. Ire., 1666–9*, xxi.

[4] See *supra*, i.`169.   [5] Bagwell, *Ireland under the Stuarts*, iii. 94.

and dishonest as his predecessor was scrupulous and moral; in contrast also with Robartes, Berkeley favoured the Roman Catholics. Otherwise he had no special qualification for the post, and his rule was memorable chiefly for his altercations with the corporation of Dublin.[1] To his surprise, he was displaced in February 1672 by Arthur Capel, earl of Essex.

Though he had served little in public employment, Essex proved to be a most fortunate choice. He knew nothing of Irish affairs, but he made a study of them; and he remained friendly with Ormonde, from whom he obtained both advice and parliamentary support. The first question to be determined was whether the oaths of allegiance and supremacy should be applied to all persons seeking membership of corporations. Essex decided to enforce these oaths as a general rule, and to dispense with them as he thought fit. He was thus trying to carry out in Ireland the policy which Charles hoped to follow in England by the Declaration of Indulgence; but Charles's enforced withdrawal of the Declaration (March 1673) had its repercussion in Ireland, where the disabilities affecting Roman Catholics had again to be enforced. Like Ormonde, Essex mediated between extremes. He did not drive the Roman Catholics into hostility; nor did he yield to the demands of Orrery and the extreme Anglo-Irish party for the establishment of a strong Protestant militia.[2] His main difficulties arose from brigandage, caused by the dispossessions of the land settlement; to Presbyterian missionaries, who penetrated as far west as county Mayo, riding up and down the country 'like martial evangelists with sword and pistol';[3] to the corporation of the city of Dublin, its faction and turbulence a serious problem for most Irish lords lieutenant; and lastly to the veiled hostilities of lord Ranelagh, the notorious farmer of the revenues, and the irregularities of lord Orrery, who, in 1668, had been impeached by the Commons on the accusation of malversation in his office of lord president of Munster.[4] Behind Ranelagh and his uncle Orrery were Danby and the duchess of Portsmouth, who had a

---

[1] Ibid. 102. [2] Ibid. 109–17.

[3] Bishop of Killala to Essex, Jan. 22, 1677, in *H.M.C. Rep.* vi, app., pt. i. 745.

[4] The impeachment had been quashed by the prorogation of parliament on Dec. 11, 1668.

scheme for making Monmouth lord lieutenant, with lord Conway as his deputy in Ireland.[1]

Nor were these the only problems. Essex wished to secure an elementary standard of honesty in the government of the country, and strove to resist the spoliation of Irish acres by English courtiers. Had the conditions insisted upon by Ormonde in 1662 been adhered to, it might have been possible for Essex to effect some reforms; but he soon found that the course of Irish administration was not allowed to run in its proper channels, and a refusal from one responsible authority might be followed by successful application to another.[2] Some officials, such as the Irish clerks of the crown and the clerks of the peace, increased their fees by instituting vexatious lawsuits; others made fortunes from extortion; all of them were 'quick in getting pardons out of England'.[3] In general, the details of appointments and revenue were so interlocked with the exigencies of the English Court that the powers of the lord lieutenant were to a large extent nullified, a condition of affairs particularly exasperating to a zealous viceroy. In truth, Essex was completely out of place in Stuart Ireland; moreover, Charles himself was at the mercy of Ranelagh, the corrupt tax-farmer, one of the foremost obstacles to efficient administration. The result was the recall of Essex in April 1677. On his return to England he joined the Country party and threw himself into the opposition against Danby; and thus a skilled and honest minister was forced into a fruitless opposition in which he eventually sacrificed his life. But Charles, like Henry VIII, could appreciate qualities which he himself did not possess, and so, instead of appointing Monmouth to the viceroyalty, as he was urged to do, he again selected Ormonde,[4] who was entrusted with the administration of Ireland for the rest of the reign.

When Ormonde returned to Ireland in 1677 he was confronted by a great network of corruption and influence controlled by

---

[1] Bagwell, op. cit. iii. 122.

[2] Essex to Conway, May 26, 1674, in *Essex Papers, 1672–9*, i. 229.

[3] Essex to Arlington, May 23, 1674, ibid. i. 233.

[4] Charles may have been influenced by the opposition of the duke of York to the appointment of Monmouth, who was Danby's nominee. *Essex Papers, 1675–7*, 125–7.

the tax-farmers. Before leaving England he had, for the second time, made his own terms with Charles,[1] and he came with the intention of summoning parliament in order to obtain a grant. To this, the tax-farmers objected that any additional levy might make more difficult the collection of the revenues for which they had contracted.[2] Nevertheless, he thought that a parliament was necessary in order to clear up the remaining anomalies and grievances of the land settlement; so he had a Bill drafted with the object of introducing greater security of tenure in Connaught and Clare, where many titles were in dispute. He also proposed to offer a Bill of Oblivion in order to end factious litigation, and he had in view also some modification of the Hearth Tax, to mitigate the evil practice whereby the collectors distrained on the bed and pot of defaulters. Once again there was a prospect that Ireland might benefit by sympathetic rule, and Ormonde's third administration might have been the most fruitful of all, but in the autumn of 1678 England was dragged into the whirlpool of the Popish Plot, and everything had to be sacrificed to the supreme object of keeping Ireland quiet. It was one of Ormonde's major achievements that he preserved his country for the Stuarts in these stormy years 1678–82. By a series of proclamations[3] the Roman Catholics were ordered to bring in their arms; Roman Catholic institutions were dissolved, and the Protestant militia was strengthened and armed. That complete order was maintained in Ireland served in a measure to discredit the Plot in England.

In the earlier versions of the Plot Ormonde had been included among those who were marked out for assassination; but soon his moderation made him suspect, and for this reason he incurred the implacable enmity of Shaftesbury, who was encouraged by correspondents in Ireland to hope that he might be lord lieutenant.[4] Ormonde's offence was not that his measures were too severe, but that they were not severe enough; for if the Irish had been goaded into rebellion, this fact would have provided conclusive proof that the Plot was a genuine one. How slender were the supports of English rule in Ireland during this crisis was

---

[1] *Ormonde*, iv. 532. [2] Bagwell, op. cit. iii. 125.
[3] *Steele*, ii. 888, 889, 891, 895, 897, 898, Oct. 14–Dec. 12, 1678.
[4] *Shaftesbury*, L. no. 31, Nov. 30, 1680.

revealed by a report to the English Committee of Intelligence in August 1680,[1] when it was shown that there was danger of rebellion on the part of those who had lost or forfeited their estates, and that the Protestant militia was of negligible strength, because most of the soldiers were tenants and married persons concerned only with their farms, while others were old and unserviceable; and so not above 2,000 men were fit for active service. There was neither ammunition nor stores; all the forts, except that at Kinsale, were in ruins; the country was defenceless both against foreign invasion and internal tumult. That such an Ireland should have remained undisturbed[2] during the frenzy of the Popish Plot is one of the greatest tributes to the statesmanship of Ormonde; and when, in May 1682, he was at last able to leave Dublin for London, he could at least congratulate himself that he had not lost his ship.

It was Ireland's good fortune that she had comparatively little history[3] in the reign of Charles II. It was otherwise with Scotland. The Roman Catholic interest in Ireland was not destroyed until the Revolution; in Scotland, the Restoration witnessed the beginning of a strenuous attempt to impose prelacy on the national Protestant Church. Ireland benefited by the rule of Ormonde and Essex; Scotland was for long at the mercy of Lauderdale and Sharp. Neither country possessed those secular institutions which, in England, interposed between sovereign and subject, and accordingly in both of them could be discerned more clearly than elsewhere the real principles and implications of Stuart rule.

The northern kingdom received favourable notice from some travellers. Praise of a disinterested character was bestowed on it by an Italian Jesuit[4] who spent twelve years there, two of them in prison. He remarked on the variety of Scottish products —salmon, coal, linen, salt, and cattle, almost everything, in fact, *praeter vinum et aromata*. He was impressed by the existence in

---

[1] *Add. MS.* 15643. *Minutes of the committee of intelligence*, Aug. 8, 1680.

[2] This was one of Shaftesbury's greatest disappointments. *Ormonde*, iv. 580.

[3] In November 1670 the *Dublin Gazette* ceased to appear because there was no news. (*Cal. S.P. Ire., 1669–70*, viii.)

[4] *Introductio ad relationem missionis Scotiae 1660* in *Rome Transcripts* (*P.R.O.*), 98.

such a poor country of four universities; two of them, St. Andrews and Aberdeen, on the Paris model, and one, Glasgow, on that of Bologna; he admired also the architecture of Glasgow Cathedral. Of the fourteen Scottish bishoprics he noted with pride that no less than thirteen had been founded by popes. He marvelled at the great length of Scottish sermons, and at the custom, not abandoned until the nineteenth century, whereby beadles paraded the streets during the hours of divine service in order to arrest the 'stravagers' or wandering absentees. But this description is exceptional in two respects—it was written by one who had been in Scotland, and it is not abusive; for most of the contemporary 'characters' of Scotland were compiled by strangers who collected their epithets at home.

Scotland was poor, not in the sense that it was declining from prosperity, but in the sense that it had never been prosperous. Crown lands there were worth only £50,000 Scots, or about £5,500 sterling per annum; the total yearly exports, consisting mainly of fish, salt, and hides, did not, at the Restoration, amount to more than £200,000. The population was sparse, great tracts of land were uncultivable, inland communications were undeveloped, and there was a scarcity of capital. Holland was Scotland's best foreign customer, and through the staple at Dort or Campvere were conveyed regular shipments of salt, skins, stockings, and plaiding; but the two Anglo-Dutch wars made serious inroads on this trade, and Scotland was forced to look for other markets, an ambition not realized until, with the union of the parliaments, she was admitted to a full share in the English colonial trade. In spite, however, of these disabilities, Scottish enterprise, assisted to some extent by English capital and Huguenot co-operation, succeeded in establishing a number of capitalist ventures, including a bank, sugar refineries, paper, rope and soap works, and a linen company.[1] Exports of coal to England steadily increased, and in 1670 amounted to 50,000 tons;[2] Scotch linen was also in demand, and was hawked by pedlars whom English constable and justice tried in vain to expel. But for the religious difficulties and the absence of

[1] For this see W. R. Scott, *Joint Stock Companies*, and T. Keith, *Commercial relations of England and Scotland*. For Scotland and the English Navigation Acts see *supra*, i. 245.　　　　　　　　[2] *Grey*, i. 232.

adequate 'vents' for her products and manufactures, Scottish prosperity might well have advanced in the reign of Charles.

This poverty necessitated a lower standard of life than that which prevailed in England, but there were other things which accentuated the contrast between the two countries. In the northern kingdom the nobility had never been tamed as in the south; in consequence the Scottish nobility were still almost medieval—numerous, powerful, turbulent, litigious, and oppressive.[1] Many of them despised their countrymen, and some looked to England for bribes; hence, few of them had the making of national leaders. Hence also, political life was practically non-existent, and the third estate was not merely powerless but despised, because composed almost entirely of tradesmen; nor was there a real middle class, since the lairds or small gentry were scarcely represented in the Estates at all. An example of the contempt in which the Scottish burgesses were held was provided in one of the agitations against Lauderdale (1673–4) when they sent a remonstrance to Charles, which induced Atholl to express indignation that 'vermine and mechanick fellows dare offer such things to His Majesty'.[2] No English peer could have spoken thus of the English House of Commons.

In this void there was only one great national institution—the Kirk, and the ministers were the only functionaries whose influence was unrivalled and uncontested. Nowhere else had the teachings of the Calvinist reformation been worked out to such extreme conclusions; no other race could have deduced so logically the consequences of the Fall and the imminence of the reign of Anti-Christ. Witness a 'tolerable Sunday' as passed by a Presbyterian diarist contemporary with Pepys:

1. May 1659. This morning being in Humbie, after familie duty done, I went to Church and heard Mr. James Calderwood lecture on Math. XXIII, 13. Observation 1: that Our Lord denounceth their woes rather to terrifie his Disciples than to curse the Pharisees. . . 3. That no sin is more odious to God than hypocrisie. 4. That

---

[1] Strongest in territorial influence was the family of Campbell (earl of Argyle) in Argyleshire and the Isles. Many of the boroughs were controlled by noble families, e.g. Cupar by Rothes, Dundee by Crawford, and many of the northern boroughs by Huntly.

[2] Quoted by O. Airy in E.H.R. i. 458.

the kingdom of God is shut upon us all by nature. . . . Thereafter he preached on Matthew V, 4. From the cohesion obs. 1. That such as are sensible of povertie of spirit are always great mourners. 2. That a mournfull spirit is verie agreeable to the Ghospell. 3. That the mourning which the Lord requires is ane inward serious bitter mourning. 4. That those who do thus mourne aright are blissed. Afternoon, he preached on Deut. X 4 and Exodus XX 2. Ane catecheticall question wherein the morall law is conteined. The morall law divided in two tables. 3 opinions concerning that morall law. . . .

After sermons I went home to Humbie and after retirement went about familie dutie.

This was a tollerable good day to me.

A verie filthy rain all day.[1]

Such a religious outlook could not be transformed into episcopalianism merely by the imposition of bishops. In the south and west, notably in Lanarkshire, Renfrewshire, Ayrshire, Dumfriesshire, and Kircudbrightshire, there was maintained an uncompromising hostility to the ecclesiastical system imposed by the Restoration settlement; but elsewhere, especially in Aberdeenshire and the east, episcopacy was quietly accepted, and only Papists[2] and Quakers remained outside the fold. Even in the conformist districts of Scotland, however, episcopalianism was generally little more than a thin disguise for Presbyterianism; for, in spite of bishops and surplices, much of the discipline and worship of the native church was retained. Kirk sessions met wherein laymen, presided over by their ministers, took cognizance of lesser scandals; for more serious matters there were presbyteries, meeting once a month, and provincial synods meeting twice a year, the latter presided over by the bishop. Lastly, appeal might be made to that supreme tribunal, the General Assembly, meeting once a year, at which the king was personally represented. Thus the old hierarchy of representative institutions was preserved almost intact, and into this the bishop

---

[1] *Hay of Craignethan's Diary, 1659–60* (ed. A. G. Reid, 1901).

[2] Then as now there were communities of Roman Catholics throughout the Highlands, but there is little information about them. For a general account of Catholicism in Scotland in this period see A. Bellesheim, *History of the Catholic Church in Scotland*, trans. D. O. Hunter Blair, iv ch. ii.

fitted as a 'perpetual moderator'.[1] But while room was found for the bishop, everything conspired to exclude the graceful ritual characteristic of Anglicanism, leaving Scottish episcopalianism too exotic for the native temper and insufficiently catholic to redeem it from provincialism. This is accounted for in part by the poverty of Scottish ecclesiastical architecture. The Reformation had led to the destruction of many ancient fabrics; only one cathedral on the mainland was left intact, and though Scotland retained her castles, she lost her parish churches. The new structures were unworthy of the old; for, in the country, they were sometimes little better than cottages, and in the towns they were bricked and tiled, and often fitted with galleries. The gallery provided increased accommodation; but its precipitous elevation was no substitute for the gradual ascent of nave, chancel, and altar.

That the enforcement of episcopacy did not destroy the old roots beneath the surface is shown by the continued importance of witchcraft in the national life. In no other country was the injunction *Thou shalt not suffer a witch to live* more faithfully observed than in Scotland, where the Old Testament was interpreted and applied with a literalism unmatched save in Holy Russia. Had the bishops been men of enlightenment, commissioned to wean the country from the judaic Calvinism of the preceding century, they might have set themselves against the cult; but their rule brought no diminution of this superstition, and the Devil retained his hold on the minds of the peasantry. The government did not at first countenance the parish witchhunters; indeed in 1662 arrests for witchcraft were prohibited, except on a warrant from the Council;[2] but this was not generally enforced; for, after a brief lull, there was a recrudescence, and in 1678 the superstition became an epidemic.[3] If it be proved that the instruments of Charles's government in Scotland were not themselves believers in witchcraft, then the conclusion might follow that they hoped to conciliate the populace by pandering to devil-worship; but even among educated Scotsmen of the

---

[1] For this see *A short account of Scotland* by Rev. T. Morer, from which extracts were printed in *Selections from the records of the Kirk Session, Presbytery and Synod of Aberdeen* (Spalding Club, 1846), lxv–lxix; also G. Grub, *An ecclesiastical history of Scotland*, iii. 215–19.

[2] *P.C. Reg. Scot. 1661–4*, xlii.   [3] Ibid., *1676–8*, xxxv.

time, few were sceptical. Sir George Mackenzie, the cultured and 'bloody' lord advocate, may have had his doubts, but he kept them to himself.

In England, though the cult was by no means extinct,[1] yet the pursuit of possessed persons was not carried out with the system and thoroughness of the north. This is amply illustrated by Scottish literature. The reader of Wodrow,[2] Law,[3] and the Justiciary trials[4] cannot fail to be impressed by the absolute uniformity in the confessions of accused persons, so uniform that they might almost convince one of the existence of demoniac influence, as they certainly convinced contemporaries. But the methods employed to obtain confessions account for their uniformity. These methods were pricking by pins (in order to find the anaesthetized spots) and deprivation of sleep, producing delirium in which the victim might well give an affirmative answer to any question; and as these practices were applied to the very young and the very old, witch trials easily proved the ramifications of a satanic clientèle into every parish of Scotland. Moreover since there was no segregation of the insane, the lunatic had then opportunities for a public career now denied him, and one maniac might bring ruin or death to many sane persons. Incube and succube; devil dances and pulpit blasphemies in churches brightly illuminated at midnight; cattle-rot produced by the incantations of old women with hooves or without shadows; nightmares and premonitions; all the natural order of things converted into a wild phantasmagoria of magic, fairy tales and crude falsehood were united in the hysteria through which the nation passed before the native intelligence could assert itself.

This daily contact with the other world was maintained by those possessed of second-sight; by midwives, who sometimes secretly baptized their charges in the name of the Devil, and also

[1] See, for example, sir M. Hale, *A trial of witches at the assize held at Bury St. Edmunds, March 10, 1664* (1682).

[2] Robert Wodrow, *The history of the sufferings of the Church of Scotland from the Restoration to the Revolution*, 1721–2.

[3] Robert Law, *Memorialls, or the memorable things that fell out within this island of Britain from 1638 to 1684*, ed. C. K. Sharpe, 1818.

[4] *Records of the proceedings of the Justiciary Court of Edinburgh*, ed. W. G. Scott-Moncrieff.

by those who were deaf and dumb. Of the deaf-mutes there were two categories—those afflicted by God from birth, and those whose disability had been brought later in life by Satan. Both were 'mediums', their prototype being the damsel of the Acts of the Apostles who possessed a spirit of divination. Such a damsel was the servant-maid employed by sir George Maxwell of Pollock, whose affliction, dating from birth, enabled her to detect and reveal the secret assaults of the Evil One on her master. When, in 1677, sir George sickened and turned the colour of clay, she knew that some one was busily working at his image in clay, and made signs that she could discover the source of the malady. Accompanied by one of the laird's friends she went to the house of a witch's son, and there by candle-light she revealed, under a bolster, a clay image of sir George, not yet dry. The young man in whose premises the image lay was accused, with his sister, of sorcery. Both confessed, describing the extraordinary guise in which the Devil had appeared before them, accompanied by six women; how the Devil had formed the face of the image, and had stuck pins into its right side—a statement confirmed by the fact that sir George had experienced pain in his right side.[1]

From this successful discovery the servant-maid embarked on a career of witch-hunting, and in the following year a whole batch of her victims was burnt at Paisley. She then appears to have recovered her speech; whereupon she was pressed to declare how her powers of divination had been acquired. In answer, she denied correspondence with Satan, and accordingly her believers thought that she must have the gift of second-sight. Others, however, suspected the inspiration of the Evil One, so the maid was committed to the Canongate prison, where she still plied her trade, and revealed to an Edinburgh bailie how his wife was bewitched by two old women on the Castlehill. After being questioned by the privy council she was ordered to be transported as a cheat; but no ship-master could be found to give a passage to such a dangerous person.[2] So the Maid of Pollock survived, dividing Scottish opinion into two camps according as her exploits were fathered on God or the Devil; a pardonable division of opinion, since the distinction between those two powers was then a subtle one.

---

[1] Law, *Memorialls*, 119–27.　　　　　[2] Ibid. 128–31.

The judicial system of Scotland was an amalgam of medieval and Roman law elements. At the head of the structure was the hereditary justice general who exercised his office by deputies. A supreme court—the Court of Justiciary—was set up in 1672, consisting of five lords of session presided over by a lord justice clerk, all holding office during the royal pleasure. Local courts were held by the sheriff, whose office was then hereditary; his deputy did not necessarily have legal qualifications. Juries might be imprisoned for their verdicts. The Scottish privy council constantly interfered with the administration of justice, either by convening a case to be heard before it, or by granting special commissions to private and sometimes interested parties for the trial of offenders or crimes. Jurisdiction, civil and criminal, was also exercised by the lords of regality and barons within their regalities and baronies, who acted by deputies chosen by themselves. Procedure was quite unlike that of the English common law, the law of Scotland having been modelled on that of Rome during the 'Reception' of the preceding century. Thus, in addition to the king's advocate or public prosecutor, there might be private prosecutors, and it was possible for an aggrieved party or one of his relatives to initiate and conduct a prosecution. Written depositions of witnesses were admitted as evidence, and the testimony of women was excluded, except in cases of witchcraft; in political trials torture was frequently applied in order to obtain confessions, and there was no remedy such as the English habeas corpus. Owing to shortage of prison accommodation for recusants the Bass Rock had to be taken over in 1671 as a prison.[1]

The statute law of Scotland was not much more ferocious than that of England; but the judicial proceedings in the Scottish capital reveal a condition of things not unlike that associated with fifteenth-century England. Crimes of violence were specially numerous; 'hamesucken', or forcible entry into enclosed premises, was frequent; at least one peer of the realm stole title-deeds;[2] a sheriff court was reduced to confusion when the accused covered

---

[1] *P.C. Reg. Scot., 1669–72*, 392. For a full account of the Scottish judicial system see *Records of the Proceedings of the Justiciary Court of Edinburgh*, ed. W. G. Scott-Moncrieff, Introduction.

[2] Ibid., i. 88.

his accusers with a pistol;[1] a territorial magnate obtained a commission of fire and sword against a neighbour and (after executing justice) sent the heads of his victims to the privy council for public exhibition.[2] In many parts of the Highlands the king's writ did not run. An illustration of this may be cited from the indictment presented in 1674 against Macleod of Assynt, then a prisoner in the Tolbooth.[3] On his own initiative he had levied a tax on all ships entering Loch Inver; he had captured a neighbour and detained him for three days *tanquam in privato carcere* until he paid his ransom; he then garrisoned his house at Ardvreck (Loch Assynt) and defied the sheriff. The climax came in 1671 when a commission of fire and sword against him was granted to the earl of Seaforth and lord Lovat, a threat which caused Macleod to 'convocate' 400 armed men (presumably Macleods) and put up a stout defence against Seaforth and his 800 clansmen, who, with the help of a battering-ram, besieged Ardvreck for fourteen days. In the course of an address to the besiegers Macleod announced that he did not care a plack for the king. The trial was a lengthy one, but the accused's counsel appears to have served him well, for the verdict was Not Proven.

The Highlands remained a continual source of anxiety to Stuart administrators. Some degree of organization and control was ensured by the clan system, and if the chieftain could be won over, the clansmen would follow; so in 1664 council revived the old expedient of summoning the chieftains once a year to Edinburgh in order to give bonds for the behaviour of their dependants; but this was difficult to enforce, as so many chiefs feared to approach the capital lest they might be arrested for debt.[4] Even more troublesome were those who belonged to no clan and lived entirely by robbery, going about the country in the guise of cattle drovers. There were also lawless districts; for example, the whole of Lochaber was practically outside the sphere of civil jurisdiction, and Caithness was rent by the feuds of the Sinclairs and the earls of Sutherland.[5] Against this lawlessness the Scottish executive was impotent, but what arms could not enforce was accomplished to some extent by a book. In 1684 a Gaelic version of the Psalms

---

[1] *Records of the Proceedings of the Justiciary Court of Edinburgh*, i. xvii.
[2] Ibid. i. 127.   [3] Ibid. ii. 226–8.   [4] *P.C. Reg. Scot.*, 1669–72, xxv–xxvi.
[5] For these feuds see *Records of the Proceedings of the Justiciary Court*, i. 264.

began to be circulated in the Highlands;[1] and if the clansman could not read, he might at least chant.

In contrast also with English institutions was the structure of the Scottish constitution. The three estates, clergy, tenants-in-chief, and burgesses, were represented. Of these, the bishops remained lords of parliament until 1689; the tenants-in-chief, as in England, were divided into the greater and lesser tenants, the former receiving a special summons as lords of parliament, but the latter never joined forces with the burgesses, so there was no coalition of those classes which, in England, served to create a powerful House of Commons. The burgesses were elected by the town councils of the royal boroughs, and were therefore representative of civic oligarchies, having little or nothing in common with the nobility and gentry or the bishops; for this reason the Scottish parliament conformed more to a feudal convention of estates than to an English parliament; and so, while in the south parliament was pressing its claim to be the 'grand inquest of the nation', that in the north was divided by rigid barriers into compartments, each concerned mainly with the affairs of one class. This exclusiveness was intensified by the practice of delegating important duties to commissions, of which the most important was the Lords of the Articles, a committee representative of each estate, in which was done much of the preliminary work for later confirmation by the whole assembly. By their personal influence the Stuarts were able to exercise great control over the choice of Lords of the Articles, and through them to exert pressure on parliament itself; moreover, with such a wily Commissioner as Lauderdale, it was possible for the king to direct that, when a Convention of Estates was summoned to grant a supply, care should be taken that nothing else was discussed. Such were Lauderdale's instructions in the summer of 1678, when Charles hoped to raise a large force in Scotland.[2]

Even thus, there were 'rivals'[3] to the Scottish parliament. In England the word 'Act' was generally confined to the legislative enactments of parliament; but in Scotland the word was constantly used of the decisions of bodies which in different degrees

[1] Ibid., 1673–6, xxxiii–xxxiv.
[2] *Add. MS.* 23242 (*Lauderdale Papers*, vol. i), f. 64, June 13, 1678.
[3] R. S. Rait, *The Parliaments of Scotland*, 9.

shared the parliamentary prerogative. These were the Scottish privy council, the convention of Royal Boroughs, and the general assembly of the Church of Scotland. In the privy council the programme of parliamentary business was prepared; whatever was capable of enactment was then drafted into Acts by the Lords of the Articles. Of the other rivals, the convention of Royal Boroughs was a parliament devoted exclusively to the affairs of the boroughs, their rights and privileges, their commercial relations with the foreigner, the incidence of taxation in the towns, and the regulation of weights and measures. Here the burgesses formed decisions which they presented to parliament in their capacity of members of the third estate; to this extent, their interests were focused on one class of problem, and so were deflected from questions of national policy.[1] Lastly, the general assembly of the Church of Scotland, by its inclusion of laymen, both noble and commoner, was on a more national basis than the English Convocation, and served to give a voice to two classes practically excluded from parliament—the clergy and the lairds.[2] In consequence, the assembly might debate matters of wider import than the discipline and doctrine of the Church, and could even discuss the conduct of the executive; but its period of greatest power[3] was already past.

After the Restoration,[4] policy was at first directed not by the Scottish council sitting at Holyrood, but by a committee of council in London, in which were included Lauderdale, Monck, Ormonde, and Manchester.[5] That it was possible thus to control Scotland from a distance was soon demonstrated; for the activities of the first representative parliament of the reign (that of 1661) reflected not so much the subservience of the legislature as the expert management of the government; and the Act Rescissory[6] testified more to the zeal of Clarendon[7] than to the loyalty of Scotland. Indeed there could have been little opportunity for debate, so many measures were rushed through. In its second

[1] For its economic importance see Miss T. Keith, *Influence of the Convention of Royal Boroughs on the economic development of Scotland* in *S.H.R.* x, no. 39.
[2] Rait, op. cit. 15.   [3] i.e. 1639–51.
[4] For the Restoration in Scotland see *supra*, i, ch. iv.
[5] *P.C. Reg. Scot., 1661–4*, vi.   [6] See *supra*, i. 176.
[7] For Clarendon's share in the imposition of episcopacy on Scotland see the *Memoirs* of sir George Mackenzie of Rosehaugh (ed. 1821), 52–61.

session (May 8–Sept. 9, 1662) parliament ratified the re-establish-
ment of episcopacy already decreed by king in council, and imposed a test on all office holders in the form of a declaration that
both Solemn League and Covenant and National Covenant were
illegal. Then followed a joint campaign of council and parliament against recalcitrant ministers; but this unanimity was
impeded for a time by the rivalry of Lauderdale and Middleton,
of whom the latter hoped to exclude the other by the clause in
the Scottish Act of Indemnity[1] excepting twelve persons. When
the twelve were balloted for, Middleton succeeded in procuring the inclusion of Lauderdale's name. But he was no match for
Lauderdale in dexterity. Before the Act and the list of the twelve
excepted persons reached him, Lauderdale gained the ear of the
king; the ruse was therefore foiled, and in 1663 commissioner
Middleton had to resign in favour of Rothes.

The session of 1663, the third of the Restoration parliament,
was presided over by commissioner Rothes, acting as the instrument of Charles and Lauderdale. Four acts were passed which
tightened still further the Stuart hold over Scotland—that conferring on the sovereign the right to tax imports at will;[2] that
restoring the Lords of the Articles to their former privileges at
the expense of parliament;[3] an Act for raising a force of 20,000
foot and 2,000 horse;[4] and finally a Bill imposing heavy fines on
all absentees from the parish church.[5] The working of the constitution as now perfected was thus explained by Lauderdale:
'nothing can come to parliament but through the Articles, and
nothing can pass in the Articles but what is warranted by His
Majesty, so that the King is absolute master in parliament both
of the negative and affirmative.'[6] Now that parliament was out
of the way the council began its long campaign against dissent by
the imposition of heavy fines and the quartering of troops on the
peasantry; and, in the hope of obtaining some relief from the
overwork involved in securing conformity, the council (in 1664)
adopted Sharp's suggestion to revive the Court of High Commission. Its activities, however, did not last longer than two

---

[1] *Acts of the Parliaments of Scotland* (1820), vii. 415, Sept. 9, 1662.

[2] Ibid. vii. 503–4.   [3] Ibid. vii. 449.

[4] Ibid. vii. 480–1.   [5] Ibid. vii. 455–6.

[6] *Lauderdale Papers*, i. 172, quoted by R. S. Rait, op. cit. 78.

years.[1] These events showed how quickly constitutional progress could be made backwards.

That Scotland was known to be out of sympathy with the anti-Dutch policy of Charles II's government was used as a pretext for increased harshness to the Presbyterian dissentients of the south-west. Between eight and nine hundred persons had been placed by the Scottish Act of Indemnity in a special class, for whom there was to be pardon only on payment of a fine. It was thought in 1666 that the time had come for the exaction of this fine; accordingly soldiers were established in the houses of these delinquents until the money was paid, and a further use was found for the military in the harrying of the field conventicles conducted by the ejected ministry. The officers employed in this service had mostly served their apprenticeship in Muscovy, and their handling of unarmed peasants showed proficiency in semi-oriental methods. At last the inevitable rebellion took place. In November 1666 sir James Turner, the leader of a detachment of soldiers, was taken prisoner, and his captors formed the reckless resolve of marching on Edinburgh in the desperate hope that they would find sympathizers there. At Rullion Green, in the Pentlands, colonel Wallace with 900 men faced the government troops under sir Thomas Dalziel (Nov. 28). The rebels put up a brave fight, but having few arms they were overpowered; about fifty were captured, to whom were added thirty stragglers, and all were given up to justice.[2]

Justice was then in the hands of a privy council which was prepared to seize this opportunity of providing a sanguinary object-lesson. The contention that the insurgents had voluntarily surrendered to quarter was brushed aside; it was enough that they had been caught in the act of rebellion. For weeks the boot and the gallows ministered to Scotland's Bloody Assize. Dalziel was then sent to the south-west to replace the humanitarian Turner, and even Sharp and Rothes had reason to be satisfied with the reports of his doings.[3] But a temporary relief was provided by the fall of Clarendon in 1667; for with him went Sharp's main support, and for a moment Scottish episcopacy appeared

[1] P. Hume Brown, *History of Scotland*, ii. 393.   [2] Ibid., ii. 395–8.
[3] The persecutions were accompanied by a policy of disarming the shires of Lanark, Ayr, Wigtown, and Galloway. *Steele*, ii. 2306–7.

to be without friends in England. Another change was the removal of Rothes from office, and his appointment to the chancellorship, in spite of his protest that he knew neither Law nor Latin. A Militia of 20,000 men was raised in readiness to march wherever Charles ordered—'never was king so absolute as in poor old Scotland.'[1]

Scotland had a share in the experimental toleration which accompanied Charles's secret alliance with France. In June 1669 was issued the first Letter of Indulgence, which granted this moderate relief to ministers 'outed' by the proscription of Protestantism, that, provided their former cures were vacant, and if they accepted episcopacy and the royal supremacy in ecclesiasticals, they might be restored.[2] This attempt at reconciliation appears to have done more harm than good, since very few of the recusants took advantage of it, most of them preferring ostracism to episcopacy; while, on their side, the Scottish bishops resented even these concessions, and condemned the Indulgence because its acceptance implied a recognition of secular supremacy in the Church. For his remonstrance[3] against the Indulgence Burnet, archbishop of Glasgow, was cited before the council, removed from his see, and replaced by Leighton. Meanwhile, these years of vacillation coincided with suggestions for the union of the two countries. An Act of 1667[4] had appointed commissioners to treat concerning liberty of trade, and in 1669 a Scottish parliament was summoned to take part in discussions of the proposed union. But on neither side was there confidence or even friendliness. Lauderdale, who had been appointed lord high commissioner in October 1669, went to Scotland in order to enforce the policy which he had hitherto directed through Rothes, and he believed that his own and his master's interests would be better served by keeping the two kingdoms separate; for otherwise his powers would be reduced to those of a secretary of state, and Charles would, in emergency, have less opportunity of using Highland troops against rebellious Englishmen. So the project of union was abandoned.[5]

[1] Quoted by O. Airy in *E.H.R.* i. 446.
[2] *Reg. P.C. Scot.*, *1669–72*, 38–40.
[3] *Lauderdale Papers* (ed. Airy), ii, app. 1–2.   [4] 19–20 Car. II, cap. v.
[5] Scottish commissioners to treat of union were appointed in July 1670. On

These hints of conciliation only served to make differences more acute. Politics intruded more and more into sermons, and the Covenanters now began to appear armed at their meetings. In the often-quoted words of Leighton, it was 'a drunken scuffle in the dark',[1] a scuffle in which the advocates of compromise were invariably trampled upon. Dependent solely on Charles, Lauderdale now governed the country absolutely, managing the short sessions of parliament with such dexterity that there was no time for opposition to shape itself, while the bishops threw the weight of their influence against all suggestions of compromise. There was a faint glimmer of a nationalist movement when, in November 1673, the duke of Hamilton demanded that Scottish grievances should be taken into consideration, and some of his supporters even talked of impeaching the commissioner; but this movement was personal rather than constitutional, and Lauderdale parried the attack by successive adjournments of parliament. Hamilton and some of his party came to London in order to present their grievances; they were coldly received, however, as they were thought to be in league with Shaftesbury;[2] and they were unwilling to reduce their charges to writing, as that would have rendered them liable to the charge of leasing making. In June 1674 Lauderdale was made earl of Guildford in the peerage of England; in December of the same year Leighton resigned. To the Scottish privy council were now added Monmouth, Danby, Finch, and Ormonde, who, together with Lauderdale, were deputed to conduct Scottish affairs from London in such a manner as to strengthen Charles's power in both countries.[3] In September 1677 sir George Mackenzie of Rosehaugh, the 'Bluidy Mackenzie', was appointed lord advocate, and the Scottish officers of state were informed that they held office only during His Majesty's pleasure, and not for life.[4] These changes coincided with an increasingly vigorous campaign against the Covenanters.

In the conduct of this campaign there can be detected a certain

March 6, 1671, there was a council minute to the effect that Charles had adjourned the meetings of the commissioners until further notice. (*P.C. Reg. Scot., 1669–72*, 306.)   [1] *Lauderdale Papers* (ed. Airy), iii. 76.

[2] O. Airy, *Lauderdale* in *E.H.R.* i. 452.

[3] *P.C. Reg. Scot., 1673–6*, iv.   [4] Ibid., *1676–8*, 233.

harshness or deterioration in the character of Lauderdale, who now set himself to complete the work begun by Rothes; that is, to cause such discontent as to provide a pretext for the maintenance of a standing army.[1] The penal statutes already in force against Roman Catholics were accordingly directed against Covenanters; and many named malcontents were ostracized by the issue of 'letters of intercommuning' which forbade intercourse with them. A measure still more effective was the Act of the Council of 1674 imposing on all masters and landlords the obligation of signing a bond giving security for the behaviour of their employees and tenants. This was extended in 1677 to include all persons residing on their lands, and was enforced on the whig landlords of the south-west, including the duke of Hamilton. When it was objected that no security for the opinions and conduct of dependants could be given, Lauderdale completed a plan said to have been first suggested by the bishops,[2] namely, to utilize the military prowess of the Highlander not against the foreigner, but against the Scot. It was accordingly decided to quarter a Highland Host[3] on Ayrshire. Before the Celtic warriors were ready, the south-west had again relapsed into its uneasy quiet; but Lauderdale refused to see a deputation of Ayrshire gentlemen who came to protest that the shire was at peace; and in December 1677 Charles authorized the issue of commissions to the lords Atholl and Perth for the raising of Highlandmen, while the Scottish bishops prepared their strategical notes on 'what is fit to be done for suppressing disorders in the west'.[4] By thus pitting the Celtic cattle-dealer against the Saxon husbandman it was hoped by those responsible for the government to precipitate a racial quarrel in which the armed men would have the best of it. The two races were bitter enemies in Ireland; the one might now be used against the other in Scotland.

About 6,000 clansmen mustered at Stirling in January 1678, and were joined by 3,000 of the Militia. As they marched south they were quartered on the peasantry, special attention being shown to the duke of Hamilton's tenants in Lanarkshire.

---

[1] P. Hume Brown, *History of Scotland*, ii. 404-5.

[2] *Lauderdale Papers*, iii. 95.

[3] J. R. Elder, *The Highland Host of 1679*, 39, and *P.C. Reg. Scot.*, *1676–8*, xiv sqq.   [4] Dec. 21, 1677, in J. R. Elder, op. cit., Appendix.

Renfrewshire and Ayrshire were occupied by this army of invasion, which made no distinction between those who had signed the Bond and those who had not. After six weeks of plunder the Highlanders were anxious to return home with their booty; and as they had not succeeded in causing a rebellion, it was resolved, late in February, that they should retreat; so their cart-loads of utensils, furniture, and money were conducted across the Forth, and the internal embellishments of several Highland mansions were improved in consequence. There had been little bloodshed, but much robbery with violence, and, as all the horses were seized, the land could not be ploughed; in consequence, many Scots migrated to northern Ireland.

'The patience of the Scots under their oppressions', wrote Andrew Marvell, 'is not to be paralleled in any history.'[1] But there were limits. In 1668 an attempt had been made on the life of archbishop Sharp by one James Mitchell. Six years later Sharp recognized Mitchell in the street, and had him arrested. The privy council, promising that his life would be spared, extracted some kind of confession from him, and for a time he was imprisoned on the Bass. In 1676 he was again brought to trial, this time on the accusation that he had taken part in the Pentland Rising. He was tortured on one leg with the boot (at the suggestion of the archbishop), and when it was proposed to apply the same treatment to the other leg, some of Mitchell's friends sent a letter to Sharp intimating that, if he persisted in ordering torture, 'he would have a shot from a steddier hand'.[2] The threat succeeded for the time; but two years later Mitchell was again tried, this time in the Justiciary Court on the original charge of the attempted murder of Sharp. The prisoner's advocate pleaded the pardon, but Lauderdale refused to have the original record of the privy council's pardon brought into court, and, as Sharp insisted on his victim, Mitchell was executed. Vengeance was not long delayed. On May 3, 1679, Sharp was pulled out of his coach as it was crossing Magus Muir and murdered. More than enough retribution was exacted for this crime. After assisting at the torture of prisoners, Mackenzie wrote thus to Lauderdale: 'remember [remind] the king that king Alexander II killed

[1] June 10, 1678. *Works of Andrew Marvell*, ed. Grosart, ii. 631.
[2] Law, *Memorialls*, 85–6.

4,000 for the death of one bishop of Caithness . . . and what law had he for that?'[1]

This incident coincided with another event which helped to strengthen the case for a standing army. Observance of the anniversary of the Restoration (May 29) was by Statute the duty of all Scotsmen. This date, a dolorous one for Scotland, was chosen in 1679 for a demonstration at Rutherglen, near Glasgow, when all the Acts of the government were burnt. A few days later the insurgents, a band of about 250 men, defeated Graham of Claverhouse and the royalist troops at Drumclog, near Strathaven. Charles's government acted promptly. Monmouth was appointed captain-general of all the royal forces raised or thereafter to be raised in Scotland;[2] Irish troops were ordered to be moved north for transhipment,[3] and the Militia of all the eastern Scottish counties was hastily assembled. Before the end of June 1679 Monmouth was assured of as many thousands of troops as the whigs had hundreds. Having been repulsed from Glasgow, the rebels mustered on the Clyde at Bothwell Bridge, where the dissensions of the ministers divided them into two hostile camps, one party declaring for the king's interest 'according to the Covenant', while the other was for repudiating that interest altogether.[4] Even more ominous was the fact that when they engaged the troops of Monmouth it was on the Sabbath Day (June 22, 1679). Monmouth's offer of peace on condition of laying down their arms was rejected by the advice of the ministers, with the result that soon one more Scottish defeat was attributable to interference by the clergy. Though holding a strong position on the south side of the river, the rebels were badly manœuvred by their inexperienced commander Robert Hamilton, and they were sharply divided even at the moment of battle. It needed only Monmouth's cannon to complete their defeat. Thereupon Monmouth showed a quality of mercy to which the north was unaccustomed; but the executions afterwards ordered by the council attested the severity, not of strength, but of weakness:[5] for while the rebels had been defeated, on the other hand

[1] *H.M.C. Rep.* v, app. 316.   [2] *Add. MS.* 23244, f. 5.
[3] June 13, 1679. *P.C. Reg.* 68.   [4] Law, *Memorialls*, 150.
[5] For the perturbation of the Scottish privy council at this period see *P.C. Reg. Scot., 1678–80*, 481–5, 495.

the musters of Militia had shown so many defections that this force could no longer be relied on to crush native discontent. The problem, therefore, was either to remodel the Militia or raise a paid army. Thus the government of Scotland in the summer of 1679 was in a position almost identical with that of James II after the 'victory' of Sedgemoor.

Contemporary Englishmen, however indifferent they might be to the fate of Scottish covenanters, might well have discerned in the melancholy history of the northern kingdom a foretaste of what was in store for them. English hatred of Presbyterianism was strong, but not so strong as hatred of slavery. Already in the summer of 1678 the Scottish Estates had made a liberal grant for the raising of regiments of foot, horse, and dragoons,[1] and Charles believed that there were great, untapped sources of military strength in the north.[2] To supplement the dragoons there were the law courts; and an illustration of how effectively these might be used was provided just after the battle of Bothwell Brig. An Edinburgh jury acquitted some men of the charge of having taken part in the rebellion; whereupon an assize of twenty-five noblemen and gentry was impanelled in order to try the jury. This assize gave their verdict that the jurymen had been guilty of an error of judgement, whereupon the offenders were committed to prison.[3] That Charles might attempt to enforce on England what was already accomplished in Scotland had for long been present in the minds of the English opposition, as witnessed by the reiterated attacks on Lauderdale. These attacks were renewed in May 1679, when the Commons petitioned for his removal, and in June the duke of Hamilton presented a petition from a section of the Scottish nobility attributing the Scottish unrest to the iniquities of the hated minister.[4] A year before (May 1678), when Hamilton protested in the king's presence against the imposition of the Bond, Charles remarked that the Koran might yet be imposed.[5] Thus, in 1678–9, the opposition in Scotland and that in England were united against Lauderdale,

[1] *Acts of the parliament of Scotland*, viii. 221–9.
[2] *P.C. Reg. Scot., 1676–8*, 402.
[3] *Cal. S.P. Dom., 1680–1*, 385, 388, July 1681.
[4] *H.M.C. Rep., MSS. of the duke of Hamilton* (supplement), 99–100.
[5] Ibid. 97.

and the Exclusion party could depend on some support from Scotland,[1] where the extremists were in favour of disowning not only the duke of York but Charles himself. This was illustrated in June 1680 when there was affixed to the cross at Sanquhar (Dumfriesshire) a declaration repudiating Charles Stuart because of his perjury and breach of the Covenant.

At this moment therefore it seemed not impossible that a new Bishops' War would give a lead to English republicanism. But Charles was bending, not breaking, under the strain, and there was soon to be a recoil. The removal of Lauderdale helped to effect this. His health was failing, and in October 1680 he resigned his offices; two years later he died. A new and even darker period of Scottish history had commenced in November 1679 when the duke of York went to Edinburgh as commissioner to the Estates.

Scotland and England might long have remained divided because of their antipathies, had not the policy of the Stuarts brought them together in a common suspicion of the real intentions of that House. In a 'well-conditioned' country such as Scotland it was not difficult to enforce a system of government wherein every national institution was placed at the mercy of a capricious prerogative; but, in England, where these institutions had deeper roots, the process would be longer and more difficult. The Scottish covenanters may have been bigots as well as rebels; but at least they were monarchists, for whom Stuart rule had brought both disillusionment and persecution; the turn of the English moderates was yet to come. The Scots had given a lead,[2]

[1] It is likely that Shaftesbury communicated and corresponded with Hamilton and other Scotsmen, but the correspondence does not appear to have been preserved. It is referred to in *Shaftesbury*, vi *a*, 349.

[2] Cf. *A new year gift for the Whigs* (1684):

> The Scotch Covenanters, to rouse up our knaves,
> Have given us a signet, as they did before;
> When the bishop's brains against the coach-naves,
> They dashed out, to show what a God they adore.

This ballad was printed *in extenso* by sir Charles Firth in *S.H.R.* vi, no. 23. Cf. also the pamphlets regarding Scottish affairs published by the whigs just after the Revolution; notably, *An account of Scotland's grievances by reason of the duke of Lauderdale's Ministry. . . .* and *The Scotch mist cleared up* (in *State Tracts relating to the government of Charles II*, 1693).

but could not maintain it; Englishmen, on the other hand, were better equipped for the contest by their greater wealth, their ancient parliamentary traditions, and their guarantees for the liberty of the subject. Before describing the crisis of 1678–81, in which the two countries shared a common interest, it is necessary to return to England and consider each of these three subjects in turn.

XII

REVENUE AND TAXATION

THE increasing wealth of England in the reign of Charles II was due mainly to the steady development of overseas commerce, and was evidenced most obviously by the greater amount of taxation which the country was able to bear. This expansion was revealed also in a more scientific study of fiscal problems, and in the launching of experiments for facilitating the extension of credit. It is the purpose of this chapter to consider the financial expedients of Charles's governments, and the beginnings of a more adequate system of administering the national finances.

The Convention Parliament voted[1] to Charles for his life the subsidy of tonnage and poundage on wine imported and on woollen cloth exported, each at prescribed rates. Appended to this grant was a Book of Rates, containing a monetary valuation of hundreds of commodities of import and export, on which a poundage of one shilling in the pound was levied. Thus, of imports: oranges and lemons were valued at £1 per thousand; Irish cattle at £2 10s. each; anchovies at 7s. 6d. per small barrel; silk from the East Indies at 15s. per pound; Virginia tobacco at 1s. 8d. per pound; Brazilian tobacco at 10s.; cotton-wool from foreign countries at fourpence per pound, and that from English plantations free. Among the 'outward' rates were: apples, fourpence per bushel; butter, 'good or bad', £3 per barrel; rabbit skins, 15s. per hundred; and beer 2s. per tun. These rates were somewhat arbitrary; nor was any account taken of market fluctuations. The subsidies on wine and cloth together with these Customs duties on imports and exports provided the most important source of hereditary revenue at the Restoration, when their yield was estimated at £400,000 per annum. For the first four years of Charles's reign, the average return was barely £300,000; there was some falling off during the two Dutch wars, but after 1674 there began a steady increase until the Customs yielded between £500,000 and £600,000. This coincided with an increased revenue from Excise, and explains why Charles, in the

[1] 12 Car. II, cap. xix.

later years of his reign, and James II throughout his reign, were not dependent on parliamentary grant.

Attempts were made to prevent frauds in the payment of these dues. The Act[1] of 1660 empowered Customs officers to break into suspected houses; that[2] of 1662 authorized them to search ships inward and outward-bound, and provided that dutiable goods should remain in store until the duties were paid. But legislation was often evaded, nor was it easy to obtain a conviction, even where smuggling was proved; so the government had to enlist the support of the judiciary and the officials of corporate towns in its campaign for the enforcement of these regulations. Thus, in a smuggling case tried before him, sir Matthew Hale, chief baron of the Exchequer, was enjoined in a communication from the lord high treasurer to see that the officers were 'countenanced';[3] so also members of parliament serving for maritime boroughs were asked to obtain information of frauds on the Customs, and report to the Treasury.[4] Mayors, aldermen, and justices were exhorted to assist the Customs officials.[5] There was certainly need for these exhortations, for on at least one occasion the soldiers who helped to effect seizures were themselves sent to prison by the lord mayor of London.[6] Other causes helped to impede the efficiency of this service. The men who acted as tide and land waiters, searchers, and gaugers were appointed by recommendation only; their salaries were small (most of them received less than £50 a year), and they might be dismissed without reason; consequently they were recruited from those unfit for other employment. For many years one of the normal duties of a member of parliament was to obtain posts in this service for the more 'decayed' unemployables among his constituents. 'When anyone fails in business,' it was said,[7] 'or a gentleman wants to part with an old servant, interest is made to get them into the Customs as if into a hospital.' That this was no exaggeration can be seen from such an instance as that of the member of the Chiffinch family, aged 13, who had to be removed from his post of searcher at Gravesend, because

[1] 12 Car. II, cap. xix.   [2] 14 Car. II, cap. x.
[3] Cal. Tr. Bks., 1660–7, 263.   [4] Ibid. 266.
[5] Steele, i. 3319.   [6] Baschet, 145, Apr. 29/May 9, 1680.
[7] Shaftesbury, iii. 105.

he paid no attention to his duties.[1] In spite, however, of its imperfect personnel there grew up in London and the outports a great preventive service, and soon the Customs became one of the most important branches of the civil administration.[2]

The Excise, first introduced by Pym in 1643 and exacted during the Commonwealth, was regulated by Acts of the Convention Parliament, the effect of which was to confer on Charles for life one moiety of a tax on ale, cider, beer, aqua vitae, coffee, chocolate, sherbet, and tea; the other moiety being granted in perpetuity to the crown as compensation for Charles's surrender of the Court of Wards.[3] By an Act[4] of 1663 brewers were required to give notice of setting up or enlarging their tuns or vats, and every one retailing excisable commodities was obliged both to obtain a licence, and to give security for the payment of the dues. Additional Excise duties were granted in 1671[5] and 1677[6] for six and three years respectively. The yield from these taxes amounted at first to an average of between £250,000 and £300,000; but, immediately after the English withdrawal from hostilities in 1674, there was a remarkable increase; for, in the year following the conclusion of the treaty of Westminster, the return from this source alone amounted to more than £700,000. Thereafter, the average was £400,000, and in the reign of James it rose to about £500,000.[7]

Whether from its supposed origin, or because it was the most obvious of the indirect taxes paid by the consumer, this was one of the most unpopular of taxes. In 1660 there were so many obstructions to its exaction that the king had to issue proclamations ordering his subjects to pay it;[8] in the same year, at several Quarter Sessions, men were sent to prison for assaulting Excise officers.[9] Justices going on circuit were asked to include in their charges to grand juries a reference to the obligation of the

---

[1] *Cal. Tr. Bks.*, *1681–5*, 226.

[2] For the cost of the Customs establishments in London and the outports see *supra*, i. 50–51. For the administration of Customs revenue between 1671 and 1814 see B. R. Leftwich, in *Trans. R. H. Soc.*, series iv, xiii.

[3] 12 Car. II, cap. xxiii and xxiv. See also *supra*, i. 159.

[4] 15 Car. II, cap. xi.   [5] 22–3 Car. II, cap. v.

[6] 29 Car. II, cap. ii.

[7] For the figures see Dr. Shaw's introductions to the *Cal. Tr. Bks.*

[8] *C.J.* viii. 157, and *Steele*, i. 3210, 3260.   [9] *Carte MS.* 222, f. 49.

subject to pay these dues;[1] and in all disputes between brewers
and excisemen, the principle had to be observed that 'the law
being in His Majesty's behalf, and his revenue the public concern,
the interpretation ought to be in his favour, and no frivolous
excuses admitted'.[2] Frequently the privy council summoned to
its presence justices of the peace who had given a decision
whereby the Excise revenue might suffer; in one case, where the
justices of a city were suspected of favouring the brewers, council ordered that the magistrates and deputy-lieutenants of the
county should be joined with the city magistrates for the administration of better justice in such disputes.[3] An additional complication was introduced by the fact that the collectors of Excise
were not normally government officials, but paid employees of
the Excise farmers, to whom they were personally responsible.
The government was therefore intervening to protect one class
of private person against another class, in its own interest and
in that of the farmers. The result was constant confusion and
irritation.

Serious loss to the revenue arose from the dependence of the
government on the farmers; but, before the farming system is
condemned, it should be recalled that, in the absence of a civil
service, it was inevitable, and in some cases it worked equitably.
Between the granting of a tax by parliament and the collection
of the money there was a considerable interval; it was here that
the farmer was useful, for his first business was to make an advance of money on the security of the tax. He was generally a
capitalist, or speculator, or one of a syndicate able to lend a
capital sum and pay a rent, in return for which he recouped
himself from the proceeds of the tax assigned to him. Once
having made his bargain with the Treasury, the farmer would
not normally have to reveal the amount of his gains; but if he
demanded 'defalcations', that is a rebate in his cash payments to
the government on the ground that the yield of the tax was below
expectations, then he might have to produce accounts, and
content himself with a definitely assessed profit. An illustration

[1] *Cal. Tr. Bks.*, *1660–7*, 215.
[2] Ibid. 722–3. Lord treasurer Southampton to the justices of Middlesex
on the acquittal of a brewer in an Excise case, March 1666.
[3] The city was Worcester. *P.C. Reg.* 61, Nov. 18, 1668.

of this was seen in Michaelmas 1667 when a lease of the Customs fell in. The out-going farmers contended that owing to war, plague, and fire they had incurred serious losses in the last two years (1665–7) of their five years' farm. When their case was heard at the Treasury, counsel on their behalf submitted that they had paid the full rent for the first three years, and that their expenses of collection had amounted to £120,000 per annum. To this the solicitor-general replied that £50,000 per annum was a reasonable amount for expenses. Eventually, the king ruled that the farmers were to keep their profit for the first three years, and render an account for the last two, in respect of which they were to be 'savers, but not losers', that is, to be allowed only expenses of management. Charles assessed their expenses at £70,000 per annum.[1]

Until 1671 the Customs were farmed,[2] and part of the proceeds was always pledged in advance for the loans of ready money made by the farmers; there was also a deduction in respect of interest on these loans. An example may be quoted from the arrangements made for the new farm commencing in Michaelmas 1667, when sir John Wolstenholme and others were granted a lease of the Customs for four years at a rent of £350,000 for the first three years, and £370,000 for the fourth.[3] From the monthly payments of about £30,000 advanced by the farmers, there had to be deducted a sum of £16,000, made up of £8,000 for the payment of tallies struck on the preceding farm to the amount of £214,213, and another £8,000 per month for repayment of an advance of £200,000 made by the new farmers. In effect, therefore, the lease started with a load of debt, from which it could not be cleared for at least two years, during which time about half the total yield was hypothecated.[4] Arrangements for managing the revenue were constantly bound up with such outstanding claims; and on at least one occasion these loans at 'devouring' interest had to be paid off by the sale of crown property.[5]

[1] *Cal. Tr. Bks., 1669–72*, 106–16, July 1669.
[2] For the appointment of the commissioners (Sept. 24, 1671) see ibid., *1669–72*, 935. For their instructions, ibid., *1672–5*, 35.
[3] *Cal. S.P. Dom., 1668–9*, 34.
[4] Report of the retrenchment commission, Oct. 1668, in *Add. MS.* 28078, f. 11 sqq.
[5] For example, when, after the death of lord treasurer Southampton,

Another consequence of the farming system was that great gains were reaped by men able to supply the one thing needed by all seventeenth-century governments, namely, ready money. Many London goldsmiths amassed wealth in this way; notable examples are sir Robert Viner and Edward Backwell, but on the other hand these men were hard hit by the Stop of the Exchequer in 1672. In the provinces small men built up great estates; in Ireland, lord Ranelagh appears to have accumulated a huge fortune from his profitable farm of the Irish revenues. Even more, the farmers were sometimes able to exercise some influence on policy, because, as they had a contract with the government, they could insist on measures necessary for securing strict observance of its terms; so also, in regulations for trade, the government had to bear in mind its obligations with the farmers. Thus, in April 1669, the farmers of the Customs protested against the Order in Council of March 13, 1668, whereby the king dispensed for a year with such parts of the Act of Navigation as restrained the import of timber, and gave liberty to his subjects to buy sixty foreign vessels to be naturalized for this trade. Against the proposed relaxation, it was urged by the farmers that, as double or aliens' duty would not be payable on the cargoes of these vessels, the Customs would be the losers. But, on the report from the Council of Trade, this objection appears to have been set aside.[1] So also when the Dover Composition Trade[2] was renewed in 1661 the Council of Trade reported that the farmers would not extend dispensation to the colonies, owing to the loss which they might incur; so this trade was limited to foreign ports.[3] When, in 1673, the lord lieutenant protested against the Act prohibiting all direct trade between Ireland and the plantations, it was urged by the Customs commissioners that, owing to the cheapness of Irish provisions, Ireland would be able to undersell England in the West Indies, and so Irish prosperity would be on the basis of

Clifford became a commissioner of the Treasury, he leased the Customs to a friend, alderman Bucknall, who was already one of the farmers of Excise. Knowing that the crown was anxious to raise money on the Customs, Bucknall and his partners made their own terms. This led to a quarrel between Bucknall and Clifford; whereupon Clifford 'broke' Bucknall's lease, and repaid him his loans from the sale of the king's fee farm rents. *Add. MS.* 28078, f. 392.

[1] *Cal. S.P. Dom., 1668–9,* 290.

[2] *Supra,* i. 234–5.

[3] *P.C. Reg.* 55, June 10, 1661.

English ruin.[1] The same reason had already been adduced in 1661 by the Customs farmers against the proposal to relax the Navigation Acts in favour of Scotland.[2]

Nevertheless, some of the worst abuses in the system were remedied; and it was due mainly to Danby that many debts were paid off, and the yield from the two main sources of hereditary revenue was increased. In the absence of facilities for credit, he could not dispense altogether with the farmers, but he secured a larger measure of control over them. Thus in 1678, in return for an advance made by Richard Kent, Receiver of the Customs, he undertook that the charges on this fund would not exceed £430,000 per annum, or £530,000 if the Wine Duty were restored. Out of his receipts Kent was to make certain regular payments, including a weekly payment of £2,500 to the treasurer of the Navy, and the salaries of judges and ambassadors; his recompense was to be 8 per cent. interest on his Customs receipts.[3] This arrangement recalls the fact that, in practice, the greater part of the Customs had come to be allocated to the Navy. A Bill[4] for making this allocation statutory was introduced in May 1675; later in the same year it was proposed to annex this provision to a Bill for raising a supply for twenty ships,[5] but this scheme was afterwards negatived,[6] possibly because a majority realized that it was superfluous to make statutory what was already the custom of the executive.

An increased measure of government control can also be traced in the history of the Excise, but here even more serious difficulties had to be faced. Until 1683 the Excise was farmed in three areas—London, the five counties round London, and the rest of the country;[7] throughout these districts were farmers and sub-farmers appointed by the lord treasurer or commissioners of the Treasury from persons nominated at Quarter Sessions. A special body of commissioners was deputed to administer the Excise; they appointed gaugers, having power to enter enclosed premises in order to search for unexcised liquors. Disputes with brewers

---

[1] *Essex Papers* (*Camd. Soc.*), i. 54, Feb. 10, 1672/3.
[2] *Cal. S.P. Dom.*, *1661–2*, 74, Aug. 30, 1661.
[3] *Cal. Tr. Bks.*, *1676–9*, 856, Oct. 1678.   [4] *Grey*, iii. 102.
[5] Ibid. iii. 459.   [6] Ibid. iv. 187, Mar. 5, 1676/7.
[7] *Cal. Tr. Bks.* vii, pt. i. Dr. Shaw's Introduction.

and inn-keepers were to be referred to Quarter Sessions, but if the justices failed, or neglected to adjudicate, then appeal was to be made to the sub-commissioners, and from them to the commissioners. Leases of farm were to be for three years.[1] This system does not appear to have worked as intended. Farms were leased to untrustworthy persons,[2] and sometimes even to brewers, who made considerable profit during the Plague and Great Fire from the excessive defalcations which they claimed and were allowed;[3] there was also mismanagement by the sub-commissioners, who sometimes kept large sums of money in their hands without account.[4] For long, the deficiencies in the returns from this source of revenue were a source of anxiety to the Treasury, deficiencies due to two main causes—the difficulty in securing reliable farmers and competent sub-commissioners, and the great number of illicit or 'crock' brewers. There were plenty of facilities for brewing one's own beer; it was done by cottagers, by keepers of prisons,[5] by Oxford and Cambridge colleges. Trinity College, Cambridge, opposed the exaction of Excise on its home-brewed beer,[6] so it is not surprising that, among the humble, evasions of the tax were regarded as a venial offence. The loss to the revenue from this source was said to be £30,000 per annum.[7]

Danby's object was to obtain greater control over the Excise farmers. In the lease commencing in 1674 they had to advance security of £65,000, to pay in their daily cash, and to account for the king's share of all fines. Comptrollers of Excise were to sit with the sub-commissioners as collectors of receipt, to inspect gaugers' returns, to sign acquittances, to demand accounts of the sub-farmers, and to inform the Comptroller in London of any impediment in the collection of the tax.[8] Thus government control was mingled with private enterprise, and stricter accountancy was insisted on; in this way the yield was improved. This fact, together with the expansion of trade, the increase of wealth, and the maintenance of a higher standard of living, accounts for the steadily increasing returns from Customs and Excise.

[1] 12 Car. II, cap. xxiii.
[2] *Cal. S.P. Dom.*, *1661–2*, 420.
[3] Ibid., *1668–9*, 134.
[4] *Cal. Tr. Bks.*, *1660–7*, 322.
[5] Ibid., *1672–5*, 805.
[6] Ibid., *1660–7*, 444.
[7] Ibid., *1672–5*, 776.
[8] Ibid., *1672–5*, 538, 571.

The third branch of the hereditary revenue—Hearth Money —was introduced by an Act[1] of 1662, which granted to the king, his heirs and successors, a tax of 2s. per annum on each fire-hearth or stove. All householders were required to deliver to the constables and head boroughs an account in writing of their hearths and stoves, and the justices were ordered to cause these accounts to be enrolled and sent to the Exchequer. The constables collected the money, deducting 2d. in the pound for expenses of collection; the high constables paid it to the sheriffs, deducting 1d. in the pound, and the sheriffs to the Exchequer, deducting 4d. in the pound. The Act exempted houses of less annual value than 20s. and stipulated that the revenue from this source should not be charged with pensions. By an Act[2] of 1663 provision was made for the better keeping of accounts; and in the following year the crown was empowered[3] to appoint officers for the collection of this tax who, together with the constables, were authorized to enter and search houses. All houses having more than two chimneys were now brought within the scope of this legislation.

The Hearth Tax was difficult to collect, and the revenue from it was liable to great fluctuations. In the first year of its levy only £34,000 was brought in, increased by 1667 to nearly £200,000. It was farmed in 1667, and thereafter produced an average of about £170,000. Like other branches of Charles's revenue, it was saddled with debt, the farmers having agreed to pay a certain proportion to the city of London in repayment of loans to the king.[4] Considering its comparatively small yield, it was probably the most unwise fiscal measure of the later Stuarts because of the inquisitorial system necessary for its enforcement, and also the great inequalities in its incidence. Some people walled up their chimneys, or gave false returns, or induced justices and constables to connive at exemption;[5] others divided up large houses into tenements, the occupants of which pleaded exemption on the ground of poverty.[6] Cottagers who had no vote at elections complained that they had to pay 2s. a year for a stone 'not worth twopence which the Chimney villains call a hearth'; men

---

[1] 14 Car. II, cap. x.
[2] 15 Car. II, cap. xiii.
[3] 16 Car. II, cap. iii.
[4] Cal. S.P. Dom., 1668–9, 138.
[5] Ibid., 1663–4, 371.
[6] Modern Reports, iii. 94.

having estates of 40s. a year had often to pay as much as those having estates of £50, or £100.[1] In spite of these complaints, the Treasury in 1665 gave rulings which made the tax even more harsh; ovens only were exempted; owners, if not paupers, had to pay in respect of empty houses; stopped-up chimneys were to pay; and the levy was to be enforced on free schools, mills, and garrisons. Smiths, braziers, and pewterers were liable unless they could prove that their hearths were used solely for the purposes of their trade.[2] In consequence of these strict regulations, there grew up a trade in the 'discovery' of untaxed hearths.[3]

There were also special abuses in the farming of this tax. In April 1668 the farmers demanded defalcations for Plague, Fire, and War; also for Exchequer charges and assaults on their employees.[4] The government did everything in its power to secure the co-operation of local magistrates in order to ensure easier collection of the tax, and similar pressure was brought to bear on the judges. When, in 1670, the chief baron of the Exchequer was asked why he did not give more assistance to the chimney sub-farmers against those who failed to pay, he answered that it would be vexatious to issue process against a man in Cornwall for twelvepence; whereupon Ashley reminded him that the revenue was made up of twelvepences.[5] To this the chief baron replied that the chimney farmers should be commissioned by the Treasury, for then they would be accountants on oath, and distress could be levied on defaulters—a sound suggestion, for the deficiency in this revenue was caused not so much by failure of the subject to pay as by misappropriation or withholding of funds by the private persons entrusted with its collection. These were so extensive that, in January 1668, a treasury warrant was issued to take all the farmers of the Chimney Money into custody, except sir Robert Viner.[6] So notorious was the mismanagement of this tax that, as early as 1666, the Commons offered to compound for it at eight years' purchase, on an estimated annual value of £200,000; but Charles refused.[7] Later in the reign Halifax demonstrated to the king how he was being cheated by

---

[1] Cal. S.P. Dom., 1675-6, ix. [2] Cal. Tr. Bks., 1660-7, 689.
[3] For an example, ibid., 1667-8, 28. [4] Ibid., 1667-8, 296.
[5] Ibid., 1669-72, 352. [6] Ibid., 1667-8, 217.
[7] Diary of J. Millward, Add. MS. 33413, Oct. 15 and Nov. 8, 1666.

the farmers; and it was hoped by the whigs that the duke of York would be implicated in the revelations.[1] Thus, harshness in its incidence and abuses in its collection helped to make this tax the most unpopular of all Stuart expedients; moreover it was an intrusion not into an Englishman's castle, but into his kitchen, and so helped to destroy some of the glamour traditionally associated with Stuart rule. It was abolished immediately after the Revolution.

Customs, Excise, and Hearth Money were the main sources of hereditary revenue in the reigns of Charles and James. They were supplemented by receipts from a large number of miscellaneous sources, none of them producing a regular return comparable in amount with the sources above enumerated. An Act[2] of James I had given the crown power to seize two-thirds of recusants' estates. After his enforced withdrawal of the Declaration of Indulgence Charles was induced to consider this method of raising money, so in 1674–5 the Treasury issued commissions to certain persons in each county with power to seize the king's two-thirds.[3] But in July 1675 it was reported that little or nothing had been done in the matter—whose fault it was the Treasury did not know.[4] There were also the forfeited estates of persons convicted of treason; these were generally solicited by courtiers, sometimes before conviction had been secured—an abuse explicitly condemned by a clause in the Bill of Rights. Consequently the revenue from forfeitures like that from recusants was negligible in amount. Most important of these miscellaneous sources was the revenue from royal lands or territorial rights pertaining to the crown. Among these were the rents from lands in the duchies of Cornwall and Lancaster, and a mass of quit-rents and other dues known as the Fee Farm rents, these latter being estimated at about £50,000 per annum. This does not mean that £50,000 in respect of these rents was paid into the Treasury, for a certain proportion was applied locally;[5] but this amount represented the gross annual sacrifice made by Charles when he consented to the Act[6] for their sale. The Act vested these

---

[1] *Cal. S.P. Dom.*, *1683*, 66, anon. to Jenkins, Feb. 20, 1683.
[2] 2 Jac. I, cap. iv.   [3] *Cal. Tr. Bks.*, *1672–5*, 694, Mar. 1674/5.
[4] Ibid., *1672–5*, 804.
[5] Ibid., *1672–5*, viii–ix.   [6] 22 Car. II, cap. vi.

rents in trustees for this purpose, and the proceeds[1] amounted to about £700,000. Most of these territorial rights and dues had accrued to the crown from Tudor confiscations, and from the enforcement of the Chantries Act of Edward VI; usually they consisted of small sums which must have been very expensive to collect. Some conception of their nature may be gleaned by reference to the contract[2] whereby the Trustees agreed with sir William Ellis for the sale of a parcel of such rents, totalling £826 per annum, for a sum of £12,800, this being equivalent to about sixteen years' purchase. Among the rents so purchased by sir William were £6 7s. 1d. in respect of a custom called 'the knowing every second year and a half' in lands at Windermere, within the manor of Cartmel; £2 8s. 4d. from Greenbank vaccary; £1 11s. 9d. from the chantry of the Blessed Virgin Mary in Spalding; and £1 3s. 4d. from a similar chantry in Batley. So these picturesque vestiges of medieval fancy and piety at last disappeared into the obscurity of private ownership.

Such was the hereditary revenue; the parliamentary revenue was more tentative and irregular. The simplest form of parliamentary grant was a statute authorizing private persons to subscribe to 'a free and voluntary present' to His Majesty, as by the Act[3] of 1661; this was declared to be a special grant and was not to be used as a precedent. The subscriptions of peers were limited to £400, of commoners to £200; the proceeds appear to have amounted to £26,500, of which the commoners contributed £13,100.[4] Resort was not again made to this method of raising money. Provision for extraordinary expenditure, such as that entailed in war-time, was most usually made by an Assessment, such as had been levied during the Commonwealth. The usual rate was £70,000 per month, granted for a specified number of months, from one to eighteen. In the statutes authorizing this levy, each county and city in England and Wales was assessed at a definite quota, and commissioners were appointed to raise this quota by a levy on all owners of real and personal property in each city or county. The general principles on which the various commissioners acted were similar to those enunciated

---

[1] *Cal. Tr. Bks.*, *1672–5*, xi.　　　　　[2] Ibid., *1672–5*, 735–7.
[3] 13 Car. II, stat. i, cap. iv.
[4] Certificate of J. Clutterbock, in *Shaftesbury*, xxxiv, no. 21.

in the Act[1] of Assessment passed by the Rump in January 1660; namely, they met within a specified time in order to agree who should act within each division of their respective areas; any two or more of those so delegated then proceeded to declare the proportion of the assessment in each parish of their division or hundred; and lastly, this sub-quota was raised by a pound rate levied in each parish by two or more assessors in that parish. The rate was imposed on lands, tenements, hereditaments, annuities, rents, and offices other than judicial, military or naval offices, or household and government offices. When an assessment was made out, it was signed and given to the sub-collector, with a warrant for its collection. For each hundred there was a head collector; for each county a receiver general; and one penny in the pound was paid to collectors and sub-collectors. Tenants who paid the tax were authorized to deduct the amount from their rent; appeals against over-assessment lay to the county commissioners, but in such controversies a commissioner was not allowed to vote in his own case.

Two general principles of assessment were recognized. First, the number of commissioners assigned to each county was large, and the Commons in 1666 objected to an increase in their number on the ground that the more commissioners the less the return, since they were likely to encumber each other and promote the interests of their friends.[2] Second, both the proportion between the total for the county and the total for the country, and that between the county assessment and that of the cities and boroughs within its limits became standardized. Objection on this score was answered by a characteristic argument. When the gentlemen of Cheshire complained that the city of Chester was under-assessed in relation to the charge imposed on the county, the solicitor general answered that 'for these hundred years' the city had been assessed at one-tenth of the county, and so it would remain.[3]

In theory, therefore, the yield from these assessments was definite and invariable, because fixed in advance. The tax-payer's fraction was estimated by 'the most able and sufficient' persons in the parish or township; and as these persons were

---

[1] *Acts and Ord.* ii. 1355 sqq.　　　　[2] *Parl. Hist.* iv. 354–5.
[3] *Cal. Tr. Bks., 1669–72*, 165.

usually substantial property-owners, they were not likely to over-estimate the share due from their class. From the smaller fry they received statements, not on oath, which they might accept or reject; or they might content themselves with a marginal comment, as in the Downton hundred (Wiltshire), when John Humby 'confessed to be neere £20', the assessors added the word 'double'.[1] Similar in its incidence and method of collection was the Land Tax[2] granted in 1677; also the Royal Aids, namely that[3] of 1664–5 for £2,477,500 and that[4] of 1666 for £1,256,347, both for the expenses of the Dutch War. It is noteworthy that the Act granting the second of these Aids definitely allocated the sum of £380,000 for the payment of seamen's wages, and enacted that if the treasurer of the Navy misapplied any part of this sum, he should forfeit treble the amount so diverted.

An older form of tax on land and property, the Subsidy, was revived in 1663, when parliament granted[5] four subsidies by the clergy and laity, a grant confirmed by the clergy in their Convocations and embodied in an Act of parliament.[6] This was the last occasion on which the clergy taxed themselves separately; for in 1664–5 Sheldon, in a verbal communication with Clarendon, agreed to surrender this ancient right of the clergy.[7] The rate was the standard one of 4s. in the £1 on the annual value of land and 2s. 8d. in the £1 on the capital value of personalty, aliens and convicted popish recusants to pay double. By the Act of 1663 the county commissioners were to direct precepts to not less than two nor more than eight of 'the most substantial, discreet and honest persons' within each hundred, parish, or other division; thereupon these select persons, under pain of a monetary penalty, were to appear in person before the commissioners and inquire into the value of the substance of all persons liable to be charged. Certificates of assessments were then to be made out and served. No oath was to be tendered, and peers were taxed by a special commission of peers. Personal property was taken to

[1] Rates paid by the tenants of Winchester College as contributions to the Royal Aid of 1666 (Winchester College muniments).
[2] 29 Car. II, cap. i.   [3] 16–17 Car. II, cap. i.
[4] 18–19 Car. II, cap. xiii.   [5] 15 Car. II, cap. ix.   [6] 15 Car. II, cap. x.
[7] The new form of grant appeared in the Speaker's address to the king on Feb. 9, 1665, when he announced the grant of a Royal Aid 'in the name of all the Commons of England'. *L.J.* xi. 654.

include sums owing from debtors, while sums due to others were deducted from the gross value of the estate.

This revival was not a success. England had grown unfamiliar with the old type of subsidy, and the experiment was not repeated. Charles complained[1] that men with £3,000 and £4,000 a year did not pay more than £16; this was because such men generally taxed themselves.[2] In the absence therefore of impartial methods of assessment, it was inevitable that these property taxes gave disappointing results. In some cases the local commissioners, in their interpretation of the phrase 'clear yearly value', deducted from the gross income all payments for hearth money, church rate, servants' wages, and cost of personal subsistence, and 'so the king's part would be little';[3] sometimes also exceptional personal expenditure, such as that for the funeral of a relative, would be adduced as a plea for a less stringent assessment.[4] There was similar elasticity in the rating of personal property in towns. Thus, in September 1663 the corporation of Bristol, consisting of the mayor, aldermen, sheriffs, and councillors, met to arrange for the collection of the subsidies granted in that year. They first considered a letter from the privy council informing them of the standard rates on land and movables, a letter containing this special request that the corporation would see to the due assessment of the subsidy, since, through long desuetude, it was unfamiliar to Englishmen. Having appointed assessors for the several wards, the corporation then proceeded to assess themselves. The mayor declared that in chattels he was worth £10; so he paid £2 13s. 4d. This was comparatively conscientious; for three of the wealthiest men in the city assessed themselves at £8, and it was publicly said that many men were being taxed at a hundredth part of their real wealth.[5]

This was the last use of the old Tudor subsidy, but the word 'subsidy' was still retained and used of assessments and other

---

[1] *L.J.* xi, 582. King's speech, Mar. 21, 1664.

[2] e.g. the letter of the lords commissioners for rating and assessing the peers to lord Rutland, asking him to assess himself. (May 18, 1671. *H.M.C. Rep.* xii, app. v. 23. *MSS. of the duke of Rutland.*)

[3] *Cal. S.P. Dom.*, *1671*, 452.

[4] Ibid. 320. Lord Conway to the commissioners for assessing a property tax, May 1671.

[5] J. Latimer, *Annals of Bristol in the seventeenth century*, 320 sqq.

taxes. An interesting example is the 'Subsidy' of 1670–1, which was intended to fall not on capital but on income and profits. Among the rates were: on lands and mines, 1s. in the £1 of annual value; on public offices, 2s. in the £1, with an allowance on one-third of income for necessary charges; on personal estates not otherwise charged, 6s. for each £6 of annual interest or revenue. There was also in this Act an entirely new tax—a levy of 15s. on every £100 of borrowed money kept on deposit by bankers, the banker being authorized to deduct 10s. on every £100 repaid to his customers. Loans were invited on the security of this Act, the lenders to have 7 per cent. interest. But this new departure was discredited to some extent by its poor yield;[1] and in practice income and profits were taxed in the Poll taxes.

To supplement these taxes, parliament on several occasions experimented with taxes having for their criterion the social or professional status of the subject, or his salary or profits of office, generally combining these things together in one Act, and so providing a primitive form of Income Tax. Thus the Poll Tax[2] of 1660 required dukes and archbishops to pay £100, earls £60, baronets £30, esquires £10, judges £20, the lord mayor of London £40, masters of city companies £10. The same Act imposed a levy of 40s. on every £100 worth of land, money, or stock; on every single person over 16, 1s.; on every one under 16, 6d.; and for every hackney coach, 10s. Social position, professional status, real and personal property, means of transport, and humanity itself were therefore the objects of taxation in this Poll. The Poll Bill[3] of 1666 imposed a similar scale, but at half these rates, money owing to the estate being taxed, but debts due therefrom being exempted, with the proviso that exemption could be claimed in respect of money lent to the government on the security of the Act of 1665 for raising £1,250,000 by an assessment.[4] Public officers taxed in the monthly assessments were, by this Act, to pay 1s. in the £1 on the profits of their offices; those not so taxed,

---

[1] 22–3 Car. II, cap. iii. The yield in 1670–1 was £59,000 and in 1671 £152,000. It had been thought that this tax would give £800,000. See *Cal. Tr. Bks., 1669–72*, x, and W. Kennedy, *English Taxation, 1640–1799*. This essay by the late W. Kennedy is a brilliant contribution to seventeenth-century economic history.

[2] 12 Car. II, cap. ix.   [3] 18–19 Car. II, cap. i.

[4] i.e. 17 Car. II, cap. i. For loans on security of the taxes see *infra*, 444–5.

3s.; on government pensions 3s. in the £1 was to be paid, and 1s. in respect of every 20s. of servants' board-wages. Some of these rates, with modifications, reappeared in the Poll Bill[1] of 1677–8, but income from administrative, professional, and judicial offices was then consolidated, and charged at 2s. in the £1. This Act derived additional importance from the fact that it appropriated the proceeds of the tax, with all loans thereon, to a war with France, and prohibited the importation of French wine, brandy, vinegar, linen, and silk for three years from March 20, 1678.

Other sources of revenue taxed in Charles's reign included (1) the profits of the Post Office;[2] (2) the wine licences;[3] (3) imported wine and vinegar;[4] (4) proceedings at law;[5] and (5) new buildings about London. The profits of the Post Office provided a perquisite for the duke of York; and rival schemes, such as that of Docwra, who proposed a penny post, were suppressed.[6] Licences for the retail of wine were issued by a body of commissioners, at such fees as they might appoint, and the revenue therefrom was not to be charged with any pension. On French and Spanish wine, and on strong waters, the Act of 1667–8 purported to raise the sum of £310,000; the later Acts (1670 and 1678) granted an imposition at definite rates, the first for eight years and the second for three; so the renewal of this levy was one of the inducements for keeping parliament in session.[7] The tax on proceedings at law, the earliest of our modern Stamp Duties, was accounted for by the various courts of justice in London and the provinces, and by town clerks and stewards of manors; in the first year of its levy, it appears to have yielded little more than £20,000.[8] In February 1677/8 the Commons resolved to tax the yearly value of buildings erected in London since 1656, some of the Commons having alleged that new

---

[1] 29–30 Car. II, cap. i.   [2] 12 Car. II, cap. xxxv.

[3] 12 Car. II, cap. xxv.

[4] 19–20 Car. II, cap. vi; 22 Car. II, cap. iii; 30 Car. II, cap. ii.

[5] 22–3 Car. II, cap. ix.

[6] For the Post Office see J. C. Hemmeon, *History of the Post Office.*

[7] Another inducement was the renewal of the Additional Excise of 1670–1 (22–3 Car. II, cap. v) which was granted for six years from June 1671 and renewed for three years in 1677.

[8] *P.R.O. Accounts*, bundle 528, no. xi.

buildings about London were a common nuisance; but no special levy for this purpose appears to have been made, except that in the assessment for 1678, the amount to be paid by Middlesex and Westminster was increased.[1] A tax on entertainments was proposed in 1670, at the rate of 1s. for each person occupying a box at the theatre, 6d. for places in the pit, and 3d. for other seats, but the proposal was opposed by the courtiers, who successfully urged that the actors were the king's servants,[2] and would be prejudiced by this levy.

Lastly, among the sources of Charles's revenue must be included the subsidy from France. At no time was this sufficient in amount to make Charles independent of parliamentary grant; it was the increase of his hereditary revenue, not French money, which eventually enabled Charles to dispense with parliament. The contributions from Louis were generally sufficient to provide comfort, where otherwise there would have been economy; and the total amount received in the course of the reign did not exceed £1,200,000, a sum which would have barely sufficed to defray the civil administration for one year. Nor was this supplementary income spent solely on pleasure; for of the £689,758 accounted for by Chiffinch[3] in 1681, over £330,000 had been paid for the Navy, £66,000 for Ordnance, and £18,000 for the repair and rebuilding of Windsor. Among the miscellaneous objects on which this money was spent were these: to the duke of Buckingham, expenses of mourning for the duchess of Orleans, £1,000; to Pepys, treasurer for Tangiers, £5,000; to the royal upholsterers, £2,700; for a George, set with diamonds for William, prince of Orange, £400. Nurseries for trees at Greenwich, repairing fences at Hampton Court, planting trees in St. James's Park, building and repairing walls in Hyde Park, providing hay for the deer in Windsor Park, and the renewal of the more shabby decorations of Windsor Castle—these were among the miscellaneous uses to which the French money was put.

Such were the main sources, hereditary, parliamentary, and exceptional of Charles II's revenue. It is difficult to estimate

---

[1] 30 Car. II, cap. i.   [2] *Parl. Hist.* iv. 456.
[3] *Cal. Tr. Bks., 1680–5,* 198. Chiffinch's account of French money, Feb. 1671–Dec. 1677.

what proportion of his income a tax-payer might have to sacrifice in taxation; since the methods of assessment differed so much, and so many taxes were non-recurrent, that the burden must have varied greatly in both place and time. Assuming the resources of a tax-payer as static, a portion of his sacrifice would vary with the enrichment or impoverishment of the county or city where he was domiciled; for the most usually recurrent of the property taxes was the assessment, in which the contribution of each administrative unit was fixed; accordingly, if one's neighbours became richer, they might have to pay a larger share of this fixed amount; and conversely, a decline in the prosperity of the administrative unit might necessitate a greater sacrifice on the part of those whose fortunes had not changed. An example of the latter class of county would be Suffolk; of the former, Kent. Local differences in rating and fluctuations in the value of land may also have helped to increase these inequalities. That there should be a regular survey of land, and a more uniform valuation of it were among the principles advocated by sir William Petty.

As the freeholder was the unit of society, so the taxes of the seventeenth century were levied mainly on the income derived from landed property. In a sense this was the price of the pre-eminence of land among articles of private possession. The yeomen and farmers paid, not on their gross agricultural income, but on the rental value of their holdings.[1] It was natural, therefore, that the landed classes generally should favour those taxes which appeared to spare the land. The Customs fell on the importer and so on the consumer; but there was a definite return for these charges, namely, the maintenance of a navy for the protection of commerce. The other great indirect tax was the Excise, and it was here that the landowners joined issue with the rest of the community. In 1660 this contest had been decided in favour of the landed classes, when the compensation for the abolished feudal tenures was saddled on the Excise, a settlement which accentuated a question of principle. On the one hand, from the point of view of the tax-payer, the Excise duties, by their incidence on common articles of consumption, might involve a

[1] Working landowners paid on the annual rental value of their land and also on their stock in the Monthly Assessments. In the Aids they did not pay on their stock. (W. Kennedy, *English Taxation, 1640-1799*, 47, n. 3).

comparative sacrifice by the poor greater than that imposed on the rich; moreover, these duties were of comparatively recent and foreign origin; they were being gradually extended, and might well result in freeing the crown from dependence on parliamentary grants. From the point of view of the crown, on the other hand, the Excise had these advantages; it was paid insensibly and continually, and its administration supplied the prerogative with an army of officials who, if they had votes, must use them in the interests of the crown. Herein were the rudiments of a party distinction, though they never quite fitted into the compartments dividing whig from tory; but it is certain at least that Excise came to be associated with absolutism, and the popular prejudice against it survived late in English history. At the same time, however, there was an increasing acquiescence in the view, popularized by Petty,[1] that Excise is the best and most just of expedients for revenue purposes, because it does not fall on sheer necessities, and is adjusted to the tax-payer's consumption of excisable commodities. By the time of the Revolution no political party could have dispensed with it.[2]

The formulation of a general theory of taxation was attempted by Petty in his *Treatise of Taxes*.[3] As a substitute for the precious metals he sought a more scientific standard of value, and found it in land and labour, the two ultimate sources of human wealth. Between these two denominations, however, he failed to establish any definite correlation; he thought, nevertheless, that each country possessed some 'easily gotten', or staple food, of which the cost of production provided a constant. Increased rent he considered was mainly due to increase of population. While it is true that Petty did not fully develop these principles, they provide some anticipation of the theories of the Physiocrats and of Ricardo. The incidence of taxation was discussed in his *Verbum Sapienti*.[4] He estimated that, towards raising the £70,000 per month assessment, men paid a tenth part of the annual value

---

[1] *Treatise of Taxes*, ch. xv.

[2] For a discussion of this subject see W. Kennedy, in op. cit. 60–2.

[3] In *Economic Writings of sir William Petty*, ed. C. H. Hull. For Petty's theories generally see Dr. Hull's Introduction, and Lord E. Fitzmaurice, *Life of sir William Petty*, 211–15.

[4] In *Economic Writings of sir William Petty*, vol. i.

of their estates, and he believed that, if the special taxation of 1665 for the Dutch War had continued for two more years, the sacrifice would have been increased to a third part. In his view, the public charge was laid very disproportionately; and, in a justly distributed system of taxation, he thought that no man need pay more than a tenth part of the annual value of his property. In this connexion, it may be noted that taxation might have been more equitably assessed had there been adopted a proposal constantly advocated by both Puritan reformers and Caroline publicists, namely, a Land Registry. Such an institution would have safeguarded title to land; it would have greatly diminished the legal cost of conveyancing, and would have provided a body of statistics for a more scientifically adjusted scheme of taxation. The Land Registry, one of the most constantly reiterated of seventeenth-century reforms, has been adopted only in recent times.

Similar improvements might have followed from the establishment of a national bank. This was frequently suggested, but there was great difference of opinion regarding the true functions of such an institution. In 1661 a Dutch writer, Gerbier d'Ouvilly, proposed[1] the foundation in England of a Bank of Exchange as 'beneficial to sovereign and people'. His bank would have a large stock, under 'fitting governors' ('to remove all jealousy of its falling into the hands of those who control the Militia'), having a coinage of its own called bank money, and empowered to lend money on the security of real estate. The proposal appears to have been not unlike that afterwards advocated, as a rival to the Bank of England, by Chamberlayne. A scheme for a Corporation Bank of Credit in London was set on foot[2] in 1682, towards which funds were invited, and for the administration of which a committee of aldermen and councillors was appointed. The scheme was that all persons having goods lying by them should bring them in chests into the large store-house attached to the bank. There they would be valued 'according to durableness and market value', and made over to the Trustees by a bill,

[1] *Cal. S.P. Dom.*, *1661–2*, 78.
[2] For this see *England's interest, or the great benefit to trade by banks or offices of credit in London*, 1682, in *Bodley* G.P. 1120, and *Corporation Credit, or a Bank of Credit made current by common consent in London*, 1682, in *Bodley, Ashmole*, 1672.

a certificate being given to the depositor, who was then entitled to receive a credit for a proportion of the value so deposited. As the credit note was assignable, it was hoped that the scheme would enable men to embark on fruitful schemes, and 'engross the commodities of other countries', thereby beating the Dutch with their own weapons. But, except for its distinguished civic patronage and a complicated system of book-keeping, this institution was little better than a pawnshop, and therefore socially inferior to those schemes, such as land-banks, where the security did not have to be kept on the premises. That the civic bankers were conscious of this disability is shown in a literary effort to commend the 'good and painful undertaking' to the country customer. This was a *Dialogue*[1] *between a country gent and a London merchant*. The merchant disabused the countryman of the idea that the adventurers Chamberlayne and Murray were behind the scheme; he dwelt on the facilities of the bank, how credit could be created, goods deposited in safety, and taken away in proportion as the loan was paid off; he so convinced his inquirer that the dialogue ended with this tribute from the prospective client: 'if this be the constitution of the Bank, I must confess you have satisfied me that it is both Just, Safe, Useful, and Profitable.' Only the skill of the pictorial artist was wanting to depict the benevolence of the merchant and the complete satisfaction of the customer from the country.

In 1680 the English Treasury 'in its present hands' was recommended as a safe deposit,[2] on the ground that it gave 8 per cent. interest and its security was as good as that of any private person. This recalls the fact that existing government machinery very nearly provided the requisite organization for a government bank; indeed, it was only because an impossible task had to be performed by Charles's financial administrators that they did not succeed in grafting some kind of permanent bank on to the Exchequer.[3] This short-lived experiment origin-

---

[1] *Bank Credit* . . . 1683, in *Bodley, Ashmole*, 1672.

[2] Godolphin to the prince of Orange, May 4, 1680, in *Prinsterer*, v. 397.

[3] For this see W. A. Shaw, *The beginnings of the national debt*, in *Historical Essays of Owens College, Manchester* (ed. Tout and Tait); also Dr. Shaw's introductions to *Cal. Tr. Bks.* for the reign of Charles; also R. D. Richards, *Early history of banking in England*.

ated in the practice whereby the Exchequer began to administer loans as well as revenues. For example, there were the deposits made by the farmers when they negotiated their farm; next there were the private advances on such regular sources as the Customs, a security specially favoured by the bankers; then there were loans to which contributions from the nation were specifically invited, the security for which was placed on a definite tax. In 1662 Southampton and Ashley introduced an innovation[1] which helped to increase the confidence of the lender, namely the system of paying out 'in course'. At first, this appears to have been applied only to payment of tallies struck on the Customs receipts; it was intended to displace the older and more haphazard method whereby one man was served before another because of his importunity; or a little paid out to every one because there was not enough to pay in full. The innovation was intended to secure payment only according to strict, chronological sequence; and accordingly, the man who lent on the Customs might apply for repayment in a year or eighteen months, with a reasonable hope that his claim would not be sacrificed to that of some other lender.

Soon, the principle was extended, and Exchequer procedure was greatly developed by the reforms associated with the name of sir George Downing. It was by his initiative that certain innovations were embodied in the Act for the Additional Aid[2] granted by the Oxford parliament of November 1665, an Aid by which it was hoped to raise £1,250,000 as a further subsidy for the war. Against the strenuous opposition of Clarendon, Downing succeeded in carrying a clause whereby it was enacted that all money raised by this Bill should be applied only to a definite purpose, namely for carrying on the war. By this appropriation clause some limitation was imposed on the powers of lord treasurer Southampton, who had faithfully striven to make ends meet by supplementing one source from another; but nevertheless he set himself to carry out the revised procedure, though he complained of the difficulty of doing so, because payments had to be made 'in course' as registered; moreover, without his knowledge, this fund was soon saddled with com-

---

[1] *Cal. Tr. Bks., 1660–7*, 358, Feb. 3, 1662.
[2] 17 Car. II, cap. i.

mitments registered by the king and the duke of York.[1] But that such an appropriation clause should have passed the Commons was of importance, because it reflected the suspicion that funds intended for the war were being diverted; and it was thus one of the earliest suggestions of criticism of the executive by the Cavalier Parliament. Once having secured a statutory appropriation of supplies, Charles's parliaments extended the principle; for in the following year they assigned £30,000 to the Guards[2] (thereby giving some legal colour to the existence of a standing army); in the Poll Bill[3] of 1677 they appropriated the proceeds to a war with the French king, and in the Assessment[4] of £619,388 voted in 1678 they allocated this sum to the disbandment of all the land-forces raised since September 29, 1677. In 1677 an Assessment[5] of £584,978 had been granted for the express purpose of building thirty ships-of-war. Thus the principle of appropriation of supplies had taken root long before the end of Charles's reign.

Appropriation of a tax to a defined object, and payment 'in course' of all expenditure defrayed therefrom were thus two important innovations in English fiscal practice. Even more important was the revival of a project first attempted in the Poll Bill of 1660, namely, that of inducing the public to lend money on the security of one of the national funds. In the Additional Aid of 1665 these three principles were for the first time united—appropriation, payment 'in course', and an appeal to the public for loans on the security of this more precisely regulated fund. There was a fourth innovation which may be attributed definitely to Downing, namely, that the repayment orders accompanying the Exchequer tallies were made assignable by endorsement. The effect of this last provision was that a holder of tallies needing ready money before the assigned date of repayment could now take his tallies and orders to a goldsmith-banker and have them discounted. Between 1667 and 1671 many of these 'orders of loan' were issued by the Exchequer,

---

[1] *Cal. Tr. Bks., 1660–7,* 712, Jan. 5, 1666.

[2] 18–19 Car. II, cap. i, par. xxxi.

[3] 29–30 Car. II, cap. i. The appropriation is embodied in the title of the Act.

[4] 30 Car. II, cap. i, par. i.　　　　　　　　　　[5] 29 Car. II, cap. i.

and when the 'Stop' came in 1672 most of them were in possession of the bankers. It is possible, therefore, to discern in the
terms of this Additional Aid of 1665 the germ of three things—
a national debt, in the invitation to lend money on the security
of a portion of the national revenues; a national bank, in the
reorganization of the Exchequer system, whereby its repayments
of borrowed money became more automatic and less capricious,
thereby encouraging the lender and the investor; and lastly,
a paper currency, because these early Exchequer Bills were
negotiable instruments, and so might serve as a substitute for
currency. Had this scheme[1] succeeded, the monopoly of the
goldsmiths would have been destroyed, and England would
have had a national institution for the creation and circulation
of credit. Colbert tried to do the same thing for France when
in 1674 he established the *Caisse des Emprunts* for short-term
loans, redeemable in definite sequence; but the French experiment also failed.[2]

These facts have been cited to show that considerable progress
was made in fiscal administration in the reign of Charles, and
that some of the most notable financial achievements of the
Revolution whigs were not without their backing of earlier
experiment. But, as in so much else, this reign stands between
two worlds. On the one hand it was still thought by some that
the king should 'live of his own'. On the other hand, the enor-
mously increased demands on the executive made this older ideal
no longer possible of fulfilment. So too with accountability; on
the one hand the king had his hereditary revenues for which he
had to render no account, while on the other he was obliged to
demand more and more money from parliament, for which a
rendering was required. The king was still a landed proprietor
and not yet an official; the Civil List was still mixed up with the
normal expenses of peace administration and the exceptional
expenditure necessitated by war. In these circumstances both
confusion and misunderstanding were inevitable, and these

[1] For this see R. D. Richards, op. cit., 59 sqq.; W. A. Shaw, *The beginnings
of the national debt* in *Owens College Historical Essays*, and J. Beresford, *Sir
George Downing*, ch. 12.
[2] Germain Martin, *L'histoire du crédit en France sous le règne de Louis XIV*,
i. 92–4.

things should be taken into account when the difficulty of Charles's task is gauged. The scheme associated with the name of Downing was an attempt to adjust the older financial system to the newer needs of the state; but it was foredoomed to failure, because the parliamentary provision for Charles's revenue was so inadequate as to make bankruptcy (as then understood) inevitable. That bankruptcy was merely being staved off is seen from the steady increase of debt in the first twelve years of the reign, until in 1672 it amounted to more than £2,000,000, when a suspension of payments had to be resorted to. In addition, even had there been no debt, it is doubtful if a Stuart could have acquiesced in a scheme, such as Downing's, which subjected payments to strict routine.

One illustration in support of this last assertion may be cited; it had its origin in the following way. As many of the farmers and collectors were guilty of embezzlement or failure to account for their receipts, parliament in 1667–8 passed an Act[1] requiring the payment of 12 per cent. interest on such overdue accounts. The enforcement of this penalty explains the motive of a petition to the privy council in 1673 from one David Powell, Receiver for an eighteen-months Assessment in the county of Montgomery, who alleged that the money collected (£988) had miscarried on its way to London. These arrears were charged to Powell; but interest in the debt was assigned to Killigrew (the court jester) by the king, who may have thought that this was not a very valuable gift. As security for the debt Killigrew thereupon took over part of Powell's estate, and sold some of the debtor's goods; he then demanded the full 12 per cent. interest allowed by the Act. Powell petitioned[2] that the interest should be reduced to 6 per cent. This example has been selected because it shows how even from a debt an importunate courtier might profit. On the royal assets, whether forfeitures, reclaimed lands, or revenues, the demands were more continuous and rapacious. The generosity of the king on these occasions contrasts with the niggardly attitude to humbler applicants; for example, the widow of Charles I's shoemaker, to whom £1,100 was owing. Her claim was ordered to be paid out of the leather forfeitures, from which highly speculative source she received

[1] 19–20 Car. II, cap. vii. [2] P.C. Reg. 64, May 14, 1673.

only enough to support her in prison, where she was confined for debt.[1] Charles's private expenses were not excessive, nor were his women associates costly if one thinks in terms of millions, but the hangers-on and courtiers were an equally insidious source of profligacy, because their importunity was as secret and personal, and might be rewarded from any branch of national revenue. Many historians have emphasized the brilliance of Charles's Court, or his guiltlessness in the financial affairs of his reign; but behind these attractive things there is the background of dishonoured government bills, imprisoned creditors, and starving sailors.

The king's personal generosity crowned a wonderful edifice in which each compartment was kept completely separate. This meant that the different sources of revenue were reserved for separate commitments; thus, the assessment raised from one county would be allocated to the Wardrobe; or one month of Customs revenue would be assigned for a particular debt; or a pension might be placed on the Chimney Money, or on the Excise, with the result that if there was a shortage in one of these separate funds, the payments therefrom might fail.[2] Experience showed which were the more secure, which the less reliable funds. Customs and Excise were the soundest, the first being favoured by the goldsmiths for their loans, while the second was a good basis on which to assign the pension of a favourite. Chimney Money was highly speculative, owing to fluctuations in yield. The result was that there might sometimes be effected transfers of security from one fund to another—changes called *virements* in French finance; for example, Lord Mandeville, in 1668, asked that his pension of £1,000 per annum should be transferred from the Chimney Money to a better source.[3] Or the Exchequer officials might have to go round looking for a fund on which some payment could be placed; and in spite of the 'in course' system, it seems generally to have been possible for both the king and the duke of York to secure priority for a pension or payment, even though the fund allocated was already burdened with debt, and encumbered with registered claims. This is why the seamen suffered so much in the Second

[1] *Cal. Tr. Bks.*, 1669–72, 1044.
[2] Ibid., 1669–72, 7.
[3] Ibid., 1667–8, 441.

Dutch War. Parliament had definitely allocated £380,000 for their wages, but who was to see that such a sum was applied for that purpose? Moreover, the seamen were far off, and obscure persons at best; while near at hand there were the Gentlemen of the Bedchamber, the Groom Porters, the Pages of the Backstairs, to name only some of the more reputable of those who frequented the Court.

Not dishonesty, but clumsiness and wastefulness were the characteristics of financial administration at this period. Only gradually was there being evolved the experience and public opinion requisite for the creation of a system more fitted to cope with the rapidly-expanding needs of the state. Not yet was the fiscal administration regarded as the prerogative duty of government departments, or civil service; for so long as there were tax farmers, there was an element of private enterprise and profit in the national finances; and indeed the levying of a tax might be committed almost entirely to an outside body, as for example when the Vintners advanced on loan the greater part of the proceeds expected from the Wine Act of 1667–8, and then made their own arrangements for its collection;[1] or when, at the Restoration, the proceeds of several taxes were administered by the Chamber of the city of London.[2] Perhaps the severest criticism of the executive in the whole of Stuart history was that implied by the proposal of October 1675 to lodge in the Chamber of the city the money to be raised for the building of ships. It was negatived by only 171 to 160.[3]

These things contributed to the rising flood of debt which, for a time, overwhelmed the structure. The issue of Exchequer Bills had facilitated the circulation of credit and was a perfectly sound scheme; but when these Bills were assigned on revenues already hypothecated for more than a year in advance they were really based on no security whatever.[4] Most of these 'orders of repayment' on the Exchequer had come into the hands of the

---

[1] For the irregularities to which this led see *Cal. Tr. Bks.*, *1681–5*, 118, where it is shown that those members of the Vintners' syndicate who had lost money by the first speculation of 1667–8 used their influence with parliament to have the Wine Act of 1670 passed, so that they could recoup their losses.

[2] Ibid., *1660–7*, Introduction.   [3] *Parl. Hist.* iv. 772–4.

[4] For this subject see Dr. Shaw's preface to *Cal. Tr. Bks.*, *1669–72*.

bankers and goldsmiths; a portion was held by government departments, and all these paper commitments came to be based on security already pledged up to the hilt. In January 1672 Charles issued letters patent suspending for one year all payments on asssignations in the Exchequer.[1] This measure did not involve the break-down of the finances of the nation, but it meant default in regard to a substantial portion of national debt. The Stop was renewed a year later, and its real effect was to make available for government needs the proceeds of the taxes as they came in, while leaving unsatisfied the claims due on the paper orders of loan issued in accordance with the scheme of 1665. The loss, amounting to just over a million pounds, fell mainly on the bankers, who in 1674 were given two years' interest on their capital; a more permanent provision was that made in 1677-9, when interest was paid to them by a scheme of annuities.

More than personal loss, the Stop of the Exchequer involved public discredit; for it appeared to confirm all the suspicions entertained of Charles's financial administration in the Second Dutch War, and it was partly responsible for England's withdrawal from the Third. Another consequence was that further financial experiment had to be postponed until after the Revolution.

[1] Ibid., *1669-72*, 1172, Jan. 20, 1671/2.

XIII

THE CROWN IN PARLIAMENT

THE central theme in the history of Charles II's reign is the attempt to establish a clearly defined relationship within the trinity which consisted of crown and both Houses, and was known as the crown in parliament. That the king was an essential part of the legislature; that he had supreme control over the Militia and all forces by land and sea; that his supremacy in ecclesiastical matters was not abridged by the abolition of the court of High Commission—such were among the principles enunciated by Statute in the first session of the Cavalier Parliament. To the restored monarch, more foreign than English in his education and sympathies, indifferent to the vague constitutionalism enshrined in the native common law, such a settlement must have seemed eminently just; for it appeared unreasonable that the polity of England should present an exception in the well-ordered ranks of European states. Herein was the true significance of Charles's somewhat fitful Catholicism—it suggested links with the oecumenic church and still more with the equally oecumenic and sacrosanct principles of government then being applied abroad, notably in France. Charles had been deprived of his birth-right for twelve years, and though much of his exile was passed in the Low Countries, where there were some local traditions of independence, he was yet taught to associate absolute kingship with order, and political experiment with anarchy. Of English patriotism, or respect for English tradition, there was no trace in his career.

Charles must have found some confirmation of his theory of kingship in the language of those who came into contact with him. Clarendon made no secret of his conviction that the roots of the late rebellion could not be destroyed 'until the King's regal and inherent power and prerogative should be fully avowed and vindicated, and till the usurpations in both Houses since the year 1640 were disclaimed and made odious'.[1] Men more learned in the law helped to confirm this doctrine of royal pre-eminence. Thus lord Guilford, citing Bracton, Britton,

[1] *Clar. Cont.* iii. 164.

and Fleta, contended that the king alone has supreme and ordinary jurisdiction in the state, all others having merely delegated jurisdiction; while from Tudor precedent he argued that the king is supreme governor in all ecclesiastical as well as temporal causes.[1] More generally, Guilford defended the prerogative on the ground that 'a King is above ambition, and it will be easy to obtain justice from one who hath almost all that he desires'.[2] The royal power was so extensive that its limits should not be inquired into—such was the expressed opinion of secretary Coventry in the House of Commons.[3] Its activities were also entitled to the protection of secrecy, for it was 'the law of the land' that no one might expose to public knowledge anything concerning the government without the king's licence.[4] According to Danby, peace and war, punishment and mercy, jurisdiction and its concomitants, all belonged to the king and to no one else; the phrase 'the body politic' was a trick of the lawyers.[5] It was generally agreed that the crown was not one of the three estates; to contend that it was an estate of the realm was a whig heresy.

The clergy provided even more strenuous advocates of the prerogative. At a meeting of Convocation of the University of Oxford in July 1683 a decree was passed condemning certain 'pernicious books and damnable doctrines'. Among the doctrines so condemned were these: that civil authority is derived from the people; that there is a contract between the ruler and his subjects; that a ruler who becomes a tyrant forfeits the obedience of his subjects; that the king is one of the estates of the realm; that covenants and associations are legal.[6] Unlike the lawyers, the churchmen had no reserves in their political theory, and they based their doctrines on something stronger than tradition—namely the Bible. It was a not inconsiderable part of Charles's achievement that he availed himself of the religious sanctions with which the Divine Right school

[1] *Add. MS.* 36086, f. 22.   [2] *Add. MS.* 32520, f. 221.
[3] Feb. 1673, in the debate on the Declaration of Indulgence. *Parl. Hist.* iv. 521.
[4] Jeffreys, at the trial of Henry Carr for printing and publishing *The Weekly Packet of Advice from Rome. State Trials* (1730 ed.), iii. 57.
[5] *Add. MS.* 28043, f. 102.
[6] *H.M.C. Rep. Kenyon MSS.*, 163–6.

surrounded the throne; he confirmed these sanctions by the assi-
duity and success with which he touched for the King's Evil,
and no one could have worn more gracefully than did he the
halo with which Anglican devotion sanctified the royal head.

If it is impossible to define the limits of Charles's prerogative,
it is possible at least to describe some of the paths which con-
verged on it. Religion, sentiment, and expediency all found a
meeting point in the crown; even the much vaunted common
law tradition of England seemed to direct a finger in the same
direction; for had not Bracton declared: *parem non habet Rex in
regno suo?*[1] From this primordial dictum it had been argued in
the preceding century that the royal prerogative was above
human laws.[2] But unfortunately there was a disputed right of
way in this legal path towards absolutism; for elsewhere Bracton
had stated: *Rex habet superiorem, scilicet Deum; item curiam suam,
videlicet comites et barones, quia comites dicuntur quasi socii regis, et
qui habet socium habet magistrum.*[3] Here was an entirely different
conception of kingship, already well known to critics of the
prerogative. Lord President Bradshaw at the trial of Charles I
had quoted it to support his two contentions, that the function
of parliament was to redress the people's grievances, and that
in Saxon times parliaments had frequently called kings to
account.[4] Similar views were taught by Algernon Sidney on
the strength of the same authority.[5] This apparent inconsistency
in Bracton arose from the interpolation in a defective manuscript of a marginal gloss or comment—an explanation first suggested by a seventeenth-century Englishman, who contended
that the passage was an addition made to the text by someone
in sympathy with the ideals of Simon de Montfort.[6]

This has been quoted as one of the many instances where the
authority of secular tradition was invoked with somewhat
ambiguous results. Less ambiguous were the conclusions

[1] Bracton, *De Legibus Angliae*, f. 5 *b*.
[2] By Thomas Cromwell and Robert Cecil, *Parl. Hist.* (1751 ed.), iv. 191
and 465.   [3] *De Legibus*, f. 34 *b*.
[4] *Trial of king Charles I* (ed. J. G. Muddiman), 115–17.
[5] *Discourses concerning government* (2nd ed. 1705), 263–4.
[6] John Turner, in his reprint (1684) of *The Soldier's Catechism* (originally
printed 1644). In Prof. Woodbine's edition of Bracton (ii. 110) the passage
is classified as one of the 'addiciones'.

deduced from the maxim, the king can do no wrong. This was reiterated not by the churchmen, but by the lawyers, and connoted a legal rather than a moral irresponsibility. It related especially to the king's commands in writing under the Great Seal. As such commands were public and authenticated, it was possible for the subject to see for himself whether they were legal or not; if legal, he had to obey them; if illegal, it was his duty not to obey them. Consequently, any of the king's grants might be contested in one of his courts of justice. This, the more academic interpretation, imposed on the subject the requirement of finding out or testing the legality of the sovereign's commands, while absolving the crown from the duty of ascertaining whether these were legal before enunciating them; in a sense therefore this interpretation of the maxim amounted to no more than this, that everyone, except the king, is supposed to know the whole law of England. 'Every Englishman', it was said in the House of Commons, 'is born a common lawyer.'[1] But there was a more important deduction, destined to be brought into sharper prominence by the events of Charles's reign. This was that the king can do no wrong in the sense that his responsibility has to be apportioned among his ministers; accordingly, from a seemingly absolutist maxim, was deduced the doctrine of ministerial responsibility. Hence one of the most sacred rights of the Commons—the right to impeach: hence also their right to discuss and criticize the king's speeches, since these were put into his mouth by his ministers. But Charles strove to avert the attempt to attack him through his agents by exercising an undoubted right of his prerogative—the right to pardon, and it was Danby's plea of such a pardon which prompted the declaration in the Act of Settlement that no pardon under the Great Seal was pleadable in bar of an impeachment. Before a constitutional monarchy could be achieved, it was necessary to restrict not only what the king might do but what he might forgive.

From this fundamental maxim a third deduction was made, namely, that the king must not give reasons for his acts. His legal immunity was already so complete, that for him to explain or condone his conduct was to sacrifice that immunity, and to

[1] *Grey*, iv. 137.

descend from the throne to the tribunal. The Tudors had all avoided this trap; some of the Stuarts were always falling into it. James I wrote books and made speeches in the attempt to explain himself; Charles I was forced into the false position of having to protest his innocence and good faith; James II, convinced that he could bring even the most obstinate to his way of thinking, conducted an electioneering campaign, and made the worst mistake a king can commit, that of composing his own speeches. Alone of the male Stuarts, Charles II appreciated and respected this essential element of the prerogative, knowing as he did that a king who argues or excuses himself is lost; but so strong were the forces ranged against the unique but obsolescent system which he so skilfully directed, that even he was guilty of serious lapses, as when in October 1675 he gave his promise to parliament that, if a supply were granted, he would be more economical in future.[1] The worst lapse was in February 1673, after a prorogation during which he had caused his chancellor to issue writs for the filling of vacant seats. Having made his speech, he appears to have got up again with the extraordinary preamble 'One thing I forgot to tell you', and then proceeded to explain what he had done.[2] The Commons promptly unseated all the members so elected, and solemnly recorded the principle that it was for them to issue such writs.

When they granted to Charles the Customs and Excise for life, the legislators of 1660 may not have foreseen how this grant would ultimately absolve the crown from the necessity of recourse to parliament; later, they may have thought that some guarantee was provided by the Triennial Act[3] of 1664, which enacted that parliaments should be summoned and held 'once in three years at the least'. This Act contained no provision for its enforcement, and its violation by the crown commenced in April 1684, three years after the dissolution of the Oxford Parliament. But in a sense it was fortunate that such a life annuity was voted, because it spared Charles the necessity of raising money without parliamentary consent, and so helped to confirm the claim of the Commons to be the sole initiators of money grants. In this respect the aims of the Puritan Revolution were

---

[1] See *infra*, 534-5.   [2] *L.J.* xii. 526, Feb. 5, 1673.
[3] 16 Car. II, cap. i.

vindicated; here indeed was the most substantial link between the conduct of Charles Stuart and the principles formulated by the Long Parliament of 1640. One of the first acts of James II was to break this link, for he began his reign by levying Customs and Excise duties before the meeting of his parliament. But not only did Charles preserve inviolate this sacred right of parliament; he allowed also a parliamentary investigation of national expenditure in the Second Dutch War,[1] and in practice he devoted the greater part of the yield from the Customs to the needs of the Navy. He paid at least nominal respect to the privileges of the Commons, and he did not publicly resent criticism of his speeches. In these respects Charles acted as a constitutional monarch, and to that extent he made more easy the task accomplished by the statesmen of 1689. This process was further facilitated by an English institution not usually associated with constitutional progress—the Tower of London. Unlike the Bastille and other prerogative prisons, the Tower was not merely a place of confinement for personages arrested on a royal warrant, because it received into its custody persons committed on the warrant of either House of Parliament; and so, at least in the reign of Charles, the Tower served at times as a national repository for the safe custody of those whose temporary seclusion from public life was desirable.

Otherwise the relations between king and Commons showed a steadily increasing tension, ended by the personal triumph of Charles and the apparent discredit of parliamentary institutions. Though annihilated in the reaction of 1681–5 and reduced to impotence in the reign of James II, the whig opposition had nevertheless placed on record many of the fundamental principles on which sovereignty was afterwards to be based. These doctrines were formulated mainly in discussion or criticism of certain prerogative rights exercised by the crown, including (1) absolute control over the military forces of the kingdom, (2) the right to maintain ministers in office, (3) the right to summon, prorogue, and dissolve parliament, (4) the right to appoint judges during pleasure, (5) the right to veto legislation, and (6) the right to declare war and make peace, and, in general, to control the foreign policy of the country without recourse to parliament.

[1] See *supra*, i. 317.

The first was contested only to this extent, that a standing army was thought by the opposition to be illegal, in spite of the reference in the statute of 1661 to 'the Militia and all forces by land and sea'. Here parliament was trying to undo what the Restoration legislators had effected. The second, appointment to high offices of state,[1] and retention of unpopular ministers, was not opposed as a general principle, but only in particular cases where the Commons tried in vain to use their weapon of impeachment. Both Clarendon and Danby were, it is true, removed; but not directly at the suit of the Commons; Lauderdale on the other hand remained, impregnable in his master's support. The third right, that of summoning, proroguing, and dissolving parliaments, did not become a matter of concern until comparatively late in the reign. In 1668 sir Richard Temple brought in a Bill which conferred on the chancellor the power to issue writs in the event of parliament not having been summoned within three years, but he was ordered to withdraw it.[2] The Commons took a very different view during the Exclusion controversy; for in December 1680 a committee of the whole House resolved to introduce a Bill for the more effectual 'securing and sitting of frequent parliaments as one means to prevent arbitrary power'.[3] The fourth right was contested by the Commons in their demand, reiterated at the time of the Popish Plot, that judges should hold their offices not *durante beneplacito*, but *quamdiu se bene gesserint*.[4]

Of the fifth right, that to veto legislation, Charles made a very sparing use; nor would its exercise have been discussed had he not, in at least one instance, acted in a somewhat unusual manner. Only two public Bills were vetoed—one for confirmation of the office of Register of Sales[5] (1662) and a Militia Bill[6] (1678). In neither instance did the Commons show resentment, and in

---

[1] On appointment to all but the most important offices the duchess of Portsmouth exercised some influence. In 1671 Andrew Marvell wrote of her: 'all promotions, spiritual and temporal pass within her cognizance'. (Marvell, *Works*, ed. Grosart, ii. 394). These promotions included deaneries and even bishoprics.   [2] *Parl. Hist.* iv. 410.

[3] *C.J.* ix. 682.   [4] Ibid. ix. 682, and *infra*, 605.

[5] *L.J.* xi. 473. For the veto generally see C. E. Fryer, *The royal veto under Charles II* in *E.H.R.* xxxii.

[6] *L.J.* xiii. 394; also *infra*, 604–5.

the latter they tried to find out wherein their Bill had offended. But there were two occasions when a Bill ready for the royal assent was 'lost'; the first being a Bill for the stricter observance of the Sabbath[1] (1663), and the second a Bill for repealing the Elizabethan statute on which the penal legislation against the Dissenters was based.[2] Charles's complicity in the second 'loss' was suspected, and this unusual method of quashing legislation was keenly resented by the whigs of the Oxford Parliament (1681), one of whom lamented that the earlier loss (that of the Sabbath Observance Bill) had not been more strictly inquired into at the time, since the one mishap might have given some kind of precedent for the other. The result was a resolution for a conference with the Lords on the constitution of parliaments in the matter of passing Bills,[3] but Charles did not again have occasion to exercise ingenuity in the elimination of inconvenient legislation.

This moderate use of the veto helped to preserve the right intact, and in practice Charles quashed many bills by the expedient of proroguing or dissolving parliament. The result was the evolution of an almost stereotyped relationship between crown and Commons. On the one hand, the Commons held out the bait of a subsidy in return for some legislative conces- sion; on the other hand, the crown strove, by its friends and agents in the House, to secure a grant without such concession, and when these expedients failed, the king prorogued parlia- ment in the hope that delay would put the legislators in a better frame of mind; or else dissolved it, in the hope that the country would return a House of Commons more likely to repose faith in the executive. Charles skilfully utilized the English sentiment for royalty in his calls upon the confidence of the two Houses; he played assiduously on this harp until there was no string left; but his Commons showed more and more clearly that, while they regarded the king as a gentleman, they believed Charles to

[1] Ibid. xi. 577. It was 'taken from the table and is not now to be found'. Each peer gave his oath that he had not removed it.

[2] On Dec. 17, 1680, the Commons accepted the Lords' amendments to this Bill, *L.J.* xiii. 719. For the debates in the Oxford Parliament on its loss see *Parl. Hist.* iv. 1308.

[3] *Parl. Hist.* iv. 1311–13.

be a trickster.[1] The unfailing courtesy preserved throughout this relationship was a distinctively English achievement.

In regard to the sixth right, that to control foreign policy, the Commons knew that they could not dictate the crown's alliances, mainly because they were handicapped by a certain limitation implied in their writ of summons, the formula being: *ad consentiendum et deliberandum de quibusdam arduis regni negotiis*. The word *quibusdam*, contrasted with the Lords' *omnibus*, seemed to infer that certain exalted matters of state might be withheld from their cognizance, and the classical example was Elizabeth's refusal of the Commons' claim to discuss her marriage. But in the Third Dutch War the Commons made clear their disapproval of Charles's foreign policy, and in May 1677 they debated an address for a defensive and offensive alliance with Holland, a debate in which precedents were quoted to prove that, in the past, the crown had sometimes acted on the advice of parliament in making its treaties. This was objected to by secretary Coventry as a knocking at the prince's door, instead of the customary scraping, but the Commons were not to be deterred; and they coupled their address with an intimation declining a further supply until His Majesty's alliances were known.[2] Charles's reply was an uncompromising refusal to allow the slightest invasion of his fundamental power of making peace and war.[3] But the king himself was at the mercy of the very exceptional circumstances which controlled European policy in the crucial years 1677–8; and when parliament again met on January 28, 1678, he announced that he had formed an alliance with Holland. He appeared to yield still further; for in April he made known to the House the terms of his alliances.[4] These concessions were not changes of principle on the part of Charles, but were strategic moves in the negotiations with Louis XIV, whereby Charles was using the English demand for war with France as a means of extorting money from the French king. Herein was his most notable failure; he thought that he could

---

[1] e.g. in the debate of May 1677 Sacheverell was reported to have said: 'When peace was made with Holland, we desired it exclusive to France. It was said then: "trust the King"; and you were deceived then. Will you be deceived twice?' *Parl. Hist.* iv. 876.   [2] Ibid. iv. 870–9.

[3] *C.J.* ix. 426.   [4] See *infra*, 554.

yield to the Commons and also secure the foreign subsidy; but not even the wiliest of diplomats could have combined these two things in the crisis of 1678. Moreover, Charles's failure was an ungraceful one. His trickery was revealed to each of the two parties which he wished to dupe, and the shame of these proceedings helped ultimately to secure for the Commons an effective control over the foreign policy of the crown.

Charles yielded in the matter of the Dispensing Power, and his control over foreign policy broke down temporarily in 1678; but otherwise he preserved intact all the prerogatives with which his crown was endowed. Nor did he do anything to diminish the national veneration for the throne, however much his personal conduct may have aroused criticism. To the end he retained firm hold of a sceptre which at many moments seemed certain to slip from his hand, and he surmounted innumerable difficulties not by industry, but by inactivity; not by force, but by a histrionic gift and a supreme sense of tact. But, unknown to himself, his reign was steadily preparing the way for the constitutional government of modern times. From the core of the privy council there was evolving an administrative machinery controlled by experts; parliament became securely entrenched as an essential element in English life because of the gradual realization that its activities were the concern of the nation; still more, the events of the reign made Englishmen politicians, and there can be no real measure of parliamentary government until some standard of political education has been achieved. This political education was almost continuous between at least the years 1640 and 1688. The Long Parliament instituted rule by a single House; Protectorate and Commonwealth were little more than a series of experiments in adjusting the powers of the executive to the control of the Commons; at the reaction of the Restoration England seemed to be heading direct for absolutism, in the crisis of 1678–9 for revolution or republicanism, and throughout these years there was no lengthy intermission in the meetings of the House of Commons. Charles quickened the cause of constitutionalism by the suspicion which his conduct created, but he retained his throne by sheer political genius, and bequeathed to his brother the strongest prerogative in modern English history. The measure of James's failure is the measure of Charles's success—a success personal, solitary, and unique.

If there was doubt in regard to the extent of the powers enjoyed by the crown there was still more in regard to those of parliament. The theory still survived that parliament had first been instituted by king Alfred, but there was little agreement about the limits of its functions, advocates of contrary opinions finding support for their views in the heterogeneous mass of legend and tradition which had been readily devoured by lawyers and parliamentarians in the struggle against Charles I. An extreme view was that vouched for by the semi-spurious *Mirror of Justices*, and afterwards endorsed by Algernon Sidney— that parliaments were ordained to hear and determine 'all complaints of wrongful acts done by the king, queen or their children, and such others against whom common right cannot be had elsewhere'.[1] A more moderate definition was that given by the antiquarian Petyt:[2] 'it is called parliamentum, because every member of the court should speak his mind, "parler le ment" '; in other words, a national council. It was at least certain that parliament was a court; that its origins were lost in the mists of antiquity; that the Lords, as perpetual legislators, were free from arrest in civil suits for their lives, and that this privilege extended to the Commons and their servants during a parliamentary session, and for a period of forty days before and after it. Either House might adjourn on its own initiative, and Charles sometimes adjourned parliament; but in both instances there was no session; on the other hand, by royal prorogation a session was constituted, and Bills which had passed either or both Houses but had not yet received the royal assent had to be commenced again at the next session.

A privilege shared by both Houses was the right to commit a member to custody when he infringed the rules or traditions of the House. From the point of view of a member of either House this might well prove a disability; for it was a sacred principle that in those cases the law courts had no jurisdiction. In 1677 Shaftesbury argued in the Lords that the length of the preceding prorogation had automatically dissolved parliament; a Court

[1] *A just and modest vindication* . . . in *State Tracts*, pt. i (1689), 181.
[2] *Lex Parliamentaria* (1689), cap. i.

majority thereupon ordered him and three other peers to ac-
knowledge their error, and beg pardon of the king and House.
On refusing, Shaftesbury and his fellows were committed to
the Tower. He applied for a writ of habeas corpus, his counsel
contending that to the courts of Westminster pertained the right
of adjudging the validity of a commitment by either House, as
well as the right of determining whether the Journals of Lords
or Commons constituted records, or what was a session of
parliament. In general, it was urged on Shaftesbury's behalf
that, when the liberty of the subject is restrained, the proper
place 'of appeal is the King's Bench; and, in particular, this
committal by the Lords was tantamount to depriving the king
of the advice of one of his peers. But these contentions proved
of no avail against the general principle that offences in parliament cannot be adjudged elsewhere than in parliament, and to
this extent therefore membership of either House involved a
sacrifice of the protection afforded by the courts.[1]

Another important privilege common to Lords and Commons
was that whereby each House had the right to determine its
own composition. This was impugned by the Commons in their
dispute with the Lords over the impeachment of Danby (1679),
when the former challenged the right of the bishops to be present
during the trial. Here the Commons failed to substantiate their
claim. The Lords in this reign made at least one important
decision regarding their membership; for in the Freschville
peerage case (1677) they enunciated the principle that a parliamentary barony is not created by a mere writ of summons; nor
is the blood of the recipient ennobled thereby; for there must
be proof that the summons was obeyed.[2]

On the composition of their own House the Commons exercised an equal measure of control. They denied the crown's
claim to limit or determine the franchise, as in the case of
the borough of Newark, when the king granted a charter which
confined the franchise to the corporation. The Commons in
1677 unseated the two members so returned, and thereafter the
crown did not attempt to declare who should vote. They also
determined when a writ should be issued for a by-election; they

[1] *English Reports*, lxxxvi. 792–800.
[2] Sir W. R. Anson, *Law and Custom of the Constitution* (4th ed.), i. 199–200.

decided all doubtful or double elections, and in at least one instance (that of the burgesses of Bristol) they subsequently admitted a candidate who had at first been rejected. This case had its origin in 1661, when lord Ossory (son of the duke of Ormonde) and sir Humphrey Poole were among the candidates for the suffrage of Bristol. Poole retired from the contest and 'resigned his interest' to Ossory; but a double return was made of these two, and the Commons chose Ossory. In 1666 Ossory, on his elevation to an English peerage, was called to the Lords; whereupon it was debated whether Poole should be admitted on the former double return, or whether there should be a writ for a new election; but, as Poole was a loyalist, he had the support of the Court, and the Commons decided to have him on the strength of his very dubious election of 1661.[1] This exclusive right to determine the legality of the returns made to their chamber was vindicated in the case of *Barnardiston* v. *Soame*. In the Suffolk by-election of 1672 sir Samuel Barnardiston was returned by a large majority of Dissenters and tradesmen; but the sheriff (Soame), whose sympathies were with the defeated candidate, made a double return, on the ground that Barnardiston's majority was due to the 'rabble', who presumably were not forty-shilling freeholders. Barnardiston (who was admitted by the Commons) obtained a verdict and damages in the King's Bench[2] against Soame; but, on a writ of error, this was reversed in the Exchequer, one judge stating that the misfeasance alleged was only 'pepper and salt and nothing'.[3] In 1689 the case was carried to the Lords, who affirmed the judgement of the Exchequer. In consequence, the sheriffs acquired this special protection that, as to declaring the majority, they were the judges, and no action could lie against them at common law for what they did judicially; more indirectly, but of even greater importance, the Commons were confirmed in their right to determine on the returns of elections and on the conduct of returning officers.

A still more valuable right was enjoyed by both Houses—that of freedom of debate. Outside the walls of parliament both peer

[1] *Diary of J. Millward* (*Add. MS.* 33413), Oct. 5, 1666.
[2] *State Trials*, vii (1730 ed.), 428 sqq.; also *English Reports*, lxxxvi. 615–17.
[3] *Grey*, iv. 141.

and commoner were at the mercy of the harsh treason laws, and
their most casual words might be seized upon by spies and informers; but within these walls the only tribunal was that constituted by their fellow members, and to that extent debate was
free from outside interference. There was much personal solicitation and, of course, there was bribery; but the independent peer
or commoner suffered no punishment for either his speech or his
vote. Here again Charles avoided the mistakes made by his
father; and, however arbitrary his acts, he never violated those
twin sanctuaries at Westminster, where the conduct of his executive was the theme of active debate.

If each House be considered separately, it may be noted that
among the special privileges enjoyed by the Lords were these:
(1) right of personal access to the sovereign; (2) right of voting
by proxy; (3) right to trial by one's peers in cases of treason
and felony; and (4) right of recording in the Journals a protest
against a decision of the majority. The exercise of the first
privilege called for circumspection, as Charles did not tolerate
fools gladly; and his treatment of the earl of Bristol, who brought
accusations of high treason against Clarendon in 1663, was a
warning that the privilege must not be abused. It does not appear
to have been practised by peers other than personal friends and
ministers enjoying the confidence of the crown. The right of
voting by proxy was still exercised and, save in moments of crisis,
the attendance at the House was poor; but absentees without
excuse or proxy were sometimes fined one shilling for the poor
box. More important was the third right, that of trial by one's
peers, a privilege liable to abuse, in so far as a peer might be tried
not by neutral persons, but by a jury of friends and associates.
There were attempts at reform. In 1675 the Lords passed a Bill
amending the constitution of the court of the lord high steward,
whereby thirty peers at least were to be present at the trial, of
whom a minimum of twelve was necessary for a verdict of guilty;[1]
in 1680 the Commons introduced a Bill intended to reform procedure and to abolish the Lords' privileges under the Statute of
Scandalum Magnatum.[2] By the Trial of Treasons Acts (1696) the
peers themselves benefited by the improved procedure intro-

[1] *H.M.C. Rep.* ix, app., pt. ii. 49–50. *MSS. of House of Lords.*
[2] See *infra*, 465.

duced into trials for high treason;[1] otherwise there was no change in the principle by which peers were tried by themselves.

The fourth right, that of protest against a majority decision, was really more a convention than a right, and its exercise over a long period has proved of great value to the student of history.[2] Two such protests may be noted. In 1663 a minority protested against the restraint laid on the importation of Irish cattle, since common right and the subject's liberty were thereby invaded, and the impoverishment of Ireland was likely to follow.[3] Again, in November 1675, when a proposal for an address to the crown advocating the dissolution of parliament was rejected, a minority, including Shaftesbury, Halifax, Buckingham, and Wharton, protested; alleging that, according to the ancient laws and statutes of the realm, there should be frequent parliaments, and that it was unreasonable for any body of men (such as the then House of Commons) to engross so large a measure of the nation's confidence, 'since the mutual correspondence and interest of those who choose and are chosen must admit of great variations in course of time'.[4] On both these questions—restraint of the import of Irish cattle, and the continuance in power of the Cavalier Parliament—the minority showed a wisdom that would be applauded to-day, but the names of the dissenting peers in the latter instance suggest that the protest was not absolutely disinterested, and that it was really a party move, intended to popularize the demand for a new parliament in which, it was hoped, the opposition would be more strongly represented. Shaftesbury was the first to realize the value of these protests for the purpose of propaganda.[5]

Other privileges enjoyed by the peers were the right of personal exemption from the taking of oaths, and the right to a special measure of protection against the slanders of others, whether peers or commoners. The first was successfully vindicated by Shaftesbury and his followers in April 1675, when Danby

[1] See *infra*, 514.
[2] They were collected and published by Thorold Rogers in his *Protests of the Lords*.
[3] *L.J.* xi. 571, July 24, 1663.
[4] *L.J.* xiii. 33, Nov. 20, 1675.
[5] Turberville, *House of Lords in the reign of Charles II*, in *E.H.R.* xliv.

attempted to secure the passage of his Non-Resistance Test.[1]
Even when trying one of their fellows the Lords each gave his
verdict not as a sworn juryman, but on his faith and allegiance
to the king; and as a witness in the law courts he gave evidence
not on his oath but on his honour. Thus while successive Houses
of Commons saddled themselves with oaths and obligations, the
Lords, as born legislators, maintained their freedom from commitments, a privilege saved for them in 1675 by a minority in the
Lords and a majority in the Commons; nor, until 1678, were they
required to take the oath against transubstantiation, a requirement which automatically disabled the Catholic peers from
membership of the House. As regards the second privilege, the
old statute *De scandalis magnatum* acquired a new lease of life in
the passions aroused by the events of the reign. Every lord of
parliament was, in law, a great officer of state, because he was
required to support the king by his advice; and the statute *De
scandalis magnatum*[2] gave them a special protection against critics
and enemies. In 1676 this was suddenly revived from desuetude,
though at first the lawyers were doubtful whether juries would
respect such a medieval implement; experience, however, soon
showed that juries were specially liberal in their assessment of
damages sustained by maligned peers. It could be used even
against a fellow peer, as in the case of *Shaftesbury* v. *Digby* (1676),
when the former obtained £1,000 damages for this statement
made to him by Digby: 'You are not for the king, but for sedition
and a commonwealth, and by God we will have your head at
the next sessions of parliament.'[3] It was a moderate price for such
language. A few months later a Dr. Hughes had to pay £4,000
for these words spoken of lord Townshend: 'he is an unworthy
man and acts against law and reason'. Hughes appealed, on the
ground that the damages were excessive, and because one of the
jury had admitted that they awarded lord Townshend such vast
damages so that he would have the greater opportunity of showing himself noble by remitting them; but the court dismissed the
appeal, on the ground that the judges always construed in favour
of these actions, so as to ensure that the peers would not have to

---

[1] See *infra*, 532–3.
[2] 2 Ric. II, cap. v.
[3] This case was tried in the Common Pleas. *Modern Reports*, ii. 98.

exact vengeance themselves.[1] But the full potency of the action of *Scandalum magnatum* was not revealed until 1684 when, in the case of *Duke of York* v. *Titus Oates*,[2] the jury assessed the damages at £100,000.

Protected against the criticisms of both equals and inferiors, the Lords, who seldom numbered more than a hundred at their sessions, permitted themselves a certain degree of informality in their proceedings—an informality sometimes enlivened by the remarks of the king, who began to attend the debates with some regularity in 1670, when the Divorce Bill of lord Roos was discussed. From his station, not on the throne, but by the fire-place, Charles did not scruple, by interjection and even solicitation, to influence the course of debate; he never succeeded, however, in breaking up the solid phalanx of the bishops. On at least one occasion the House insisted that a certain minimum of public decency should be maintained by its members; as when, in February 1674, Buckingham was ordered to cease cohabitation with the countess of Shrewsbury, an order to which Buckingham promised obedience 'on his honour', each party giving security to the amount of £10,000. But there were limits to this personal interference by the Lords as a corporation. In 1678 lady Mohun, a daughter of lord Rutland, was injured on the knee by a candlestick thrown at her during a quarrel with a lady friend. She drew up a petition to the Lords on a breach of privilege, which her father solemnly presented to the House. The Lords referred the petition to the law courts, and did not accept the king's offer to conduct a personal investigation of the extent of the injuries.[3]

By the readmission of the 26 spiritual peers in the summer of 1661 the total membership of the House of Lords was raised to 170; in 1685 the number was 181. Fresh honours were conferred, most notably at the Restoration; and in 1681–2 for services during the critical period of Plot and Exclusion, but the total additions to the peerage in this period (64 in all) did little more than make good the 53 extinctions.[4] The existing dukedoms were increased by seven—those of Monmouth, Southampton, Plymouth, Richmond, Grafton, St. Albans, and Northumber-

---

[1] *Modern Reports*, ii. 160; also *English Reports*, lxxxvi. 850–1.
[2] See *infra*, 651.   [3] *H.M.C. Rep.* xii, app. v. 49.
[4] A. S. Turberville, *House of Lords under Charles II*, in *E.H.R.* xliv. 403.

land, all conferred on the natural progeny of the king. Of the score of Catholic peers excluded in 1678, none had played a prominent part in politics, with the doubtful exception of lord Arundell of Wardour, a signatory to the secret treaty of Dover. In talent and integrity the Lords compared very favourably with the Commons, including as they did poets, statesmen, soldiers, admirals, and lawyers; while the bishops were ably represented by Sheldon, Morley, and Seth Ward. Moreover a society which included Buckingham, Ormonde, and Halifax was at least redeemed from mediocrity, and the fiery eloquence of Shaftesbury helped to raise the standard of debate.

In contrast with that of the Lords, the prerogative of the Commons was so ill defined that it seemed capable of almost limitless expansion. No one knew how far it might go.[1] That they were in the nature of a grand jury was the description which seemed best fitted to describe the functions of its members, a grand jury which found true Bills against many offenders, but succeeded in obtaining only one conviction—that of lord Stafford, a victim of the Popish Plot. But they succeeded in vindicating several important privileges. In 1667 they obtained the concurrence of the Lords in a ruling that the Act[2] concerning Richard Strode was a general law, indemnifying all members of parliament in respect of any proposal or declaration made in parliament.[3] They also established the right to choose their own Speaker. The occasion for this arose in March 1679, when Edward Seymour (with whom Charles had a quarrel) presented himself as the Commons' choice. Charles discharged him of his trust, claiming that it was an essential element of the prerogative to refuse as well as to approve the choice of Speaker.[4] Fierce debates, two addresses to the crown, and a prorogation were the immediate consequences of this challenge; the contest was ended only when Charles accepted another choice of the Commons—sergeant Gregory, and thereafter the privilege was left inviolate.

Attendance in the House was maintained by the threat of a fine, and at critical moments there was talk of committing

---

[1] Thus in 1678 Winnington confessed in the Commons that he was unwilling to declare what the House could not do. (*Parl. Hist.* iv. 937.)

[2] 4 Hen. VIII, cap. viii.   [3] *C.J.* ix. 19, Nov. 12, 1667.

[4] *Parl. Hist.* iv. 1092 sqq.

absentees to custody.[1] The observance of greater decorum appears to have been first proposed in October 1666, when certain
reforms were suggested; as, that no member should be allowed to
walk about with his hat on, or talk during speeches, and that the
private door to the Speaker's chamber should be sealed up. The
reason for this last precaution was that Buckingham was in the
habit of coming up by the back door and listening to the speeches.
Prynne's motion for a fine of 1s. on those absent from prayers does
not appear to have found a seconder.[2] Expulsion was sometimes
resorted to,[3] and in 1678 a convicted popish recusant (sir Solomon
Swale) was expelled the House, and a writ issued for a new
election.[4] Not only his religion, but in some respects his private
conduct, might bring the member into clash with the House, and
before its dissolution the Cavalier Parliament attempted to apply
strict tests to its members. These tests related to popery, bribery,
taking the sacraments, conversing with foreign ministers, public
hospitality, and attendance at conventicles or mass.[5] Dissolution
prevented these proposals being carried into effect; but it is
significant that a parliament which began as an assembly of
courtiers, and contained a high proportion of paid dependants
of the crown, ended its sessions on a high note of personal
responsibility.

Apart from the official records entered in the Journals, the
expressed opinions of members in the House were, in theory,
secret and informal—secret in the sense that the public was
excluded, and there was no regular means for reporting speeches;
informal in the sense that a speech must not be read from written
notes. The surviving records of speeches in Charles's Houses of
Commons are due mainly to the note-taking of Anchitell Grey.[6]
An important step was taken in 1680, when it was ordered that
the votes of the House should be published, in spite of secretary
Jenkins's objection that the practice was unbecoming the gravity
of the Commons, and was 'a sort of appeal to the people'.[7] But

[1] *C.J.* ix. 558, Dec. 18, 1678.
[2] *Diary of J. Millward (Add. MS.* 33413), Oct. 13, 1666.
[3] *Parl. Hist.* iv. 589.   [4] Ibid. iv. 1003.   [5] *C.J.* ix. 500, June 1678.
[6] His *Debates of the House of Commons from the year 1667 to the year 1694* were
published in ten volumes in 1769. An important record of debates by
J. Millward (1666–8) will be found in *Add. MS.* 33413.
[7] *Parl. Hist.* iv. 1306.

the Commons were at first very sensitive to anything savouring of public criticism of these printed votes; for in November 1680 they attempted to find the culprit who, in a coffee-house, had appended the comments 'a damned lie' and 'voted like rogues' to their votes on the succession.[1] As parliamentary oratory acquired a great measure of publicity, an increasing use appears to have been made of written notes; indeed, speeches were sometimes read, a practice which dated back to the Long Parliament of 1640, when orators sometimes read their declamations 'out of a hat', or 'behind a friend'.[2] Soon, the printed oration rivalled the printed sermon.

Such were the powers and privileges specially distinctive of each of the two Houses. These were given sharper definition by their numerous conflicts with each other, in the course of which some principles of importance were enunciated. The rights to initiate money grants and to enforce ministerial responsibility were the two major rights on which the Commons insisted most strongly, leaving to the Lords the judicial functions of a supreme court, and the duty of trying those persons who might be impeached by the Commons. This division of powers was not always easy of application, as instanced by the case of *Skinner* v. *The East India Company* (1668). Skinner, an interloper, was aggrieved at the confiscation of his ships by the agents of the East India Company. Having made a direct appeal to the king in council, he was referred to the House of Lords, who, after hearing his case, awarded him £5,000 damages against the Company. The Commons immediately acted on a petition presented by sir Samuel Barnardiston, a deputy governor and a member of the House. They voted that Skinner's action in taking his common plea to the Lords originally was not agreeable to the laws of the land, and tended to deprive the subject of his rights under these laws; also, that the action of the Lords in taking cognizance of the suit, and giving damages against the Governor and Company was unwarranted. Meanwhile, Barnardiston was summoned to the Lords (May 8) for his contumacy in petitioning against their award, and sentenced to a fine of £300. The dispute between the two Houses was continued in the autumn session of 1669. On the one hand, the Lords contended that, as the case had arisen

[1] *Grey*, vii. 430.   [2] *Letter from an ejected member to Sir J. Evelyn* (1648).

from acts committed overseas, it was not (except by a legal fiction) cognizable in the common law courts; on their side, the Commons challenged the Lords' entertainment of an action which had not come before them by way of appeal, and their punishment of Barnardiston for having petitioned against their judgement. The dispute was ended only by the erasure of the record in the Journals; but the Lower House by resolution affirmed the right of every commoner to present a petition to the House in case of grievance, and the right of the House to judge and determine of such petitions.[1] In effect, the victory lay with the Commons; for the Lords did not again act as a court of original jurisdiction in a matter cognizable by Westminster Hall.

In another dispute, however, the Commons proved to be in the wrong, and were encouraged to maintain an impossible position, so that the prorogation of parliament might be ensured. A plaintiff named Dr. Shirley, having lost his suit in Chancery, brought an appeal to the Lords, the defendant being sir John Fagg, burgess for Steyning. The Commons voted this a breach of their privilege, since thereby one of their members (Fagg) had to submit to the judgement of the Lords. They sent Fagg to the Tower for having presented himself in answer to the appeal, and they took into custody those serjeants, being members of the House, who had pleaded in this suit at the bar of the Lords. The Lords (May 17, 1675) insisted on their right, as Lords in Judicature, to receive and determine in time of parliament appeals from inferior courts even where a member of the Lower House was concerned; at the same time defining their status to be that of 'Lords in Parliament where His Majesty is highest in his royal state, and where the last resort of judging on writs of error and appeals in equity in all cases and over all persons is undoubtedly fixed and lodged'.[2] To this, the Commons replied that the definition implied a diminution of the dignity of the king 'who is highest in his royal estate in full parliament'[3]; moreover, they contended, the Lords were wrong in denying the House of Commons to be a court. But the Lords persisted in their attitude, in which they were encouraged by the eloquence of Shaftesbury, who warned his compeers that they would quickly grow burdensome if they grew useless: 'you have now', he said, 'the greatest

---

[1] *Parl. Hist.* iv. 422–6.   [2] *L.J.* xii. 694.   [3] *C.J.* ix. 354.

and most useful end of parliaments principally in you, which is not to make new laws, but to redress grievances and maintain the old landmarks. The House of Commons' business is to complain, Your Lordships' to redress not only the complaints from them that are the eye of the nation, but all the other particular persons that address themselves to you.'[1] The result was that the Commons did not again contest the right of the Upper House to hear appeals in which members of the Lower House were concerned, and so the supreme appellate jurisdiction of the Lords was tacitly recognized.

Of even greater importance were those disputes in which the right of the Commons to control taxation appeared to be infringed. In 1671 the Commons sent up to the Lords a Bill levying impositions on foreign commodities. The Lords, having received petitions from merchants who believed that their interests would suffer by the application of certain clauses in the Bill, proposed a conference thereon with the Commons. This was agreed to; but the representatives of the Lower House insisted on the resolution of their House 'that there is a fundamental right in the House of Commons alone in Bills of rates and impositions on merchandise, as to the matter, the measure and the time'.[2] In reply, the Lords argued that their writs of summons required them to treat and give counsel on the great and arduous affairs of the kingdom without exception; nor was there any record that they had ever divested themselves of any portion of this right. Moreover, when they sent a Bill down to the Commons they never challenged the right of the Lower House to make amendments; why should not the Commons reciprocate in the matter of a Bill sent up by them? Historical precedents were quoted on both sides,[3] and the Commons introduced this alternative argument, that if the Lower House had no precedent to justify its sole control over taxation, equally the Upper House had none to show how it had acquired supreme powers of judicature, to the exclusion of the Commons; to which the Lords properly replied that their judicature dated from a time before the existence of the House of Commons, when the peers constituted the

---

[1] Shaftesbury's speech in the Lords, Nov. 1675, in *Add. MS.* 32094, f. 389.
[2] *C.J.* ix. 239, April 20, 1671.
[3] Ibid. ix. 240–4; *L.J.* xi. 494–8.

grand council of the nation. This contest was ended by adjournment.

For the Commons the issue was a vital one, and they established their right. In 1678 they sent up a Bill of Supply for the disbandment of forces raised since September 1677. The Lords, in view of the situation abroad, introduced an amendment, extending the time for disbandment. The amendment was rejected by the Commons, and in July they placed on record their resolution 'that all aids and supplies to His Majesty are the sole gift of the Commons, and all bills for granting such aids ought to begin with the Commons; and that it is the undoubted and sole right of the Commons to direct, limit and appoint in such Bills the ends, purposes, considerations, conditions, limitations and qualifications for such grants, which ought not to be changed or altered by the House of Lords'.[1] The Commons, therefore, not only claimed the sole right to impose taxation, but denied to the Lords the right to amend any measure which directly or indirectly involved a charge on the subject. This principle has never since been surrendered, and thereafter the Lords retained only the right to reject such Bills—a right which they exercised with momentous consequences in 1909. Already the Commons had realized one use to which their privilege might be put, namely the device of 'tacking' a controversial measure to a money Bill in order that it might pass the Lords without amendment, and impose on the crown a choice between the alternatives of rejection or supply. A notable example was the measure prohibiting certain French imports for three years which was tacked to a Poll Bill[2] in the session of 1677-8. But it is to the honour of Charles that this practice was discouraged; for in May 1678 he announced that in future he would veto all Bills containing several matters tacked together, no matter how important they might be.[3]

In order that the vigorous political life of Charles II's England may be appreciated, it is now necessary to turn to the franchise, the elections, and the external influences that might be brought to bear on the elected representatives.

The House of Commons, as constituted in 1661, contained

[1] *C.J.* ix. 509, July 3, 1678.   [2] 29-30 Car. II, cap. i.   [3] *L.J.* xiii. 223.

509 members, made up of two burgesses from each of the 197 boroughs returning two members, one each from five boroughs[1] returning one member, two from each of the two universities, four from London, two from each of 39 counties, and 24 members from the Welsh counties and boroughs. These members were increased to 513 in Charles's third parliament (1679) by the addition of four members from the palatine county of Durham —two from the county and two from the city. The election of knights and burgesses was regulated by custom and statute. By a statute[2] of Henry VI's reign knights of the shire were required to be 'notable knights, or such esquires or gentlemen-born of the same county as are eligible to be knights'; and the franchise in the counties was, since the fifteenth century, the standard qualification of a freehold of at least 40s. annual value. There was greater latitude in the qualifications required of a burgess. By statute, a man was ineligible for a borough which he did not inhabit, but this disqualification was seldom insisted on; in effect any one was eligible, provided he was over 21, neither an alien nor a clergyman, not attainted of treason or felony, nor of unsound mind, and 'magis idoneus, discretus et sufficiens'.[3]

In contrast with the county franchise, that in the boroughs was bewildering in its heterogeneity. Generally, it was widest in the scot-and-lot and pot-walloper boroughs; narrower in the freeman boroughs, and narrowest of all in the corporation and burgage boroughs. As an example of a very wide franchise Preston may be cited, where, by determination of the Commons in 1661, it was declared to reside in 'all the inhabitants'. The Commons may have established this very liberal franchise from their belief that the corporation of Preston was 'presbyterian'.[4] So, too, in those boroughs where the qualification was the payment of 'scot-and-lot', or the possession of one's own hearth, the franchise might be wide enough to include persons in receipt of poor relief. In the freeman boroughs, the freemen had originally

[1] The five boroughs which each returned one member were Abingdon, Banbury, Higham-Ferrars, Monmouth, and Bewdley.

[2] 23 Hen. VI, cap. xv.

[3] For the franchise before 1832 see E. Porritt, *The Unreformed House of Commons*. For elections to the parliaments of 1679–81 see E. Lipson in *E.H.R.* xxviii.

[4] Sacret, *The Restoration and municipal corporations* in *E.H.R.* xlv.

been those householders having the right to trade; but, by the seventeenth century, when votes were coming to be in demand, means were found for restricting the number of freemen, and the more coveted privilege was beginning to be conferred on non-residents by making them honorary freemen. The same process can be seen in corporation boroughs, where a landed gentleman might be appointed to the office of mayor or recorder. Equally amenable to manipulation were the burgage boroughs, where the franchise went with certain tenements or holdings, which might be houses, or (as at Droitwich) shares in salt-pits. In the corporation boroughs, as at Bath, the vote was exercised by a small corporation, kept in existence almost solely for the exercise of this right, and an election might represent little more than the opinion of an enterprising mayor or bailiff; for example, at Hasle-mere, the bailiff explained the principle thus: 'it lay in his little pate to return whom he would'.[1]

It was mainly in consequence of these anomalies that the greater territorial families were able to exert control over many boroughs. In the west the duke of Beaufort was supreme; for he united the lord lieutenancies of three English counties (Here-fordshire, Gloucestershire, and Monmouthshire) with the lord lieutenancy of every Welsh county. In Cornwall and Devon the earl of Bath (Grenville) was building up his territorial influence; the Lancashire boroughs had to reckon with the earl of Derby, and many of the Wiltshire boroughs were controlled by the earl of Ailesbury. In the north the most notable borough-monger was the duke of Newcastle, whose influence extended through Northumberland, Nottinghamshire, Staffordshire, and Derby-shire. It was often through the Militia that this power was exer-cised. That it would be used in the service of the crown was generally assumed; indeed the captains of the Militia were con-sidered the strongest bulwarks against the 'sedition' and dissent of the towns; and the monarch who had the support of the Militia was strong indeed.

But, as early as 1675, an instance was provided of how a deter-mined and influential landlord could, with the help of the Militia, turn elections against the Court. In that year a knight of the shire had to be chosen for Norfolk, the two candidates being

[1] Porritt, op. cit. i. 53.

sir R. Kempe and sir N. Catlyn, the former backed by the lord lieutenant (lord Townshend) and the deputy lieutenants; while the latter was put up by the loyal party and gentry against his will. Hitherto, Townshend had been distinguished for his loyalty, his influence, and his zeal in sending fanatics to prison. For whatever reason, he had now turned momentarily against the Court, and speedily demonstrated what he could do. He joined forces with sir John Hobart, an old Cromwellian; and the two made up their minds that Kempe and not Catlyn would be returned.

Having found out that many of Catlyn's friends were in the habit of dining at the *King's Head* in Norwich, the lord lieutenant commenced his campaign by an invasion of that hostelry, and so forced the enemy to transfer their head-quarters to the *White Swan*, 'a very inconvenient place'; the Militia had therefore won the first round. At the appointed day of election (the city being packed with voters) the writ was read by the sheriff, and the two rival knights stood on chairs before the assembled freeholders; but as the shouts for each seemed to be equal, the second round was considered indecisive. For a short period there was a truce, and the rival candidates rode about the market-place, while the sheriff retired to the grand jury chamber in order to settle 'such a method in the carriage of the business as might be equal and indifferent'—in other words the real contest was about to begin. After a speech on behalf of Kempe by sir John Hobart, it was resolved to draw up a written agreement, the essence of which was that the two sets of persons entrusted with the duty of recording the votes should be placed so close together that each could act as a check on the other, and so prevent electors from voting twice. Hobart, acting as electioneering agent on behalf of Kempe, penned the agreement, and the managers then set up two distinct polls, the lord lieutenant presiding over that for Kempe. Soon it was noticed by Catlyn's managers that some freeholders were voting twice at Kempe's booth; whereupon complaint was made, and the written agreement was invoked; but when this was produced, it was found that Hobart had omitted the vital clause which enabled each set of managers to keep an eye on the proceedings at the rival booth; moreover the lord lieutenant repudiated the agreement altogether, so there seemed no reason why the supporters of Kempe should not record their votes twice. It was now a race against time. Catlyn set up an extra booth, in order to get as many votes as possible, and proposed to continue the poll until late in the evening, as so many freeholders had not yet voted; but Kempe's party had the advantage of a good start, and accordingly the lord lieutenant sent to the grand jury chamber, and asked the sheriff to cast up the votes. The sheriff did so and pronounced that Kempe had a majority. When the result was announced, many of Kempe's voters said that they had voted not for the candidate, but for the lord lieutenant's sake, or on behalf of some colonel or captain in the Militia; the genuine supporters of Kempe appear to have been either 'fanatics' or Roman Catholics. 'You see how the Militia of Norfolk govern this county.'[1]

Not unnaturally, Townshend was removed from his lord lieutenancy, and thereafter he devoted himself to turning the Norfolk elections against the Court.[2] In this way was created a whig and a powerful whig. His career provided an anticipation of how the power usually exercised on behalf of the crown might be used with equal force against it; and when Charles completed the remodelling of the boroughs, he little realized that thereby he had strengthened that local influence of the nobility and landlords which was so soon to be directed against his own House. James II ruined his cause not by his constancy to Jeffreys or father Petre, but by alienating the country gentry.

The above account of a Norfolk election suggests that management rather than oratory was the deciding factor. This might be amply illustrated from the records of borough elections. In the year 1679 there were two general elections, both of which aroused intense national interest; and, at the first of these, many members of the preceding (the Cavalier) parliament were unseated, and their places taken by whigs. Abingdon had been represented since 1660 by sir John Stonehouse, who, whatever his views, appears to have maintained silence at Westminster for nineteen years; so at the general election of September 1679 a Mr. Dunch of Pewsey was put up against him. The franchise was popular, and as the corporation was in favour of the sitting member, all the tenants holding of the borough were informed that

[1] *H.M.C. Rep.* vi, app. 371–2.   [2] *Cal. S.P. Dom.*, *1682*, 54 sqq.

if they did not vote for Stonehouse their fines would be raised, or they would not have their leases renewed. On the day of election (Sept. 6) crowds walked through the main street shouting 'A Dunch, a Dunch'. This cry was reiterated at the election, when the mayor granted a poll. The result showed 297 for Mr. Dunch, and 171 for sir John Stonehouse. The mayor and his brethren then retired to the council chamber to discuss the matter. Many queries were raised. What was the 'constant practice' of previous elections? What was the extent of their charter? Dunch then appeared in person to demand his return; but the mayor was playing for time, so he adjourned the proceedings until the following Monday. On Monday morning Dunch entered the town with 100 horse and 200 foot, all shouting 'A Dunch, a Dunch'; so the mayor again adjourned, and at 5 p.m. he told the corporation that he had examined the poll and found 171 was greater than 297, so he declared Stonehouse their burgess. After publicly announcing this return, he was hissed all the way to his house by the women and children, shouting 'A cheat, a cheat'; and next day the clamours for Dunch were so vociferous that the mayor was obliged to keep himself 'incognito' in the nettles behind the town hall until the dreaded Dunch had gone back to Pewsey. So sir John Stonehouse was again returned to Westminster, where he maintained his reticence throughout the remaining parliaments of Charles II and in the parliament of James.[1]

The tactics of the mayor of Abingdon were at least simple and straightforward; elsewhere more ingenuity had to be exercised. Witness sir John Reresby's account[2] of his election as burgess for Aldborough in 1673. At that time he noted the existence of two parties—the Country party, professing to protect the subject from over-taxation and to secure his privileges and liberties; and the Court party, committed in the abstract to these principles, but anxious that the king should have a sufficient revenue. Sir John noted also that an increasing number of men wished to enter parliament; for those in debt thereby obtained protection from their creditors, while others found in membership of the

---

[1] *Letter from a friend in Abingdon to a gentleman in London* (in *Bodley G. Pamph.*, 1678).

[2] Reresby, *Memoirs* (ed. Browning), 91–2, 95–6.

House an avenue to Court favour. At the Aldborough by-election he had five rival candidates, of whom the most formidable was one Benson, who, beginning as clerk to a country attorney, had risen to be clerk of assize of the northern circuit, and now (through the favour of sir Thomas Osborne) was possessed of an estate worth £2,500 per annum. The traditional franchise at Aldborough was vested in nine electors, owners of nine burgage houses; but on the eve of the election the lord of the manor contended that formerly there had been 24 houses each conferring a vote. Hitherto he, as owner of these houses, had given only one vote in respect of them; but now he proposed to sell or alienate them so as to create as many votes. These 24 votes were acquired by the enterprising Benson. Reresby stood by the other burgage votes, of which he obtained a majority, while Benson was returned by his 24 houses; and, as the other candidates had retired from the contest, the field was cleared for Reresby and Benson. The result was a double return, in the traditional form—*executio istius brevis patet in quibusdam indenturis huic brevi annexis*, which Benson on his own initiative altered to *in quadam indentura*. But, because of this alteration, he lost his case when the double return was examined by the House of Commons, and so in this tortuous way Reresby became a burgess for Aldborough.

Sometimes an association of electors would undertake in writing to support the candidates selected by a majority of themselves, and also to induce as many electors as possible to join in the association, so that at the Polls there would be less opportunity for dissension, faction, or expense. Such an association was formed in Herefordshire, one of its declared objects being to propose and elect only persons well-affected to the government.[1] Or reference might be made to the wishes of some territorial magnate; in other cases, the election might be influenced by bribery, direct or indirect. An example of the latter was a written communication to the Mayor of Poole intimating that, if the writer were elected, he would oppose taxation.[2] A gift of money was sometimes made to a borough after election; or an offer might be made on condition of election, as when admiral Spragge

[1] The articles of association (undated) are in *Add. MS.* 11051, f. 227.
[2] *Grey*, i. 232.

offered £300 to the burgesses of Dover for this purpose.[1] Voters
became accustomed to this association of their vote with some
return, either in money, or privilege, or (at least) entertainment;
and so the expenses of elections increased considerably. Danby's
organized jobbery served to enhance the commercial value of a
seat, and justified the dictum of Shaftesbury: 'men that buy dear
cannot live by selling cheap'.[2] As there was a greatly increased
demand for seats after the Restoration, successive elections were
more keenly contested, and that for Bedfordshire in the spring of
1679 was said to have cost the candidates £6,000.[3] At other places
there might have to be social enterprise, as at Buckingham, where
the rival candidates (one of them a peer) danced all night with
the wives of the burgesses, and the noble competitor assured his
dance partners that his lady would welcome their acquaintance.[4]
It was in 1679 that the word 'representation' first came into
general use as a political term;[5] the word 'mob' had already been
acclimatized.

Indeed, the old parliamentary boroughs provided the best
training-ground for political strategy, because, as scarcely any two
were alike, they each offered opportunities for individual treatment. Some might be taken by assault, others by a slow under-
mining, others by a ruse, most of them by money. The procedure
of elections provided additional opportunities. Thus, there was
often doubt where the poll was to be taken, and a candidate might
lose the election by shepherding his supporters to the usual place,
and find too late that it had been changed; or the election might
be held at night (as at Bedford in 1685); or the voting might be
adjourned so often that many electors went away in disgust.[6] Or
the candidate who had lost his election on one franchise might
demand his election on another, and win on it.[7] In cases of doubt
(and these were numerous) the sheriff made a double return,
leaving the House to decide the election. This right was after-

---

[1] Porritt, op. cit. i. 158. For this election see also A. F. W. Papillon,
Memoirs of T. Papillon, 126.

[2] *Parl. Hist.* iv, app. vii.

[3] *H.M.C. Rep.* vii, app. 471, *Verney MSS.*

[4] Ibid. 478.

[5] *Hatton Correspondence* (*Camd. Soc.*), i. vii and 182.

[6] Luttrell, *Brief Historical Narration*, i. 341.

[7] e.g. the Tamworth by-election of 1670, *Grey*, i. 243-4.

wards used by the House to increase the strength of the party in power.

There were other and more insidious influences. By statute, the boroughs were obliged to pay wages to their burgesses. This had fallen into desuetude; and Andrew Marvell was probably the only person still in receipt of this allowance from his borough (Kingston-upon-Hull). When, in March 1677, the Commons ordered a Bill to be brought in for the repeal of this statute, it was mentioned in debate[1] that some burgesses had threatened to serve writs on their constituencies for arrears of wages in the event of their not being returned at the next general election. Another influence was that of the crown. This had long existed in the Cinque Ports and in ports and dockyard towns, where there was a tradition in favour of Court nominees, as instanced at the Liverpool by-election of 1670, when the king commanded a prospective candidate to desist, as he wished the seat for the Customs farmer sir William Bucknall.[2] Elsewhere this influence was more sparingly exercised; though it was felt as early as the election of April 1660, when the personal preference of Charles was cited in the favour of at least one candidate.[3]

These illustrations suggest not so much that the old franchise was corrupt, as that it had never been designed to withstand the invasion of the intruder armed with money, or influence, or ingenuity; for at first the boroughs had returned to parliament not politicians who valued the privilege, but burgesses whose travelling expenses had to be paid; and in this way the complicated franchises which at first returned the unwilling now became the battle-ground of the ambitious. The abuses of the system were so patent that there was a demand for parliamentary reform on the part of the more independent members within the Commons, and of more independent statesmen without, such as Shaftesbury. In January 1667 the House discussed certain regulations with a view to their embodiment in Bills. These included the requirements that voters should be such as had taken the sacrament; that only those having lawful votes should be allowed to attend elections, and that no soldiers should be present in the polling

[1] *Grey*, iv. 177, and Marvell, *Works* (ed. Grosart), ii. 525.
[2] *H.M.C. Rep.* x, app., pt. iv. 117.
[3] *Add. MS.* 11051, f. 229.

booths except those who had votes, and then only if unarmed.[1] Complaint of the increasing expenses of elections was made in January 1674, when members blamed the competition of non-residents;[2] in November 1675 a residential qualification was suggested by sir John Bramston, who pleaded also for a more equal distribution of seats.[3] The result was the adoption of a resolution[4] that if a candidate, after the issue of a writ and before the day of election, should give to a voter or voters meat or drink exceeding £5 in value in any place other than his dwelling-house, his election should be void. This maximum of £5 was raised to £10 in April 1677.[5] But 'dry' elections were regarded with disfavour by the more conservative, and were thought by some to be a device for 'introducing Presbytery by way of small beer', as well as damaging the king, by reducing his revenue from Excise.[6]

The whigs were the earliest advocates of parliamentary reform; but after the Revolution of 1689, when they became strongly entrenched, they lost heart for the cause, which was later taken up by the tories. One of the first acts of the first whig parliament (that of March 1679) was to draft a Bill[7] for regulating abuses of elections. The main provisions of this Bill were these: (1) limitation of the county franchise to persons having an estate in fee of at least £200; (2) creation of a standard franchise in the boroughs (except London, York, Norwich, Exeter, and Bristol) consisting of all householders paying scot-and-lot who had resided for at least one year in the borough for which they voted; (3) a penalty of £500 and disability from sitting in parliament on any one giving bribes or rewards for votes, and disfranchisement of the borough where the bribery was committed; (4) no suit to be prosecuted for wages by any burgess in respect of his service in parliament, and all arrears of such wages to stand discharged; (5) sheriffs, mayors, and bailiffs to complete the election at the appointed time and place without adjournment; (6) persons inducing a returning officer to make a false return, and returning

---

[1] *Diary of J. Millward (Add. MS.* 33413, Jan. 17, 1667).
[2] *Parl. Hist.*.iv. 658.   [3] *Grey*, iv. 2.
[4] *Parl. Hist.* iv. 784–5, Nov. 12, 1675.   [5] *C.J.* ix. 411.
[6] *Savile Correspondence (Camd. Soc.)*, 118.
[7] Printed *in extenso* in *Somers Tracts*, ed. 1748, pt. i, vol. i. 63–6.

officers making a false return for some valuable consideration, to incur a penalty, and the election to be void; and (7) in order to secure the benefits of successive parliaments, no future parliament to have continuance for more than two years.

This Bill may have attempted too much; for it combined a sweeping reform of the franchise with an effort to guarantee frequent parliaments. Unfortunately, there was no provision to secure that parliaments should even be summoned, an elementary safeguard not achieved until the Mutiny Act imposed on William III the necessity of annually renewing the legal status of his troops. Equally notable was the scheme of reform attributed to Shaftesbury.[1] There was an idealist object in this scheme—so to amend and strengthen the parliamentary constitution that it would be impervious to the attacks of fraud and corruption. He thought it of dangerous consequence that the crown should have the power to determine the franchise of a borough, as it had attempted to do with Newark.[2] More urgent, the anomalies and varieties of borough franchise should be brought to one head by 'a touch of the supreme authority', and there should be one uniform system in all these constituencies. Next, rotten boroughs should be disfranchised, and their members transferred to more populous centres; with this redistribution, it would not be possible to have a repetition of such a measure as the prohibition of Irish cattle, which, Shaftesbury contended, was passed by the votes of certain counties having an excessive proportion of borough votes to their share. Next, as the old 40s. freehold qualification was assessed on the value of money in the fifteenth century, it should be raised so as to correspond with its modern equivalent. So, too, as the electors ought to be men of substance, the person elected should have a good estate, in order to ensure his faith and honesty; for which purpose he should be worth at least £10,000, all debts paid, and should be of at least forty years of age. Lastly, there ought to be secrecy of voting; the electors coming in at one door, recording their votes at a table, and leaving by another.

Shaftesbury's House of Commons would thus have been an assembly of middle-aged plutocrats; men of gravity and circumspection, too old for folly or extravagance, and so rich that they

[1] *Somers Tracts*, pt. i, vol. i. 66–72.   [2] *Supra*, 461.

could be neither bribed nor bullied; primitive and pioneer whigs, with at least one Puritan in their ancestry, and a fortune acquired in a career of business rectitude. It was a type in the making; but the temper of Charles's reign did not favour its full development.

Such were the means by which men entered parliament, and the chief proposals for reform. On the members of the Commons Charles did not scruple to exercise his influence. This might take the form of a personal letter to members on whose support he could rely. Such letters were sent on April 1, 1675 to ten members, asking them to be present in their places 'for the King's interest', when 'His Majesty will communicate his good and pious resolutions of returning all things in Church and State to their legal state and condition'.[1] Before the opening of the autumn session of the same year Charles sent similar letters, expressing his alarm at the rumour that he did not intend to have a sitting of parliament, and asking his supporters to be present in good time, *preferably a day or two before the opening*.[2] This suggests that, like the Country party, the Court party was beginning to discuss the plan of campaign before the meeting of parliament. The Commons protested against this practice;[3] but it was resorted to again in March 1681, when the king commanded all his servants in the House to promote expedients in place of exclusion.[4] On an earlier occasion, when the Commons were pressing their right to appoint a committee to inspect war expenditure, Charles sent out the lord chamberlain to bring in the loyalists from the places where they were presumed to be engaged— namely the theatres and houses of ill fame.[5] More directly, the influence of the crown was exercised by the distribution of offices to members, on the implied condition that they would vote in the right way. Danby reduced this to a system. In May 1678, when the Commons renewed their attack on Lauderdale, the king ordered all his servants to attend the House, 'and such as

---

[1] These were sent to sir T. Peyton, sir F. Windham, sir Job Charleton, colonel Sandys, sir C. Fisher, sir Humphrey Winch, sergeant Jones, sir Henry Vernon, sir Francis Crompton, and sir T. Hanmer. *Coventry Papers* (*Longleat*), 83, f. 78.   [2] Sept. 21, 1675, ibid., f. 95.

[3] In their address that summons should be by proclamation only. *Parl. Hist.* iv. 780.

[4] *Prinsterer*, v. 490.   [5] *Pepys*, Dec. 8, 1666.

either did not attend, or voted not according to their duty, he would turn out one after another'.[1] On this occasion sir William Lowther was dismissed from his post in the Customs for voting against the Court, which 'threw so great a terror into many members of the House' that the attack on the hated Scottish minister was 'minced'.[2]

This abuse was not allowed to pass unchallenged. Agitation against office-holders in the Commons had begun in 1675, when a Bill was introduced to make the holding of a public office in time of parliament incompatible with a seat in the House,[3] a proposal again discussed in 1679. On two occasions also[4] a test was proposed for administration to members, requiring them to declare whether they had received money for their votes, or whether they had been ejected from office because of their votes. The agitation culminated in May 1679, when sir Stephen Fox was forced by the Commons to reveal the names of those members of the late parliament to whom he had paid money from secret service funds.[5]

Public interest in this matter was stimulated by the appearance of a biographical compilation entitled *Flagellum Parliamentarium* (sometimes attributed to Marvell), containing the names of 178 members who in the period 1661–72 were alleged to have received 'snip', that is, a share of the spoils.[6] This parliamentary *Who's Who* was modelled on an earlier and equally candid publication, *The Mystery of the Good Old Cause* (1660), in which was contained a list of those members of the late Long Parliament who had held civil and military office contrary to the Self-Denying Ordinance. No feelings were spared in the *Flagellum*, and under the names of prominent politicians were to be found such summary descriptions as these: 'a poor Scot, therefore a knave'; 'a private forsworn cheat in the Prize Office'; 'a pimping groom of the bed-chamber'; 'king's jeweller, a great cheat at bowls and cards'; 'once a poor factor to buy malt, now a farmer

---

[1] *Lauderdale Papers (Camd. Soc.)*, iii. 131.
[2] *Lauderdale Papers (Add. MS.* 23242), ff. 28–9.
[3] It was rejected by 145 to 113. *Grey*, iii. 53.
[4] 1675 and 1678.
[5] *Parl. Hist.* iv. 1137–42; see also *infra*, 589–90.
[6] See also E. S. De Beer, 'Members of the Court Party in the House of Commons', in *Bulletin of the Institute of Historical Research*, June 1933.

of the revenues'; 'a poor ale-house keeper's son, now has the Faculty Office and is one of the Masters of Requests'; 'a beggarly fellow that sold his vote to the Treasurer for £50'; 'Navy contractor'; 'son of Harbottle'; 'commissioner for Irish Claims'; 'the first mover for Chimney Money'; 'pays no debts, has a son in the Guards'. Such were the 'Court Cullies' of this libellous anthology. When it is recalled that French money was soon to supplement Court bribery, the wonder is that such an assembly contrived to maintain some degree of independence; but then the English House of Commons was a peculiar institution, and neither Charles II nor Louis XIV quite understood it.

The most notable failure of the Commons of Charles's reign was their inability to make full use of the weapon of impeachment. 'It is strange', complained a member, 'that all our addresses cannot remove a single obnoxious person',[1] a confession of impotence, it is true; for in this contest of wits the House was no match for the wiliest of monarchs. Nevertheless the Commons showed an uncouth strength before which even Charles yielded. He would not surrender Clarendon to their wrath, but he sent his minister into banishment; nor did he release Danby from the Tower until long after his last parliament had been dissolved. He resisted the attempt to dictate his foreign policy, but yielded in time to avert revolution; he disbelieved in the Popish Plot, but nevertheless he went the way of his Commons, even in their delirium. From Charles Stuart these were striking tributes. The Revolution settlement was peaceably effected because so many of its principles had already been enunciated in the parliaments of this reign, and because, in spite of the interludes of Cromwell and James II, these parliaments were the heirs of the Puritan revolution, and the ancestors of the Convention of 1689.

[1] Speech of Powle, May 1675, in *Grey*, iii. 214.

XIV

LIBERTY OF THE SUBJECT

MUCH is heard of the rights of seventeenth-century Englishmen, but less of the many duties that were silently enforced. The state was then thought of not as an instrument of social service, nor as an establishment for the political education of the masses; but as the armed force providing ultimate sanction for the enforcement of law and order. There was no abstract right to work, nor right to live; but there were innumerable obligations —the obligation to conduct one's trade in the manner prescribed by common and statute law; to serve one's turn in unpaid parochial office; to clear out one's ditches or mend the roads; to present one's neighbours for their sins; to eat fish on Fridays and in Lent; and, when destitute, either to live precariously on the dole meted out by churchwarden or overseer, or to retreat, under the blows of the constable, to the place of one's birth, there to die and be buried in woollen. 'Authority is the main point of government': this maxim, popular with the compilers of children's copy-books, adequately summarized the relationship between ruler and ruled. A more amplified version of the same principle may be seen in this report from the constable of a well-behaved village:

The poor are provided for; the stocks and whipping post are in good repair; hues and cries duly pursued; highways and bridges in repair; warrants executed; watch and ward duly kept, and all things belonging to my office are in good order to the best of my knowledge.[1]

A host of local functionaries and institutions co-operated in securing this state of affairs. Among these was the lord lieutenant, who combined executive with military functions. He was the king's vice-regent in the shire; he commanded the local militia; he was the custodian of the county archives, and, as head of the commission of the peace, he provided the link between the crown in council on the one side and a network of local officials on the other. His office was almost invariably conferred on one of the greater landlords or nobles, for whom it provided training in

[1] Quoted in S. and B. Webb, *English Local Government: the Parish and the County*, 471, n. 1.

administrative duties; in this way did the Howards, the Stanleys, the Cavendishes, the Herberts, and the Townshends acquire, within the bounds of their own counties, that practical experience in the handling of men which no other country could provide. His position was quite unlike that of the autocratic noble in provincial France;[1] for not only was his conduct under the close supervision of the privy council, but he had to act in conjunction with his deputy lieutenants, with whom he held regular meetings, at which petitions were heard and decisions made. There the disposition of the militia regiments was regulated; orders were issued for the levy of distraint on persons failing to provide their due quota for this territorial force, and the county share of the militia assessment was apportioned among the hundreds and corporations within their jurisdiction. Questions involving important principle had sometimes to be decided at these meetings, such as whether the clergy should be assessed and charged for the militia in respect of their spiritual estates;[2] and in moments of crisis, such as during the two Dutch Wars, the lieutenancies had to organize home and coastal defence.[3] These bodies often influenced the elections to parliament;[4] and in the scope of their deliberations they were themselves not unlike local parliaments. Together with the country gentry, the lord lieutenant and his deputies were the strongest support of the crown.

On the justices appointed by commissions of the peace devolved by far the greater part of the administrative and judicial work of the county. Hard-worked and unpaid, they have provided an endless source of surprised or admiring comment by foreign observers. Three qualifications were required of a justice: a competent estate, a good reputation, and a tolerable education.[5] By competent estate was meant a freehold of at least £20 per annum; good reputation was synonymous with receiving the sacrament according to the usage of the church of England at

---

[1] Thus, he could not dismiss an officer of militia, since these were appointed by His Majesty's commission. The marquis of Worcester had to be reminded of this fact in February 1676. (*Coventry Papers, Longleat*, vol. 83, f. 97.)

[2] Journal book of the lieutenancy of Norfolk, 1661–74, in *Add. MS.* 11061, f. 8. The Norfolk lieutenancy decided this question in the affirmative.

[3] See *supra*, i. 253.   [4] See *supra*, 474–6.

[5] E. Bohun, *The justice of the peace, his calling* (1693), 13.

least once a year; and tolerable education meant an elementary knowledge of Latin. In practice, therefore, only the notorious among the landlords were debarred from office.

The duties of the justice may be enumerated according as he acted singly, or with another, or with all his colleagues of the county in general sessions. In his single capacity he could order the imprisonment of vagabonds and trespassers; he committed seditious persons, and he might declare a price at which an article should be sold. He could administer oaths, including that of allegiance; and by his warrant he authorized the churchwardens to levy a fine of one shilling on absentees from church. Two justices sitting together could license ale-houses, punish offenders against the numerous statutes regulating the cloth-manufacture, inflict fines on all persons using unlawful or unjust weights and measures, and enforce the greater part of the poor law regulations, including the levying of the poor rate, and the removal of paupers to their last place of settlement. In quarter sessions, the justices of the county took cognizance of all breaches of duty by parish officials; they received presentments on all matters concerning county structures, including gaols, roads, and bridges; they tried recusants, traders forestalling the market, persons breaking the gaming laws by keeping greyhounds or other sporting dogs; labourers who violated the statute of Apprentices, or erected cottages on the waste without licence. They made affiliation orders, and could punish by fine or imprisonment; they might also inflict a sentence of banishment to one of the plantations, the choice being generally left to the privy council.[1] For an increasing number of human activities the tacit or written approval of the justice or justices came to be necessary; and the statutes of Charles's reign imposed many additional duties on these country gentlemen, who depended for their legal knowledge on compilations written specially for their use, such as that of Dalton.[2]

[1] e.g. in 1682 the justices of Devon ordered four rogues to be banished, and asked the council to assign a suitable plantation. The Board thought either Jamaica or Barbados. (*P.C. Reg.* 69, Nov. 29, 1682.)

[2] M. Dalton, *The Countrey Justice*, first printed in 1622. For good accounts of the duties of the justices see S. and B. Webb, op. cit., *The Parish and the County*, and E. Trotter, *Seventeenth-century life in the country parish*, 211 sqq.

The variety of these functions may be illustrated by example. Thus, in 1664, the Hertfordshire sessions condemned a Quakeress to pay a fine of £20 or suffer six months' imprisonment; three Quakers who stood mute were ordered to be transported to Barbados; in 1668 a man was fined £22 for exercising the craft of brewer without having served an apprenticeship. The Hertfordshire justices received an indictment of a man for using false and scandalous words about a woman, namely, that she was a witch, and did bewitch his ale; in 1671 they heard a petition from a lame and diseased man who had been imprisoned for nearly three years because he did not frequent the parish church. There were also prosecutions for Sabbath-breaking and non-observance of Lent. More commonly, the work was administrative. Children chargeable on the parish were boarded out; fit persons for farming the Excise were recommended; persons impoverished by fire were given a licence to beg for alms; and orders were made for the mending of highways and bridges, and the scouring of ditches.[1] At the Shropshire sessions in January 1661 the business included the grant of an ale-house licence, and of a licence to build a cottage; a maimed soldier was assigned a pension; two 'settlements' of paupers were declared, and several Scotch pedlars were ordered to be punished and deported. In January 1685 they heard a complaint from prisoners in the county gaol alleging ill usage by the gaolers, and petitioning for relief from exorbitant charges; in answer, the justices ordered that the charges ordered by the statute[2] of 1670-1 should be enforced, and that, in accordance therewith, a list of the authorized fees should be hung up in gaol.[3] Urban areas had their special problems. Thus, at the Middlesex sessions of August 1686, the churchwardens of St. Clement Danes were ordered to attend, in order to show how many poor children they had put out to be apprenticed at the charge of the court; two years later, the justices visited the workhouse in Clerkenwell to see the condition of the poor children there. Much time was spent by the Middle-

---

[1] These examples have been taken from *Hertford County Records* (1581–1698), ed. W. J. Hardy, i. 166, 202, 217, 226.

[2] See *supra*, i. 119, 120.

[3] *Shropshire County Records*, ed. sir O. Wakeman and R. L. Kenyon, 71, 102, 108.

sex magistrates in hearing and determining the numerous petitions from scavengers and rakers for the money due to them. Disputes between apprentices and masters also provided much business for the court.[1]

The justice was the link between the county and the parish; indeed it was in the complete dovetailing of the functionaries of the one into the supervision and control of the other that the excellence of the old system was to be found. There were about 10,000 parishes in the England of Charles's reign. These were as heterogeneous in size and population as the 40 counties, but it was exceptional for a parish to have more than 500 inhabitants. Its affairs were regulated by four classes of unpaid officials—the churchwardens, the constable, the surveyor of highways, and the overseer of the poor. The churchwardens, generally two in number, were chosen in accordance with ecclesiastical rule; in dignity and responsibility they were its most important officers. The constable, as the corporal embodiment of 'law and executive authority', was the person with whom the wrong-doer came into earliest and closest contact. A surveyor of the highways was chosen by the constable and churchwardens; he inspected bridges and roads and saw that repairs were effected, for which purpose he was authorized, together with two or more substantial householders of the parish, to lay an assessment of not more than sixpence in the pound in any one year.[2] The overseers of the poor were, in theory, required to see that an adequate stock was provided on which the willing poor could be set to work; in practice they appear, at this time, to have done little more than supplement the churchwardens' doles by small payments to the impotent poor. Of the humbler officials the parish clerk, who held office for life, acted as caretaker of the parish church; the sexton and bell-ringer held office during satisfactory performance of their duties. In some parishes there was a beadle, who acted as assistant to the constable; and here and there was to be found the dog-whipper, who expelled dogs from church, and occasionally applied his ministrations to the more somnolent or disorderly of the congregation. Some parishes boasted an organist, a spare-

[1] Calendar of Middlesex sessions books (R.O.). See also E. G. Dowdell, *A hundred years of Quarter Sessions (1660–1760)*, 1932.
[2] 14 Car. II, cap. vi.

time occupation, usually rewarded with a salary of £2 10s. per annum. Thus in the parish was to be found not only an ecclesiastical unit, but a centre of administrative activity and disciplinary control.

It is because the churchwardens had to keep accounts that records of their activities have survived. In many parishes they assisted the farmer by paying money for the destruction of vermin, at such rates as 1d. for a fox's head; 4d. for a polecat; 2d. for a stoat, and 1d. for a dozen of sparrows. There is one recorded payment for 149 dozen sparrows. Not all their payments were in cash; for occasionally a sum might be spent in providing a draught of sack for the preacher; or a comparatively large sum might be spent on the conciliatory meal offered to the archdeacon when he made his visitation. More commonly money was spent on beer for workmen and ringers. There were many occasions on which the services of supplementary ringers were required; and 1688 was their golden year, because they officiated at four extraordinary occasions: Queen's being with child (6s.); birth of the prince of Wales (6s.); rejoicings for the prince of Wales (6s. 6d.); ringing for the prince of Orange (6s.). In addition to these national occasions, there were parish events commemorated by special expenditure, generally in beer; as 'when the organ came home'; 'when they had set up the organ'; 'when the bell was taken down'; 'when the plumber made a bargain for the lead at the top of the tower'; 'when we made the bargain with the bell founder'.[1] Money was also spent in giving alms to licensed beggars.[2] More exceptionally, the churchwardens bore the cost of removing undesirable persons, as witnessed in these successive entries:[3] 'given to a woman to remove out of the parish, 1s.; spent to remove her, 6d.'

[1] Most of the above examples have been taken from the accounts of the churchwardens of Abbotsbury and Puddle Hinton (Dorset), for access to which I am indebted to the kindness of Rev. Canon Moule and Rev. W. Newman respectively. Lists of such local records will be found in *Ecclesiastical records of the Diocese of Birmingham* (Birmingham, 1911), and *Shropshire Parish Documents* (Shrewsbury, 1903). Derbyshire has been done very thoroughly by J. C. Cox in *Churchwardens' accounts from the fourteenth to the seventeenth century*; for Durham see *Durham Parish Records* (Surtees Society, 1888). There is a good bibliography by Miss E. Philips in *E.H.R.* xv.

[2] See *supra*, i. 121–2.   [3] Chirbury accounts, in *Shropshire Parish Records*.

The unwanted were generally removed by the constable. His duties were numerous and exacting. He had to see that the king's peace was kept, for which purpose he arrested all that went offensively armed, or committed riot; he apprehended felons, and, when resisted, raised the hue and cry; he executed the statutes for punishing rogues and idle persons; he kept a watchful eye on sporting dogs and their furtive owners, on gaming-houses, and on all who sleep by day and walk by night. Among the rogues and vagabonds were included not only those who would now be classed as tramps, but many wayfarers of a superior degree, such as scholars and seafaring men that beg; persons using unlawful games or telling fortunes; counterfeit Egyptians; jugglers, tinkers, pedlars, and chapmen, if not provided with a sufficient testimonial; all proctors and patent-gatherers (except for fire); pretended collectors for gaols or hospitals; fencers, bear-wards, minstrels, players of interludes; released prisoners begging their fees; persons going to and from the baths and wandering out of their way; labourers leaving their parishes, or refusing to work for wages reasonably taxed; servants quitting service in one place to seek it in another; all wanderers infected with plague.[1] The sentence on these intruders into the parish was a simple one: they were stripped from the waist upwards, and 'whipped till their backs be bloody'. They were then sent from constable to constable until their place of birth was reached; or, if that were unknown, to the place where they had last spent a whole year; otherwise to the house of correction or gaol, there to be employed or put to some service. On completion of the statutory punishment, a testimonial, signed by the minister and constable, was handed to the rogue; this document was framed on the following model:

W. W. a sturdy vagrant beggar (aged about 40 years) tall of stature, red-haired and long, lean-visaged and squint-eyed, was this 24th day of A. in the 22nd year of the reign of our gracious sovereign lord king Charles the Second etc. openly whipped at T. in the county of G. according to the law for a wandering rogue; and is assigned to pass forthwith from parish to parish by the officers thereof the next streight way to W. in the county of B. where he confesses he was born; and he is limited to be at W. aforesaid within twelve days

[1] *The Compleat Constable* (1692).

next ensuing at his peril. Given under the hands and seals of C. W. minister of T. and J. G. constable there.[1]

Exceptions were allowed in favour of expectant mothers and persons desperately sick.

As the constable expelled strangers from the parish, so on its immobile inhabitants he exercised a vigilance whereby every exuberance or deviation was sternly repressed. He saw to it that all ale-keepers were licensed, and, on a warrant from the justice, he levied a fine of 3s. 4d. on all persons engaged in bear-baiting or common plays on Sundays. Sunday was his busiest day; for he had to apprehend all who violated it by attending wrestlings, shootings, bowlings, ringing of bells for pleasure, masques, wakes, church-ales, dancing, or any sport or pastime, the penalty on persons over 14 being 5s. He had to satisfy himself that no drover or carrier plied his trade on that day, that no meat was killed, and that no one travelled except by licence from a justice. In church, he had to apprehend any one disturbing a lawful minister by brawling, and he made a note of absentees from service in order that they might be committed to the justices. He could break open doors in search of conventicles; nor did he have to produce a warrant, 'I arrest you in the king's name' being sufficient introduction.

They [the constables] are bugbears to them that wander without a pass. Poor soldiers are now and then helped to a lodging by their means. They'll visit an alehouse under colour of search, but their desire is to get beer of the company. . . . It's a thousand to one if they give a soldier two pence, but they will send in their bills 'given sixpence'.[2]

Nor was this all. The constable had to assist the Excise officers in their pursuit of offenders; he was also a sanitary inspector, a billeting officer, a rate collector, a revenue official on the look-out for private tobacco-crops, a hunter of poachers, and an inspector of weights and measures. That he had so many duties, and that there was no material incentive to encourage competence, may account for his many mistakes; but that he should have functioned at all is a tribute to the sense of order and

[1] W. Brown, *The duty and office of high constables, petty constables and tithing-men* (1677), 26-7.
[2] D. Lupton, *London and the country carbonadoed and quartered* (1632), 317.

discipline inherent in the humblest of Englishmen. Parliament
was a wonderful institution; but the unpaid parish constable
was much more remarkable.

Another administrative unit was the manor. The manorial
organization, where it survived, was of importance mainly for
the copyhold tenants holding in fee simple, in fee tail, or for life
or lives 'at the will of the lord after the custom of the manor'.
Uncertainty mingled with custom in the services of those who
owed suit and service to a manorial court, and there was the
greatest divergence of opinion regarding the status of the copyholder; some, with Fitzherbert, holding that he was really a
villein, in possession of a base fee, while others considered him
fully emancipated from every incident of villeinage, save his
obligation to attend the lord's customary court. The manor
itself was loosely defined as 'a thing compounded of demesnes
and long services', in distinction from a lordship, in which a
man might have services but not demesnes.[1] In consequence of
Edward I's *Quia Emptores* the subject could create a new copyhold but not a freehold, a restriction partly responsible for the
gradual decay of the manor.

The lord's jurisdiction was nominally exercised in three courts
—the court of freehold tenants, where the steward was only *primus
inter pares*, and the jurors gave judgement; the court of copyhold
tenants, sometimes called court baron, sometimes customary
court, where the steward was the sole judge, and the jurors were
merely jurors of presentment; and lastly the court leet, generally a hundred court in private hands. The first of these courts
was still summoned, but it was often difficult to obtain the attendance of freeholders. The distinction between the other two was
sometimes ignored, and one court, generally called a court leet,
served for the miscellaneous jurisdiction of those manors which
were still active.

These court leets were disciplinary institutions of some
importance. The presentments made by the homage covered a
very wide range, such as the withholding of due services, pur-

---

[1] *The relation between the lord of a manor and the copyholder*, also *A manor and
a court baron*, in Manorial Society Publications, nos. 17 and 3 respectively.
See also S. and B. Webb, *English local government: the manor and the borough*,
13–21.

prestures on land or water, erection of walls or hedges to the annoyance of the people, diversions of roads or streams, encroachments on the highways, eavesdroppers standing under walls or windows to hear tales, breakers of hedges, keepers of brothels, common haunters of taverns, butchers selling bad meat, ostlers asking unreasonable prices for their hay, millers taking excessive toll, and artificers failing to produce good work. Stray cattle might be 'presented'; also diseased horses, poachers, persons taking away the spawn of fish, artificers conspiring to raise wages, unauthorized persons using such luxurious material as velvet, fur, damask, or chamlet. Many of these offences, now known as common nuisances, are regulated by sanitary and board of health authorities. The court leet could not imprison as it had no gaol; but it punished by fine, and as a court of first instance it referred serious cases to the general sessions or the assizes. Here also were appointed the constable who kept the king's peace within the manor; also, in some instances, the ale-conner and the poundkeeper; while in market towns within the leet jurisdiction there might be inspectors of weights and measures, scavengers, dogmuzzlers, clerks of the wheat, fish, or butchery market. To some extent this jurisdiction overlapped that of the parish, but throughout England the latter was gaining at the expense of the former.

Side by side with the jurisdictions of county, parish, and manor was that of the church. This was exercised in the courts of the archdeacon and bishop, and in such archiepiscopal courts as the court of Arches; the Prerogative or Testamentary court, and the court of Peculiars (Canterbury); and in the Consistory, the Prerogative, and the Chancery courts of the archbishop (York). In the reign of Charles there was much ambiguity in regard to the spheres of the lay and clerical courts; but it was generally agreed that to the church pertained the probate of wills, in so far as personalty was concerned; the administration of intestates' estates; all cases loosely defined as matrimonial; suits for tithes and church rates; moral offences, whether committed by clergy or laity. They might determine at what age a person is capable of making a will, and when they granted probate to the executors of a boy of 15, the King's Bench refused to interfere.[1] The fre-

[1] *Modern Reports*, ii. 315.

quency with which the lay tribunals issued prohibitions to clerical courts, inhibiting them from proceeding further in cases brought before them, is sufficient to attest the dubiety surrounding the jurisdiction[1] of the church; and that so much of this jurisdiction should have remained is evidence not only of the lack of clarity in our judicial system, but of the strength of survivals.[2]

The recusant of Elizabethan and early Stuart times had felt the heavy hand of the court of High Commission; but this court was abolished in 1640, and, thereafter, dissent was dealt with by the justices in secular courts, in accordance with the statutes which handed the recusant over to the lay power. In consequence, a great field of activity was removed from the church courts (which nevertheless did not surrender their jurisdiction in matters of heresy and recusancy); in practice, therefore, the ecclesiastical tribunals were concerned not with bringing dissenters back to the fold, but with testamentary cases, and with the duty of imposing on the communicant strict standards of conduct and morality. For the smaller fry there was the court held by the archdeacon or his deputy, who at regular intervals conducted a visitation so exacting in character that at times it must have seemed an inquisition; for, on these occasions, he commenced with the minister. Was he a man of orderly life? Did he observe all the canonical requirements? Did he neglect his duties of preaching and catechizing? Then came the turn of the churchwardens. Did they keep the church fabric in good repair? Were the pulpit and ornaments clean? Were their accounts in order? Through a descending scale of parish clerks and sextons the ordinary laity were at last reached; and here there was plenty of scope for a conscientious archdeacon. He inquired into absentees from church, including those who left their pews after the first lesson, or neglected to receive communion; sabbath-breakers, brawlers, swearers, ne'er-do-wells, and unbaptized children were all good game for him; he was inquisitive about married couples living apart and unmarried ones living together; he saw to it that legacies left to the church were paid thereto;

---

[1] In practice the ecclesiastical law consisted mainly of all the old canon law which had not been repealed by statute.

[2] For this see *Report of the ecclesiastical commissioners of 1832*; also Claude Jenkins, *Ecclesiastical Records*.

that unlicensed persons did not keep school; that wills were proved, or letters of administration taken out. Accused persons protesting their innocence had to do canonical purgation, either by personal oath or, more often, by the oath of their neighbours; convicted persons might be required to do penance, as by standing up in church and confessing the fault. Such a penance might be preceded by forty days' excommunication. The archdeacon could also punish by fine, as 2s. for not paying marriage dues, or for not producing a marriage certificate. Whatever escaped through the sluices controlled by constable and justice was captured in the finer mesh of the archdeacon's net. The one set of authorities dealt with positive wrong-doing, the other with acts of omission and frailty. It was chiefly the unmarried mothers of England who provided this medieval functionary with an excuse for his continued existence.[1]

Similar in their scope were the presentments made to the commissary and consistory courts of the diocese, when the churchwardens were required to pass in review the condition of churches and churchyards; the state of repair of rectories and glebes; the absences of the rector or vicar; whether holy and fast-days were observed; if any refused infant baptism; or if any were unlawfully married or divorced, or remained in a state of excommunication; if any schoolmasters, physicians, surgeons, or midwives were pursuing their calling without licence; whether any one was under suspicion of immorality.[2] Diocesan courts decided matters also of purely spiritual discipline; they had power to suspend or deprive clergymen; they might declare a marriage void, or separate a married person *a mensa et thoro*. Much of their business related to the disposition of personal property by will. Superior to these were the courts of the two archiepiscopal provinces. The prerogative courts of Canterbury and York granted probate to executors and administrators within the jurisdiction of the province, wherever the deceased had had personal

[1] For the archdeacon see examples of churchwardens' presentments, such as those for Berkshire, in Bodley. Also S. A. Peyton, *Oxfordshire Peculiars* (*Oxford Records Society*), and *Act book of the archdeacon of Taunton* (*Somerset Records Society*, xlii, ed. C. Jenkins).

[2] These are taken from the *Articles to be enquired of within the commissarship of Westminster* (*Bodley*, B. 7, 9. Linc.).

property exceeding a certain amount in more than one diocese; the court of Peculiars had jurisdiction over those deaneries and peculiars which were outside episcopal control; the court of Arches had appellate jurisdiction over all the diocesan and most of the peculiar courts of the province of Canterbury. Crowning the whole edifice was the court of Delegates, originally established by Henry VIII, a tribunal composed of clergy and laity, to which appeal might be made from any of the lower courts.

By a reference to some of the appeals taken to the Delegates[1] in this period it is possible to form some conception of the jurisdiction of the church. Thus, in February 1664 they heard a case of some general interest. Shortly after the Restoration a person named Josiah Slader intruded himself into the rectory of Birmingham. His conduct was displeasing to the parishioners; for he was disaffected; he preached among Quakers; he was guilty of swearing, gaming, and perjury; he performed juggling feats in public, in which he purported to cut off his son's head and put it back again. Such were the allegations made by thirty-seven inhabitants of Birmingham in their petition to the bishop of Lichfield and Coventry. On account of doubt regarding his ordination, the bishop suspended him (Oct. 1662). Meanwhile, there were rumours that Slader's ordination papers were forged; whereupon the court of Arches inhibited him, until it should be determined whether or not he was lawfully ordained. The case then appears to have been considered by the Arches, which annulled the bishop's suspension, and gave costs against the Birmingham plaintiffs, reserving the question of Slader's orders (July 1663); but a few months later, the same court found that Slader was an intruder; that he was guilty of the offences charged against him, and that he was 'a mere layman'. Slader appealed to the Delegates (Feb. 1664), who upheld the decision of the Arches, decreed that Slader be sequestered from his living, and ordered the mesne profits to be paid to the churchwardens. It is of interest that in the course of the proceedings the appellant moved for a prohibition on the ground that forgery was triable by common law; but the prohibition was denied, because the forgery was 'touching an ecclesiastical matter'.

[1] For these see H. C. Rothery, *Return of all appeals in causes of doctrine and discipline made to the high court of Delegates* (1868).

A case where the verdict of the Delegates is not on record was that of a parishioner in a village of the Salisbury diocese named Robson who, in the consistory court, charged White and Harris with committing adultery. The charge appears to have been proved to the satisfaction of the court, which sentenced both parties to be canonically corrected, and cited the two for the imposition of penance. The female defendant Harris did not appear; but shortly afterwards she was allowed to come into the consistory court with three neighbours as compurgators, who swore on oath that she had not committed adultery with White. The situation was now somewhat complicated; but the bishop's deputy adopted a middle course: he pronounced that she had purged herself sufficiently; and he restored her, so far as he could, to her former good name; but at the same time he warned her not to be seen in the company of White except in church or market-place. He gave her a testimonial to this effect. Thereupon the unsatiated Robson appealed to the Arches against the admission of Harris to purgation, and her absolution from the sentence of penance originally imposed upon her; but the Arches upheld the proceedings of the consistory court, and gave costs against Robson. Whether he eventually recovered these from the Delegates is not known.

Altogether thirty-seven cases were taken to the Delegates, including one from the consistory court of Dublin; some of these were carried the whole way from the archdeacon's court by way of consistory court and Arches. Two appeals were lost by persons who were alleged to have secured their livings by means of forged credentials; another offence penalized was that of teaching boys without a licence; in another case it was ruled that the archdeacon's court could punish any one not attending church, in spite of the plea that the matter pertained to lay jurisdiction. A study of these cases tempts one to conclude that, apart from their probate administration, much of the work of these spiritual courts was made by the busy-body and informer. These are to be found in every society, but there was unlimited scope for them in the times of the later Stuarts. It may be added, however, that, with the foundation of societies for the reformation of manners, such as those instituted after 1689, a somewhat different attitude to moral offences was gradually introduced.

Such were the jurisdictions, lay and clerical, with which the average offender was most likely to come into contact. Of the tribunals at Westminster the court of Common Pleas was that nominally reserved for pleas of subject against subject and for cases where the crown was not plaintiff; in practice, however, much of its work was being 'poached' by the King's Bench and Exchequer, of which the first had originally been instituted for pleas of the crown, and the second for cases arising from the administration of the revenue. In effect, therefore, by the seventeenth century these three central tribunals were common law courts, their respective provinces not very clearly defined, save that the King's Bench was the superior, and was that wherein the crown instituted proceedings against the more serious political offenders. Moreover, many cases between subject and subject were disposed of in circuit under the *Nisi Prius* procedure, and the judgement of the central court was generally based on the finding of the local jury. Of the political trials there are few absolutely authentic records; for some of the State Trials, notably after 1678, appear to have been edited with party bias, and this is one of the most serious impediments in the way of an impartial account of the events of this period.[1]

There was more dubiety and debate about the functions of the fourth of the central courts—that of Chancery. Its functions were thus described in the earl of Oxford's case (1615):

The cause why there is a Chancery is for that men's actions are so diverse and infinite that it is impossible to make any general law which may apply with every particular act, and not fail in some circumstances. The office of the chancellor is to correct men's consciences for frauds, breach of trust, wrongs and oppressions of what nature soever they be, and to soften and modify the extremity of the law which is called Summum Jus.[2]

To illustrate from example. Chancery reviewed decrees of tithe;

[1] The first edition of the *State Trials* appeared in 1719, an edition very rarely met with; the second appeared in 1730. The reporting and editing of the trials of 1679–83 were done mainly by Robert Blaney, who may have tampered with some of the evidence. For this see J. G. Muddiman, *State Trials, the need for a new and revised edition* (1930). The opinion of the present writer is that the contemporary material does not make possible the completion of an absolutely dependable edition of the *State Trials*.

[2] *English Reports* (Chancery), xxi. 486.

enforced the customs of such cities as London and York, wherever the orphans of freemen were concerned; gave relief where conveyances were defective; adjudicated in breaches of trust and in construction of wills; and in general entertained all cases where the subject was aggrieved either by the enforcement of the letter of the law, or by unjust practices under cover of the law. By the issue of an injunction it could restrain any one from doing an act otherwise lawful. Chancery could determine what were or were not superstitious uses; and wherever a charitable use was intermixed, it decreed what was charitable and what superstitious, the latter being given to the crown. It was also a court of appeal from customary courts, from the vice-chancellor's courts of the two universities, and from the palatine courts of Chester and Durham. It had incurred the enmity of great common lawyers, such as Coke, because it was supposed to administer laws alien to the native jurisprudence, and because it frequently issued injunctions to the prejudice of common-law courts. Its abolition had been advocated by many Puritan reformers, because of its expense and delay, and since it seemed to be a jurisdiction outside the common law, and hostile to it; but, after 1660, its prerogative was seldom impugned, and its prestige was enhanced by such a lord keeper as Bridgeman, one of the greatest conveyancers of the century, and by lord chancellors such as Shaftesbury and Nottingham, of whom the one acted with such fairness and justice as to win the praise even of his enemies, while the other prepared the way for Eldon by the measure of system and uniformity which he introduced into the administration of equity. Nottingham is remembered by lawyers to-day as the 'Father of Equity'.

The historian is familiar with those suits where constitutional principle was involved; but something may also be gleaned from cases which, though of primary interest to the lawyer, provide evidence of social conditions. Among such are the cases relating to personal status, as illustrated mainly from questions of professional privilege or personal disability.

For example, a practising physician was chosen constable by the officers of his parish. A writ of privilege was thereupon moved for him in the King's Bench on the ground that his profession exempted him from parochial office. The privilege was refused, on the ground that a physician is in a different status from an attorney or barrister-at-law; for while these attend public courts, he is exercising a private calling.[1] A similar motion was made on behalf of the archdeacon of Rochester, praying that he might be discharged from an office to which he had been appointed by commissioners of Sewers in respect of lands which he held in Kent. On his behalf it was argued that the office was a mean one, and that the lands were let to a tenant. The privilege was granted, because he was a clergyman, and the land let in lease.[2]

Cases of interest for the history of the legal profession were those of maintenance and barratry. The statute legislation of the later middle ages abounded in prohibition of those two offences, prohibitions based on the principle that it is immoral to profit by the financial encouragement of other men's suits, or to defend a suit where there is reason to believe that it is an unjust one. Insistence on the second of these principles might have seriously hampered the growth of at least one branch of legal practice. To quote from an example. A was arrested at the suit of B in an action for debt. When the case came for trial, C, a barrister-at-law present in court, solicited the suit, 'when in truth at the same time B was indebted to A in £200', and A did not owe B anything. When it was shown that C had several times entertained B in his house, it was thought at first that his offence was maintenance; but when it also transpired that C had several times brought actions on behalf of B where nothing was owing, the court found C guilty of barratry. This distinction was embodied in the judgement that a man may lend money to another in order to help him to recover a just right at law; but if he lend money to promote and stir up suits, that is barratry.[3] Litigation as an object of speculation was therefore discouraged.

The courts insisted on a difference between the status of a lunatic and that of an idiot, a difference clearly illustrated in the case of *Prodgers* v. *Frazier*.[4] Here both sides recognized the right of the king to grant the custody of an idiot to whomsoever he pleased, without account; but it proved to be otherwise with a lunatic. An idiot was afflicted *a nativitate*, and could at no time

[1] *Modern Reports*, i. 22. Case of Dr. Pordage.
[2] Ibid. i. 282. Case of Dr. Lees.
[3] Ibid. iii. 97.
[4] Ibid. iii. 43.

have views on the administration of his property; he was therefore at the mercy of the person to whom his custody was allotted;
but a lunatic might have lucid intervals, in which he could call
his administrator to account. So the custodian of a person of
unsound mind kept accounts of his stewardship only if the misfortune of his charge did not date from birth; but with a 'natural
fool' he took the profits without waste or destruction and found
his charge in necessaries.[1]

Another question affecting status was the relationship between
master and apprentice. The law was clear that a master could
punish and correct the apprentice; but some justices were not
certain whether an apprentice who beat his master could be
discharged of his apprenticeship, until this was affirmed by the
King's Bench on appeal from the general sessions of Bristol.[2] A
freeman of London might turn away his apprentice for gaming.[3]
Wherever a capital sum had been paid by the apprentice at the
signing of his indentures, a portion of this was to be repaid on
his dismissal for negligence. It was held also by the courts that
a master might summon his servant from a conventicle or an
ale-house, and might use a moderate amount of force in so doing,
because the lord had the right to beat his villein without cause;
but if he commanded another to do it, then an action for battery
would lie.[4] Occasionally also there filtered through from the
church courts a case affecting the relations of husband and wife.
Thus, for a box on the ear and bad language, a spiritual court
awarded a woman £4 a week alimony against her husband, who
thereupon moved for a prohibition, on the ground that he had
chastised his wife for a reasonable cause, as he was allowed to do
by common law. The church court replied that it had jurisdiction *de saevitiis*; to which the husband rejoined that subsequent
reconciliation had taken away that *saevitia*.[5] In practice, however, the right of the spiritual tribunals to try such cases was
rarely contested.

Another sphere of litigation not without interest to the student
of social history is that of slander. The great number of such cases
in the later seventeenth century suggests that public fame and

---

[1] *English Reports* (Chancery), xxii. 488.　　[2] *Modern Reports*, i. 286.
[3] *English Reports* (Chancery), xxi. 1065.　　[4] *Modern Reports*, ii. 167.
[5] *English Reports* (Common Pleas), cxxiv. 414.

reputation were coming to be more highly prized, and that the remedies provided by the courts were more frequently invoked. When a shoemaker brings an action against a man for calling him a cobbler,[1] it is clear that social differentiation has proceeded far; indeed, modern society reposes on these subtle distinctions. Generally, for success in these actions, it had to be shown that material loss had ensued, or was likely to ensue; thus a man might with impunity be called a bungler, but if the words were spoken with reference to his trade, then the word was actionable. But it was not so with a peer; for any slander about him was actionable under the statute *De scandalis magnatum*, even if it did not expressly imply inaptitude for his hereditary office of adviser of the king.[2] There was considerable doubt whether the epithet 'papist' was libellous; some thinking that, like the word 'heretic', it related to something spiritual, and was therefore cognizable in the church courts; others held that at one time it would be actionable to use such an epithet, though not so at another time; for the meaning of a word may change, as shown by the term 'knave', formerly meaning a servant, and now libellous if used of an attorney. In 1683 the King's Bench gave a verdict in favour of sir T. Clarges against a defendant who had called him 'papist' at a parliamentary election.[3] So, too, there were epithets which, when applied to one person were libellous, but not necessarily so when used of others. Thus, it was libellous to say of a farmer that 'he owes more than he is worth', or of a tradesman, 'he is broke, and run away'. On the principle perhaps that there is no libel like the truth, each occupation acquired a special susceptibility, and had to be accorded protection against imputations touching on that susceptibility.

One of the most important questions of status was that of the soldier. The professional soldiers of the later Stuarts were not distinguished for stature or personal appearance; indeed, some of the garrison which came back from Tangier were decrepit men of 60 and 70; in consequence, the army was not a caste. Nor, at first, did they have buildings permanently allotted for their use, and it was not until 1684 that a beginning was made in the establishment of Chelsea Hospital, for the accommodation of

---

[1] *Modern Reports*, i. 19, where a judge stated that such an action had been brought.   [2] Ibid. ii. 165.   [3] Ibid: iii. 26.

400 aged or disabled soldiers. The standing army was not illegal, but it was extra-parliamentary, in the sense that while several statutes recognized its existence, either directly or by implication, no parliamentary provision[1] was made for its maintenance, as was made for Militia and Navy; even more, a red coat was anathema to every English patriot, because the recollection of army rule was still fresh.

In theory, the soldier did not sacrifice any of his civilian rights when he entered the army; and in practice he shared with the civilian a strong objection to anything with 'martial law in it'. In the summer of 1673 there was assembled on Blackheath an army for transport to the Continent; the men composing it were to be disciplined by the Articles of War promulgated in the preceding year. Their attitude to such restraints may be inferred from the following letter:

The soldiers at Blackheath are almost ready to mutiny on the rumour that they are to fight alongside the French. Men are wondering who dared to print the Articles of War . . . they scruple the oath in it, and say that to swear at large to obey the King's commands is strange; for then he may command things for which the persons that do them shall afterwards be hanged. The words of this horrid oath are:—'I, A.B. swear to be true and faithful to my sovereign lord king Charles . . . and to be obedient in all things to his General or Lieutenant General for the time being, and will behave myself obediently towards my superior officers in all that they shall command me for His Majesty's service, and I do further swear that I shall be a true, faithful and obedient soldier, every way performing my best endeavours for His Majesty's service, obeying all orders, and submitting to such rules and articles of war as shall be established by His Majesty.'[2]

That English paid soldiers should have objected to this 'horrid' oath is one of the most striking tributes to the pre-eminence of common-law traditions; for in some general way, these men on Blackheath believed that, unlike foreigners, they had over them the protection of Magna Carta and the Petition of Right; more-

[1] For an exception see *supra*, 444.

[2] Henry Ball to Williamson, July 18, 1673, in *Letters to Williamson*, ed. Christie (*Camd. Soc.*), 117. At the trial of lord Russell in 1682 it was argued that the King's Guards are not his Guards in law, but are merely a company of men in the king's pay. (*Burnet*, ii. 375).

over, soldiers, like sailors, were still tried by civil courts for offences not cognizable by courts martial, and the sphere of military jurisdiction was much narrower than it is to-day. It was also more vague; for there was considerable doubt whether, in law, desertion was punishable as a felony;[1] and there existed a court—the court of Chivalry or Marshal's court—which could deal with matters not pertaining to common law. But this court was in abeyance, and its reputation was bad. Nevertheless, as the crown imposed, by proclamation and articles of war, a more comprehensive and definite system of discipline,[2] there grew up a clearer distinction between soldier and civilian, and so was created the nucleus of military law. The Stuarts had no difficulty in obtaining from their judges a ruling that by statute law desertion was a felony. This evolution may be summarized thus: at the Restoration, a deserter might be punished by fine or imprisonment in the court of a justice; in the last years of the reign he might be hanged as a felon, in one of the places of execution under the jurisdiction of the tribunal which sentenced him; in the reign of James II he might be hanged as a felon, by sentence of a civil court, but in a special place, selected by the crown—in the view of his regiment.[3]

This confusion was increased by the distinction between discipline in time of peace and in time of war, between service at home and abroad, and by the fact that two different terms, martial law and military law, were often used for the same thing. Martial law was properly the suspension of common law in time of emergency, and so might concern any one; in 1678 it was defined as 'the law which dependeth on the King's will and pleasure, or his lieutenant's in time of war'.[4] Military law, on the other hand, was a set of rules, regulating the discipline of the soldier in his pro-

---

[1] For this see Holdsworth, *History of English Law*, vi. 225–30.

[2] C. Walton, *History of the British Standing Army*, 531. For the subject generally see Clode, *Military Forces of the Crown*.

[3] Herbert C.J. objected to this on the ground that the execution could legally take place only in Middlesex. The court was informed of the king's will—that the execution should take place in Plymouth, before his regiment; and soon afterwards Herbert was removed from the King's Bench, and replaced by Wright. (*Modern Reports*, ii. 124, *Rex v. W. Beal*.) For an execution in Covent Garden before a regiment see Luttrell, *Brief Historical Relation*, i. 400.

[4] Chamberlayne, *Angliae Notitia*, quoted in C. Walton, op. cit. 533.

fessional capacity; a code not yet clearly defined, but in process of formulation by edicts. Within the limits of these edicts, commanding officers enforced their jurisdiction in courts of inquiry and in courts martial; but punishments amounting to loss of life were not inflicted by these in peace time; so in this respect at least the scope of such tribunals was substantially limited, a restriction for which the old respect for Magna Carta and the Petition of Right was mainly responsible. Had Stuart relations with the legislature been harmonious, it would have been possible to end this anomalous state of things by legislation; but parliament could not take this work in hand till after the Revolution. The Mutiny Act, by its subjection of the soldier to a definite military code, ended the old confusion; and it had this important corollary, that an army not definitely and annually authorized by parliament is illegal.

The scope of military law in this period may be illustrated from surviving records of courts martial. In Tangier,[1] the discipline appears to have been that of an army in time of war, and was dispensed by courts consisting of four captains, four lieutenants, and four ensigns, presided over by a senior captain; its commission was derived from the warrant of the Governor and Commander of the Garrison. Here the most usual penalty was corporal punishment, varying from 31 to 39 lashes for such diverse offences as wounding another soldier, selling provisions, pawning uniform, and assaulting a Frenchman. To ride the wooden horse with muskets attached to each heel appears to have been a favourite punishment; this was inflicted on a private who, when in drink, disobeyed a sergeant. Refusal to obey an officer was punished by dismissal from the service, and a drummer who refused to beat his drum when ordered to do so had to stand at the gibbet with a rope round his neck, and a placard on his chest, on which the offence was inscribed. The most serious case heard by the Tangier courts was that arising from a mutiny in October 1677, when two soldiers went to the Governor's house and demanded the release of one of their companions who was imprisoned for disobedience. The ringleader was shot on the spot by the Governor, and the other was shot by order of a court

[1] 'Tangier Courts Martial', 1676–83, in Worcester College, Oxford, MS. no. 121.

martial. These records suggest that the Tangier garrison was more than usually turbulent, and that the discipline, though more severe than that prevailing in the army at home, was much less severe than that afterwards exercised.

The gradual imposition of a distinctive code on the soldier helped to disabuse men of the notion that in some way Magna Carta had provided one uniform law for all Englishmen. In other respects also the reign of Charles II is of great importance in the history of English law. To the Puritans we owe the earliest experiments in legal reform; and though it was long before the more far-reaching proposals of Commonwealth visionaries could be adopted, the legislation of Charles II owes a substantial debt to that of the preceding age. Outside of parliament there were public-spirited men like Petty who believed that the energy thrown by the Commons into penal legislation against dissent might be better employed in the promotion of measures for the advance of trade and national well-being; others would have had the law itself simplified, and in 1666 a Bill was introduced into the Commons for reviewing all the statutes and bringing them to one head,[1] but it appears to have been dropped. Another reform was that of trying to reduce the excessive number of attorneys. Both puritan and cavalier legislators tried their hand at this, but with the same result. Thus, a committee of the Commons, after hearing the evidence of the judges, proposed to limit the number of attorneys to a certain quota in each county; but it never reported.[2] More serious defects in legal administration were the numerous harsh punishments for minor offences, and the comparative impunity with which perjury and forgery might be committed. Sir William Temple protested against the sanguinary laws for common thefts, because these deprive us of so many subjects and do not cure the disease;[3] other writers echoed these views.[4] Had perjury and forgery been felonies in law, the Popish Plot might never have been concocted; that they should be felonies was advocated by at least one writer.[5]

---

[1] Oct. 5, 1666. *Millward's Diary.*

[2] *H.M.C. Rep.* ix, app., pt. ii. 20, Feb. 14, 1673; see also *supra*, i. 132–3.

[3] Sir W. Temple, *Works* (1770), iii. 55.

[4] e.g. *England's Wants . . . by a true lover of his country* (1668), in *Bodley, Godwin Pamph.* 1125.   [5] *Brief reflections upon . . . forgery and perjury* (1685).

Nevertheless, some important legal reforms were effected by statute. An Act of 1665 provided that in all actions, real, personal, or mixed, the death of either party before verdict and judgement should not be allowed for error, provided the judgement was entered within two terms after the verdict.[1] A measure which helped to lessen delays in the execution of justice was the statute of 1664–5 which decreed that judgement on a verdict of twelve men in any action or suit should not be stayed for a technical error, such as a mistake in the Christian name or surname of plaintiff or defendant.[2] So, too, vexatious lawsuits were discouraged by the provision that in personal actions where the jury awarded damages of less than 40s. the plaintiff should not have greater costs than the amount of the damages awarded him.[3] A ruling was given on the period of time after which the death of an absentee might be presumed; seven years of such absence abroad, without evidence of existence, was the period made statutory in 1666.[4] Another limit recognized by the law was that prescribed in the Gaming Act of 1664, whereby any one losing more than £100 in a game of chance was not bound to pay.[5]

Of greater importance were the Statute of Frauds[6] (1677) and the Act for better securing the liberty of the subject[7] (1679), usually known as the Habeas Corpus Act. The first of these, with the intention of diminishing opportunities for fraud and perjury, enacted that, in future, all parole leases of lands and interests of freehold should have the force of estates at will only, and also that devises of freehold lands or tenements must be in writing, and signed by three or four witnesses. Declarations or creations of trusts in lands or tenements were also to be in writing and signed, and the validity of contracts for the sale of goods above £10 in value was subject to certain alternative stipulations, including the requirement that a note or memorandum of agreement should be signed by both parties. So too with wills. A nuncupative will (that is, by word of mouth), where the estate

---

[1] 17 Car. II, cap. viii. [2] 16–17 Car. II, cap. viii.
[3] 22–3 Car. II, cap. ix. [4] 18–19 Car. II, cap. xi.
[5] 16 Car. II, cap. vii.
[6] 29 Car. II, cap. ii. See also Holdsworth, *History of English Law*, vi. 384–97. [7] 31 Car. II, cap. ii.

exceeded £30, was invalid unless proved by three witnesses on oath, and made during the last sickness of the testator, an exception being allowed in favour of soldiers and sailors in actual service.

The legal importance of the Statute of Frauds has sometimes been exaggerated by historians, who have been tempted to think that it effected a revolution in conveyancing. Already, before the passing of the Act, transactions relating to land were generally in writing; for estates of importance this was almost invariable. Moreover, the statute gave rise to several technical abuses in conveyancing; and, in general, it was possible for Chancery to drive a coach-and-four through it. In reality, it provides a good instance of the piece-meal character of English legislation; how an abuse may be remedied not by a sweeping reform, but by a limitation of the abuse. Until 1863 there was a common-law rule whereby neither party to a civil suit could give sworn evidence at the trial, a rule which at times provided considerable scope for the suborned witness who, in return for money, would give false evidence on oath; consequently, the framers of the Statute of Frauds, instead of allowing the principal parties to give evidence, merely insisted that in certain contracts, something more than parole evidence should be forthcoming. For the sale or purchase of goods over £10 in value, a safeguard was provided by the requirements as to written contract, acceptance, or delivery; but for goods under £10, the subject had still to take the risk of losing his case on the sworn evidence of the perjurer. Hence the Statute of Frauds is of profound importance to the student of history; for it reveals how widespread was the menace of perjury, and only with this knowledge can the Popish Plot be understood.

There was also a moral as distinct from a legal significance in Shaftesbury's Act for better securing the liberty of the subject and for prevention of imprisonment beyond seas.[1] Part of this moral significance lies in its date—1679, one of the really critical years in the history of England, when the Commons were fighting a fierce battle against the king, and when additional security for the liberty of the subject, no matter how slight, was a

[1] For a good account see Holdsworth in op. cit. ix. 112–25; also J. Patterson, *Commentaries on the liberty of the subject*, ii. 205–18.

tremendous achievement. This Act, commonly known as the Habeas Corpus Act, was the culmination of a series of efforts to make statutory what had long been a common-law right, and to facilitate the exercise of that right by providing that no one should be imprisoned in a place where the writ could not easily be served. In this respect it was the most notable statute of the century, and it appears to have passed the Lords by a mistake in the count.

The writ of habeas corpus could be demanded from the King's Bench by or on behalf of a prisoner; by its terms, the gaoler or detainer was required to produce the body of the prisoner, with the date and cause of his detention, to the judgement of the court issuing the writ. In practice there were many difficulties in applying this remedy. For example, the writ was sometimes refused by courts other than King's Bench, and as a rule was issued only in term-time; again, a second and even a third writ might have to be applied for; still more, the prisoner might have been transported to one of the Channel Islands (as was Prynne), and a whole winter might pass before the writ could be served. In effect, therefore, a political prisoner might be placed in custody and kept there for a long period before trial, and it was in the interests of the Stuarts to restrict, as far as possible, the application of the remedy, because it was often deemed inadvisable that the cause of commitment should be investigated by the courts. In 1676 a London alderman named Jenkes was committed for a speech at the Guildhall in which he urged the common council to petition for a new parliament. As he was arrested in vacation the writ was refused by Chancery; and his release was due to the initiative of Rainsford L.C.J., who told the chancellor (Finch) that the writ was of right.

Repeated efforts had been made to remedy these defects by statute, and it is notable that some of these date from the period immediately following the banishment of Clarendon. A prisoners' transportation Bill[1] was introduced in 1669–70, and again[2] in 1673–4, together with a habeas corpus Bill, the object of which was to amend the working of the writ, and to make illegal the imprisonment of English subjects beyond seas or in Scotland. These provisions were embodied in Shaftesbury's Act,[3] which-

[1] *H.M.C. Rep.* viii, app., pt. i. 142.
[2] Ibid. ix, app., pt. ii. 42. [3] 31 Car. II, cap. ii.

required sheriffs, gaolers, or other detainers, within three days of the service of the writ (except in cases of treason and felony), to produce the prisoner before the court to which the writ was returnable, and at the same time to certify the cause of commitment. In vacation, a petition for the writ might be directed to the lord chancellor, or to any of His Majesty's judges. Persons committed for criminal matters were not to be moved from one prison to another, but by writ of habeas corpus or other legal writ.

It was characteristic that the Act did not introduce any new principle, and that it achieved only a partial remedy. Its limitations were clear; for it did not regulate the amount of bail that might be demanded; nor did it apply to treason or felony; nor was there any provision whereby the court might investigate the truth of the facts alleged by the gaoler. These deficiencies were chiefly evidenced in the later administration of the bankruptcy legislation and the laws enforcing military service; but in practice the judges of the eighteenth century extended its scope, and what had hitherto been informal was made statutory in 1816, when the remedy acquired its present form. Before that date, it had been invoked in many cases not only of imprisonment but of wrongful detention, whether of wives or children, or of persons reputed to be insane; and herein is its true significance, that it provides the right to public investigation in all cases where the liberty of the subject is unwarrantably restrained.

Of the laws which limited the liberty of the subject, the most notable were those relating to treason and the press. The law of treason was based on the statute of 1353, which had reduced the crime to seven definite heads, with a proviso that parliament might in future adjudge any political offence as treason. But while this Act protected the king against war and violence, it did not deal with conspiracy, until the conspiracy had become open war. Parliament and judicial bench combined to remedy this defect, with the result that many things, including riots, came to be construed as overt acts tending to expose the king to danger, or to deprive him forcibly of some part of his authority. Hence the so-called law of constructive treason; hence also the potency of this weapon in the hands of a determined executive; for a servile bench might be trusted so to interpret the law as to secure the removal of a political opponent, on the ground that his words or acts were likely to prejudice the powers or safety of the sovereign. This was the weapon with which the later Stuarts removed many of their critics.

The first statute of the Cavalier Parliament was a treason Act.[1] This defined treason within the terms of the Statute of 1353, and included in the category of overt acts all printing, writing, preaching, or malicious and advised speaking calculated to compass or devise the death, destruction, injury, or restraint of the sovereign, or to deprive him of his style, honour, or kingly name. Overt acts had to be proved by two witnesses; but at the trial of the Regicides in 1660 it was ruled by Bridgeman that two witnesses were not required for each overt act; one witness proving one such act, and another witness proving another being sufficient.[2] In 1668 there was provided a good illustration of how far the law of treason could extend. Early in that year Peter Messenger and fourteen other apprentices tumultuously assembled themselves in Moorfields under colour of pulling down houses of ill fame—such was the allegation in the indictment of high treason preferred against them; though it was well known to the court that the affair was merely an apprentices' riot. Kelyng L.C.J., who was not devoid of sympathy for the accused, defined treason in these terms:

By levying of war is meant not only when a body is gathered together as when an army is, but if a company of people will go about any public reformation, that is High Treason . . . for they take upon them the royal authority; the way is worse than the thing. These men do pretend that their design was against bawdy houses; now for men to go about to pull down houses with a captain and an ensign and weapons; if this thing be endured, who is safe? It is High Treason because it doth betray the peace of the nation . . . for if every man may reform what he will, no man is safe.[3]

These words admirably describe two things—a judicial construction of the law of treason, and the panic fear with which, for long after the Restoration, the government regarded everything that seemed likely to result in a mass movement. The jury gave a verdict that Messenger and three others had met in a riotous

[1] 13 Car. II, stat. i, cap. i.　　　　[2] See *supra*, i. 197–8.
[3] *State Trials* (1730 ed.), ii. 583.

manner; the judges then deliberated whether this was treason or not. They decided that it was, Hale only dissenting; accordingly these four men suffered death in the barbarous manner then prescribed for those convicted of this offence. It is not surprising, therefore, that when, after 1681, the attack on the whigs was launched, the judges were able to prove that almost anything was treason. Thus in 1681, when Shaftesbury was indicted at the Old Bailey, Pemberton L.C.J. stated that, according to the Act of 1661, the intention to levy war on the king was now treason; and so also were words, if they imported any malicious design against the king or government.[1] Two years later Algernon Sidney was convicted on the opinions expressed in his unpublished writings. Perhaps the most extraordinary case of all was that of Rosewell, a nonconformist preacher, who in 1684 was found guilty of high treason on the evidence of two women, who swore that, in a sermon, he had compared Charles to Jeroboam, and asked why people flocked to the king on the pretence of being healed. In this case, the attorney-general had pressed for a verdict on the ground 'that the government is greatly concerned in the matter'. This is noteworthy as one of the few trials at which Jeffreys acted with fairness; for in face of the jury's verdict he suspended judgement, and shortly afterwards Rosewell obtained the king's pardon and was discharged.[2]

A man accused of high treason was therefore at the mercy not so much of the law as of the judge and jury which tried him; but even if these were impartial he was handicapped by the method of procedure. He did not receive a copy of the indictment until the day of the trial; nor was counsel allowed him; he had therefore to conduct his own defence, and without preparation of any kind. It was here that Jeffreys showed himself at his worst; for he railed and jeered at men struggling to exculpate themselves from all sorts of hearsay evidence levelled against them by enemies and perjurers. These and other defects were not remedied until 1696, when the Trial of Treasons Act[3] allowed counsel to the accused, and required two witnesses for each overt act.

Censorship of the press, originally exercised by the Church,

[1] See *infra*, 629.　　　　　　　　[2] *State Trials*, iii. 982-3.
[3] Holdsworth, op. cit. vi. 232-4.

had long been controlled by the crown, and was placed on a statutory basis by the Licensing Act of 1662.[1] This Act prohibited the printing or importing of any books or pamphlets containing doctrines contrary to the principles of the Christian faith, or to the doctrine and discipline of the Church of England, or tending to the scandal of government or governors in church or state. For purposes of inspection, all books had first to be entered at Stationers' Hall, and were licensed according to their subject—law books by the lord chancellor; books of history or affairs of state by one of the principal secretaries of state; books of heraldry by the earl marshal, and all others by the archbishop of Canterbury and the bishop of London. This Act remained in force until 1679, when its place was taken by a proclamation[2] ordering the seizure of all libels against the government, and the apprehension of their authors and printers; with a reward of £40 for informers. In 1685 the Act was renewed, and eventually expired in 1695. The noted Roger L'Estrange was appointed in 1663 to enforce these licensing regulations, after he had distinguished himself by his devotion to the royalist cause and by his extreme views on the functions of the censorship. Before he was appointed 'surveyor of imprimery' he had enumerated[3] most of the seditious opinions which he thought an efficient censorship should suppress; among these were the following: (1) that the execution of Charles I was justified; (2) that the king is one of three estates; (3) that in cases of necessity sovereignty resides in the two Houses; (4) that the power of the crown is fiduciary; (5) that the king's person, as distinct from his authority, may be resisted; and (6) that the king has no supreme power in ecclesiastical matters. L'Estrange became the greatest of the tory pamphleteers; prolific, unscrupulous, and completely deaf to ridicule.

The rights of the subject in regard to printing and publishing were properly summed up by Scroggs when he declared that there was no such thing as liberty of the press.[4] This was made

---

[1] 14 Car. II, cap. xxxiii.   [2] Oct. 31, 1679, *Steele*, i. 3699.

[3] In his *Considerations and proposals in order to the regulation of the Press*. This was issued in June 1663; in August he was appointed 'surveyor of the imprimery'.

[4] *State Trials* (1730), iii. 57. Trial of Henry Carr for printing and publishing a libel, July 2, 1680.

more explicit by Jeffreys in his pronouncement that the law forbade the publication of anything concerning the government
without the king's licence.[1] Already the courts had illustrated
how the doctrine was applied. In 1664 L'Estrange forced his
way into the premises of a printer named Twyn, where he seized
the sheets of a book *A Treatise of the execution of Justice*, probably
an apologia for the execution of Charles I. Twyn was indicted
for high treason, convicted, and executed.[2] As the state was protected, so was the church. In the same year as Twyn was executed Benjamin Keach was indicted for libel at the Aylesbury
Assizes, the libel relating to his book *The Child's Instructor*, wherein
were these statements: that infants ought not to be baptized; that
laymen might preach the Gospel, and that Christ would reign
personally on earth in the latter day.[3] His sentence was fourteen
days' imprisonment, a fine of £20, and the pillory. His book was
burnt in front of him by the common hangman.

Expression of personal opinion was therefore strictly limited
by the law of treason and the law of the press. In 1678 a statute[4]
was passed taking away the old writ *De haeretico comburendo*; but
this left intact the rights of the spiritual courts to punish heresy,
and of the common law courts to punish blasphemy.[5] In theory
the church courts still had the right to punish recusancy;[6] but in
practice the civil courts now administered all the penal legislation
against Dissenters and Catholics. In effect, therefore, the control
of opinion was almost altogether removed from the church and
vested in the state. This was not without importance in the
history of toleration since, in its imposition of particular doctrines,
the state had at least the argument of expediency in its favour;
on his side, the subject might, in the interests of public security,
subscribe to doctrines which he would have repudiated if
tendered to him by a priest. In this way did theological opinion
merge with social safeguard; and the process was further assisted
by the fact that, unlike the theologian, the statesman insisted on
doctrines few in number and straightforward in expression.
Three doctrines came to be enforced on all who desired the full

---

[1] *State Trials* (1730), iii. 57.   [2] Ibid. ii. 524–9.
[3] Ibid. ii. 546.   [4] 29 Car. II, cap. xxix.
[5] For an instance see *English Reports*, lxxxvi (King's Bench), 189, Taylor's
case.   [6] See *supra*, 496, 499.

privileges of English citizenship, namely: (1) that there is no transubstantiation of the elements in the sacrament, (2) that the invocation of the Virgin Mary or of any other saint, and the sacrifice of the mass as practised by the church of Rome are idolatrous, and (3) that these affirmations are to be understood 'in the plain and ordinary sense of the words'. The first of these doctrines was imposed by the Test Act[1] of 1673 on all office-holders; all three were imposed by the Act of 1678[2] on members of both Houses, and on sworn servants of the king and queen. Together with the oaths of allegiance and supremacy, and the taking of the sacrament at least once a year according to Anglican practice, these doctrines constituted the state religion of England until 1828-9. They were enforced for a political, not a religious object, and by penalties not spiritual but civil. Protestantism and patriotism were therefore wedded by indissoluble bonds, and if Anglicans themselves had no very clear-cut theology, they were committed to emphatic opinions about the essentials of the rival system. English independence was therefore preserved not by forging new weapons, but by selecting the strongest weapons of the enemy and throwing them in his face. To this extent also were the opinions of Hobbes[3] put into practice, and the cause of toleration was hastened not by the laxity of the state, but by its strictness in the enforcement of those few doctrines which seemed requisite for national security.

There was another respect in which the views of Hobbes found illustration and vindication in the legislation of the Stuarts, namely, in the policy adopted towards corporations. Hobbes[4] had compared the municipal franchises to the worms which eat into the intestines of the body politic; the Corporation[5] Act of 1661 and the writs of *quo warranto* make the words of Hobbes seem like prophecy. By this Act five obligations were imposed on all holders of municipal offices,[6] and the commissioners appointed to administer the Act were authorized not only to impose these obligations, but to remove officials at their discretion, even where they had complied with the statutory requirements. One of

---

[1] For the Test Act see *supra*, i. 368-9.
[2] 30 Car. II, stat. ii, cap. i. For this see *supra*, 467, and *infra*, 574.
[3] For Hobbes see *infra*, 741-6.   [4] *Leviathan*, ch. xxix.
[5] 13 Car. II, stat. ii, cap. i.   [6] For these see *supra*, i. 198.

Prynne's last services was to oppose this Bill.[1] Within the period of three years allotted to the commissioners, the crown succeeded in 'purging' several boroughs, generally with the help of local commissions composed of country gentry, presided over by the lords lieutenant; and in this way a threat was directed against the whole principle of parliamentary representation. After the lapse of the commissioners' powers, the executive continued to make use of the statute; but difficulty was experienced in obtaining suitable persons as substitutes for those ejected, and the increasing practice of occasional conformity permitted the entry of men whose loyalty was nominal. But by the issue of a *quo warranto* for alleged misfeasance, the crown was enabled to remodel several charters; moreover, it was possible to levy blackmail on a borough, by threatening forfeiture unless some technical defect was compounded for in money.[2] That Clarendon had done so was one of the accusations against him.[3] The crown soon saw how far it might go, and how it might depend on the support of the country gentry. Thus, the charter of Gloucester was forfeited in 1671;[4] in the following year a *quo warranto* was directed against Northampton, because of its disrespect to the earl of Peterborough 'who had honoured them by accepting' the office of Recorder;[5] and the franchises of Nottingham tottered in the balance because the duke of Newcastle did not find the corporation sufficiently obsequious.[6] In its progress towards constitutionalism, England had to go through a long process of 'purging' —first of parliaments; then boroughs; next, justices, lords lieutenant, and universities; the purging stopped short only at the church and the army. It was James II who carried out this process most conscientiously; even the man who showed visitors round the tombs in Westminster Abbey was removed from office.[7]

The process of remodelling the boroughs enabled and encouraged the landed gentry to impose their yoke on the municipal

[1] He wrote a pamphlet against it and was censured by the Speaker, *Steele*, i. 3313, July 15, 1661.

[2] For a good account of this subject see R. H. Sacret, *The Restoration government and municipal corporations* in *E.H.R.* xlv.

[3] See *supra*, i. 315.   [4] *P.C. Reg.* 63, Nov. 3, 1671.

[5] *H.M.C. Rep.* xii, app., pt. vii. 98.

[6] *Coventry Papers* (Longleat), 83, f. 106.

[7] N. Luttrell, *Brief historical relation*, i. 368.

corporations; for they were frequently intruded as mayors or recorders. Hitherto, the recorder was presumed to have legal qualifications; but under the new and more aristocratic dispensation these might be done without. Such was the conclusion to be deduced from the case of lord Hawley (1671). He had been 'put in' as recorder of Bath by the Corporation Act commissioners in 1663; but the corporation removed him in 1669 because he had been absent for five years without reasonable excuse, and was *nullo modo peritus in lege*. The court of King's Bench issued a *mandamus* restoring him to his office; and some curious arguments were adduced for this course. The phrase *nullo modo peritus in lege* was too general; there were precedents where recorders, ignorant of the law, had given erroneous judgements; and were they ineligible because of that? As for the five years' absence, this was no disqualification; by analogy, a park keeper does not forfeit his office for non-attendance, unless a deer is killed in his absence.[1] The analogy was an apt one. The Stuarts imposed 'park keepers' on the boroughs; thereby strengthening that class which was to prove most inimical to themselves, and laying the foundations of the political power exercised by the landed families of the eighteenth century.

Liberty of the subject was controlled and determined by these courts and laws; it was influenced also by the character of the men who served on juries, or sat on the bench. That jurors should be substantial freeholders was a generally accepted principle, because poor men might be more easily influenced, or might fail to discern the matters in question; accordingly, an Act[2] of 1664–5 required that in trials of issues they should be worth at least £20 per annum in freehold lands. But this was often difficult to enforce, especially in London, as the estates of the city belonged mainly to great nobles and corporations;[3] in consequence, for the political trials of Charles's reign, Middlesex juries were sometimes empanelled from persons not all of whom were freeholders. Most of the Stuart judges had clear notions

---

[1] *English Reports*, lxxxvi (King's Bench), 98–9.
[2] 16–17 Car. II, cap. v.
[3] At the trial of lord Russell the court refused to uphold the objection that some of the jury were not freeholders of London: *The Tryals of W. Walcot, W. Hone, lord Russell . . .* (1683), 32–5.

of the qualifications of the ideal juryman; and, had Jeffreys had
his way, he would have enlisted the help of personal servants
of the king in cases where the crown was prosecutor, in spite
of an opinion to the contrary in that 'straggling'[1] book, Coke's
Institutes. When a jury gave substantial damages to the tory
lord mayor sir W. Pritchard against the whig sheriff Papillon,
the lord chief justice made a significant remark: 'You seem to
be persons that have some sense upon you and consideration for
the government';[2] still more, when juries which had convicted
papists were called upon to convict whigs, it was clear that the
weapon which had served indirectly against the Court might be
used with equal efficacy against its enemies. By their remodelling
of the corporations after 1681 the Stuarts could be nearly as sure
of their juries as they were of their judges; such was the moral
to be deduced from the following interchange of courtesies between Jeffreys and Oates, when the latter was on trial for
perjury (1685):

> *Oates*. We know how juries have gone a'late.
> *Jeffreys*. Ay, very strangely indeed, *Mr.* Oates, and I hope so as
> we shall never see them go again.[3]

The epidermis of Oates was soon to bear eloquent testimony to
the significance of Jeffreys' remark.

But it was characteristic of the reign that, in the midst of legal
abuses, there was secured one of the most important judicial
reforms of modern times. This was the principle of the inviol-
ability of the jury for its verdict. In 1670 two Quakers, Penn
and Mead, were indicted at the Old Bailey for preaching in the
streets. Despite the directions of the recorder, the jury (whose
foreman was Bushell) gave a verdict for acquittal. For this they
were fined; and their foreman, in default of payment, was committed to prison with some other members of the jury. A writ
of habeas corpus was applied for and obtained from the court
of Common Pleas, the judges of which court discharged Bushell
on the ground that to find against the evidence or direction of
the court was not sufficient cause to punish a jury.[4] One of the

---

[1] *The Tryal and Conviction of John Hampden Esq.* (1684), 2–4.
[2] *An exact account of the trial between sir W. Pritchard and T. Papillon* (1689), 32.
[3] *The Tryals, Convictions and Sentence of Titus Otes upon two indictments for
Perjury* (1685), 10.   [4] *English Reports*, cxxiv (Common Pleas), 1006–18.

jurymen then brought an action against the recorder for false imprisonment; but it was ruled that an action does not lie against a judge for what he does judicially, though erroneously.[1]

Under the Commonwealth, judges had held office during good behaviour; but, at the Restoration, they again became wholly dependent on the crown. With the development of a concerted opposition in the Commons, it was inevitable that attention should have been directed to the relations between crown and bench, and as early as 1674–5 a Bill was introduced for making the tenure of judges *quamdiu se bene gesserint*, instead of *durante bene placito*.[2] The matter became of increasing moment during the Popish Plot, when it was not their severity but their occasional moderation which brought on the judges the condemnation of the House. On December 23, 1680, a report was received from a committee appointed to review the proceedings of the judicial bench; the result was a series of resolutions condemning certain recent proceedings, including these:[3] (1) the conduct of Scroggs and Jones in discharging the Middlesex grand jury when a Bill had been presented indicting the duke of York as a popish recusant; (2) the infliction of a fine of £1,000 on one who expressed the opinion that the English constitution consisted of three estates; and (3) the extraordinary charge given at the last Assizes of Kingston by baron Weston, who was alleged to have stated: 'Zwingli set up his fanaticism, and his disciples are seasoned with such a sharpness of spirit that it concerns magistrates to keep a sharp eye on them.' These words, resolved the Commons, were 'a scandal to the Reformation'. As a result of these and other revelations the Commons resolved that Scroggs and Weston should be impeached, and that judges should hold office only during good behaviour. A lead to the movement had already been given by Sacheverel in February 1678, when he objected that the judges did as the Court directed, and cited facts to prove his contention.[4] Moreover, England had old and memorable traditions about her judges. Edward I had conducted a great inquiry into their conduct in 1288, with drastic and salutary results; and his predecessor king Alfred was said to have kept his judicial bench

---

[1] *Modern Reports*, ii. 218.
[2] *Grey*, ii. 415.
[3] *C.J.* ix. 688 sqq.
[4] *Grey*, iv. 140–1.

spotless by periodical hangings of whole batches of unjust judges.[1]

The Stuarts frequently consulted with their judges; for example, before the trial of the Regicides in 1660, they had to confer with the solicitor-general and attorney-general, so that there might be no hitch in the proceedings.[2] In revenue cases this was a frequent procedure.[3] More serious, and more customary in the reign of James, was the practice of removing judges whose conduct was not in accordance with the wishes of the executive, and substituting for them others on whom reliance could be placed. For this purpose there was good material to hand. In private litigation the judges might have to decide against the validity of one of the king's grants, or they might quash an indictment by the crown; but, where the interests or the supposed interests of the Court were concerned, the judges, almost without exception, were tools. Sir Matthew Hale was a notable exception, but his puritanism and punctiliousness savoured of an earlier age; lord keeper Guilford proved himself a man of humanity and judgement, until he was called upon to try whigs, such as Stephen College. Scroggs hounded many innocent victims of the Popish Plot to their death; until, in the trial of sir George Wakeman, when the queen's honour was concerned, he suddenly changed round, and impugned the evidence of Oates and Bedloe. It was the need for the right kind of judge which caused the elevation of sir Francis Wythens to the Bench in April 1683, after distinguished service for the crown against Fitzharris and Shaftesbury. Sir Francis Pemberton, who succeeded Scroggs as lord chief justice of the King's Bench, had already imperilled his career by a reputation for impartiality; but he succeeded in living this down, for at the trial of archbishop Plunket he refused the prisoner time to collect his evidence; and at the indictment against Shaftesbury he prohibited the grand jury from inquiring into the credibility of witnesses. All of these were men of legal acumen and judicial fairness, except wherever the government was concerned. The same is true of Jeffreys, whose most famous exploits belong to a

---

[1] *The triumph of justice over unjust judges* (1681). This is based on *Horn's Mirror.*

[2] Pollock, *The Popish Plot,* 279.   [3] See *supra,* 423–4.

later reign. With the general rehabilitation of the Stuarts he has come to be regarded as a misunderstood and maligned man; he has even been credited with a sense of humour,[1] and other virtues may yet come to light. But the Stuart taste in judges as in personal friends was peculiar, and the apologist of Jeffreys needs consummate literary skill.

Such were the main institutions and laws for preserving or restricting the liberty of the subject in the reign of Charles. They attest the great strength of survivals in English national life, and provide evidence of a degree of corporate intelligence and responsibility such as no other race had attained. Many of them were to be strained to breaking-point in the years 1675 to 1688, and so the narrative of events must now be resumed.

[1] H. B. Irving, *Judge Jeffreys*, 43.

XV

DANBY AND THE PARLIAMENTARY OPPOSITION, 1674–8

IT has been seen that in three respects England was better qualified than the sister kingdoms for a contest with the Stuart prerogative—in her comparative wealth, her unique parliamentary institutions, dominated mostly by landowners, and her great common-law traditions, which habituated Englishmen both to acquiescence in order and discipline, and to resentment of encroachment from without. These exceptional advantages gave weight to the claims of the Commons, claims which had steadily become more insistent after the first symptoms of suspicion had entered into the minds of the legislature; and, by the end of the year 1674, the Lower House could look back on a considerable measure of achievement. The Second Dutch War, which was embarked on at the solicitation of the Commons, had ended the domination of Clarendon, and with it the conception of the rigid state; the Third Dutch War had been concluded by pressure from the Commons, and had resulted in a fierce but unorganized attack on the men who shared Clarendon's power among them. Of these men Clifford had died in less than a month after his resignation from office (Aug. 18, 1673); Arlington, his rival, resigned his secretaryship to Joseph Williamson in September 1674 and, as lord chamberlain, tried thereafter to gain the favour of the Commons, and to supplant those who had superseded him; Buckingham, no longer bound to the Court by the ties of office, was now setting up as the apostle of Protestantism and Patriotism, while retaining his close personal attachment to Louis XIV. Shaftesbury, fooled in the secret negotiations with France, but resolved not to be fooled further, was now the most vehement declaimer of the Popish interest, talking publicly of exclusion, of the menace of a French invasion of Ireland, and the necessity of a royal divorce and marriage with a Protestant. Lauderdale, still secure in his master's favour, was the solitary survivor from the wreckage.

Of the other great personages the duke of York was the most

consistent but the most undecided. Had he been gifted with political acumen, had he even possessed any real knowledge of the country over which he was one day to rule, he might easily have created a powerful following of his own, as there were always Dissenters ready to welcome his alliance against Anglicans; but he had neither resilience nor flexibility, the two essential qualities for political success in this reign; and even his virtues, namely industry and intense seriousness of purpose, were being exercised at the one period of English history when these things had their dangers. In contrast with him was the duke of Monmouth, who 'seemed born as if only for love', and was then combining his escapades and gallantries with the chancellorship of the university of Cambridge, everywhere showing promise that he would perpetuate the unconventionalities and personal charm of his father. He had already distinguished himself in arms; within a few years he was to become a serious element in politics, because of two things, his Protestantism and his illegitimacy. The events of the Popish Plot placed a substantial premium on the first, while the second commended him to those who thought that a weak claim to the throne was the best guarantee of constitutional rule.[1]

The third personality of importance at this time was William, prince of Orange. He did not inspire love, nor had his career in arms shown higher qualities than determination; but he had this asset, that by some Englishmen he was accepted as the only man able to save Europe from the domination of France and Popery. Now that England had deserted the ranks of his enemies William was determined that she should become one of his active allies; and after his defeat at Seneff in August 1674 he devoted himself to this object. In September, in response to Charles's friendly overtures, he sent to England an agent named Sylvius, nominally to secure the renewal of his uncle's good graces as a preliminary to a separate Dutch peace with France, but really in order to guide the anti-French feeling of the Commons into

---

[1] And nobler is a limited command
Given by the love of all your native land,
Than a successive title, long and dark,
Drawn from the mouldy rolls of Noah's Ark.
Absalom and Achitophel.

active co-operation against Louis XIV. Though fully aware of the prince's correspondence with the opposition, Charles showed unfailing indulgence; and in November of the same year he sent Arlington and Ossory on a conciliatory mission, with an offer of the hand of the twelve-years-old princess Mary. The prince refused the proposal, nominally on the ground of the princess's youth, and the possibility that the duke of York might yet have an heir; but really because the offer was represented to him by his English correspondents as a trap.[1] From this point dates that Dutch pressure on English politics which, coupled with the whig opposition, was to result in the Revolution.

Increasing solicitude for an undiminished prerogative caused William to sacrifice a certain amount of popular support; but his agents had not found it difficult to stir up anti-French feeling in this country. During the Third Anglo-Dutch War the prince had helped to discredit Stuart policy by aiding the circulation of a pamphlet[2] attacking the Anglo-French alliance; and the successful result of these activities was evidenced by the fact that in February 1674 the Venetian envoy noted the existence of a Dutch party,[3] distinguished by hostility to the duke of York, and committed to the cause of a legitimate and Protestant succession. There were other groups, not unconnected; all of them supplying rallying points for a concerted opposition. Thus, lord Holles was an almost traditional nucleus for associations of Presbyterians and old Commonwealth's men, none of them very enduring; Buckingham also tried to create a following out of similar material, but without much success; Shaftesbury led the party which advocated the king's divorce and marriage with a Protestant; when this failed, he pressed for a dissolution of parliament, led the exclusionists and backed Monmouth. More moderate men favoured severance of the French connexion and maintenance of good relations between crown and legislature. From such shifting groups the Country party had begun to take shape in the autumn session of 1673, when a determined opposition was

---

[1] *Mignet*, iv. 325.

[2] *England's appeal from the private cabal at Whitehall to the grand council of the nation.* The original was composed by the imperialist envoy Lisola; the translation was by Pierre du Moulin, who was in the pay of William.

[3] *Ven. Trans.* 14/40. Feb. 20/March 2, 1674.

led in the Commons by lord Cavendish, William Russell (afterwards lord Russell), William Sacheverell, sir William Coventry,
sir T. Lee, and sir T. Meres, and in the Lords by Shaftesbury
and Halifax. Opposition to Arlington, Buckingham, Lauderdale, and the French alliance was in effect opposition to the
Court, a fact which accounts in part for the term Country party;
but the name at first denoted not so much the aims of a nationalist movement, as of men who, untied by office or personal favour,
demanded a more disinterested and economical management
of the affairs of state.

.Hitherto Charles's policy, if such a phrase may be used, had
been influenced mainly by the duke of York and by Arlington.
The zeal of the one and the pliability of the other had resulted
in the Declaration of Indulgence, the enforced withdrawal of
which was the only public rebuff ever suffered by the king. In
consequence, the pathway to Rome *via* toleration was now
barred, and the Test Act was as sacrosanct as Magna Carta, a
lesson not lost on Charles, for whom this meant the termination
of a period of experiment. But at the very moment when the
complete failure of this experiment left the crown exposed to an
opposition steadily becoming more formidable, fortune placed
in his hands a minister whose services are commensurate with
those of Clarendon. This was sir Thomas Osborne, who was
born in Buckingham's county (Yorkshire) in 1632. He had
combined hostility to Clarendon with the foundation of a personal interest at Court, based on Anglicanism and Cavalier
loyalty; more distinctive was his financial aptitude, his competence in all matters of accountancy. Appointed joint treasurer
of the Navy in 1668 and sole treasurer of the Navy in 1671, he
resolutely set himself to the task of paying off debt, and diminishing the opportunities for fraud. 'A pay was made of old
tickets' is a frequent entry in the journal[1] which he commenced
in September 1671; he also introduced a more regular routine
by accounting weekly to the Navy Board. In June 1673 he
succeeded Clifford as lord high treasurer, and by strict order
and retrenchment he succeeded in diminishing the rate of interest on government loans. He restored a measure of national
credit by providing for the payment of interest, amounting to

[1] *Add. MS.* 28040. These entries occur frequently after f. 12.

£77,000 per annum to the bankers after the Stop of the Exchequer; he obtained better terms from the farmers of Excise, securing from this source alone an increase of £20,000 per annum; and, by good management, he improved the yields from the Hearth Tax and the Irish revenues, measures which resulted in clearing off old debts and enriching the hereditary revenues by more than £100,000 per annum.[1] In this work of reconstruction he was at first helped by the rapid expansion of English trade immediately after England's withdrawal from the Third Anglo-Dutch War; but this was not steadily maintained, and so he was obliged to insist on a policy of retrenchment. He was created a privy councillor and viscount Osborne in 1673, and a year later he became earl of Danby.

During his tenure of office Danby's activities helped to strengthen the association between the White Staff and responsibility for government policy, thus illustrating the change whereby the purse-bearer displaced confessor, favourite, and lawyer. Southampton was the last of the old lord treasurers, for whom the post was the crowning reward of devoted service; the personal opportunities of the office had been snatched from Clifford by the Test Act, and were now to be utilized to their fullest extent by his successor. Successful accountancy and an accommodating manner established Danby in Charles's confidence, and by March 1675 he was chief minister. Considering his impregnable Anglicanism he had unusual supporters, these at first including York and Buckingham; and so far as he had any political mentor, it was Lauderdale, whose alliance he secured, and whose silent methods of governing Scotland he admired.

Danby had a definite policy. He was for alliance with the prince of Orange and a commercial understanding with Spain; he knew of no advantages from a French alliance,[2] and he believed that Louis should be kept strictly to the Triple Alliance. That the English and Irish revenues ought to be maintained, and embezzlement stamped out, were for him matters of principle.[3] He recognized the two alternatives: that Charles must either 'fall into the humours of the people' and accept the con-

---

[1] For his financial reforms see *supra*, 427–8; also A. Browning, *Life and letters of sir T. Osborne, earl of Danby*, i, cap. v, vii and viii.

[2] *Add. MS.* 28042, f. 13, 'Memo in year '77 for the King'.   [3] Ibid., f. 15.

trol of parliament; or he must have sufficient revenue to dispense
with parliament. By conserving the national finances he hoped
to establish royal independence; by bribing the lesser members
of the Commons he obtained the votes of the obscure, even
though they cost him the diatribes of the eminent; for he rejoiced
more in the votes of ninety-nine silent legislators than in the
conversion of one notable opponent. He was not the first
English statesman to use bribery or influence, but he was the
first to realize the value of organized system and personal
mediocrity in the methods and material of politics, with which
aids he contrived to establish Charles's absolutism on a basis,
if not of consent, at least of negotiation and influence. Nor was
this all. Knowing that the fitful breezes of toleration were
dreaded as the likely forerunners of a popish hurricane, he proposed to steer the ship-of-state on the never-failing current of uncompromising Anglicanism; the absolutist edifice which Charles
and Louis had thought to balance on the slim shoulders of
soliciting priests and metropolitan *demimondes*, he would rest
securely on the broad backs of the English bishops. Herein he
showed common sense, his most characteristic quality.

Charles had enough personal honour to cause him feelings of
regret that he had been obliged to abandon the French alliance;
accordingly in July 1674 he informed the French ambassador
that he would prorogue parliament until April 1675. He thus
obtained a respite of a few months; but his difficulties had to be
faced in more intensified form in the spring of 1675, when Ruvigny
pressed for a dissolution. It was Danby who opposed this suggestion most strenuously; for he knew that both the urgent needs
of the fleet and the clamours of the opposition made a session
absolutely essential. Through the duke of York a hint was
conveyed to Ruvigny that a renewal of the French subsidy was
the only possible alternative.[1] But the ambassador's offer of
£100,000 for a prorogation of at least one year was not acceptable to Charles, because Danby's preparations now made it
permissible to hope that parliament would be more compliant.
These preparations consisted of proclamations, issued early in
1675, reinforcing the laws against conventicles, and imposing

[1] *Mignet*, iv. 330-1.

severe penalties on Englishmen attending mass, even in privi-
leged places, or receiving Catholic orders.[1] With these concessions to intolerant Anglicanism Danby won over the Court
and Lauderdale to his design of parliamentary reunion, a
design in which Charles at last acquiesced; so the Commons
were carefully 'nursed' before their reassembly in April 1675.
The lord treasurer had already bribed them with edicts against
popery and dissent; Spanish money was ready for distribution
in order to induce them to press for war; Dutch money was
available for the policy of mediating peace terms which, if not
accepted by Louis, might furnish a pretext for compelling England to enter the fray. The arrival of the Spanish ambassador
Ronquillo had been preceded by that of a Jewish paymaster;
and van Beuning took a house in Westminster, where he entertained on a lavish scale. Louis sent over £100,000; not for
Charles, but for the reconciliation of the enemies of France in
the Commons and the encouragement of her friends; while
Danby began to dole out bribes and offices in a system which
combined judgement with economy. On the Continent the
summer campaign had already begun, when Louis, first in the
field, appeared in Flanders with an army of 70,000 men, backed
by the most highly equipped organization ever known in Europe.

The stage having been set, parliament reassembled for its
thirteenth session on April 13, 1675, after a prorogation of nearly
fourteen months. In his speech Charles asked the legislators
what they thought was still wanting for securing religion and
property, and restoring that right understanding which had been
disturbed by the pernicious designs of ill-intentioned men. As
he had demonstrated his zeal for the Church of England, he
commended for consideration the condition of his Fleet. Finch
followed suit by assuring both Houses that the king's solicitude
for the Church arose from his conviction that it best suited
with monarchy; the revived laws against Dissenters had lost
none of their strength, while those against Papists were now
edged with new rewards for informers. What more would they
have? A strong fleet and the compulsory limitation of new
buildings about London were the measures in which the crown
hoped to secure the concurrence of the legislature.[2] The response

---

[1] *Steele*, i. 3608 and 3609.   [2] *L.J.* xii. 653–5.

of the Commons was not conciliatory; for they began with addresses praying for the recall of British subjects in French service (April 19) and for the removal of the duke of Lauderdale (April 23).[1] Against Lauderdale the chief accusations were: (1) the opinion attributed to him that royal edicts have the force of laws, an opinion implying a justification of the Declaration of Indulgence, and (2) his part in procuring the settlement in Scotland of a militia of 20,000 foot and 2,000 horse, obliged to be in readiness to march into any part of His Majesty's dominions.[2] Burnet was called in to give evidence of Lauderdale's assertion that Scottish troops might be used to enforce the Declaration of Indulgence, and Irish Papists to suppress the Scottish Covenanters.[3] In reply, Charles refused either to part with his Scottish minister or to recall his troops still serving with the French flag; but he undertook not to send any more men to Flanders.

The Commons had lost the first round; the second began on April 27 when sir Samuel Barnardiston, supported by Arlington and the leaders of the Country party, brought in articles of impeachment against Danby on accusations as vague as those already cited against Lauderdale. He had, it was alleged, violated the ancient course of the Exchequer by perverting the method of receipts and payments; he had engrossed the sole power of disposing revenue into his own hands; moreover, he had declared that a new proclamation was better than an old law.[4] In regard to those charges relating to Danby's conduct as treasurer, the Commons became involved in a mass of technical detail, and had eventually to accept the assurance of sir William Coventry: ' 'Tis a hard thing that all the king's ministers of state must answer all circumstances of law; if so, then 'twill follow that no great officer of state but must be a studied lawyer.'[5] The opposition was evidently not agreed that the charges could be pressed home, and after further investigation they had to be dropped.[6] Another success was scored for the lord treasurer when the Bill to incapacitate parliament men from holding office of benefit was rejected by 145 to 113.[7]

How evenly parties were divided and how strongly personal

[1] *Parl. Hist.* iv. 678, 684.   [2] *Grey*, iii. 28–9. See *supra*, 411, 413.
[3] Ibid. iii. 30 sqq.   [4] *C.J.* ix. 324.   [5] *Grey*, iii. 62.
[6] *Parl. Hist.* iv. 695.   [7] Ibid. iv. 698, April 29.

feelings had been aroused was shown when the question of a
further address for the recall of British soldiers abroad was first
put to the House in grand committee (May 10); for 135 were
counted on each side, and when the numbers were disputed,
there was a scene in which periwigs were torn off, swords were
drawn, some honourable members spat in the faces of their
opponents, while others put their feet on the mace, which lay
under the table (its usual place when the House was in grand
committee). When the tumult seemed likely to result in casual-
ties, the Speaker restored quiet by wrenching the mace from
under the feet of the disorderly and placing it on the table,
thereby terminating a riotous committee meeting and restoring
a House of Commons.[1] Order being restored, sir T. Lee moved
an engagement on the honour of each member that he would
proceed no further in the matter after the House had risen; and
when this motion was passed each member, standing in his place,
gave his promise.[2] On the original question being again put on
May 11, it was negatived by only one vote.

These events did not augur well for the measure which the
Court hoped to make law in this session, a measure whereby a
non-resisting test was to be imposed on all office-holders, including members of parliament, who, in the terms ultimately approved
by the Lords, were to be required to take this oath:

I do declare that it is not lawful on any pretence whatsoever to take
up arms against the King; and I do abhor the traitrous position of
taking up arms by his authority against his person, or against those
that are commissioned by him, according to law, in time of rebellion,
and acting in pursuance of such commission. I do swear that I will
not endeavour any alteration of the Protestant religion, now established in the church of England, nor will I endeavour any alteration
in the government in church or state as it is by law established.

The Bill[3] imposing this oath passed the Lords, in spite of strenuous opposition from Shaftesbury; indeed its passage elicited a
protest from fifteen peers who objected that the measure was an
invasion of their privilege acquired by birth, and therefore

[1] *Essex Papers* (ed. C. E. Pike), ii. 9.
[2] *Grey*, iii. 128–9.
[3] For its terms see *Rawl. MS*. A. 162, f. 54. See also *H.M.C. Rep.* ix,
app., pt. ii. 51–2.

inherent in and inseparable from their status.[1] What would be the fate of the Bill in the Commons was a question of equal moment for Court and Opposition. Its intention was obviously to confine office-holding and even membership of the two Houses to high episcopalians and the old Cavalier party, 'and to fight the old quarrel over again now that they have the arms and forts of the nation'.[2] If it passed, the constitution would have become static; for political criticism or opposition might thereby have been construed as violation of an oath, and with this weapon England could have been reduced to the uneasy quiet of Scotland. Accordingly, for Shaftesbury and the opposition a prorogation was more than ever imperative, and an opportunity for this soon presented itself, because the case of *Shirley* v. *Fagg* suddenly diverted the two Houses into a hot contest over their privileges.[3] The Houses were still contesting this point when, on June 9, they were prorogued until the following October.

Thus, Danby's first political experiment had met with only qualified success. He had, it is true, escaped impeachment, but he had failed to obtain a supply, and his abortive non-resistance test had served to make public the real designs of his ministry. He had created the nucleus of a tory party by his alliance of crown and church; but indirectly he had also given cohesion to an opposition, determined to subordinate the crown to parliament. By his audacity he had limited and clarified the issues; but his supporters would have to be held together by rewards, while his opponents would become more united in their insistence on constitutional principle. In this way did Danby help to create the distinction of whig and tory. He might have been sacrificed at this point but for two things—his skilful administration of the finances, and the exceptional yield from the Excise in the years 1674 and 1675 whereby Charles's hereditary revenue for 1674–5 rose to £1,400,000.[4] For the first time in his reign Charles was solvent and could therefore afford to take a risk.

But this state of affairs was transitory, and Charles was soon

---

[1] *L.J.* xii. 677. Among the protesters were Buckingham, Shaftesbury, Salisbury, Delamere, and Wharton.

[2] *Letter from a person of quality* in *Parl. Hist.* iv, app. v.

[3] For this see *supra*, 470.

[4] *Cal. Tr. Bks.*, *1672–5*, Introduction, xviii–xix.

restored to his position of perilous oscillation. With the death of Turenne, and increasing French exhaustion in the summer of 1675, the menace from Louis XIV became perceptibly less, and the continuation of the war by Orange and his allies grew more desperate. In these circumstances the English parliament became a factor of international importance. If it remained long enough in session, Dutch and Spanish bribery might prevail on a majority of its members to force Charles into hostilities against France; but a long prorogation would remove this possibility, and so facilitate the peace for which Louis was now so anxious. Charles's negotiations with Louis were therefore renewed; and it was eventually (Aug. 17, 1675) agreed that parliament should meet in October and be given an opportunity to vote money, unconditioned by clauses directed against France. If it failed to do so, Charles was to dissolve parliament, and during the cessation of its activity to receive an annual subsidy of £100,000, which sum, together with the enhanced yield from the hereditary revenues, might serve to make him independent of parliamentary grant, and so free to choose his own policy. A condition attached to this agreement was that William of Orange should be discouraged from undertaking his proposed visit to England.[1]

Accordingly, the Commons were given one more chance. Their session, which opened on October 13, 1675, was preluded by the customary duet of king and lord keeper,[2] when Charles asked for supplies to take off the anticipations of his revenue—these having been caused mainly by the war and the building of ships; this demand he coupled with the extraordinary admission that, while he had not husbanded his financial resources in the past so well as he might, he was resolved that there should be improvement in future. Equally conciliatory was Finch, who reported the King's resolve to enter on terms of strictest endearment with his parliament, to take its counsel in weighty affairs and acquaint it with all the royal wants and necessities. He adjured all the members of parliament to behave like those who deserve to be called king's friends; and, now that the faith was absolutely secure, they were invited to concern themselves with

---

[1] Charles at first demanded 500,000 écus, but eventually agreed to accept 400,000 écus, the equivalent of £100,000. *Instructions Données*, ii. 183, 238.
[2] *Mignet*, iv. 366–70.   [3] *L.J.* xiii. 4–5.

matters of commercial and domestic importance—'a little time
will serve to make many excellent laws, and to give you the
honour to be the repairer of all our breaches'. On returning to
their House, the Commons looked at each other for some time,
until sir T. Meres asked the Speaker to recapitulate the substance of the king's speech, a request which was properly
declined.[1] Waller then hinted at the inconsistency between the
king's admission of ill-husbandry and the doctrine that the king
cannot err. This personal admission of wrongdoing was an
innovation for which the Commons were unprepared.

Their subsequent proceedings show how evenly divided and
efficiently organized were the Court and Country parties, the
former controlled by Danby with the two secretaries of state
(Henry Coventry and sir Joseph Williamson), while the latter
looked for leadership to Shaftesbury, who included Buckingham
among his lieutenants. In committee the Commons refused
by 172 to 165 to grant a supply for taking off the anticipations
on the revenue (these were estimated at £800,000) on the ground
that the anticipations were directly due to a war (the Third
Dutch War) and that war was not theirs.[2] On October 21 a Bill
for appropriating £400,000 from the Customs to the use of the
Navy was read a second time and committed; it was resolved
also that twenty ships, at a cost of £300,000, should be built, and
only by a narrow majority was it decided that this sum should be
deposited in the Exchequer, and not in the Chamber of the city
of London. Otherwise, the Commons did little but discuss
grievances; including the falling of rents and the increase of
atheism (not unconnected); the bribing of members (against
which a test was proposed), and even their own continued existence. 'A standing parliament', said the septuagenarian sir
Harbottle Grimstone, 'is as grievous as a standing army.'[3] 'I am
afraid of a dissolution,' said sir John Birkenhead, another
venerable legislator, 'because God is my witness, I am afraid
the next will be worse'[4] (*laughed at*). Dissolution of parliament
now seemed the only means of eliminating Danby's influence,
and in the Lords a motion for an address to the king to dissolve
parliament was supported by the duke of York, together with

[1] *Grey*, iii. 290.
[2] *C.J.* ix. 359.
[3] *Grey*, iii. 341.
[4] Ibid. iii. 342.

Buckingham, Shaftesbury, Essex, Holles, and Townshend[1]—a conjunction which suggests that Papists and Dissenters were once more bedfellows. Charles was tempted to adopt this policy; but, on the other hand, he knew that many members of the Commons were of noble family, and therefore attached to the monarchy; whereas a new parliament might be composed of 'Presbyterians'.[2] It was therefore deemed inadvisable to dissolve; but a revival of the dispute of *Shirley* v. *Fagg* provided once more a pretext for prorogation. On November 22, 1675, parliament was prorogued for the unprecedented period of fifteen months.

The conditions attached to the payment of the French subsidy had not been completely fulfilled, but Louis grudgingly agreed to perform his part of the bargain, and the first quarterly instalment was promised for March 1676. This concession may have been owing to Ruvigny's knowledge that, just before the prorogation of November, Charles was being pressed by Danby to conclude an engagement with the Dutch.[3] Relations between Charles and Louis were now regularized by a secret treaty (Feb. 16/26, 1676) in which both kings bound themselves to give no aid to the enemies of the other, nor make any treaty without the participation of the other. Danby was unwilling to countersign this treaty,[4] though he had made a feint of entering into negotiations; even Lauderdale at first refused to be a party to it, but he eventually witnessed Ruvigny's signature to the treaty as copied by Charles and sealed by him on February 16, 1676. This secret engagement renewed all previous treaties between the two monarchs, and expressly named the States General as the power with which neither king would treat, except conjointly. Thus, having failed to secure peace by mediation, and having successfully resisted efforts to drag him into war on behalf of the Dutch, Charles now renewed the old intimacy with Louis, so enabling the French king to achieve by diplomacy what he appeared unable to obtain by arms. Having divided Charles from Protestant England, Louis now strove to detach the Dutch from Spain, the prince of Orange from the States General, and the princes of

---

[1] *L.J.* xiii. 33, Nov. 20, 1675.
[2] *Baschet*, 132, June 12/22, 1676.
[3] Ruvigny to Louis XIV, Dec. 30, 1675/Jan. 9, 1676 in *Mignet*, iv. 377.
[4] *Mignet*, iv. 381–6; *Instructions Données*, ii. 163, and 197–200.

Germany from the Emperor, and thus secured his immediate ends by fomenting discord among his numerous enemies.

The conclusion of the treaty was followed by the recall of the aged Ruvigny, who was glad to quit a post possibly the most difficult of any in the service of France. He was succeeded by Honoré Courtin, whose earlier experience of England led him to avoid the ceremonial 'entrée'. His instructions[1] provide an apt comment on the relations between the two monarchs, and contain a glimpse of English history as seen by the interested foreigner. 'England', he was told, 'may, properly considered, be reduced to the king, the duke of York, the royal ministers, and "l'ésprit de la nation en général".' Charles's withdrawal from the Dutch War proved (according to these instructions) that he is not master in his own house. Lauderdale is most in the royal confidence; Arlington has unfortunately drifted away from the French alliance; Buckingham, though out of office, is important and has a special affection for the French king. Danby's appointment was due solely to his favour with the duke of York and to his ability in restoring the finances; he considers himself strong enough to be independent, and has been joined by the duchess of Portsmouth,[2] in spite of the presents she has had—diamonds, and (at Charles's request) the territory of Aubigné. Another lady worth watching is Hortense Mancini, duchesse Mazarin, who, having run away from her husband and established herself at the English Court, has induced Charles to intercede on her behalf for an increase in her alimony and the return of the jewels she left behind. She may succeed in casting her spell over Charles and, unless carefully handled, will use her influence against France; so, although her demands are grossly unjust, Courtin is to assure her *en termes généraux* of Louis's solicitude on her behalf. Thus one of the major problems of French diplomacy was the French women at Charles's Court.[3]

English dislike of France, Louis said, was owing to France's

[1] *Instructions Données*, ii. 169–97, April 5/15, 1676.

[2] Possibly because Danby gave her money with which to buy jewels. *Essex Papers*, i. xi.

[3] In June 1676 Courtin reported that the duchess of Portsmouth was losing favour at Court and was likely to be displaced by duchesse Mazarin. He suggested that the latter should be sent back to France. (*Baschet*, 132, May 29/June 8, 1676.)

greatness, especially at sea, and to a fear that, on the basis of the French alliance, Charles might become absolute. Courtin was therefore to persuade the king to manage his revenues with such economy that he might dispense with parliament. The ambassador was to discourage the projected marriage between William of Orange and Mary Stuart; but he was to promote the interests of that prince; for it was desirable that he should acquire sovereign power in order that the States General might be detached from their alliances, and thus there would be one republic less in the world. Courtin was also to quieten English qualms about British troops in French service, and to see that Charles rendered good service as a 'benevolent mediator'.

The French ambassador, who was endowed with a sense of humour, did his best to carry out these difficult tasks. His first concern was with the maritime advantages which England was deriving from her neutrality. He protested against English ships supplying Spanish and Dutch ships with stores in the Mediterranean; in reply, he was assured by Charles that merchants would do anything for gain. Courtin was then asked to induce his master to remit, in favour of English ships, the tax on English merchandise imported into France, a demand supported by Lauderdale (a proprietor of Scottish coal-pits) on the strength of the old Franco-Scottish alliance. But this failed. If Lauderdale's demand were granted, wrote the French secretary for foreign affairs, 'every Englishman would call himself a Scotsman'. Courtin's main achievement was his part in the completion of an Anglo-French maritime treaty,[1] signed in Paris on February 14, 1677. The occasion for the treaty was this. Many English ships were doing a profitable trade with Dutch cargoes, protected by the flag; in some cases Dutch ships were manned by English crews in order to escape confiscation; both classes of ship were being seized by the French,[2] on the excuse that they were really Dutch, whereas Scottish and Irish ships with Dutch cargoes were

---

[1] *Dumont*, vi, pt. ii. 327–9; *Instructions Données*, ii. 205–10. It was followed by a proclamation (May 26) enforcing neutrality in English waters. Contraband, that is munitions of war, was to be searched for in outgoing English ships. *Steele*, i. 3631.

[2] For lists of ships captured by the French see *A list of several ships belonging to English merchants* . . . in *Bodley, G.P.* 1120.

usually spared. As a sop to English interests Louis made some important concessions in this treaty. Contraband was clearly defined; English ships were allowed to trade between neutral ports and enemy ports, or between enemy ports; and it was expressly declared that the goods of enemies of France (except contraband) found on English ships should not be confiscated, even though they formed the main part of the cargo.[1] In other words English ships might carry Dutch cargoes without molestation from the French, a concession of more value to our carrying trade than the winning of several naval battles, particularly as it was granted at a time when the two commercial rivals of England were engaged in a fiercely contested war with each other. In this way French dependence on English neutrality proved of direct value to English trade; and it was partly due to Louis XIV that this country was able to make serious inroads on the Dutch monopoly of the carrying trade.

Other concessions were demanded of Louis. In February 1677, when peace terms were first outlined by the assembled representatives at Nimeguen, it was seen that the Dutch wanted Maestricht and the principality of Orange; Spain and the Emperor demanded restitution of all their lost territories; the duke of Lorraine sought for restitution; while Denmark and Brandenburg asked for an indemnity. The exorbitance of these demands showed that the allies were hoping for action on the part of the English parliament, then due to meet after the fifteen months' prorogation; and so pressure on Charles was increased at the moment when his financial difficulties were at their most serious point. In the previous November he had failed to obtain a loan from the city of London; and he confessed to Courtin that he was over a million pounds in debt, £200,000 of this being attributed to the cost of suppressing Bacon's rebellion in Virginia and the loss in Customs revenue directly due to that rebellion.[2] These figures may have been exaggerated; but they induced Louis to offer him, for the year 1677, the same sum as had already been paid for the cessation of parliamentary activity in 1676, namely, £100,000; together with an additional sum if he would prorogue parliament until 1678.[3] On the other hand, Danby urged the

---

[1] Cl. viii of the treaty.   [2] For this see *infra*, 670-1.

[3] *Mignet*, iv. 430; *Instructions Données*, ii. 215.

necessity for a session, because the additional excise granted in
1670–1 was due to expire in June 1677, and there was still just
a chance that the Court party in the Commons would be strong
enough to obtain a supply. Between these two alternatives
Charles vacillated. No sooner was it known that he intended to
summon parliament than Louis sent 200,000 livres to Courtin
for 'his service in parliament'; that is, for countering the propaganda of van Beuning, and (in conjunction with the duke of York,
Shaftesbury, and the Country party) for subsidizing opposition
to Danby, if the latter showed anti-French tendencies. Alterna-
tively, Courtin was to direct his efforts at embroiling the two
Houses so that nothing definite would result from the session.[1]
The solution of the European conflict was therefore to be sought,
not at Nimeguen, but at Westminster; French money was to
assist the early training of English party politicians, and the
greatest monarch in Christendom eagerly waited for a revival
of *Shirley* v. *Fagg*.

The long recess (Nov. 1675–Feb. 1677) provided a breathing
space. Charles, in the summer of 1676, set the fashions of evening
rowing and bathing in the Thames, diversions in which the
women do not appear to have taken a part; indoors, the monarch
whiled away the hours after dinner by beating time to his favourite song, the 'Récit du Sommeil', sung by French voices to the
accompaniment of clavichord and flute;[2] or dallied with the
duchesse Mazarin, to the disparagement of the more feminine
charms of the duchess of Portsmouth. The duke of York could
not conceal his hopes that the parliament would be dissolved; if
it must meet, he thought that the 'Presbyterians' should be made
use of in order to divide the two Houses;[3] nor was he alone in
thinking that dissolution was overdue, for this view was shared
by Arlington, Ormonde, and prince Rupert. Lord Holles suggested an alliance between himself, the duke, and the French
ambassador as a rival opposition to that of Shaftesbury; but the
duke refused to be a member of a cabal.[4] Danby talked of joining

---

[1] *Mignet*, iv. 434, letters of Louis XIV to Courtin, Jan. 17/27 and Jan. 23/
Feb. 2, 1677.
[2] *Baschet*, 133, June 22/July 2, 1676.
[3] Ibid. 133, Aug. 1/11. Courtin's conversation with the duke.
[4] Ibid. 134, Jan. 11/21, 1677.

forces with Lauderdale in the headship of a Protestant and anti-French interest.[1] Shaftesbury, who had been repeatedly advised to leave London, moved from Exeter House in the Strand to a house in Aldersgate Street, where he so busied himself with the affairs of the Green Ribbon Club that its votaries began to be noted in the streets of London from the distinctive badge which they wore.[2] Courtin, who complained that one can never depend on anything in England, urged Louis to send money in good time —at least three weeks before the opening of parliament, 'the time when the cabals form'.[3] Every one was busy, except the king.

Nor was interest in public affairs confined to the grandees. An alderman named Jenkes was committed for what was considered an inflammatory speech;[4] and there were fears that the election of a new lord mayor in November would be the occasion for attacks on the duke of York, now the most unpopular man in England.[5] Throughout the country there was apprehension lest the unusually long intermission of parliament might forebode some change of consequence; hence the tide of anti-French and anti-papist feeling steadily rose. Its height may be gauged from the popularity of Andrew Marvell's *Account of the growth of popery and arbitrary government in England*, a book first published in 1677, the contents of which were so outspoken that the government offered a reward of £100 for the discovery of its author. This book gave emphatic expression to the dominating feeling entertained by humbler Englishmen at that time—the feeling of suspicion. It was Marvell's thesis that for some years there had been a design to change the lawful government into an absolute tyranny, and convert the established religion into 'down-right Popery'. 'Were it either open Judaism, or plain Turkery, or honest Paganism, there is yet a certain bona fides in the most extravagant belief... but this [Popery] is a compound of all the three, incorporated with more peculiar absurdities of its own, and all this deliberately continued by the bold imposture of priests under the name of Christianity.' Added to this was the French slavery, which men had been trying to introduce since

---

[1] *Baschet*, 133, Nov. 23/Dec. 3, 1676.

[2] Ibid. 133, Oct. 23/Nov. 2, 1676. For the Green Ribbon Club see sir G. Sitwell, *The First Whig.*   [3] Ibid. 133, Nov. 23/Dec. 3, 1676.

[4] See *supra*, 511.   [5] *Baschet*, 133, Oct. 23/Nov. 2.

that day in May 1670 when the king went to meet his sister at Dover. These words were potent because they confirmed a vague dread.

When, on February 15, 1677, the fifteenth session of the Cavalier parliament was opened, Charles offered further securities for liberty and property, at the same time reminding his listeners of the need for providing an adequate supply. Lord chancellor Finch followed with a speech containing a hint that foreign policy was outside the sphere of parliament, the proper concern of which was the peace of church and state; he appealed also to their patriotism by deprecating those 'ill meant distinctions' between Court and Country.[1] On this, as on other occasions, the verbosity and innuendoes of the chancellor helped to destroy the good impression created by the tact and reticence of the king's speech. The campaign commenced in the Lords, where Buckingham, supported by Shaftesbury, Salisbury, and Wharton, spoke for a dissolution, on the ground that by the fifteen months' prorogation parliament was automatically dissolved, since the statute[2] of Edward III required that parliaments should be holden every year once, and more often if need be; but their motion for dissolution was rejected; and the four peers, having refused to ask pardon for their contempt of the House, were committed to the Tower. In the Commons the majority of the Opposition maintained that, while the prorogation was illegal, the parliament was a legal one nevertheless.[3] Thus unexpectedly the leaders of the Country party in the Lords had played into the hands of Danby and the Court, an initial success followed on February 21 by a vote of supply of £600,000 for building ships, and on March 12 a renewal of the additional Excise. This last measure had passed the Commons in spite of strenuous opposition from Meres, sir William Coventry, and Powle.

Danby now succeeded in passing through the Lords one of the most curious Bills ever considered by the legislature. This was a Bill for securing the Protestant religion by educating the royal children in the Protestant faith. Together with safeguards for the election of bishops, there was a test for the next successor to the throne, in the form of an oath against transubstantiation, an oath which was to be tendered within fourteen days of the death

[1] *L.J.* xiii. 36–7.   [2] 4 Ed. III, cap. xiv.   [3] *Parl. Hist.* iv. 825–34.

of the then king by a deputation of nine bishops who, for this purpose, were to remain about the Court until commanded by the sovereign to administer the oath. As their vigil was limited to fourteen days, no great strain was imposed on the patience of the episcopal quorum.[1] To this Bill the Commons gave two readings, in the course of which its potential dangers were brought to light. It was objected first of all that it was based on two hypotheses: that the king would die or forsake the Church of England. This was tantamount to imagining both the death and the wrongdoing of the king, thereby committing treason and violating the constitution at one stroke; for 'if once an offence be sheltered under error of the King, you may seek impeachments elsewhere than in the House of Commons'.[2] It was objected also that the measure would subordinate the crown to the mitre, and it was now a thesis among churchmen that the king was not king but by their magical unction. The Bill was therefore 'a great invasion of the prerogative'; it strove to promote a good end, but by entirely unconstitutional means, and although it was committed, 'it died away' (Marvell). An even worse fate befell another Bill for preserving the Protestant religion, sent down from the Lords on April 4. Under the mask of sharper penalties on Dissenters, this measure, while retaining the Test, discriminated in favour of Papists, and so it was unanimously rejected at the first reading, on the ground that its title was entirely different from its contents.[3]

But the attention of the Commons was soon directed to an even more serious quarter. A great French offensive was launched in Flanders in March 1677; and by the end of April Louis had scored a series of successes which provided an effective reply to the peace proposals of the allies, whose representatives were then negotiating at Nimeguen. Valenciennes and Cambrai were taken, and the prince of Orange was defeated at Cassel.

[1] For the terms of the Bill see *Rawl. MS.* A. 162, f. 23. See also *H.M.C. Rep.* ix, app., pt. ii. 81–2, March 1, 1677.

[2] Vaughan's speech, March 27, 1677, *Grey*, iv. 321.

[3] This Bill appears to have provided for the registration of Roman Catholics and their exemption from the penal laws on their paying 52s. each, together with 5 per cent. of their revenues and submitting to a new oath of fidelity. (*Baschet*, 135, April 4/14, 1677.) See also *H.M.C. Rep.* ix, app., pt. ii. 82–3.

This threat to the Netherlands caused the Commons to draw up an address[1] to the king (March 10) requesting him to strengthen himself with such stricter alliances as might secure his kingdoms and preserve the Netherlands; and, in quick succession, they voted three addresses (March 29, April 13, April 16) urging active measures against France; for which purpose the king was authorized to borrow £200,000 on the additional Excise, with an assurance of further supplies if he conformed to the spirit of the addresses.[2] Charles continued to ask for money; but would not commit himself to the policy pressed upon him,[3] and in the midst of this deadlock both Houses were adjourned on April 16 to May 21.

By a mixture of evasion and inflexibility Charles had succeeded in preserving the French interest, not only against Danby and a section of the Court, but against the demands of an opposition now national in character. But it was no easy task. With some truth he confessed to Courtin that he was sacrificing the love of his subjects in the interests of Louis;[4] and he begged the French ambassador to urge his master to secure peace before the winter. Throughout the summer of 1677 there was no respite; for the campaign against his neutrality was directed from a triple front. In June the Imperial envoy Waldstein arrived in London in order to supplement the efforts of van Beuning and of Borgomaniero, the newly arrived Spanish ambassador; and it was the avowed object of these three emissaries to induce Charles to enter into an offensive alliance against France. But Charles refused to exchange his mediation for war. Meanwhile French successes and Orange defeats served to prolong hostilities, which could be terminated neither by Louis's attempts to obtain a separate peace with the Dutch, nor by increasing disagreement among the allies. Charles's determination to control his own foreign policy was to undergo still further test.

When the session was resumed on May 21 Sacheverell led the debate on alliances, calling for a statement of what leagues had been made since their last meeting.[5] Secretary Coventry's reply

---

[1] *C.J.* ix. 396.
[2] Ibid. ix. 408, 419–20, 423.
[3] Ibid. ix. 418, 422.
[4] *Mignet*, iv. 445.
[5] *Grey*, iv. 355.

that alliances were not to be talked of in public incited the Commons to go into full committee for the purpose of more free debate, which resulted (May 25) in an address[1] declining a further supply until His Majesty's alliances were made known, and again urging the king to form a defensive and offensive alliance with Holland. Charles's reply was a direct refusal to allow any invasion of his fundamental power of making peace and war; nor would he have the manner or circumstances of leagues prescribed to him.[2] With this definitive pronouncement he adjourned parliament (to July 16). There was a scene in the Commons when the Speaker, on rising to announce the adjournment, was called back to his place by several members in a manner which recalled famous episodes earlier in the century; and only by securing and removing the mace could he bring the meeting to an end.[3] When it reassembled on July 16 parliament was again adjourned until December 3, and did not resume proceedings until January 28, 1678.

Charles knew that he was risking the gravest discredit that a statesman can incur—that of refusing to embark on a war for which there is a popular demand—but he had his reasons for avoiding concession to war fever, as he had some experience of the amount of financial support he might expect once the fever was past. At a secret interview with Courtin in June 1677 he drew up a memoir[4] advocating a separate peace between Louis and the Dutch, on the basis of the retention of Franche Comté by Louis, and the creation of a strong Flemish barrier, guaranteed by England. His debts, he confessed, amounted to £2,200,000; without French aid he would be forced back on parliament, and so the war would be prolonged. After some negotiation, Courtin at last induced Charles, in return for the promise of two million French livres, to delay the meeting of parliament until April 1678. Danby was privy to these negotiations, and had delayed the settlement by insisting on a larger sum.[5] This was Courtin's last negotiation in England, for in August he was succeeded by Barrillon, whose embassy was to last until 1688.

Another event decisively influenced the peace negotiations.

---

[1] *C.J.* ix. 425.   [2] Ibid. ix. 426, May 28, 1677.
[3] *Grey*, iv. 390.   [4] *Baschet*, 136, June 11/21, 1677.
[5] *Mignet*, iv. 498–500; *Instructions Données*, ii. 215.

This was the marriage of the prince of Orange. Three years
before he had been the most popular man in Holland; now, by
his repeated failures, he was risking the allegiance of his com-
patriots,[1] and there seemed a chance that the States General
might even conclude peace without his participation. The help
which he had not hitherto obtained by threat and bribery, he
might now secure less directly but more effectively by marriage
alliance with the dynasty which held the casting vote in the
European deadlock. On consulting Temple regarding the good
policy of such an alliance and the personal character of the
princess Mary, William was warmly reassured on both points
by the English ambassador, ever intent on securing good relations between English and Dutch. Both Danby and Arlington
eagerly seconded the proposal as the measure best fitted to
restore Protestant confidence, and impede the progress of French
influence; but the final decision lay with Charles, who confided
to Barrillon his reasons for approving the match.[2] The alliance,
he said, would remove the suspicions in England that his friendship with France was intended to bring about a change of
religion, suspicions mainly due to the rash conduct of the duke
of York, who alone was responsible for English jealousy and
dislike of France. By bringing William into the family these
suspicions would be allayed, and the ground would be removed
from anti-Court cabals. It was true, remarked Charles, that
the prince ought to have asked the consent of Louis before
addressing himself to the princess;[3] but on the other hand, by
the measure of public confidence thereby created, the marriage
was as much in the interests of Louis as of Charles. Both the
French ambassador and his master experienced some difficulty
in following this explanation; which amounted in effect to this,
that as Charles now had a closer personal association with
Protestantism and respectability, he might enjoy a larger
measure of the nation's confidence, and was therefore all the

[1] The revival of the Republican party in the United Provinces was noted
as early as 1675 in a memoir entitled *Relation of the present state of affairs in the
United Provinces* [*S.P. For.* (*Holland*), 198]; see Miss M. Lane's account of
this document in *E.H.R.* xxx. 304 sqq.

[2] *Mignet*, iv. 509–10.

[3] *Baschet*, 137, Oct. 18/28.

more worthy of a French subsidy. As the reasoning seemed specious, Barrillon tried to induce both the duke of York and the duchess of Portsmouth to use their influence against the match.[1]

The betrothal of William and the princess Mary was announced on October 22, 1677, and was speedily followed by the wedding. In this way did the zealous convert of the treaty of Dover link the destinies of his House with the leader of European Protestantism and the most formidable of Louis's enemies. What were Charles's real motives in consenting? There may have been secret reasons; but it was obvious that this alliance with Dutch Calvinism provided some kind of rampart against the anti-popish opposition. It also imposed a brusque and ambitious son-in-law on the duke of York; to that extent it was Charles's revenge on a brother whom he disliked. With greater certainty the immediate effect of the union can be stated. Louis insisted on having Condé, Valenciennes, and Tournai, which he considered necessary for the defence of Artois and Lille; the Dutch, now more confident, refused to assent to the acquisition of these three towns by France.[2]

Curiously enough, this alliance did not appear to imperil the French subsidy; and if, by its means, the prince of Orange could be induced to turn his thoughts to peace, then both the senior rulers would benefit. Its effect, on the contrary, was to harden the prince's determination. There was another miscalculation. Just as Charles and Louis thought that Orange would yield because of his defeats, so Charles and Orange thought that Louis would yield in spite of his successes. Disillusionment came when Louis rejected the joint proposals sent to him by Charles and his nephew, these being based on the cession to France of Franche Comté, Cambrai, Aire, and St. Omer, in return for the surrender, by France, of Maestricht (to the Dutch), Charleroi, Oudenarde, Ath, Tournai, Condé, and Valenciennes (to Spain), and the restoration of his duchy to the duke of Lorraine. Louvois told the English ambassador Montagu that Louis would rather make war for a hundred years than sacrifice Valenciennes, Condé, and Tournai; and that if necessary he would rather

[1] Ibid. 137, Oct. 22/Nov. 1, 1677.
[2] *Instructions Données (Hollande)*, i. 354–5.

pawn his jewels than suffer the English parliament to meet.[1] The marriage therefore did not appear to bring the end of the war any nearer; and so Charles was restored to his position of unstable equilibrium between Danby and Barrillon, forced to choose between the alternatives of an uncompromising legislature and a foreign subsidy. As the time for the reassembling of parliament approached, the trepidation of Charles increased. He seemed to lose some of his buoyancy; he talked to Barrillon of the time when he would retire from active politics, and (most ominous of all) he even lost some of his healing power, so that those who came for his ministrations had to take their chance.[2] The French subsidy seemed farther off than ever; while close at hand were the coffee-houses, the clubs, and the town dinners, where, from cup, pot, or bottle, the legislators were fortifying themselves for the rigours of the coming campaign.

Faced with the prospect of another period of continental travel, Charles yielded to the counsels of Danby; and on December 31, 1677, the English plenipotentiary, Lawrence Hyde, signed a treaty with the States General (in agreement with the prince of Orange) whereby the two contracting powers undertook to restore a general peace on the principle of French retention of Franche Comté, Cambrai, Aire, and St. Omer, and her surrender to Spain of Sicily, with Charleroi, Courtrai, Ath, Oudenarde, Condé, Tournai, and Valenciennes.[3] The kings of France and Spain were to be induced, by force if necessary, to accept these terms, for which purpose Ostend was assigned to England as the base of an expeditionary force of 11,000 infantry and 1,000 cavalry; and thirty English ships of war were to be fitted out, part for the Mediterranean, part for the Channel. British troops in French service were to be recalled. This instrument was ratified by the Dutch on February 20, 1678. Differences on both sides, however, prevented the fulfilment of the conditions of this treaty, which was intended to be the preliminary to a more general offensive and defensive alliance of England

---

[1] Montagu to Charles II, Dec. 19/29, 1677, in *H.M.C. Rep.* ix, app., pt. ii. 453.　　　　[2] *H.M.C. Rep.* vii, app. 494 (Verney Papers).

[3] *Dumont*, vii, pt. i. 341. For a full account of these negotiations see C. L. Grose, *The Anglo-Dutch Alliance of 1678* in *E.H.R.* xxxix; also C. Brinkmann, *Relations between England and Germany* in ibid. xxiv.

and Holland in European waters. Such a general alliance was signed at Westminster on March 2, 1678, and was ratified by the States on March 28. But it was never ratified by England, because the real executive (i.e. Charles) had no desire for an alliance with the Dutch, and was merely playing for time. There were, therefore, two treaties between England and the States: one intended to force peace on France and Spain in certain terms; the other designed to safeguard the interests of the two Protestant powers in Europe against aggressors. To both, the Dutch had committed themselves; but the English government gave its full sanction to neither.

Ostensibly, therefore, Charles had yielded to the popular demand; and the treaty of December 31, 1677, appeared to detach him from France. To Barrillon he explained that he consented to these measures in order that he might have the credit for them;[1] otherwise, he would be forced by parliament to adopt them; at the same time he pressed Louis to concede a two months' truce in the Netherlands, not for the advantage of the Allies, but for the benefit of the English king's domestic affairs.[2] Diplomacy had indeed reached a high point of subtlety. On the one hand Charles had entered into an offensive alliance with the Dutch; he had summoned parliament for December 1677 instead of April 1678; he had married his niece to the prince of Orange—such was his public policy. On the other hand he continued the secret negotiations with Versailles, whereby he proposed to leave Louis a free hand in return for a subsidy. In other words, Charles was proving an apt pupil at the game of saying one thing and meaning another; but in this instance he played the game too long, even for his patient instructor and paymaster.

In the midst of these negotiations parliament was adjourned from December 3, 1677, to January 15, 1678, and finally to January 28. This gave Danby time to make preparations for securing a working majority in the House. When parliament met, the speech from the throne enumerated the efforts that had been made to secure an honourable peace by mediation; the benefits derived by England through her abstention from

---

[1] *Mignet*, iv. 529.
[2] Montagu to Charles, Dec. 31, 1677, in *H.M.C. Rep.* ix, app., pt. ii. 454.

hostilities; the recent alliance with Holland; the recall of British troops from France, and the necessity of fitting out a large fleet. In the pursuit of this policy Charles had spent more than the sums received from the two special parliamentary concessions, namely, the grant for building ships and the authority to borrow £200,000 on the Excise. The rebellion in Virginia,[1] a war with Algiers,[2] and the cost of a dowry for his niece had added to his expenses. Having done these things, he looked for a plentiful supply and the renewal of the impost on wine.[3]

The Commons, irritated by the successive adjournments of the House, opened with an acrimonious debate[4] on the Speaker's refusal to submit these adjournments to the approval of the House. Thanks were then voted to the king for his speech, with an address (Jan. 31) that no treaty of peace be considered until France was reduced to her frontiers of the Pyrenean treaty; that, until then, commercial intercourse with her should cease, and that meanwhile the king should communicate his alliances to the House. Charles replied that to reduce France to the Pyrenean treaty was a determination not for him but for Providence.[5] 'In sum, Gentlemen, the right of making and managing war and peace is in His Majesty; and if you think he will depart from any part of that right, you are mistaken.' Having heard this clear-cut pronouncement, the Commons then proceeded to debate a supply for a war against France; but in the course of the debate there emerged a new and more insidious fear. They were proposing to raise money for red-coats; but to what use might not these red-coats be put? They were enabling the king to take some one by the beard, but whose beard?[6] The Cavalier Parliament had become as suspicious of Charles II as the Long Parliament of his father. The Commons tried at first to compromise by voting only £600,000 for the setting out of 90 ships and 30,000 troops, though the Speaker assured them that three millions would be required;[7] they eventually agreed (Feb. 18) to raise a million for 'an actual war' with the French king, £600,000 of which was to be raised by a Poll Tax, and the remainder by a levy on new buildings erected about London since 1656. Thus

---

[1] See *infra*, 670–1.   [2] See *supra*, i. 279–80.   [3] *L.J.* xiii. 130–1.
[4] *Grey*, v. 7–17.   [5] *C.J.* ix. 431–2, Feb. 4, 1678.
[6] *Grey*, v. 89.   [7] Ibid., v. 177.

the king received a grant; but it was coupled with a strict appropriation clause, and with a prohibition of the import of French
wine, linen, and brandy for three years.[1]

The inadequacy of this supply, the stringency of its appropriation, and the frank avowal of suspicion by members of the
opposition such as Sacheverell, so disturbed Charles as to cause
him to express the opinion that the opposition had been bribed.
His conjecture was right. Louis had now set in motion a vast
organization for sowing dissension among his enemies, and now
that his former ally was a potential opponent he resolved that
he would be disappointed in his hopes of parliament. In January Barrillon had been joined by the younger Ruvigny, so that
French influence was now directed from a double front—the
former to control the Court, the latter to control the Commons.
For the expenditure of the large sums entrusted to him Ruvigny
had no difficulty in obtaining coadjutors in such members of
the Country party as Buckingham, Holles, Russell, and (after
his release in February) Shaftesbury. Meanwhile, Danby borrowed £60,000 from the London bankers in January for a campaign of counter-bribery; there were also Dutch and Spanish
paymasters, and in consequence only the ultra-scrupulous remained unbribed. The position was therefore one of unusual
complication. Charles was anxious mainly to keep England out
of the war with France, and thereby qualify for the promised
French subsidy; Louis, engaged in sterilizing all political activity against himself, knew that parliament might well prove too
strong for the English king; so he turned his attention to the
Country party with presents of money[2] and assurances that if
they helped him in parliament he would not attack their liberties
or religion. Danby on behalf of the Court was anxious to
obtain a large parliamentary grant for the war, unfettered by
conditions. The opposition, hitherto clamorous for war against
Louis, now began to fear that the troops for which they voted
might be turned against themselves, and accordingly some of
them found it in their interest to act in accordance with French
dictates. Behind it all was this dominating uncertainty: Charles
had ostensibly yielded to the Commons; but did not this yielding
conceal some subtle design?

[1] See *supra*, 437.   [2] *Instructions Données*, ii. 259, 265, 268–72.

The game continued to be played for some months. Charles urged Louis to surrender his claim to places on the Scheldt; but instead of listening to proposals for compromise Louis with 70,000 men captured Ghent and Ypres in the early spring of 1678, thus completing his north-eastern frontier, and placing the Spanish Netherlands at his mercy. Accordingly, the terms of the Anglo-Dutch treaty had to be carried out, and Charles was obliged to send several battalions to Ostend under the command of the duke of Monmouth, a measure which he explained to Barrillon as merely a popular demonstration, intended to appease the English thirst for war, and not an indication that he desired war. To the same confidant he expressed also his disgust at the bellicose attitude of his brother, when neither of them had a *sou* to spare for the raising of troops; moreover, he knew that nothing good could come from Anglo-Spanish military co-operation in Flanders, as Spanish military personnel was notoriously defective.[1] Thus by the end of February 1678 Charles had sent to the Continent an expeditionary force intended to co-operate with Spanish troops, in whom he had no confidence, against a power on which he had no intention of declaring war, and with which he desired to continue his secret alliance in return for a subsidy. He would remain master of his foreign policy as long as possible.

When on March 14, 1678, the Commons debated the state of the nation and the removal of evil counsellors, seriousness was mingled with platitude as never before in the history of the House. Colonel Birch produced for the third time his comparison of Louis XIV with a glass bottle which might easily be broken with an English crab-tree cudgel; sir John Ernly, after remarking that every tub must stand on its own bottom, asked his listeners: 'An house is on fire; will you not quench it?' Russell, after insisting that the saddle must be set on the right horse, asked for a committee to consider their deplorable condition and their apprehensions of popery and a standing army; sir Charles Wheeler reminded them that inquiry into evil counsellors began the former civil troubles. Some members thought that 'we were in jest', others that 'we are in the dark'.[2]

---

[1] *Mignet*, iv. 541, and *Baschet*, 139, March 25/April 4.
[2] *Grey*, v. 223–30.

More clear expression of the national temper was revealed in
the words of the aged sir Philip Warwick: 'I have feared the
greatness of the French king these forty years. . . . I am willing
(like Balaam's ass) to crush my master's foot when an angel
stands in the way.'[1] The impotence or paralysis of which the
Commons gave evidence was really due to this, that their war-
like temper was almost completely neutralized by the interplay
of powerful forces, including bribery by Danby and Ruvigny;
the fear that a Stuart alliance with Orange might result in joint
action against dissentients in both countries; the dread of a
standing army; and, above all, intense suspicion of both Charles
and Danby, even when they seemed most conciliatory. Behind
the scenes were double sets of diplomatic negotiation, each of
unparalleled complexity;[2] the one set intended to group England
in a triple or even quadruple alliance against France, so that
English opinion might be conciliated, and the other to secure
French money for English neutrality. These two objects did
not seem inconsistent; since by ranging himself with the allies
and obtaining a war vote from his parliament, Charles's bargaining power with Louis appeared to be increased. Both sets
of negotiations failed. The failure of the negotiations with the
States General and Spain was probably intentional, but at least
time was gained; the failure of those with France was uninten-
tional, and proved to be of disastrous consequence, because they
came to light.

These proceedings, together with the short recess of March
26–April 11, enabled Charles to dally still longer with his appre-
hensive Commons. On April 29 a long speech by lord chancellor Finch[3] reciting Charles's peace efforts as mediator, and
inviting the advice of both Houses on the defensive and offensive
alliances then being negotiated with the Dutch, evoked a request
from the Commons that the king would communicate, for the
benefit of the House, all the leagues and treaties mentioned in
this speech. While awaiting this information the Commons discussed evil counsellors, the growth of popery, and the breaking

[1] *Grey*, v. 230.
[2] For a full account of these see C. L. Grose, *The Anglo-Dutch Alliance* of
1678 in *E.H.R.* xxxix. 349 and 526; also A. Browning, *Life and Letters of
sir T. Osborne, earl of Danby*, i, ch. xii.   [3] *L.J.* xiii. 206–7.

of civilian heads by red-coats, who 'might fight against Magna Carta',[1] and devoted the greater part of a day to hearing evidence about concealed priests and chapels in the county of Monmouth.[2] On May 2 the offensive and defensive league of December 31, 1677, and the proposed league of perpetual defence with Holland were read in the House, which, after considering them, voted that they were not pursuant to their addresses.[3] At the same time the king was urged to enter into a quadruple alliance with the Emperor, Spain, and the States General[4] for the vigorous conduct of war against France. This was followed on May 7 by another address for the removal of Lauderdale; but Charles kept his Commons to the main point—supplies; in spite of their expressed opinion that the whole affair was 'a work of darkness'.[5] Charles would neither declare war on France nor disband his troops; the Commons were unwilling to grant money either for their maintenance or disbandment. After two short adjournments the Commons found a loophole through which they hoped to escape from the dreaded red-coats; for on June 4 they voted £200,000 for the disbandment of the army (provided this was completed by the end of June), and an additional £200,000 for the expenses of the fleet. This time-limit was subsequently extended to July 27. The additional sums granted for paying off the extraordinary charges of Navy and Ordnance and for the dowry of the princess of Orange were merged into a consolidated act[6] for raising £619,368 by a land-tax, which passed the Commons on July 8, and received the royal assent on July 15.

Having secured the impotence of England by setting parliament against the king, Louis next succeeded in setting the States General against the prince of Orange. This was not a difficult task, especially as, in the projected permanent alliance between England and the States, there was said to be a secret clause providing for reciprocal assistance in dealing with rebel-

---

[1] *Grey*, v. 287.   [2] *C.J.* ix. 466–70.   [3] Ibid. ix. 475, May 4, 1678.

[4] On March 26 a conference on this subject was held by Danby with the Imperial, Spanish, and Dutch envoys; Charles later gave it to be understood that he would declare against France if parliament granted him the money. But because of Charles's ambiguous attitude the alliance never ripened.

[5] Col. Birch's description (*Grey*, v. 385).   [6] 30 Car. II, cap. i.

lious subjects in exile. D'Estrades, one of the French agents, made good capital out of this rumour, and thereby helped to widen the cleavage in Dutch sentiment, so that the prince of Orange found himself pitted against a strong peace party in his own country. When Louis offered to surrender Maestricht, to renew the commercial treaty of 1662, and to sacrifice the severe tariffs of 1667 in favour of the moderate ones of 1664, Amsterdam took the lead in the demand for peace, since this would now bring the restoration of commercial relations with France on exceptionally favourable terms. In effect, therefore, French diplomacy was willing to surrender her exceptional weapon against Dutch prosperity in return for peace and frontier possessions. On May 15, in spite of opposition from the prince of Orange, the States General announced its intention of sending an extraordinary ambassador to the French king.

At this point a patriotic king would either have declared war on France, or would have used his mediation to secure what is called 'the balance of power'; but Charles, it must be repeated, had only one object—money. Through no fault of his, he had failed to arrive at a satisfactory arrangement with the Dutch, whose polity was complicated and difficult of comprehension; so he fell back on France, where conditions were at least more easily understood.

For some time there had been secret negotiations with France. On January 9, 1678, Danby had written to Montagu complaining of the difficulties into which Charles was forced by the cessation of the subsidy, and concluding with these significant words: 'Unless some balm from heaven be applied to the wound I do not see but that it must bleed very suddenly.' Danby later erased the words 'from heaven'.[1] The balm consisted of six million livres a year for three years, in return for which Charles was to use his influence with Spain and the Dutch to procure peace. This audacious proposal was made in a letter sent by Danby to Montagu on March 25, to a draft of which Charles, in his own hand, added the postscript: 'I aprove of this letter.' The negotiation lapsed; but when in May there were clear

---

[1] A copy (with alterations in Danby's later handwriting) will be found in *Add. MS.* 38849, f. 118. For a full account of a complicated subject see A. Browning, *Life and letters of sir T. Osborne, earl of Danby*, i, chs. xi and xii.

indications of Dutch willingness to accept a separate peace, Charles decided again to make what capital he could out of his now threadbare mediation, and at the same time to fortify himself against a malignant opposition. After a week's negotiation, a secret treaty was signed on May 17, 1678, by Charles and Barrillon, whereby the English king undertook to maintain absolute neutrality during the continuance of the war, and to withdraw his troops from the Continent in the event of the allies not accepting the French terms within two months. The 3,000 troops raised for Scotland were to be retained,[1] and parliament was to be prorogued for at least four months from the date of the expiration of the two months. In return, Barrillon undertook to pay six million livres, the first half payable two months after signature of the secret treaty, the remainder by quarterly instalments thereafter. The preamble to this secret engagement recited that Charles had been urgently solicited by the States General to use his good offices with Louis to induce him to keep open the terms offered in April 1678, in spite of any subsequent successes of French arms; ostensibly therefore this bargain was in the interests of the Dutch, a presumption which would prove useful if by chance its terms had to be made public. Neither Danby nor Lauderdale signed the treaty.

Within a few days Louis realized that it would not be necessary to spend this money; for on May 22 he received from the States General a letter announcing willingness to negotiate terms on the basis of those proposed in April at Nimeguen. Louis thereupon granted the Dutch a truce of six months to date from July 1. Peace seemed assured; but Louis renewed his demands that to his ally Sweden should be restored those of her possessions which had been captured by the elector of Brandenburg. To enforce this demand, Louis would have had to invade Germany and occupy Cleve and Mark, territories in close proximity to the Dutch frontier; a prospect which revived the war spirit among the allies, and with it the hopes of Orange that the proposed separate peace would be abandoned. Even the States General were unwilling to accept peace on such terms, and so the war trumpets of Europe were once more in full blast. The project of a permanent Anglo-Dutch alliance

[1] *Baschet*, 139, May 18/28, 1678.

against France was therefore resumed, and Temple was sent to The Hague, where, on July 16–26, 1678, he secured the adhesion of the States to a joint ultimatum in which France was given a fortnight to yield her demand on behalf of Sweden, and come to terms[1] on the conditions already laid down in the Anglo-Dutch treaty of December 31, 1677. Temple was surprised when the document was repudiated in London; he knew only one of the two sets of negotiations.

It might seem that these events were sufficient to destroy the secret Anglo-French treaty; but this compact was still in being, and Charles was reminded of his undertaking to disband his troops by the middle of June. To this he replied that if he dismissed his troops then, and France meanwhile made any important conquest in Flanders, he would be in danger of expulsion from England as a traitor. Additional English regiments were accordingly sent to the coast for transport to Flanders; and Danby continued to quibble over the interpretation of the stipulation that the troops should be dismissed at the end of two months from the signature of the secret treaty. Publicly therefore Charles was maintaining a free hand in the European impasse; but secretly he was on the alert for every chance of grasping the French subsidy which for so long had dangled before him. Even the demand for Swedish restitution seemed to offer such an opportunity. England had the troops; she had also an available princess (Anne) for a Swedish matrimonial alliance; so Sunderland was sent over to Paris in order to realize these assets. But it may be doubted whether Louis really intended to hold out on behalf of Sweden; it is certain that he was relieved when the Swedish agents announced that they would not insist on such restitution. Freed from a troublesome allegiance to his ally, Louis was therefore able to sign peace with the Dutch on July 31, 1678, followed later by treaties with Spain (Sept. 1678), the Emperor, Brandenburg, and Denmark (Feb. and June 1679).

Even thus, Charles did not give up hope. In October Sunderland returned after a fruitless mission, and Charles reduced his demand from six million livres to three;[2] but, once more, he had over-estimated the generosity of Louis. In the midst of a great

---

[1] *Dumont*, vii, pt. i. 348.   [2] *Mignet*, iv. 704.

European pacification, the position of England now seemed one of innumerable possibilities. When other nations were in the last throes of resistance to the all-conquering arms of France, England, hitherto a naval power, had suddenly raised an army. To what use could it be put? For a joint campaign with the Emperor and the northern powers on behalf of Sweden? Or, in conjunction with France, for a war against the Emperor and the northern powers? Or for a war against France and Holland?[1] If these seemed too speculative, the army might be used at home to secure the king in a non-parliamentary absolutism. Charles, it is true, had not succeeded in obtaining the French money, but he kept his army, the gift of a House of Commons which was now in terror of the weapon it had placed in his hands. All the fears and hatreds steadily accumulating for more than a decade were now to be unloosed in wild panic, and a fierce storm preceded the calm for which Charles yearned.

[1] *Baschet*, 141, Sept. 23/Oct. 3.

XVI

THE POPISH PLOT, 1678–81

I. THE EARLY STAGES OF THE PLOT, AUGUST 1678—FEBRUARY 1679

THE summer of 1678 abounded in omens that great events were impending. 'There seems a more than usual concernment among all men,' wrote Andrew Marvell, 'as if some great, and I hope good thing were to be expected.'[1] The fourth of the five acts in the second Caroline drama was about to be staged; and men looked eagerly for the raising of the curtain which would reveal whether the scene was laid in Rome or Paris. In the heavens something uncommon was afoot; for in that year there were three eclipses of the sun and two of the moon,[2] and in April of the preceding year there had appeared a blazing comet, the effects of which were still awaited with apprehension.[3] Astrologers prophesied 'frenzies, inflammations and new infirmities proceeding from cholerick humours',[4] as well as 'troubles from great men and nobles';[5] while readers of literature less ephemeral than the Almanacs were assured that a great trial would be brought on England by the Papists, those worshippers in the outer court; indeed it was alleged that the late archbishop Ussher, when predicting these trials, had swooned at the thought of what was in store for the nation.[6] Even in the occult world there was more than usual activity, for a great revival of witchcraft occurred in Scotland, and in August the Devil himself presided at a general convocation of witches, attended by a warlock who, originally a presbyterian minister, had conformed when the bishops came in.[7] Charles would need that gift of second-sight, with the possession of which his clan was sometimes credited, and with which he appeared at times to be endowed.

Plotting was one of the spare-time occupations of the seven-

---

[1] May 23, 1678, in *Poems and Letters*, ed. Margoliouth, ii. 226.
[2] Dove, *Speculum Anni*, 1678.   [3] W. Andrews, *News from the stars*, 1678.
[4] Dade, *A prognostication* . . . , 1678.
[5] J. Partridge, *Calendarium Judaicum*, 1678.
[6] *Strange and remarkable prophecies and predictions of the holy, learned and excellent James Ussher*, 1678.   [7] Law, *Memorialls*, 145.

teenth century, one of the undesirable things that have disappeared with washed faces and outdoor games. Messages were
often composed in cypher that might quite well have been
written in plain script, considering the jejune character of their
information and the ease with which the cypher could be unravelled; but the disguise helped to create the atmosphere of
consequence and secrecy, so stimulating when men combine for
the achievement of some undisclosed object. Another factor
helped to foster the plot mentality; namely, that few men applied
reasonable tests for determining the truth of a statement.
Rumour and hearsay were often taken for proofs; in the courts,
a prisoner was generally assumed to be guilty before he was tried,
and personal animus did not debar one from giving evidence.
It was an age of oaths, perjurers, and informers; when every one
was scrupulously religious, and personal honour still undeveloped.
A third contrast has to be noted. We live in an economic age, and
seek to interpret the past in terms of that age. But in the England
of Charles II the Scarlet Woman was more prominent than the
Economic Man.

Venner's Rising, the Derwentdale Plot, the Plague and Fire
of London, the disgrace of Chatham; all these in succession
helped to put the nation into a state of mind in which anything
might be believed. In both England and Ireland plots were of
almost regular recurrence. Hidden in garden or thatch, Irishmen sometimes found bundles of mysterious documents containing evidence of gigantic conspiracy; one such bundle found in
1673 was found to be written 'in perfect Irish-English and some
parts have no sense'. 'Had I troubled you with a narrative of
every little plot I have been informed of,' wrote the bishop of
Ferns on this occasion, 'it would have been endless; for as those
of the Roman persuasion have been perpetually forward to in-
vent plots and conspiracies which they pretend those of the
fanatic party are engaged in, so those others have not been un-
fruitful of the like inventions against the Romanists.'[1] This was
almost equally true of England. Sir John Bramston, a knight of
the shire for Essex, was the victim of a plot engineered by a hostile
neighbour named Mildmay, who employed a Portuguese adventurer to swear that a papal visitation was held at Bramston's

[1] *Cal. S.P. Dom., 1673*, xlv.

house, attended by the knight, who (according to the sworn evidence) received both dispensation and a pension.[1] In January 1674 Shaftesbury made a violent speech in which he said that there were about 16,000 papists round London ready to execute a desperate stroke, and that no one was sure of his life; at the same time a boy of 13 was examined by the Lords with regard to his discovery in the streets of a letter from a Roman Catholic containing plans for the destruction of both Houses by gunpowder. This juvenile witness had *un résolution qui n'est pas de son age*; and, when the Commons were informed of these revelations, they proposed to ask the king to put the Militia into readiness, and to arm the Protestants of London.[2] Two years later the queen was informed of the accusation that popish books were being stored over the stables at Somerset House, and a search was ordered to be made;[3] this building was soon to come into more lurid publicity. In April 1678 the Commons investigated the secret ramifications of popery in the county of Monmouth,[4] a county which was afterwards to produce the informer Bedloe. England was ripe for a plot.

Among the plotmongers was Ezerel Tonge, born in 1621; the rector of St. Michael's, Wood Street, a doctor of divinity of Oxford, and an enthusiast for botany, alchemy, and the revelation of Jesuit designs. He acquired a certain amount of reputation as educator and researcher; for he taught children to write by a new method of inking over copper-plate copies;[5] he also communicated to the Royal Society his papers on the flow of sap in plants. Diffusion of interests and a certain clownishness of manner had hitherto interfered with personal success; but in the winter of 1676–7 he chanced to meet, at a house in the Barbican, one possessed in full measure of the personality and self-confidence requisite for success in a heavily overstocked market. This was Titus Oates, who, although Tonge's junior by 28 years, could, at the age of 27, look back on an extremely varied life; for this ecclesiastic was already distinguished in three distinct spheres— sanctimoniousness, indecency, and perjury. Though no scholar, he had a fund of native cleverness, and was gifted with a large,

[1] Bramston, *Autobiography (Camd. Soc.)*, 146 sqq.
[2] *Baschet*, 130, Jan. 11/21, 1674.   [3] *Cal. S.P. Dom., 1676–7*, xviii.
[4] *Supra*, 554.   [5] *Aubrey*, ii. 261.

imposing figure, impressive at a distance, and needing only a doctor's gown and bands to create what in some circles is called 'presence'. Another asset was his chin, the longest in England, supporting his mouth as by a pedestal, and helping to confer on his utterances a gravity and portentousness not confirmed by his small, shifty eyes. Having been expelled from a naval chaplaincy and from a living in Kent, Titus was in one of the penurious 'vacations' of his career, when he chanced on this meeting with Tonge, still contriving to supplement his stipend from the vapourings of his pens and his alembics. According to his own account Oates called on Tonge in order to have the counsel of that experienced theologian on 'a case of conscience'.[1]

The two combined forces and for a time appear to have tried hard to discover a real plot. Oates had already seen something of Roman Catholic society as chaplain to the Protestants in the duke of Norfolk's household, and in 1676 he became a member of a mixed Roman Catholic and Protestant club, which met at the *Pheasant* in Fuller's Rents. At this club, in spite of the rule forbidding talk of religion or politics on pain of a fine of sixpence, Oates railed against the Church of England and proclaimed that the king was only one of three estates;[2] it was also noted that he generally wore full canonicals. There he met several Jesuits; but in order to 'dive into their secrets' more deeply, he decided to become converted, and according to his version he was received into the Society of Jesus on Ash Wednesday, 1677.[3] For the purposes of his novitiate he was sent to Spain in order to bring back the body of lord Cottington from Valladolid. He was given to understand that his sole mission was to bring back the body, but a sealed packet entrusted to him for delivery in Madrid led him to assume that there was something else on hand; so at Burgos he opened the packet, and 'made himself master of all the secrets thereof'. After trying to stick down the wafer, he explained that it had come undone through being rubbed in his pocket. Armed with this knowledge, he was able to worm out still more secrets from the fathers in Madrid. Nor did he obtain only information in this mission; for he brought back to England, not the body,

---

[1] *Grey*, vi. 327.
[2] W. Smith, *Contrivances of the fanatical conspirators* (1685).
[3] *Add. MS.* 38847 (*Southwell Papers*), f. 201.

but a doctorate of divinity of the university of Salamanca, a 'rabbinical degree' which proved the best accessory in his outfit.

Another mission enabled him to perfect his knowledge of Jesuit designs. In December 1677 he was sent to the College at St. Omer, where he was known sometimes as Sampson Lucy, and sometimes as Titus Ambrosius.[1] His unusual deportment occasioned considerable mirth among the junior members of this sodality; and in a game known as 'sawing the witch' he had a pan broken over his head 'for recreation'. Owing to his seniority, he sat at a small table in Hall by himself, near the High Table; for he could not diet with the young students; there he specially distinguished himself by canting stories after dinner. At St. Omer he found plenty of evidence, and when he learned the indignation of his hosts at Tonge's translation of a book named *Jesuits' Morals*, he offered to return to England and poison Tonge. This offer, according to his own account,[2] was accepted, with the promise of a modest £50 if he succeeded; and so, when he returned to England in June 1678 he was a pseudo-Jesuit, commissioned to murder the man with whom he was co-operating in the discovery of a great plot.

With all this miscellaneous information, the allies set to work; and an indictment of 43 articles was speedily drawn up. How to bring this to the notice of the king was the next point; but they succeeded in getting into touch with Christopher Kirkby, who appears to have had some employment at Court as a chemist, and in this way they obtained some knowledge of the king's movements. On August 13 Kirkby intercepted the king as he was walking in St. James's Park; but Charles referred him to Chiffinch and passed on; the same evening Kirkby brought Tonge to the king at Whitehall, and the matter was now referred to the lord treasurer. Tonge communicated a copy of the indictment to Danby, who questioned his informant personally about the revelations.[3] Briefly, the substance of the 43 articles was that pope Innocent XI had deputed to the Jesuits supreme control

---

[1] Evidence of the Jesuits at Oates's trial for perjury, May 8, 1685, in *The tryals, convictions and sentence of Titus Otes upon two indictments for perjury* (1685), 10, 19, 25. [2] *Add. MS.* 38847, f. 204.

[3] C. Kirkby, *Discovery of the Popish Plot*, 1679; *P.C. Reg.* 66, Sept. 28, 1678; J. Pollock, *The Popish Plot*, 13, 70–1.

of the Roman Catholic interest in England for the purpose of
overthrowing king and government; money was to be provided
by the Spanish Jesuits and by the French king's confessor, père la
Chaise; two Jesuits had been paid to shoot the king, four Irish
ruffians to stab him, and sir George Wakeman, the queen's
physician, to poison him. In addition to all this, there was to be
a massacre of Protestants and a French invasion of Ireland; the
duke of York was to become king, and rule under the direction
of the Jesuits. This was the original version of the Plot; other
details were afterwards added;[1] such as that lord Arundell was to
be lord chancellor; lord Powis, lord treasurer, and Coleman
secretary of state. This design had been finally agreed upon by
the Jesuits at the *White Horse* tavern in the Strand on April 24,
1678, when Oates, as one of their trusted members, carried the
documents from room to room for the signatures. Oates was at
St. Omer, not in London, in April 1678, but that was a minor
discrepancy; for no one at that time knew his movements.

At this point a new and tragic figure entered the scene. One
of the best known of the London magistrates at that time was sir
Edmund Berry Godfrey, then in his fifty-seventh year. Of good
family, he had been educated at Westminster and Christ Church,
and had prospered in the trade of wood and coal merchant. He
had distinguished himself during the Plague by remaining at his
post, and pursuing robbers of the dead even into the pest-houses;
for these services he was presented with a piece of plate. In 1669
he was placed in custody for a few days because he had procured
the arrest of the king's physician for debt, an occasion when his
resolute behaviour still further confirmed his reputation for
staunchness of character. He was known as a strict but tolerant
Protestant; his generosity and courtliness brought him into contact with men of different faiths, including Papists; and he was
received in good society. He appears to have had some kind of
friendship or association with Coleman, the duchess of York's
secretary; and was thus an exceptional, but in some ways
mysterious man; for while he was liked and respected, his circle
of acquaintance was wider than comported with the standards
of safety. His short imprisonment of 1669 may have saddened

---

[1] For these see T. Oates, *A true narrative of the horrid plot* (1679). This
pamphlet contains 81 counts and was dedicated to Charles.

him; certainly the engraving from the only existing portrait shows a man of somewhat melancholy features. In the spring of 1678 he went to the south of France for the benefit of his health, returning in the summer of that year.

Early in September Oates and Tonge called on Godfrey with the request that he would take their depositions on oath as to the truth of the accusations contained in the papers which they brought with them. The magistrate declined to do so unless he was informed of the contents of the papers; some days later (Sept. 28) he was provided with a copy, and the depositions were then taken on oath. It appears that Godfrey, who was visibly distressed by the serious nature of the depositions, at once revealed them to Coleman (possibly as a warning), but Coleman did not profit by the hint to destroy all the incriminating letters in his possession. Meanwhile the government, possibly at the instigation of the duke of York, had decided to investigate the matter, and on September 28, at a Council meeting presided over by the king,[1] Williamson produced a bundle of papers received from Tonge, the king remarking that on August 13 he had been told about a conspiracy by Tonge, and had referred him to the lord treasurer. Danby reported that, when he sought for further information, he was informed by Tonge, in a letter of September 3, that evidence would be forthcoming if letters directed to father Bedingfield (the duke's Jesuit confessor) were intercepted at Windsor post office. Danby had tried to intercept them, but was too late;[2] for Bedingfield had himself collected the packet, and as the letters contained some 'mysterious expressions' apparently tending to an unlawful design, he had taken these to the duke of York, who brought them to the king, and in this way they were communicated to the council board. On examining them, several councillors pronounced the letters counterfeit because of the bad spelling, and because, in spite of the forced hand, they appeared to have been written by the same person. Indeed they were such clumsy forgeries that no use could afterwards be made of them.

Tonge was then called in. His manner showed nervousness, but he was assured that he need have no apprehension. He said that of his own knowledge he knew nothing, as all his information

---

[1] *P.C. Reg.* 66, Sept. 28, 1678.   [2] Pollock, op. cit. 73–4.

was from Oates. He was asked to fetch his friend, and at the afternoon session Titus was ushered in. It was not his first appearance
before the council; for in April 1675 he had been summoned
thereto with his father to substantiate his allegation against one
of the jurats of Hastings of having spoken scandalous words of
the council,[1] an occasion when he had failed to prove his accusations. On this, his second appearance, he shared none of his
friend's hesitation, his first request being that he should be put
on oath. This having been complied with, he was shown the
Bedingfield letters, and at the mere sight of a few lines he swore
to the authorship of each—this was written by Nicholas Blundell,
that by Dr. Fogarty, another by Thomas White, another by
William Ireland. The confidence of Oates, his unhesitating
answers, his wealth of detail, all these carried the council before
them; and as a result the arrest was ordered of the men whom he
named. It was not unimportant that Charles was absent from
this afternoon session (having gone to Newmarket), for the fate
of the Plot might have been very different had the king exposed
the falsehoods of the informer at this early stage. Having gained
the confidence of his audience, Oates then retailed a picturesque
anthology from the more recent incidents of his career. The
matter was now deemed so serious that a special meeting of
Council was held on the afternoon of the next day (Sunday,
Sept. 29) at which the king was present, when Charles tested
Oates on his reference to Don John of Austria, and convicted
him of falsehood; but this did not shake the confidence of the
councillors, who ordered the arrest of Coleman and the attendance of sir George Wakeman.

At the council meeting on the following day, Oates repeated his
statements, and charged the Jesuits Ireland, Grove, and Pickering with having been of the Jesuit consult at the *White Horse*
tavern. He also cited a letter from Thomas White, Provincial of
the Jesuits, as proof that sir George Wakeman had agreed to
poison the king for £15,000, £5,000 of which had already been
paid to an agent by Coleman. By this time the dimensions of
the Plot had swollen to a capacity as great as the credulity of
the informer's listeners. Twenty-four English Jesuits, nineteen
foreign Jesuits, twelve Scottish Jesuits, nine Benedictines, three

---

[1] *P.C. Reg.* 64, April 14, 1675.

Carmelites, two Franciscans, nine Dominicans, fourteen secular priests, four secular persons (Fogarty, Wakeman, Coleman, and Groves), four Irish ruffians, and two archbishops, all jumbled up mostly in multiples of three and four, appear to have been kept clear and distinct only in the ever-resourceful mind of Oates.[1]

There then elapsed a period of seventeen days (Oct. 1–17, 1678), perhaps the most mysterious in the history of England. Oates's revelations were now public property, and what the council had swallowed was not likely to be rejected by the populace. The mine was laid; it needed only a spark to fire it; but who fired the spark may remain one of the unsolved problems of history. Godfrey, who is said to have shown signs of apprehension, and to have expressed a premonition of personal danger to himself,[2] left his house in Green's Lane near the Strand on the morning of Saturday, October 12. He was seen to go up St. Martin's Lane, and was said to have asked an acquaintance the way to Primrose Hill (near Hampstead); he was also reported to have been seen at Marylebone; though there was another story that at noon he was in the company of one of the churchwardens of St. Martin's-in-the-Fields. There is no contemporary reference to his movements after one o'clock. He did not return to his house that night, and sinister rumours were soon afloat. On the following Thursday, the 17th, about 6 p.m., two men, a baker and a farmer, were passing some waste ground on the south side of Primrose Hill, when they noticed a stick and a pair of gloves lying by the hedge. On reaching the *White House* tavern, they told the landlord, who accompanied them back to the spot; where, behind the bushes, they found the body of Godfrey, fully dressed, head and face downward, transfixed with a sword, the point of which projected about six inches out of his back. His hat and periwig were in the bushes over his head, but neither his laced band nor cravat could be found. His money was intact, but his pocket-book had been removed.[3]

---

[1] *Harleian MS.* 3790, f. 46; see also *L.J.* xiii. 313–30.

[2] L'Estrange, *Brief History*, iii. 172. Elsewhere (iii. 293) the same writer says that Godfrey inquired the way to Paddington woods. L'Estrange's evidence is to be received with caution.

[3] *True and perfect narrative of the late terrible and bloody murder of sir Edmund Berry Godfrey* (1678).

The inquest was conducted next day at the *White House* tavern by the coroner for Middlesex.[1] Two surgeons described the wounds—one, superficial, on the chest; the other on the left breast, going right through the body. There was a livid circle round the neck, which appeared to show that he had been strangled; and to this cause the medical witnesses attributed his death. The murder did not appear to have been committed on the spot, for there was no evidence of a struggle; nor, although the ground was muddy, were there marks of soil on the soles of the shoes; it seemed likely, therefore, that the body had been carried there and pierced with his own sword. One of the jury stated that, on the previous Monday and Tuesday, two boys, searching the spot for a missing calf, had noticed neither body, nor stick, nor gloves. The verdict was wilful murder. After lying in state, the body was accompanied by a long procession to St. Martin's-in-the-Fields, where it was buried (Oct. 31). A commemorative medal was struck, inflammatory sermons and pamphlets poured forth, and a reward of £500 was offered for the discovery of the murderers.

This reward speedily brought forward a claimant, William Bedloe, who had already achieved an eminence in a military career nearly as high as that of Oates in an ecclesiastical; like Oates also he knew the value of a title, and boasted a captaincy of dubious origin. Moreover, he had been to Spain; he had delved into the secrets of the Catholics by pretending to be one of them, and he had been commissioned to set fire to London.[2] Writing from Bristol, he offered to give information; and when his offer was coldly received he came in person to make his revelations. On November 8, before the committee of the Lords appointed to investigate the murder of Godfrey, he related how Chepstow Castle was to be seized by lord Powis, who, with a large army, was to join with lord Belasyse and restore popery by force. He himself, according to his story, was to have been one of Godfrey's murderers; and on Monday night, October 14, he had been taken to Somerset House to see the body of the magistrate, where he noticed two men, one a servant of lord Belasyse, and the other

---

[1] The evidence taken at the inquest will be found in the above pamphlet, and also in L'Estrange, op. cit. iii. 236 sqq.

[2] Bedloe, *Impartial discovery of the horrid popish plot* (1679).

Mr. Atkins, a servant of Pepys.[1] Atkins was arrested, but was afterwards able to prove an alibi. Another arrest now helped Bedloe to make out a more substantial story. On December 21 a Roman Catholic silversmith named Prance was taken into custody on the information of a lodger in his house, the information alleging that Prance had been absent from his house for the four nights preceding the discovery of Godfrey's body.[2] This was poor evidence, especially as the lodger was in arrears with his rent; but it led to extraordinary consequences. On being confronted with Prance at a meeting of one of the Commons' committees, Bedloe claimed to recognize in him one of those who had been present at Somerset House. Prance was then lodged for two nights in an icy-cold cell at Newgate, where he was visited by an unknown person (said by L'Estrange to be Shaftesbury) who told him what to say if he would save his life.[3] Thereupon he made a confession to the effect that an Irish priest named Fitzgerald had commissioned him to murder Godfrey, as one of the queen's enemies. Three other men (according to his statement) acted with him—Hill, Berry, and Green, of whom the first two were servants at Somerset House.

Prance's story amounted to this: Godfrey was followed along the Strand on the fatal Saturday, lured into Somerset House and strangled by Green. The body was then removed to a small room in the building, and on Wednesday was taken in a sedan chair to Soho, where it was placed on a horse and conveyed to Primrose Hill. Two days later Prance recanted the whole story; but a second immersion in the condemned hole at Newgate made him reaffirm his original version. Prance, as the price of his life, then swore that he himself was one of the murderers, now turning king's evidence; in this way (possibly with the help of Shaftesbury) Oates and Bedloe used Prance to strengthen their stories, and establish the vital connexion between Godfrey's death and the Plot. It was on this evidence that Green, Berry, and Hill were afterwards (Feb. 1679) hanged for the murder.[4]

But long before these innocent men were executed, the Plot

---

[1] J. Pollock, *The Popish Plot*, 108 sqq.

[2] L'Estrange, op. cit. iii. 51.   [3] L'Estrange, op. cit. iii. 25.

[4] For a comparison between the evidence of Prance and Bedloe see J. Pollock, op. cit., ch. iv.

had grown to uncontrollable dimensions. Parliament re-assembled on October 21, when the king announced that he would forbear any opinion on the subject of the design attributed to the Jesuits. Thereupon both Houses set to work and appointed committees for the examination of witnesses; one was deputed to search the vaults under the Houses, another was to inspect the fireworks on sale at M. Choqueux's in the Savoy, and a third was to examine the letters seized in Coleman's lodging when he was arrested. The first of these committees ordered a search under all rooms for gunpowder; and, as the fifth of November approached, the underground inspections became more rigorous. Householders in the neighbourhood of Old Palace Yard reported having heard great knocking at night; so a committee was appointed to inquire into this;[1] and to make the Houses of Parliament quite secure, sir John Cotton was required to remove his coal and faggots from beneath the Painted Chamber;[2] Monmouth was set in command of sentinels at the doors, while sir Christopher Wren helped the committee to search all the walls, inside and outside, of the vaults stretching from under the Thames to beneath Westminster Hall. Houses in the vicinity were searched for arms; and in Chelsea the lodging of the bishop of Winchester was visited in order to investigate the stories of a bricklayer who had worked there eighteen months before.[3] Nor was this the end of the digging; for on a rumour that the 'plot money' (amounting to hundreds of thousands of pounds) was buried in the Savoy, the excavators busied themselves in that neighbourhood,[4] already suspect because of the firework store of M. Choqueux. No line of inquiry was left unexplored. Shaftesbury, one of the most assiduous coadjutors of Oates, solemnly recorded on paper statements made by boys of 15 and 17 of what had been said to them by a child of 6.[5] Even Pepys's nag came on the scene; for a man was sent to Gravesend to apprehend a suspicious character inquiring after it.[6]

[1] *C.J.* ix. 530, Nov. 1, 1678.

[2] The Cotton family had a house in Westminster, and the reference here is to the cellars of that house.　　　[3] *H.M.C. Rep.* xi, app., pt. ii. 16–17.

[4] *Hatton Correspondence (Camd. Soc.)*, i. 182.

[5] *Shaftesbury Papers*, vii, no. 496, Nov. 6, 1678.

[6] *H.M.C. Rep.* xi, app., pt. ii. 16. See also J. R. Tanner, *Pepys and the Popish Plot* in *E.H.R.* vii.

The firework committee examined M. Choqueux, a surgeon in the Savoy. There was an old association between the Jesuits and pyrotechnics. The name Ignatius obviously denoted something incendiary; the saint himself was known for his hot temper, and either the Jesuits or the Pope must have set fire to London in 1666, indeed a woodcut of 1667 depicted the Pope plying a pair of bellows, while London burned.[1] So great things were expected from an examination of M. Choqueux's stock-in-trade, which was found to consist of 6,914 empty serpents, 10,400 water balloons, and many empty rocket cases. From his information, it appeared that he had sold fireworks for eighteen years, and the empty cases in his possession were kept for filling whenever the king wanted a display. The 'manacles' found on his premises seemed intended for some sinister object, until he explained that they were used for screwing down candlesticks. Having noted this information, the committee ordered a guard to be set over the surgeon's house. His explosives were then carefully examined by two Ordnance officers, who reported that they were quite harmless. The committee thereupon ordered M. Choqueux to be publicly rebuked.[2]

More serious business was stirring at the committee for examining Coleman's letters. Edward Coleman, a convert to Roman Catholicism, had served as secretary first to the duke and then to the duchess of York. An enthusiast for the cause of his adopted religion, he was so indiscreet and communicative that the duke was several times advised to dispense with him altogether; but this course was never adopted. Beginning in June 1674 he wrote numerous letters to persons abroad, not about any definite plot, such as Oates was purveying, but about the general design of restoring the Roman Catholic faith in England.[3] He foolishly kept his correspondence, the veiled allusions of which might seem to imply something more serious than he intended. He may have been overcome by the high rank of the persons with whom he was in communication, or the momentous cause for which he corresponded; moreover he gave his letters a special consequence

---

[1] See *supra*, i. 307. [2] *H.M.C. Rep.* xi, app., pt. ii. 18.
[3] These letters were published in 1681 by order of the Commons under the title of *Collection of letters . . . from the originals in the hands of sir G. Treby*, 2 pts. (1681).

by using a cypher, and ensured some publicity for their contents by his vanity and garrulity. They were mostly requests for money. Thus, in September 1674 he wrote to père la Chaise asking for funds in order to increase the credit of Charles and his brother, in return for which the duke 'would afterwards perform all that His Most Christian Majesty can ask of him'. Another letter of that month referred to 'the great design', which was 'to undermine the intrigues of that company of merchants who trade for the parliament and the religion, and to establish that of the associated Catholics in every place'. This, he thought might be done with the assistance of Pope and Emperor. Written on the back of one of the letters was this memorandum: 'King's power to command his subjects' service against all acts of parliament.' A continually recurring theme in these letters was Charles's debauchery and James's merit; how money intended for the one might be put to far better use by the other. It is noteworthy, also, that his correspondents confirmed the view that money given to Charles would be wasted. Coleman was trying to obtain for James what Charles had already procured for himself by the secret treaty of Dover; but the secretary was no diplomatist, and what in the letters of royal personages was high policy, appeared an infamous plot when propounded by an ordinary person. Hence the Commons seized on statements like these: '£300,000 certain is better than the bare possibility of getting money from parliament',[1] and 'we have here a mighty work on our hands, no less than the conversion of three kingdoms, and by that perhaps the subduing a pestilent heresy which has domineered over part of this northern world a long time'.[2]

In a sense, therefore, Coleman's plot consisted in a development of the scheme concocted in 1670 between Louis XIV and Charles, with the substitution of the duke for the king. His letters supplied the proof for which the Commons were looking. Their committee spent weeks in translating and deciphering the correspondence; and the men who had suspected the existence of gunpowder in the vaults, and of high explosive in M. Choqueux's fireworks, had no difficulty in elucidating hidden works of darkness from the somewhat vague but always compromising corre-

[1] Letter to la Chaise, Sept. 29, 1675, ibid., pt. i. 111.
[2] To la Chaise, undated, but probably late in 1675, ibid., pt. i. 117.

spondence of the secretary. For example, there was a letter from cardinal Norfolk referring to the appointment of a Roman Catholic bishop for England; on the margin, one of the committee wrote: 'this confirms Mr. Oates'. Similarly, a letter from the earl of Berkshire referred to trees and gardeners; these, noted the transcriber might well be kings and governments. Southwell, who wrote a précis of the papers, declared that 'the general scope of all these letters tends to bring the Roman Catholic religion into England'.[1] In the House, sergeant Maynard declared that the letters tallied with Oates's discoveries 'as a counter tally in the Exchequer'.[2] When a shrewd government official and a trained lawyer were convinced, it is not surprising that belief in Oates became an article almost of religious belief;[3] and to doubt that Godfrey was murdered by the Jesuits was a heinous offence, punishable in the courts.[4]

From the day of their reassembly (Oct. 21, 1678), Lords and Commons exercised the functions of grand jury of the nation. Five popish lords—Arundell, Belasyse, Powis, Petre, and Stafford —were sent to the Tower; and the Commons resolved 'that there has been and still is a damnable and hellish plot, contrived and carried on by popish recusants for the assassinating and murdering the king, and for subverting the government and rooting out and destroying the Protestant religion'.[5] This was followed by debates for an address to the king that the duke of York might be required to withdraw from the king's person and counsels, many members supporting this proposal because Coleman's letters seemed to confirm the duke's guilt; but the House was mollified to some extent by the king's verbal assurance[6] that he would consent to reasonable Bills for safeguarding their rights in the

---

[1] Add. MS. 38142, f. 3. Southwell's report on Coleman's letters.

[2] Grey, vi. 295.

[3] See, for example, the Narrative of the horrid conspiracy of T. Knox, W. Osborne and John Lane to invalidate the testimonies of Dr. Oates and Wm. Bedloe. Published by the appointment of me, Titus Oates (1680). In this book (dedicated to the king) Oates attempted to refute the charge of sodomy brought against him.

[4] In June 1682 two men were fined and pilloried for printing and publishing letters which implied that Godfrey had committed suicide. State Trials (1730), iii. 501.

[5] C.J. ix. 530, Oct. 31.　　　　　　　　　　　　　　　　[6] Grey, vi. 172.

reign of his successor, provided the principle of the succession was not violated. The Lords then proceeded with their Bill for disabling the Papists from sitting in either House; on November 20 this was sent back to the Commons with an amendment exempting the duke of York.[1] Here was a severe test for the loyalty of the Commons. 'If the prince should go into another place', declared secretary Coventry, 'it would cost you a standing army to bring him home again'; sir Jonathan Trelawney urged that, by rejecting the proviso, they would drive the duke into popish hands; sir William Killigrew wept after declaring, 'I dread taking the duke from the king'.[2] Those against the proviso sat silent; it was accepted by 158 to 156. By the passing of this Bill[3] about a score of Roman Catholic peers were deprived of their seats in the Lords, including the duke of Norfolk, the earls of Shrewsbury, Berkshire, and Powis; lords Stafford, Petre, Arundell, and Belasyse.

For a moment the Commons turned from the Papists to the Army. About 25,000 troops were still under arms, and some members regarded the Plot as a trap to make them acquiesce in the existence of this standing army;[4] while others thought the soldiers little better than rioters, and there was a feeling in the House that they should be voted a grievance to the nation.[5] A Militia Bill which provided for their disbandment was rejected by the king on November 30, on the ground that by its terms the control of the Militia would be out of his power for a time, and he would not part with that control, even for half an hour; whereupon the Commons read their Bill again in the hope of finding a valid reason for its rejection, but could not discover wherein they had encroached on the prerogative. Having failed to remove the menace of the Army, they turned with fresh zeal to the Plot. On November 28 Bedloe was called in and the door of the House locked.[6] Having been given a full pardon in advance, Bedloe proceeded to relate how a Jesuit consultation was held at Somerset House on May 11 in a room near the chapel, attended by lord Belasyse, lord Powis, two French abbots, Mr. Coleman, and two others who, by the respect shown them, were persons of

---

[1] *L.J.* xiii. 365. [2] *Grey*, vi. 243.
[3] 30 Car. II, stat. ii, cap. i. See *supra*, i. 368–9; ii. 467.
[4] *Baschet*, 141, Oct. 28/Nov. 7, 1678. [5] *Grey*, vi. 266–9.
[6] Ibid. vi. 287.

quality. The queen joined them, while 'Father Walsh' and Bedloe remained in the chapel. The result of the conclave was that
the queen, though with tears, at last consented to 'taking off' the
king. Bedloe thought that the persons of quality who stood with
their backs to him might be the dukes of York and Norfolk. Then
came the turn of Oates. He had already made known to the
king his accusation against the queen, but from Charles's reception of the insult, he knew that he had overstepped the mark, and
must thenceforth depend on his reputation with a credulous
nation. So when he followed Bedloe at the bar of the House he
was a lugubrious martyr, encircled by the forces of evil which
he had exposed at the risk of his life. He complained that after
revealing the queen's designs, he had been refused pen, ink, and
paper; his father and friends had been denied access to him; the
Yeomen of the Guard had smoked in his chamber. He was in
danger of being poisoned. It would be in his interest to make no
further discoveries.

Oates was a profound psychologist. Just as he asked the
readers of one of his printed sermons to 'drop a tear in private'
because he was in danger of persecution,[1] so he stood before
the Commons, a prospective candidate for the martyr's crown.
Without a single dissentient, his audience expressed complete
confidence in him.[2] He then confirmed Bedloe's accusations
against the queen. The result was an address to the king asking
him to remove his consort and all her household from Whitehall,
a request which Charles ignored.[3] But though the king knew that
the Plot was an imposture, he was almost completely solitary in
that knowledge; and he realized that, if he resisted the tide, he
would be swept under by it. Already the heads of the victims
were beginning to fall. On November 27 Oates gave evidence
against Coleman at the King's Bench, and on December 3 he was
executed, perhaps the only victim who in any sense deserved his
fate. Three Jesuits, Ireland, Grove, and Pickering, who, on
Oates's testimony, had been present at the *White Horse* tavern
on April 24, were next tried and sentenced to death. On December 5 it was resolved to impeach the five popish lords in the

---

[1] Preface to a sermon preached at St. Michael's, Wood Street (*Bodley Pamph.* 146). This was Tonge's church.   [2] *Grey*, vi. 295–6.
[3] *C.J.* ix. 549–50, Nov. 28, 1678.

Tower. Meanwhile the Doctor, comfortably housed and in receipt of a handsome weekly allowance, was entering on the zenith of his career, and was setting up for a representative of the older English aristocracy by having engraved on his plate the arms of sir Otes Swinford, husband of the lady who afterwards married John of Gaunt.[1] He dined with the king, to the disgust of the duke of York. Even captain Bedloe could not rival this metropolitan of perjurers, and the innumerable small fry of informers filled in the few gaps left in the gigantic edifice.

Such was the national aspect of the Plot. Its reaction on each of the leading characters on the stage differed considerably. Charles was firmly keeping his legislature to a choice of alternatives—a standing army or a subsidy for their disbandment. The duke of York's position was more ambiguous. His religion and his unpopularity had been taken advantage of by the plot-mongers; but, had he been gifted with agility or imagination, he might have profited by the occasion to find allies in the chaos to which parties were reduced. But he had no gift for these things; and when he made public his opinion that his safety depended on the retention of a standing army, he was deserted by men who might have rallied round him[2] in opposition to Danby and Anglican intolerance. So too, if he had kept his alliance with Danby, the two together might have weathered the storm; but Barrillon was now directing all his efforts to their separation, in order that the impending attack on the lord treasurer might be assured of success.[3] Danby was thought by some to have encouraged the Plot as a means of ridding himself of the duke and strengthening himself in anti-Catholic hatred;[4] but, on the other hand, Oates had not hesitated to use his name, and there was a chance that he might be accused of misprision of treason if only because he had not acted immediately on the revelations made to him in August.[5] He had even more adroit enemies. Louis XIV, who had never forgiven him his conduct in the subsidy negotia-

---

[1] W. Smith, *Contrivances of the fanatical conspirators*, 15.

[2] *Baschet*, 141, Nov. 4/14 and Nov. 7/17.

[3] Ibid. 141, Nov. 14/24.

[4] Ibid. 141, Oct. 28/Nov. 7.

[5] A contemporary hinted that, for this reason, Danby had been instrumental in the murder of Godfrey (*Some Reflections upon the case of Danby in relations to the murther of sir Edmundbury Godfrey*, in *Bodley Ashmole*, F. 51).

tions, willingly lent himself to a scheme for the lord treasurer's downfall. The tool employed was Ralph Montagu, who had just been dismissed from the post of ambassador in Paris.

Montagu, a follower of Arlington and an enemy of Danby, had already (in 1676) been instrumental in bringing over to England the duchesse Mazarin in order that she might help to reinstate Arlington and displace Danby.[1] Thereafter, he strove to ingratiate himself with Charles by obtaining better terms from Louis. But meanwhile he had several grievances. Early in 1678 he had agreed with Henry Coventry for the reversion of a principal secretaryship; but Danby, in the interests of sir William Temple, refused to ratify the bargain, and so made an enemy of the man to whom he had written compromising letters. Montagu soon experienced a more serious rebuff. In a spiteful letter[2] written from Paris the duchess of Cleveland reported disparaging remarks made by him about the king; and when the ambassador left his post without leave in order to exculpate himself, he found himself dismissed from his embassy and from the privy council. He therefore joined forces with Barrillon, and obtained the promise of a large pension for his assistance in the attack on Danby; he would make public the letters, while Louis was to reveal the real intentions of the English Court, and the purpose of the standing army.[3] Having been elected a burgess for Northampton, the ex-ambassador then awaited his opportunity to produce the letters. Knowing his intention, Charles ordered the seizure of his papers, on the allegation that he had been in communication with the papal nuncio in Paris; whereupon the House took up his cause, and ordered his papers to be fetched and examined. Here was a fresh set of treasonable materials for the unsatiated Commons; Montagu for a time displaced Oates, and fears were expressed that he might share the fate of Godfrey.[4] When his box was delivered up and broken open he selected the two fateful letters sent to him by Danby on January 17 and March 25, 1678. Both letters were read to the Commons, including these incriminating words: 'in case the condition of peace shall be accepted, the King expects to have six millions

---

[1] A. Browning, *Life and letters of sir T. Osborne, earl of Danby*, i, ch. xi.
[2] *Harleian MS.* (*B.M.*), 7006, f. 171.
[3] *Baschet*, 141, Oct. 14/24.   [4] *Grey*, vi. 346.

of livres yearly for three years, from the time that this agreement shall be signed between His Majesty and the King of France, because it will be two or three years before he can hope to find his parliament in humour to give him supplies, after your having made any peace with France'. Charles's postscript, 'I aprove of this letter', appended to the original draft of the letter, was afterwards altered by Danby to 'this letter is writ by my order'. On the question being put that there was matter sufficient to impeach the earl of Danby, it was carried by 179 to 116.[1]

On December 21 the articles of impeachment were read. These included: the traitorous encroachment of royal power by treating of peace and war with foreign princes without communicating with the secretaries of state; his attempted subversion of the ancient form of the constitution by the introduction of an arbitrary and tyrannical form of government, with which object he had designed the raising of a standing army on pretence of war against France; he had continued the army contrary to the statute disbanding it; he had negotiated a peace with the French king disadvantageous to His Majesty, and tending to hinder the meeting of parliament, and had endeavoured to obtain a large sum from the French king; he was popishly affected, and had lately concealed the horrid plot and had suppressed the evidence; he had paid for unnecessary pensions and secret service the sum of £231,602 within two years; and, lastly, he had procured for himself considerable grants of inheritance of the ancient revenue of the crown.[2]

The Lords refused to commit Danby, and it seemed likely that this would provoke an interminable duel between the two Houses. Accordingly on December 30 the king, having declared: 'I think you are all witnesses that I have not been well used',[3] prorogued parliament to February 4, 1679. On January 24 the parliament was dissolved by proclamation,[4] a new one being summoned for March 6. So ended that Cavalier Parliament which, having begun its career by removing every shackle from kingship, was now, in the terrors of a nightmare plot, attacking everything sacred in the prerogative—the king's minister, the

[1] C.J. ix. 559–60, Dec. 19. See *supra*, 555–6.   [2] Ibid. ix. 561–2.
[3] L.J. xiii. 447.
[4] *Steele*, i. 3679, Jan. 24, 1679.

king's control of the army, the morality of his consort and the
loyalty of the heir presumptive.

At this point it might well be asked whether there was any
meaning in the madness through which the nation passed in these
months. Who murdered Godfrey, and why? What was the connexion between his death and the plot? Or did he die by suicide?
Was there anything serious behind Coleman's letters? Was the
Court using the plot for some sinister purpose? The problem is
not that of finding a key to fit a lock, but rather that of finding a
key-hole; for, on the evidence which was then considered good
enough to hang a man, it is possible to construct almost any theory.
It must remain a theme for conjecture rather than proof.[1]

The mystery of the plot is bound up in the mystery of Godfrey's
death. Before the cause of that death can be conjectured, it
should be recalled that medical jurisprudence was then in its
infancy; nor is there sufficient medical evidence to justify a
resumed inquest by modern experts. The inquest verdict was
murder by strangulation; but medical opinion has recently been
invoked to substantiate the view that the livid mark round the
neck was owing to post-mortem hypostasis; hence the theory of
suicide, presumably by his own sword. This latter theory may
be dismissed at once as improbable, owing to the great difficulty
which a fully dressed man would experience if he sought his
death by throwing himself on an upright sword of average length;
but there is still left the possibility of suicide by hanging. This
amended conjecture of suicide has still to face the problem of the
sword-thrust, an objection to which the murder theory is not so
liable; since the murderers might quite well have completed their
work by impaling the magistrate with his own sword.

At the outset, therefore, it is by no means certain how Godfrey
met his end, and this leads to a dual series of suggested solutions
of the mystery. A second question or rather set of questions

[1] Among the best-known contributions to the problem are J. Pollock,
The Popish Plot; A. Marks, *Who killed sir Edmund Berry Godfrey?*; J. Gerard,
The Popish Plot and its newest historian (containing criticisms of theories
advanced by Mr. Pollock), and sir John Hall, *Four Famous Mysteries*. See
also Andrew Lang, *The Valet's Tragedy*. Of contemporary sources the third
volume of L'Estrange's *Brief History of the Times* is important but not always
reliable; it favours the suicide theory.

centres in the career of Godfrey. He was one of the commissioners for recusants in the county of Middlesex,[1] appointed in accordance with the scheme of 1675, whereby the crown hoped to confiscate a portion of recusants' estates;[2] he appears also to have been entrusted by Danby with a sum of £300 for the making of a sewer by St. James's Park;[3] but neither of these facts attests more than the Protestantism and the integrity of the magistrate. Nor is there any suspicion that Godfrey was in financial embarrassments such as might account for suicide. There are two great questions about him which have never been satisfactorily answered; what were the nature of his relations with Coleman; and why did Oates choose him for his depositions? To the first query it might be answered that the relations between the two men amounted to no more than friendly intercourse; or it might be suggested that Godfrey was really a man of double life, who, behind the mask of Protestantism, was planning vast designs with his confederate. The difficulty confronting the first answer is that friendly intercourse would not usually be maintained by two such men, living as they did in very different spheres, and divided in both religion and temperament; to the second answer it might be rejoined that, if Godfrey was secretly a Catholic, he was not in a position to perform services of much value to an international schemer such as Coleman. Then, as regards Oates's choice of Godfrey. This may have been pure accident or from deliberate design. If from design, the selection may have been made because Godfrey was noted for his character and his Protestantism; or from some more subtle reason, such as that Oates had contrived to learn a little about Coleman's correspondence and his friendship with sir Edmund, knowledge which Oates might have put to several purposes, including attempted blackmail.

Already it will be seen what a large number of possible suggestions are opened up. Oates noted the extreme trepidation of the magistrate when he swore his depositions before him;[4] why Godfrey should have been so disturbed it is hard to explain; still more, why he should have communicated these depositions to

[1] *Cal. Tr. Bks., 1672–5,* 790, July 1675.
[2] For this see *supra*, 431.   [3] *Cal. Tr. Bks., 1676–9,* 1196.
[4] W. Smith, *Contrivances of the fanatical conspirators* (1685), 8.

Coleman on September 28. Again, why did not Coleman take advantage of the warning to destroy *all* his papers, since those up to October 1676 were left intact? Were there any after that date; and did these (if they existed) contain the secret? Were the papers prior to 1676 left intact because thought to be less incriminating, and so likely to divert attention from questions about the presumably more serious letters that may have been destroyed? Godfrey is alleged to have written a series of more than one hundred letters (to whom is not known) which, if discovered, would (it is held) give the secret history of the reign.[1] It will be seen, therefore, that at the very threshold of the problem there is a host of unanswered questions.

Contemporaries had a simple theory to account for the murder, namely, that the Jesuits procured it because of the damning revelations in the papers entrusted to him by Oates. This explanation is not impossible; but it is based on the assumption that the murderers were foolish, since obviously the one way of giving verisimilitude to Oates's stories was to destroy the Protestant magistrate to whom they were confided. The same criticism, though in a less degree, might be urged against the contention of a modern writer of distinction who has demonstrated that, among the nonsense sworn to by Oates, there was a germ of truth; namely, that on April 24, 1678, a consult of the Jesuits did actually take place, not at the *White Horse* tavern in the Strand, but at St. James's Palace; and as this was a profound secret, revelation of which would have implicated the duke of York, there was good reason for destroying Godfrey, whose murder was therefore 'a cruel necessity'.[2] On this theory some kind of plot was being engineered; Oates knew just enough about it to make his communications dangerous, and so the man who received the sworn information was removed, as otherwise he would have had to divulge it. But Oates copied out his depositions in duplicate, leaving one with the magistrate and taking the other to the council; and so the depositions, with their truth or falsity, were already, in a sense, public property. Nor do we know what Coleman may have revealed to Godfrey.

[1] Andrew Lang, *The Valet's Tragedy*, preface, viii–ix.
[2] J. Pollock, *The Popish Plot*, 149–54. Mr. Pollock suggests that Coleman revealed this secret to Godfrey.

The theories which attribute the guilt to the Jesuits do not satisfactorily explain the motive; though, on the other hand, it is not impossible that some rash but ardent Catholic may have thought (wrongly) that by killing Godfrey he was hushing up a great secret.

Another theory is that Oates murdered Godfrey as a means of securing for the Plot both publicity and confirmation.[1] Here the motive is more clear, for Oates himself afterwards admitted that the murder made the fortune of the Plot; but Oates does not seem the type of man who would resort to violence, and assassination would have been a clumsy weapon for a man capable of his supreme craftsmanship. A third theory is that the murder may have been quite unconnected with the Plot. As a magistrate, Godfrey had come into contact with many dangerous characters, and it is not absurd to suppose that the crime was a work of revenge on the part of one who had fallen foul of him. This theory, first suggested by Hume, has at least the merit of simplicity, and so is free from the strong objections that can be urged against almost every other hypothesis. There was at least one man who may have had a grudge against Godfrey. This was the earl of Pembroke, who, in April 1678, was indicted of the murder of one Coney, by a grand jury of which Godfrey was foreman. Pembroke was the most violent homicide of his age and Godfrey may have been one of his victims.[2]

A fourth theory may be suggested; it is based on the assumption of suicide by hanging. There is evidence that Godfrey was of a melancholy disposition, and the one common element in all the conflicting evidence about his movements before death is that he was exceedingly depressed. This may have been caused by threats of violence; it might also be attributable not to any definite threat, but to a feeling of disquiet, due as much to bad health as to the import of the depositions sworn before him; and, if the magistrate was verging on a breakdown, the affair may have been too much for him. He may have been threatened in some way by Coleman, and called upon 'to fulfil some promise or to redeem some pledge';[3] his

---

[1] This has been suggested by sir J. Stephen, *History of the Criminal Law*, i. 393. [2] This has been suggested by Mr. J. G. Muddiman.

[3] Sir John Hall, *Four Famous Mysteries*, 135. Sir John Hall, in his very interesting discussion, inclines to the murder theory.

failure to do so may account for his assassination, but it might equally well account for his suicide. More generally, a sensitive man might well have felt apprehension that he was dragged into an affair involving such great matters and such high personages, and he had already experienced how the displeasure of the mighty was not lightly to be incurred; moreover, he had been informed of treasonable designs, and he had communicated the information to Coleman, but he had not himself revealed it to the government. This was misprision of treason, and the longer he delayed action, the more perilous his position must have appeared. Still another reason for suicide may be suggested. Oates was an absolutely unscrupulous man who probably knew just a little of Coleman's activities and of his relations with Godfrey. This would be sufficient for a blackmailer, and so Oates may have chosen Godfrey for this purpose. On a broad view of the case, suicide is the most likely theory; such was the king's opinion,[1] and a slight element of confirmation is provided by the fact that Godfrey appears to have taken no food within two days of death.[2]

This conjecture of suicide by hanging is consistent with the contemporary evidence that, at the inquest, the neck was found to be dislocated.[3] But there is still left unexplained the extraordinary position in which the body was found. Why the spectacular sword-thrust? There is fairly general agreement that the sword pierced a corpse; the corpse may as well have been that of a suicide as of a murdered man. The theory of blackmail is compatible with the hypothesis that, at least after the fatal 28th of September, the magistrate was being shadowed, whether by Oates or by some one interested in his movements; hence, the man or men on his trail may have been the first to come upon him while he was still hanging. If Oates or an accomplice made this discovery, he may suddenly have realized that, for the purposes of the Plot, more could be made of sir Edmund dead than alive; and as it is likely that the discovery was made

---

[1] *Baschet*, 141, Oct. 21/31, 1678.   [2] *Cal. S.P. Dom.*, *1678*, 472.

[3] See *supra*, 567, for the contemporary sources for the evidence at the inquest, where the doctors pronounced that the neck was broken. This is repeated in *Burnet*, ii. 164. But even thus, the fact cannot be regarded as absolutely certain.

in a solitary place, it would not be difficult to pierce the body with the sword, and leave it in a position which would suggest a death as spectacular as the other incidents retailed in the depositions. This hypothesis attributes to Oates a genius for propaganda, a not unreasonable attribution; nor is it inconsistent with the little we know of Godfrey's life and temperament; and it accepts consistency of motive as the principle inspiring the actors in the drama. But endless theories might be suggested; some just possible, others having serious objections; and so the death of sir Edmund Berry Godfrey is likely to remain one of the unsolved mysteries of history.

2. PARLIAMENT AND EXCLUSION, FEBRUARY 1679–FEBRUARY 1681

In order that the complicated events of these two years may be more easily followed, it should be noted that within this short period Charles summoned and dissolved two parliaments—the third and fourth of his reign; that in each of these the Commons passed an Exclusion Bill, and that in the interval between the two parliaments (Oct. 1679–Oct. 1680) the excitement of the Plot reached its zenith. Thereafter a surfeited nation gradually quietened down, and a harassed king finally cut the knot tying him to parliament, and obtained a renewal of the subsidy from France.

Shortly after the dissolution of the Cavalier Parliament Charles tried to strengthen himself by compromise; and as he had failed to obtain money from Louis, he was obliged to be conciliatory. The most serious problem was his brother, who adopted a hint that he should leave the country, on condition that the hint was conveyed in a written command, and provided also that the illegitimacy of the duke of Monmouth was definitely declared. With these conditions Charles complied; the order was written out, and at a council meeting of March 3, 1679, Charles produced a signed declaration to the effect that he had never married any one but his consort. This declaration, having been attested by the sixteen councillors present, was deposited in the council chest.[1] The duke then went to Brussels. Charles now furnished himself with a new adviser. Robert Spencer, second earl of Sunderland, returned to England in February

[1] *P.C. Reg.* 67, March 3, 1678/9.

1679 from his fruitless embassy to France, and on the retirement of sir Joseph Williamson from the secretaryship of the northern department, Sunderland paid him £6,000 for the post (Feb. 10). On the 26th of March Danby resigned his treasurership, which was put in commission; and so against a formidable opposition Charles had at his side only the two secretaries, sir Leoline Jenkins and lord Sunderland.

This appearance of conciliation was strengthened by an adroit use of sir William Temple's reputation. With the conclusion of the peace at Nimeguen his diplomatic labours were for the moment at an end, and in February 1679 he was pressed to take a secretaryship of state, but he declined on the ground of ill health. His name was invoked, however, for the scheme whereby the privy council was remodelled, as the result apparently of his advice. By this scheme the council was to be reduced to thirty members, representative of the executive, the opposition and the landed interests, and the councillors were individually to be of sufficient prestige and influence for mediation between crown and opposition.[1] Twenty-seven members of the old council were retained in the new, which included a majority of the opposition, notably Shaftesbury, Essex, and Halifax.[2] Charles announced that he would be guided in weighty affairs by his remodelled council, whose advice would have second place only to that of parliament.[3] Such were the preliminaries with which the king prepared himself for the ordeal of his third House of Commons, the first to be returned by the nation since the loyalist enthusiasm of eighteen years before.

The general election of February 1679 was the first to be fought on distinctively party lines. On both sides there was propaganda and an unsparing use of influence. Monmouth, on the strength of his governorship of Hull and his chancellorship of Cambridge, wrote to the port and the university recommending his candidates; the secretaries wrote to the lords lieutenant on behalf of government nominees,[4] and Barrillon asked Louis to send money for beer.[5] In some constituencies electors were

[1] *P.C. Reg.* 68, April 21, 1679. [2] *Halifax*, i. 149.
[3] *L.J.* xiii. 530, April 21, 1679.
[4] *Cal. S.P. Dom., 1679–80*, 78. [5] *Baschet*, 142, March 30/April 9.

warned not to return bribe-takers or pensioners, and even in
loyalist Devon it was conjectured that scarcely one of the
old burgesses would be returned.[1] In a pamphlet attributed to
William Penn the main objects of the opposition were defined
as follows: (1) the further discovery of the Plot; (2) evil counsellors to be brought to justice; (3) pensioners of the previous
parliament to be punished; (4) measures to be adopted for
securing frequent parliaments, for the ease of Protestant Dissenters, and for safeguarding the nation from popery and
slavery. The electors were advised not to give or receive bribes
at elections; not to choose a pensioner, or a court official, or
any one who held *durante bene placito*; also to be avoided were
indigent or voluptuous persons, ambitious men, non-residents.
The votes and inclinations of former members were to be reviewed
if they stood for election. Choose sincere Protestants, men with
an eye to the improvement of industry, men of 'large principles'
who will maintain civil rights; prefer a good stranger to an ill-
affected neighbour—such was the advice in this, one of the first
clear statements of party doctrine ever put before the English
electorate.[2] That such appeals met with some response was
shown in the composition of the new House of Commons; for
it was said to contain not more than thirty or forty on whom
the Court could rely, and it differed from its predecessor mainly
in the fact that it was now possible to speak plainly of political
miscarriages without being dubbed a 'Presbyterian'.[3] The
shorter word 'whig' was now displacing that ancient term of
abuse. Barrillon noted that the new House contained a large
proportion of men having no parliamentary experience, who
swamped the old cabals.[4]

The first session of the new parliament opened on March 6,
1679. 'I meet you', said Charles to the assembled legislators,
'with the utmost desire that man could have to unite the minds
of all my subjects, both to me and to one another.' He recalled
how he had sequestered the popish lords; he cited the executions

[1] *Cal. S.P. Dom.*, *1679–80*, 78.

[2] *England's great interest in the choice of this new parliament* (1679). By
'Philanglus'. Shaftesbury may have had something to do with its composition. For a copy see *Bodley*, 22858, c. 6.

[3] *Grey*, vii. 374.   [4] *Baschet*, 142, March 27/April 6.

for participation in the Plot and for the murder of Godfrey; how he had disbanded as much of the army as he could with the money supplied to him; and, above all, that he had commanded his brother to absent himself. Money for disbanding the army, for paying the fleet (which parliament had provided for only until the previous July), and for discharging the anticipations on his revenue was earnestly solicited; and he concluded by drawing attention to the loss in his Customs revenue through the embargo on French wines and brandy.[1] Finch having followed suit at intolerable length, the Commons appointed a committee of secrecy to prepare evidence against the five noble prisoners in the Tower, and reminded the Lords of the impeachment of Danby.[2] As the Upper House decided by resolution that impeachments from the preceding parliament still stood,[3] there seemed a likelihood that the lord treasurer would be brought to trial. From these matters the Commons turned for a moment to Oates and Bedloe, from whom further revelations were recorded. Bedloe was voted the £500 reward for the discovery of the murderers of Godfrey;[4] a large bill of expenses presented by Oates was honoured, and a resolution reaffirming belief in the Plot was passed.[5]

There occurred a dramatic moment in the proceedings against Danby, when the king announced to both Houses (March 22) that he had granted the earl a pardon under the great seal, with a reminder that on a former occasion he had done the same thing for Buckingham and Shaftesbury.[6] The manner in which the pardon had been granted was explained to a committee of investigation thus: the king commanded the seal to be taken out of the bag, and directed the pardon to be sealed; whereupon the person who usually carried the bag affixed the seal, and during this process the lord chancellor (Finch) did not regard himself as having custody of the seal.[7] The Commons voted the pardon illegal, and remonstrated against the dangerous consequences of granting pardons to persons under an impeachment;[8] in this way was raised a question, not to be answered until the

---

[1] *L.J.* xiii. 449.
[2] *C.J.* ix. 572, March 20.
[3] *L.J.* xiii. 466, March 19.
[4] *C.J.* ix. 573.
[5] Ibid. ix. 572, March 21.
[6] *Grey*, vii. 19, and *L.J.* xiii. 471.
[7] *C.J.* ix. 574-5.
[8] Ibid. 575.

Act of Settlement: can a royal pardon be pleaded to an impeachment? Meanwhile the Lords ordered Danby to be taken into custody,[1] while the Commons then proposed to proceed against the ex-treasurer by Bill of attainder,[2] and objected to the amendments of the Lords which turned the Bill into one of banishment;[3] but Danby himself settled the difficulty by surrendering to the usher of the black rod (April 15), by whom he was removed to the Tower, where he was to remain for five years. There he was safe from the fury of the Commons; indeed he threatened that if he were abandoned to them he would reveal things dangerous to the Court.[4] Like Lauderdale, he had only one friend—the king.[5] A few days after Danby surrendered himself, the Commons voted a supply of £206,462 for disbanding the forces.[6]

Having failed to bring Danby to account, the Commons next turned to the duke of York; and on April 27 voted an address to the effect that the likelihood of his succession to the throne was one of the chief encouragements of the Plot.[7] Three days later Charles announced through his chancellor that he was willing to consent to laws guaranteeing religion and property in the reign of his successor, provided the succession itself was left intact.[8] Reasonable as this concession appeared, those who doubted whether there could be any security under James proved ultimately to be right. 'What is offered', said Sacheverell, 'will not do your work'; for he had seen a computation by Coleman how the king might live without parliament, and another 'how the king might have a standing army in masquerade in the fleet'.[9] With each week of the session personal bitterness against the duke increased, until on May 11 one of the members of the city of London, Thomas Pilkington, proposed that he should be impeached of high treason;[10] and a

---

[1] *L.J.* xiii. 475, March 24.　　　　[2] *C.J.* ix. 576, March 25.
[3] Ibid. 589, April 8.　　　　[4] *Baschet*, 145, May 10/20, 1680.
[5] He was given a warrant for the marquisate of Danby.
[6] *C.J.* ix. 597, April 16.　　　　[7] Ibid. ix. 605.
[8] Ibid. ix. 606, April 30.　　　　[9] *Grey*, vii. 159–60.
[10] Ibid. vii. 238. In *Sloane MS.* (*B.M.*) 2496, f. 55, there is a list of the accusations on which the charge was based. These were (1) that he had confederated with foreign powers to alter and subvert the government in church and state; (2) he was a party to the Popish Plot; (3) he made use of

debate ensued in which it was declared that the Protestant religion and a popish successor were as incompatible as light and darkness. Richard Hampden, son of the great Hampden, thereupon moved for the introduction of an Exclusion Bill, and on May 15 was read the first of the Bills for disabling the duke of York from inheriting the crown, a Bill which included the crowns of Scotland and Ireland within its scope, in spite of the fact that these kingdoms possessed legislatures. Those against the Bill on its first reading would not be counted, and so 'yielded the question';[1] on its second reading it passed by 207 to 128.[2]

The first Exclusion Bill contained a preamble to the effect that the duke of York had been seduced by the Pope's agents to enter the Church of Rome, and had advanced the power of the French king to the hazard of these kingdoms. The measure disabled him from the succession, and enacted that all acts of sovereignty committed by him should be high treason and punishable by death. On the demise of the crown, the crown should devolve on the next in succession, as if the duke were dead.

From this, the House turned to the investigation of moneys paid to members of the previous parliament by Sir Stephen Fox from secret-service funds. Forced to name the pensioners, Fox gave a long list of grants of between £200 and £500 per annum, mostly out of the Excise;[3] and the committee of investigation found that £20,000 per annum had been paid by the commissioners of Excise to members of the last parliament. Here was another plot. Sir Francis Winnington declared that several witnesses willing to make discoveries had been threatened; he was personally afraid to have any of his papers about him, lest he might be served as Godfrey was. Then came the explanations. One of the members on Fox's list (sir John Talbot) showed how he had come by the money—he had taken an Excise farm and paid the rent, when Clifford made a bargain over his head with other farmers before his lease was out; so

his control of the Post Office to prevent the examination of suspicious letters; (4) he had advised the breach of the Triple Alliance; (5) he had maintained friendship with the French king for promoting popish designs; (6) he had procured commissions in the Navy for Papists; and (7) he had tried to discredit Oates's testimony.

[1] *Grey*, vii. 260, Sunday, May 11, 1679.
[2] Ibid. vii. 314.   [3] Ibid. vii. 323–4.

the pension was compensation for his surrender of the lease.
Other members followed with equally unspectacular explanations of the payments which they had received; and the sum
of it all was a demonstration that the moneys were not really
for 'secret service' at all, but were payments consequent on an
extremely clumsy and wasteful fiscal system. These actuarial
investigations were suddenly interrupted (May 27) when Black
Rod knocked at the door and summoned the Commons to the
Lords, where the king, having passed the Habeas Corpus Amendment Act, prorogued parliament to August 14, 1679. But before
that date it was dissolved by proclamation.[1]

The balance of success as between Charles and his third
parliament had on the whole been with the king. By a pretext
of conciliation he had united his enemies with his friends in a
harmless council, and he had neutralized some of the activity
of Shaftesbury by the fiction of confidence. He had thrown over
Danby; but, as the Commons never succeeded in bringing him
to trial, there had been no damaging disclosures; moreover, the
prerogative of pardon, contested by the Commons, had not been
disallowed by the Lords; and, as most of the energies of the
opposition had been concentrated on the Papists, they had been
diverted to that extent from the crown. The Exclusion Bill had
been shelved by prorogation, and so Charles might hope to
gain something from time, the most valuable asset for a man
facing a host of enemies. Never had Charles been more solitary;
and he was also handicapped by relatives who had none of his
tact: by York in Brussels, fuming at the royal offer to restrict
some of the powers of the successor to the throne; by Monmouth,
fresh from his triumph at Bothwell Brig (June 22, 1679), a ready
tool for cleverer men; and lastly by William of Orange, now
being cultivated by Henry Sydney, envoy at The Hague, who
was acting in co-operation with Halifax and Essex.[2] Finally,
Charles was forced to acquiesce in the judicial murders which
throughout the year 1679 were removing men whom he knew
to be innocent.

These executions followed quickly on each other throughout

---

[1] *Steele*, i. 3691, July 12, 1679.

[2] For their correspondence see *Diary of the times of Charles II . . . by Henry
Sidney, earl of Romney* (ed. R. W. Blencowe, 2 vols.).

the greater part of 1679. Coleman had been executed in December 1678; then followed the Jesuits Ireland, Pickering, and Grove, together with Green, Berry, and Hill, the supposed murderers of Godfrey. In June 1679 came the turn of Whitbread, provincial of the Jesuits, with his colleagues Fenwick, Harcourt, Turner, Gavan, and the barrister Richard Langhorne, all convicted on the testimony of Oates and Bedloe. There was more game in reserve, for the popish lords were in the Tower awaiting trial. In July occurred the first misfire, when at the trial of sir George Wakeman (accused of attempting to poison the king) Scroggs, in his summing up, went so far as to question the evidence of Oates, who had not hesitated to hint at the co-operation of the queen. It was like questioning the truth of the Bible, but it had sufficient weight with the jury to induce them to return a verdict of Not Guilty. Contemporaries believed that the judge had been bribed by the Portuguese; but, on the other hand, the introduction of the queen's name may have caused the Court to give a hint to the judge. That he took a grave risk was shown by the fact that Oates and Bedloe exhibited articles against him before the privy council on the counts that he had disparaged their evidence, and had misdirected the jury; moreover popular indignation against Scroggs, because of his conduct in this case, helped to reinforce the demand that judges should hold office not *durante bene placito*, but *quamdiu se bene gesserint*. So the establishment of judicial responsibility and impartiality was due as much to indignation at the inspired fairness of Scroggs as to satisfaction with the anti-Catholic bias of his brethren.

Throughout these events the one element of continuity was the crown. Had Charles died at any time in 1679 there would probably have been a revolution; this was brought within measurable distance by the sudden and serious illness of the king in August of that year, when the duke of York had to be sent for from his exile; and for a moment it seemed that the monarchy itself would disappear in the whirlpool by which it was surrounded. But Charles quickly recovered, and it was now as necessary to get rid of the royal brother as it had been to secure his attendance; for it was known that his stay in England would do more harm than good to the Catholic cause; indeed

pope Innocent XI pressed upon him the necessity of moderation, and the desirability of postponing, in the interests of the
faith, all active measures.[1] The duke would have preferred to
stay, and would have used French support and the army in
order to establish himself securely; but at last he was induced
to depart by a bribe—the sacrifice of Monmouth, whose popularity in the summer of 1679 was, next to the Plot itself, the most
serious asset in Shaftesbury's propaganda. Having been deprived of his post of commander-in-chief, Monmouth was exiled
to Holland (Sept. 24); and a few days later the duke of York
returned to Brussels, ostensibly in order to continue his exile, but
really in order to fetch his wife and take her with him to Scotland,
where (despite the vehement protests of Shaftesbury) he was to
serve as High Commissioner to the Scottish estates. Thus early
had the balance in favour of the crown been redressed. Monmouth was removed from his adherents in England, and the
duke of York now succeeded to the prerogatives of Lauderdale.
Even the moderates were divided; for while Essex was for exclusion, Halifax was still in favour of the duke's succession, with
restrictions. Thus Charles's illness and recovery prepared the
way for the break-up of the opposition, and rallied the waverers
to the cause of monarchy and legitimacy. Before the end of 1679
it was being demonstrated also that the weapons of the plot-
mongers could be turned against themselves, as was shown by
one Thomas Dangerfield, who claimed to have discovered a
great 'presbyterian' or whig plot, the evidence having been concealed under the meal tub of his female associate Mrs. Cellier.
His disclosures, which implicated Halifax and Essex, had all
the appearance of a popish counter-move; but it proved to be a
plot within a plot, and Dangerfield then accused prominent
Catholics of having planned it.

The new or fourth parliament had been summoned for
October 7, 1679; but when it met, both Houses were immediately prorogued and then adjourned by successive stages for
a year. One reason for this was that throughout the autumn
months of 1679 Charles was trying hard to secure a subsidy
from Louis that would help him to dispense with parliament,

----

[1] Innocent XI to the duke of York, Sept. 1679, in *Add. MS.* 15395, f. 188,
quoted in Campana de Cavelli, *Les derniers Stuarts*, i. 302.

but, as the sum could not be agreed upon, these negotiations lapsed.[1] Charles's immediate object at this time was to save the succession; so he decided to rule by councillors of his own choice. Shaftesbury was therefore dismissed from the Council (Oct. 1679); and the stage was cleared when Halifax and Essex, disgusted by the long prorogation, went into temporary retirement. Having divested himself of parliamentarians, Charles now formed a ministry of courtiers to which the name The Chits has been given; this consisted of Sunderland (a secretary of state), and two young commissioners of the Treasury—Sidney Godolphin and Lawrence Hyde, of whom the latter was appointed first lord of the Treasury on November 19. These men were in office primarily as royalists and opponents of exclusion; they were nominally committed to the cause of the duke of York and the projected French alliance, and all three were in correspondence with the prince of Orange.

This, the earliest tory cabinet, was therefore an accommodating ministry, anxious above all to protect itself against sudden changes in the political barometer, primarily responsible to the king, on good terms with both York and Orange, and anxious to have something to show when parliament met. Individually, each was not without personal distinctiveness. Lawrence Hyde, afterwards earl of Rochester, inherited the great Anglican traditions of his father, and was useful as a secular representative of the Church of England; he had some ability in finance, but in character he was haughty and arrogant. Sidney Godolphin, afterwards first earl of Godolphin and minister of queen Anne, had also a good head for figures, but he had greater agility, and a certain permanent manner of unobtrusiveness. As occasion required he shed his toryism for whiggery, and the extreme caution of his political speculations ensured

---

[1] In July 1679 Charles made it known to Louis XIV that he was determined to prorogue parliament in order to give Louis time to make up his mind regarding his English policy and his interest in preserving the Stuart monarchy. *Aff. Étr. (Angleterre)*, 135, f. 70, July 24. Charles at first demanded a subsidy of six million livres, but reduced his price; the duke of York guaranteed the entire dependence of England on Versailles for two million livres a year. *Baschet*, 143, Sept. 25/Oct. 5, 1679. On Sept. 4 the duke of York wrote to Louis begging the renewal of the subsidy as his (the duke's) affairs were desperate. *Aff. Étr. (Angleterre)*, 135, f. 169.

him a considerable measure of success. More enigmatic was Sunderland. He was probably the ablest of the three; though he made some wild plunges, as when he supported the cause of exclusion, lost his post and then had to work hard for several years in order to restore himself. Endowed with a 'managing' disposition, he co-operated with the duchess of Portsmouth in the enterprise of 'mothering' Charles, so that the monarch should as far as possible be spared trouble. This tutelage he afterwards exercised with greater success on James. He was the most ingratiating and subtle of the three; a representative of that type of minister which could have retained high office only under a Stuart dynasty. The real function of this ministry was to serve Charles's object of gaining time by the fiction of concession; and even Shaftesbury was included in this policy; for in January 1680 he had nightly interviews with the king, in which a compromise was discussed, on the basis of a Protestant marriage for Charles in return for a life revenue.[1] Halifax was urged by his brother-in-law Sunderland to emerge from his retirement at Rufford in order to give some much-needed prestige to the administration;[2] there was some talk of an alliance with Holland, and there was actually signed (June 10, 1680) a treaty of union and defence with Spain,[3] limited to Europe, by which it was agreed that, if the one were attacked, the other would come to his aid within three months of being asked to do so. The Chits made no secret of their belief that this treaty would be very useful for parliamentary purposes.[4] Once more, the French ambassador found himself unable to follow the gyrations of English politics; so he decided to wait for the return of James before renewing the treaty negotiations,[5] and sent this message to Louis: 'it would be very difficult to explain to Your Majesty what is the real design of the king of England and his ministers';[6] and a few days later he had to confess that England was more concerned with horse-races and cock-fights than with anything else.[7]

During this year of parliamentary recess (Oct. 1679–Oct.

---

[1] *Baschet*, 144, Jan. 8/18, 1680.   [2] *Halifax*, i. 208.
[3] *Dumont*, vii, pt. ii. 2–4, Windsor, June 10, 1680.
[4] *Baschet*, 145, June 17/27, 1680.   [5] Ibid. 144, Feb. 12/22.
[6] Ibid. 144, March 11/21, 1680.   [7] Ibid. 145, March 29/April 8.

1680) there seemed no limit to the insanity through which the nation was passing; for no class was spared by the infection, whether the London mob, inflamed by their pope-burnings, or the landed nobility, encouraged to fear that, under a papist king, they would have to restore their church lands. 'Any who have estates in abbey lands,' declared a pamphleteer,[1] 'who desire to beg their bread, and relinquish their habitations and fortunes to some old, greasy, bald-pated abbot, monk, or friar, then let him vote for a Popish successor.' Never before were the printing-presses so busy; for men who hitherto had been content to leave politics to the gossips now turned to the printed reports of trials, and the narratives of gunpowder and incendiary plots, all of them providing crude material from which was to be created a vivid political consciousness. 'Since this damnable Popish Plot has been discovered', declared countryman Hodge in a printed dialogue, 'there have come out so many notable good and bad books on all sides that I vow to thee I am become sublime like a philosopher, and can hold out *pro* and *con* with the best of them.'[2] The autumn of 1679, with its national anniversaries and civic processions, brought the climax, and on the annual commemoration of Elizabeth's accession (Nov. 17) there was a pope-burning attended (it was said) by 200,000 persons,[3] the ritual culminating in a conflagration under the statue of queen Elizabeth. The order of the procession was thus:

Six whistlers to clear the way.

A bell-man ringing and shouting, 'Remember Justice Godfrey'.

A dead body, representing Sir Edmund Berry Godfrey, in the habit he usually wore, the cravat wherewith he was murdered about his neck, with spots of blood on his wrists, shirt and white gloves, riding on a white horse, one of his murderers behind him to keep him from falling, representing the manner he was carried from Somerset House to Primrose Hill.

A Jesuit giving pardons very freely to those who would murder Protestants.

Six Jesuits with bloody daggers.

A consort of wind music called The Waits.

Four Popish bishops in purple and lawn sleeves.

[1] *Appeal from the country to the city* (1679).
[2] *Humble Hodge and Ralph holding a Discourse* ... 1680 in *Bodley, Ashmole*, 737.
[3] *Diary of Henry Sidney* (ed. Blencowe), i. 190.

The Pope's chief physician with Jesuit's powder[1] in one hand and an urinal in the other.

Lastly, the Pope, preceded by silk banners with bloody daggers painted on them for murdering heretical kings, and behind him his counsellor the Devil.[2]

Nor was the excitement confined to London; for the Plot spread to Yorkshire,[3] where there was a conspiracy of informers (headed by one Robert Bolron, the Oates of the north) to take away the lives of prominent Catholics, including sir T. Gascoigne, who was accused, among other things, of plotting to murder the king and set fire to both London and York. Gascoigne, a man of 85, was tried in London and acquitted (Feb. 1680). Shaftesbury made frantic efforts to extend the Plot to Ireland, and urged that the English penal laws should be enforced there. When he failed to procure the passage of such measures as would goad the Irish Papists into rebellion he organized a campaign to obtain Irish informers, who for comparatively small sums could be induced to swear anything.[4] These men came out of Ireland 'with bad English and worse clothes, and returned well-bred gentlemen, well-caronated, periwigged and clothed', their brogues and leather straps changed to fashionable shoes and glittering buckles.[5] But soon these informers were being paid by the Court to give evidence against the opposition, including Shaftesbury himself.[6] Nor was the Plot confined to land. In the last days of the Third Parliament there had been talk in the Commons of a 'sea plot' in which Pepys, from his connexion with the duke of York, was said to be implicated, and in May 1679 the diarist's domestic affairs were carefully scrutinized by the House on the accusations of a

---

[1] i.e. quinine, then just coming into use.

[2] This description, with an engraving, will be found in *Bodley*, *Wood*, 417.

[3] For this see T. B. Parkinson, *The Yorkshire branch of the Popish Plot*, in *The Month*, xviii (1873). An account of the trial of Gascoigne will be found in *Bodley*, *Wood*, 426, no. 2.

[4] *Ormonde*, iv. 582 sqq. These men were drilled by Oates and by one of Shaftesbury's agents named Hetherington. The disclosures of one of them, Carey Murphy, will be found in *Cal. S.P. Dom.*, *1682*, 603.

[5] Ormonde to the earl of Arran, Nov. 17, 1681, in *Ormonde*, v. 164.

[6] For the crown's use of spies and informers see J. Walker, *Secret service under Charles II and James II* in *Trans. R.H. Soc.*, series iv, xv.

dismissed butler, who alleged that Pepys was scheming something with an alien named Morello, who had been seen at mass in Somerset House. The sum of the butler's evidence was that Pepys remained with Morello until three in the morning singing psalms; but this testimony was discounted to some extent when Pepys showed that his accuser had a grievance against him, having been dismissed for an affair with a housemaid.[1]

In truth, the history of England at this time was providing apt comment on the old proverb, 'the Devil is as bad as the broth he is boiled in'. Round Oates there surged a broth, all the ingredients of which had the same characteristic flavour. Incriminating letters were found behind wainscots or at the bottom of tubs; concocted papers were 'planted' on victims and then searched for; accused persons turned informers, and victimized others; the families of the arch-informers took up the prosperous trade of papist-hunting, or made money by informing against their own relatives; confessions were recanted and again sworn-to; both truth and honour were completely dissolved in this boiling mass. As every age has its favourite malady, so it has its special sin; whether it be corrupt litigation, as in the later middle ages, or blackmail and certain kinds of company-promoting in modern times. During the Popish Plot an outlet for pent-up evil was provided by informing. The imitators were not built on the grand lines of their original; but they kept the trade going nevertheless. Tonge's son, Simson Tonge, dabbled in the profession, and obtained small sums from patrons who induced him to swear that the original plot had been invented by his father and Oates; but this enterprise became extremely complicated when one of the parties turned traitor, and stole important papers while his confederates were being entertained to a fish dinner in the Savoy by M. Choqueux, who appears to have exchanged pyrotechnics for plots;[2] so, too, the family of Oates were proving that aptitude can be trained as well as inherited, and soon they hoped to emulate the master himself.[3] As Titus had his followers in Bedloe, Prance, Bolron, and Dangerfield, so even the unfortunate Godfrey had an

[1] *Grey*, vii. 304–10.
[2] For Simson Tonge see his affidavit in *H.M.C. Rep.* xi, app., pt. ii. 246–50.
[3] For the Oates family see *infra*, 640.

imitator in a Protestant magistrate named John Arnold, who
claimed to have been savagely attacked by Papists in Bell Yard,
Fleet Street, on April 15, 1680.[1] When originality was at an
end, the past was raked for supplies, which were heated up for
immediate consumption; from the ashes there glowed again the
Fire of London, the Gunpowder Plot, and the infamies of Mary,
queen of Scots; while above the smoke of the pope-burnings
towered the statue of queen Elizabeth, the sardonic emblem of
outraged Protestantism.

But as the Plot worked itself out the squibs failed to explode.
The assault on Arnold was construed as one more Jesuit attempt
at murder, but a surfeited populace refused to be excited by it;
Dangerfield was busy laying informations against prominent
Catholics, but his inconsistencies were too great, even for that
age; Shaftesbury, still working at his Irish Plot, announced that
he was in danger of being assassinated, but even this possibility
did not arouse the apprehension which he had expected. Oates
was not yet a bishop, nor even a doctor of divinity of Oxford;
worse still, his salary was reduced in July 1680 from £12 to £2
per week, and so he was obliged to combine his coaching of
perjurers with the ferreting out of concealed Catholic estates.
His decline had begun, a decline accentuated by acrimonious
disputes with Tonge about the proprietorship of the original
Plot. Most signal failure of all, when Shaftesbury procured the
indictment of the duke of York and the duchess of Portsmouth
as popish recusants, the judges in Westminster Hall, by collusion
with the Court,[2] discharged the juries summoned to adjudicate
on the Bills. Thus Charles had acted wisely in giving England
one year of respite from parliamentary government in order that
the excitement of the Plot might subside; but the embers were
still red, and his fourth parliament was to prove as unfriendly
as the third.

The meeting of parliament in October 1680 was preceded by
complicated negotiations, due to the unique possibilities then
confronting English diplomacy; for in the summer of 1680 England was in a position analogous to that of the earlier months
of 1678, when there had been a chance of the formation of a

[1] For Arnold see J. Pollock, op. cit., Appendix D.
[2] *Baschet*, 146, July 1/11, 1680.

general European confederation, consisting of England, the Emperor, Spain, and the States General; and already the English alliance with Spain (June 1680), coupled with the feint of overtures to the other two powers, had served to give Charles's policy an anti-French complexion. But men were now distrustful of these appearances, and so there was a chance that, whether by bribery or persuasion, the Spanish envoy Ronquillo and his Dutch colleague van Beuning might induce the Commons to insist on Charles going the whole way, and entering into active measures with the continental allies prescribed for him. Of the foreign envoys who were deputed to guide the House of Commons into the right path Barrillon was faced with the greatest number of difficulties. Hitherto French money had been directed to securing the elimination of England from decisive influence in European politics. With much difficulty, and at great cost, this object had, to a large extent, been achieved; but Louis was now at peace; so Charles's neutrality had for the moment lost its value. Money might still be spent in setting every party in England by the ears; but what did that lead to? Louis had begun by bribing the king; he was now spending money in bribing parliament; the duke of York wanted money, so also did Monmouth; and as each party was subsidized against the other, everybody's terms went up. The money was there, but not even Barrillon was sure how it should be spent.

To what useful object could French money be put? In May 1680 the French representative suggested bribing the 'Presbyterians'; but this might benefit only the prince of Orange. Money spent in defeating the objects of Charles and James might in the end benefit them more; nevertheless, money could always be usefully employed in bribing Montagu, and some clerks of the secretaries of state.[1] In July Barrillon reported that, acting on instructions, he was supporting Monmouth's cabal;[2] but a month later he noted the order that he was not to maintain close connexion with the Protestant duke.[3] A few days before he had informed Louis that as the duke of York's party was the feeblest, it might be well to support it,[4] apparently on the principle of preserving the balance of power in the internal affairs

[1] *Baschet*, 145, May 24/June 3.
[2] Ibid. 146, July 8/18.
[3] Ibid. 146, Sept. 27/Oct. 7.
[4] Ibid. 146, Sept. 9/19.

of England;[1] in November, he thought it expedient that Monmouth should imagine that France was supporting him, so that he might not suspect Louis's real design of supporting the duke of York;[2] but this piece of deception would cost more money, as Montagu (who was already being paid as a spy) was acting in the interests of Monmouth, and would demand an extra subsidy when he knew that his principal was being cheated. Late in November 1680 Barrillon announced that his main object was to prevent the union of Charles with his country;[3] but in February of the following year he urged that it was Louis's interest to preserve the monarchy in England, and that the interests of Catholicism in England were bound up with the succession of the duke of York.[4] Such is a small selection from the voluminous correspondence with the help of which Louis formulated his schemes for England.

What really were Louis's intentions? It has been contended by historians that the neutrality which Louis enforced on England was the most brilliant of his many diplomatic achievements, and that throughout his relations with England the French king was directed by motives of foreign policy. There are difficulties in the way of both views. That Louis secured English neutrality is certain; but it is not so clear that he obtained substantial benefit therefrom, since his gains by the treaty of Nimeguen were ludicrously incommensurate with the objects which had induced him in 1672 to declare war, and most of his conquests after 1678 had to be surrendered at the peace of Ryswick. Moreover, by 1678 the English Navy was in a state of temporary decay, and certainly could not have interfered with the territorial *réunions* on which Louis embarked after 1681. Nor could Louis have feared the English Army, because in numbers it was but a small fraction of his own; nor could he have valued it as an ally, because English personal dislike of France was notorious. Louis made no secret of his belief in two things: that, so far as military strength was concerned, England might be ignored,[5] and that in

---

[1] *Baschet*, 146, Sept. 20/30. [2] Ibid. 147, Nov. 18/28.
[3] Ibid. 147, Nov. 25/Dec. 5. [4] Ibid. 148, Feb. 3/13, 1681.
[5] 'Quoiqu'il n'y ait plus rien à espérer de son [of Charles II] alliance, ni à craindre de son inimitié, néanmoins l'intérêt que j'ai à maintenir la royauté en Angleterre ne me permet pas d'abandonner ce prince [duke of York]

his engagements with him Charles II had played him false.[1] So far, therefore, as foreign policy was concerned, the considered opinion of Louis XIV was that, after 1678, English neutrality was not worth purchasing; and it is probable that he was right.

It has already been seen that, in negotiating the treaty of Dover, Louis was inspired not by economic interests, nor even by consistent motives of continental policy, but by righteous indignation and a desire to assist in the restoration of Catholicism in England.[2] There was a certain profuse sentimentality and hazy idealism in the character of Louis XIV, to which even high policy was sometimes subordinated; and though, by 1680, he had to admit that the enforcement of Catholicism would have to be abandoned, he was nevertheless very anxious that the persecution of Catholics should cease, that the Catholic Church in England should be preserved, and that the interests of the faith should be maintained by a strong Catholic monarchy.[3] He had lost his faith in Charles, but he had great faith in James, and consequently he was anxious that the duke should remain by his brother's side in order to counteract the vacillation of the monarch, and to provide a bulwark for monarchy and the Catholic religion. It was for these reasons, not in order to secure English neutrality, that the subsidy was renewed in March 1681.[4] Louis XIV's calculations were based on the assumptions that Charles was politically negligible as well as unreliable, and that James was the man from whom

dans l'extrémité où il se trouve.' Louis XIV to Barrillon, Jan. 26/Feb. 5, 1681, *Aff. Étr. (Angleterre)*, 142.

[1] 'Vous le savez que je dois être persuadé par une longue expérience que je ne puis faire aucune fondement sur les traités que le roi d'Angleterre pourrait faire avec moi.' Louis XIV to Barrillon, Jan. 14/24, 1681, in *Aff. Étr. (Angleterre)*, 142.   [2] *Supra*, i. 336-7.

[3] In July 1679 Louis declared that his chief desire in regard to England was 'd'empêcher la ruine de la religion Catholique', *Aff. Étr. (Angleterre)*, 135, f. 40. In September of the same year he defined his object as 'la confirmation de la royauté et de la religion Catholique en Angleterre', ibid., f. 177.

[4] 'Je ne lui demande point d'autre reconnaissance des 500,000 écus que j'offre de lui faire payer chaque année que celle de se rétablir par la prorogation de son parlement dans la juste possession de l'autorité royale . . . de rappeler ensuite auprès de sa personne le duc de York, et j'aurais à lui demander pour mon intérêt, mais encore plus pour le sien propre et celui de sa couronne, de ne plus attirer la colère de Dieu par d'injustes persécutions des Catholiques.' Louis XIV to Barrillon, Jan. 14/24, 1681 in *Aff. Étr. (Angleterre)*, 142, f. 67.

salvation might yet come to England, assumptions which were
not challenged by Charles so long as he got the money.

Charles's fourth parliament commenced its first session on
October 21, 1680, when the king announced that the proroga-
tions had been very useful to him as he had been enabled to form
an alliance with Spain. He pointed to the danger threatening
Tangier from the assaults of the Moors and the need of money
for its defence. A further examination of the Plot having been
recommended, Charles made a plea for unity among his subjects,
because 'all Europe have their eyes on this assembly'.[1] The first
act of the Commons was to bring Dangerfield to the bar in order
to hear his revelations; they then debated the proclamation[2]
forbidding petitions against the prorogation or dissolution of
parliament; they resolved also (Oct. 27) that it is, and ever has
been, the right of English subjects to petition the king for the
calling and sitting of parliaments, and that to represent such
petitioning as seditious was to betray the liberty of the subject.[3]
Francis Wythens (later known as knight and judge) was then
expelled the House for having promoted, during the recess, an
address to the king expressing abhorrence of the petitions. Two
names were thus introduced into political terminology—Peti-
tioners and Abhorrers. After ordering their votes to be printed,
the Commons brought in a second Exclusion Bill,[4] which not
only debarred James from the succession, but declared him guilty
of high treason if he should exercise authority or return to England after November 5, 1680. This measure was read for the first
time on November 4, when Jenkins opposed it in a speech which
hinted at the nature of the support being invoked by the prerogative.[5] The Bill, he claimed, was contrary to natural justice, because it condemned without conviction and without calling the
injured party to his defence; it was contrary to the principles of
their religion, since it dispossessed a man of his right for no other
reason than that he differed in point of faith; still more, the
kings of England held their right from God alone, and no power
on earth could deprive them of it. To pass the Bill would be to
make the monarchy elective. Lastly, it was against their oath of

[1] *L.J.* xiii. 610–11.   [2] *Steele*, i. 3703, Dec. 12, 1679.   [3] *C.J.* ix. 640.
[4] For its terms see *H.M.C. Rep.* xi, app., pt. ii. 195–7.
[5] *Grey*, vii. 418–20.

allegiance; for by binding all persons to the king, his heirs, and successors, the oath included the duke as heir presumptive. Nor could there be a dispensation of such allegiance. The astute Jenkins did not scruple to insist on the dilemma which confronted the advocates of exclusion.

The second Exclusion Bill passed the Commons on November 11 and was taken to the Lords by lord Russell, accompanied by a procession composed of members of parliament, with the lord mayor and aldermen of the city of London. Barrillon noted how dangerous for the monarchy was this union of the Commons with the City.[1] The House next turned to the question of Tangier. That it might fall into French hands was admitted; but there were two difficulties confronting the allocation of a vote for its defence—the money might be embezzled; and, even more, Tangier garrison was a nest of papists. Sir William Jones summed up the general feeling when he said: 'Tangier is a place of great moment, but I take the preservation of religion to be far greater.'[2] So the upshot of this debate was a resolution to present an address to the king representing the dangerous state of the kingdom. Meanwhile, the real struggle had been transferred to the Lords, where Essex and Shaftesbury (Nov. 15) spoke vehemently for the Exclusion Bill; and the debate was prolonged late into the night, the king and members of the Commons attending as spectators. For seven hours a forensic duel was maintained between Shaftesbury and Halifax, the latter answering his opponents sixteen times, and eventually winning the day by his persistence and eloquence. In these speeches he cited the duke of York's credit in Ireland and with the Fleet; he emphasized the danger of civil war and the efficacy of limitations; nor did he hesitate to condemn the conduct of Monmouth, who was present with his supporters.[3] As the night wore on, the tension became more extreme; when at last it was clear that Halifax had won over the waverers, several peers drew their swords, while others clustered round the orator to preserve him from violence. The Lords rejected the Bill by 63 to 30.[4]

---

[1] *Baschet*, 147, Nov. 15/25.   [2] *Grey*, viii. 5, Nov. 17, 1680.
[3] *Halifax*, i. 246–8.
[4] *Parl. Hist.* iv. 1215. The protest against its rejection was signed by 25 peers, including Monmouth, Shaftesbury, Sunderland, and Essex.

This was followed by an anti-climax in the Commons, when Hotham suggested that, since their Bill was rejected, they had no means of justifying themselves but by printing Coleman's letters.[1] This they agreed to do; they also adopted Montagu's motion for an address to the king advising the removal of Halifax from the royal counsels, and that he be declared an enemy of the king and kingdom.[2] Articles of impeachment were then read against Edward Seymour, treasurer of the Navy, which alleged that, of the £584,978 appropriated for the building of thirty ships, he had lent £90,000 for the continuance of the Army, after the forces ought by law to have been disbanded.[3] The conduct of Scroggs next engaged their attention. His sins were many; he had disparaged the evidence of Oates in the trial of sir George Wakeman; he had discharged the Middlesex grand jury when the duke of York was presented as a papist; against such misdeeds there could be no remedy, said Sacheverell, so long as judges were *durante bene placito*. The impeachment of lord chief justice North was next voted on the ground that he had advised the proclamation against tumultuous petitioning.[4] Having failed in their main object, the Commons were eagerly looking about for a victim; this they found in the aged lord Stafford, one of the five popish lords in the Tower; so on November 10 they resolved to commence with him. At the trial, which began in Westminster Hall on November 30, Oates, Dugdale, and Turberville swore that he had procured a commission from the pope, and had tried to arrange the murder of the king. On this evidence the Commons secured a conviction, and their helpless victim was executed. This was the only successful impeachment by the Commons in the reign of Charles.

In the few remaining weeks of its existence this parliament succeeded in passing resolutions which in many respects anticipated the settlement achieved after the Revolution. Late in November the Lords discussed 'heads' of Bills for securing the Protestant religion, including the proposals that, if the duke came to the throne, he should have no veto, and that he should have the legal capacity only of a minor; another proposal was that the king's marriage should be dissolved, and that he should be married

---

[1] *Grey*, viii. 21, Nov. 17, 1680.   [2] *C.J.* ix. 655, Nov. 17, 1680.
[3] Ibid. ix, 658-9, Nov. 20.   [4] Ibid. ix, 662, Nov. 24.

to a Protestant.[1] They considered also a Protestant Association Bill, whereby all bishops, judges, officials and members of parliament were to be formed into an association which was to take up arms on the death of the king, and remain armed until parliament met.[2] On November 23 they resolved on these general axioms: (1) no forces to be raised without parliamentary consent; (2) the proviso exempting the duke from the Disabling Act of 1678 to be repealed; and (3) the royal veto and the principles of appointment to spiritual and civil offices to be regulated for the contingency of a Catholic succession. Herein were the rough materials from which the Lords, under the guidance of Halifax, hoped to enforce limitations as the alternative to exclusion.[3]

The Commons went farther. They discussed legislation for these objects: to secure frequent parliaments; that judges should hold office only *quamdiu se bene gesserint*, and that the illegal exaction of money from the subject should be high treason.[4] They proposed to include in the Bill for regulating the trial of peers[5] a clause abolishing the lords' privileges under the statute *De scandalis magnatum*, and another clause whereby impeachments should have statutory continuance after the prorogation or dissolution of parliament;[6] and they resolved that no member should accept any office or place of profit under the crown without the consent of the House.[7] On November 27 the Commons presented a long address hinting at supplies for Tangier as the price of royal consent to exclusion;[8] this the king rejected.[9] On January 7, 1681, they resolved that no further supply should be granted until the Exclusion Bill was passed; that Halifax had given pernicious counsels, and was a promoter of popery; and that whoever should lend money on the security of the king's hereditary revenue would have to answer for it to parliament.[10] Realizing that their time was short, the Lower House hurriedly passed resolutions (Jan. 10, 1681) that whoever should advise His

---

[1] *H.M.C. Rep.* xi, pt. ii. 209–10.　　　　[2] Ibid. 210–11.
[3] *L.J.* xiii. 684. Repeal of the proviso exempting James and provision for the meeting of parliament on the king's death were embodied in the Protestant Security Bill. *H.M.C. Rep.* xi, pt. ii. 220–2.
[4] *C.J.* ix. 682, Dec. 17.　　[5] *H.M.C. Rep.* xi, app., pt. ii. 127 and 157.
[6] *Baschet*, 147, Dec. 20/30.　　　　[7] *C.J.* ix, 695, Dec. 30.
[8] Ibid. ix. 665–6.　　　　[9] Ibid. ix. 676, Dec. 15.
[10] Ibid. ix. 702.

Majesty to prorogue the existing parliament in order to prevent the passage of an Exclusion Bill was a betrayer of the king, a promoter of the French interest, and a pensioner of France; that Monmouth had been removed from office by the influence of the duke of York, and that the presentation of the Protestant Dissenters on the penal laws was grievous to the subject and an encouragement of popery. There was an anti-climax in the final resolution—that the Great Fire of London was the work of Papists.[1] In the midst of these momentous proceedings, the ominous tap was heard at the door and parliament was prorogued to January 20, but dissolved[2] on January 18, leaving 22 Bills depending and 8 ordered to be brought in.

3. EXCLUSION AND PARTY POLITICS: THE OXFORD PARLIAMENT, FEBRUARY–MARCH 1681

By dissolving parliament Charles was taking a grave risk, but at least the air was cleared. Halifax, who had again won the favour of the Court by his victory over exclusion, was alienated by the dissolution, mainly because it shelved the Lords' schemes for limitations as the only feasible alternative to exclusion; this caused him again to retire to Rufford. At the same time the 'exclusionist juncto', Sunderland, Essex, and Temple, were dismissed from the privy council, and Sunderland's secretaryship was given to lord Conway. Of these men, Temple went into final retirement at Sheen; Essex, whose political evolution had been unusually rapid, changed from a trusted minister of Charles and friend of the Orange interest to a keen opponent of the Court and a supporter of Monmouth; Sunderland, whose disgrace was caused as much by his tactless overtures to the prince of Orange as by his support of exclusion, devoted himself, with the help of Barrillon and the duchess of Portsmouth, to the recovery of office and influence. After this shaking out, there remained among the king's advisers only the duke of York (then in Scotland, talking of civil war); sir Leoline Jenkins, secretary of state, a firm believer in divine hereditary right; and Lawrence Hyde, second son of the chancellor, the chief ministerial supporter of legitimacy.

Meanwhile a birth has to be recorded—that of the modern party system. Its gestation was a long one, and the travail that

[1] *C.J.* ix. 703–4. [2] *Steele*, i. 3724.

ensued almost rent the nation in sunder. Many ancestors contributed to the lusty vigour of this new arrival in national life. There were men who, by family tradition or sentiment, had long been accustomed to range themselves with the Court; temperamental loyalists they might be called, such as Hyde, Seymour, Ormonde, Jenkins, lords Nottingham and North.[1] In different degrees these men preferred a bad king to a good opposition; they were churchmen to whom kingship was an essential part of religion; but only two of them, Ormonde and Seymour, can be considered absolutely disinterested in their devotion to the prerogative. Opposed to them were those who, while divided in allegiance between prince of Orange and duke of Monmouth, were united in one central doctrine, namely, the sovereignty of parliament, to be guaranteed by its frequent and regular summons, by its complete control of taxation, and by its freedom from the influence of the Court. This party believed (rightly) that James Stuart would not rule as a parliamentary sovereign; that, in alliance with France, he would try to introduce popery and absolutism. Rather than have such a bad king, they would change the succession altogether, and choose either the prince of Orange, the enemy of popery and France and therefore (by implication) likely to rule constitutionally, or the duke of Monmouth, whose illegitimacy was still more likely to ensure his subservience to parliament. Intermediate between these extremes were the Trimmers, represented by Halifax, Temple, and sir Thomas Littleton, who, while devoted to liberty and constitutionalism in the abstract, were prepared to tolerate a certain amount of imperfection in kings as in everything else:

Our government is like our climate. There are winds which are sometimes loud and unquiet, and yet, with all the troubles they give us, we owe a great part of our health to them; they clear the air, which else would be like a standing pool. There may be fresh gales of asserted liberty without turning into such storms or hurricanes as that the State should run any hazard of being cast away by them. . . . The cases themselves will bring the remedies along with them, and he is not afraid to allow that, in order to its preservation, there is a hidden power in government which would be lost if it was defined,

[1] For a good analysis of parties at this time see K. Feiling, *History of the Tory Party*, 187 sqq.

a certain mystery by virtue of which a nation may at some critical times be secured from ruin.[1]

The views of Halifax did not find their fullest expression until they were given volume and force in the torrential prose of Burke; moreover, the term Trimmer savoured of compromise and so was not a good label. Baptism ensured a more assertive individuality for each of the two extremes. Both 'loyalist' and 'yorkist' seemed too generous for use by opponents of the Court party; 'tantivy' served for a time to suggest riding post-haste to Rome; but eventually 'tory' met the case, because, as it meant Irish robber and outlaw, it emphasized the duke of York's alleged association with the wild Irish. As Ireland provided the name for one party, so Scotland supplied that of the other, for the reason perhaps that English civilization did not appear to provide anything suggestive of that degree of contumely which each party stigmatized in the other. At first, the opponents of the Court may have adopted for themselves the name 'Country Party' in a mood of deliberate self-depreciation, in the same way as the 'Sea Beggars' and the 'Old Contemptibles' took pride in epithets applied to them; for the term 'Country', as contrasted with 'Court', implied a certain ostracism or social disability, similar to that which prompted the contemporary use, in France, of the word *hobereaux* for those nobles who were not received at Versailles. But this may have been too subtle; 'fanatic' was a useful substitute; then 'petitioner', and finally 'whig', or Scottish outlaw and Covenanter, a type supposed in England to be as infamous as the Irish tory, and presumed to be as uniformly sanctimonious and cantankerous as his Celtic opponent was said to be irresponsible and treacherous. So the field was left clear for the two short terms of abuse, whig and tory; and into these moulds were poured the lava-like prejudices and passions which proceeded from the Exclusion controversy and the Popish Plot. It was not in the tepid amenities of academic debate, but in the vituperation of the street, the coffee-house, and the scaffold that the distinction of whig and tory took hold on the minds of Englishmen.

The distinction, as it emerged, pervaded almost the whole field of national life, and was as potent an inspiration for the frivolous

[1] *Character of a Trimmer* in *Halifax*, ii. 297.

as for the serious. It can be traced in oaths—that of the tories being 'God Dammee',[1] while that of the whigs (following Oates) was 'So help me *Goad*';[2] in colours, red ribbons for the duke of York and blue for Monmouth;[3] in drinks, coffee for many whigs, and beer for all tories, a preference which explains the antithesis between 'sotting' and 'plotting'.[4] Each party had its favourite English sovereign; for the tories were devoted to the cult of Charles I, while the whigs found their ideal in queen Elizabeth.[5] Each attributed to the other a definite origin. The tories, from their red ribbons, were mothered on the Scarlet Woman;[6] while the whigs must obviously be descended from the first of critics, the Devil; or directly from his descendant, Titus Oates; or they had been engendered from the spread of debauchery; or the increase of luxury, as evidenced from the fact that merchants' wives now dressed like noble-women, and every servant-maid had her silk gown and holland sleeves; or from the practice of travelling to such republican places as Amsterdam and Venice; or even from the increase of free schools, where boys remained until they were 16 or 17, and were then fit only for some idle trade or the university, where they were taught to preach and wrangle.[7] These distinctions were at least such as the most unlettered could understand.

There was the same uncouth vigour in descriptions of each other. The tory was thus described:

A Tory is a monster with an English face, a French heart and an Irish conscience. A creature of a large forehead, prodigious mouth, supple hams and no brains. They are a sort of wild boars, that would

---

[1] In Oct. 1680 sir Robert Carr, in the course of remarks to the effect that there was no Popish Plot but a Presbyterian Plot, was heard to use the words 'God Dammee'. He was sent to the Tower. *Grey*, vii. 385. 'Fannees' and 'God Dammees' were respectively Fanatics (whigs) and tories.

[2] *Character of an Ignoramus Doctor* in Bodley, *Wood*, 417.

[3] Luttrell, *Brief Historical Relation* (ed. 1857), i. 111, July 1681.

[4] And better it is to be honestly sotting
        Than live to be hanged for caballing and plotting.
                    The Pot Companions in Bodley, *Wood*, 417.

[5] e.g. *Honour and carriage of our English parliaments in the reign of Queen Elizabeth* (1681) in Bodley, *Ashmole*, 730.

[6] *Character of a Tory* in Somers Tracts (1750), pt. ii, vol. iii. 282.

[7] *Dialogue of a statesman and a countryman* (1681), in Bodley, *Ashmole*, 730.

root out the constitution . . . that with dark lanthorn policies would
at once blow up the two bulwarks of our freedom, Parliaments and
Juries; making the first only a Parliament of Paris, and the latter
but mere tools to echo back the pleasure of the judge. They are so
certain that monarchy is *jure divino*, that they look upon all people
living under Aristocracys or Democracys to be in a state of damna-
tion; and fancy that the Grand Seignor, the Czar of Muscovy and
the French King dropt down from Heaven with crowns on their
heads, and that all their subjects were born with saddles on their
backs.[1]

Brainlessness and effusiveness were the two accusations most
commonly made against the tories; but the whigs were as easily
caricatured, because of their associates; whether these were
Geneva or Salamanca Doctors, *ignoramus* juries, lay preachers,
or Scottish Covenanters. They were all, of course, 'Presbyterians'; the most common accusation against them was that
they reincarnated the men of 1641,[2] and their insistence on
abstract principle brought upon them the accusation of hypo-
crisy. 'These Geneva Whigs', noted a pamphleteer,[3] 'are demure,
conscientious, prick-eared vermin.' Chief justice Jeffreys was
voicing the same opinion when he referred in court to 'snivelling
saints', with their cropped hair and demure looks.[4] They were
really Jesuits disguised in Scotch bonnets.[5] Under the mask of
scruple the whig was changing 1681 to 1649:

His principles are like chaos, a gallimofry[6] of negatives. He talks
of nothing but new light and prophecy, spiritual incomes, indwell-
ings, emanations, manifestations, sealings . . . to which also the
zealous twang of his nose adds no small efficacy. He treads the anti-
podes to everything commanded, and for no other reason but
because commanded. . . . This little horn takes a mouth to himself,
and his language is Overturn, Overturn. His prayer is a rhapsody
of holy hickops, sanctified barkings, illuminated goggles, sighs, sobs,
yexes, gasps and groans. He prays for the King, but with more

---

[1] *Character of a Tory* in *Somers Tracts*, pt. ii, vol. iii. 282.
[2] Cf. the reprint in 1681 of John Birkenhead's sarcastic *Assembly Man*
(first published in 1647).
[3] *Letter from a friend in London to another at Salamanca*, in *Bodley*, G. Pamph.,
1678.
[4] *An exact account of the trial between sir W. Pritchard and T. Papillon* (1689), 29.
[5] *The Loyal Litany* (1681) in *Bodley*, *Wood*, 417.
[6] i.e. hotch-potch.

distinctions and mental reservations than an honest man would have in taking the covenant.[1]

There was one respect, however, in which the pre-eminence of the whigs could not be challenged—they had the best horses, and they inaugurated the close connexion between English politics and the turf. The tories, it is true, could boast the university of Oxford as their stronghold; but the whigs held an even more important national fortress—Newmarket; and even Charles failed to establish a tory racecourse at Winchester.

This last fact helps to support the view that the whigs were not the socially-ineligible fanatics caricatured by their opponents, since they included a considerable proportion of both the landed nobility and the landed gentry, as well as many city merchants and rich Dissenters. From these constituent elements can be deduced two of their fundamental principles—sanctity of private property and religious toleration. They were by no means a democratic body, and it is significant that, in his second *Treatise of Civil Government*, Locke insisted on his axiom that men enter into society in order to preserve their property, and that the main object of legislation is to provide 'guards and fences' to that property.[2] What gave real direction to whig doctrine was its concerted effort to adjust a fact to a maxim; the maxim was, 'The king can do no wrong'; and the fact, king Charles II was doing a great deal of wrong. The first was an abstraction; the second a certainty; they were to be harmonized by depriving the king of the opportunity of wrongdoing, and making his legislative innocence the standard in reference to which the guilt of his servants might be judged. From this flowed most of their distinctive doctrines; such as that the judicial bench should be independent of the Court; that the military forces should be parliamentary; that ministerial responsibility should be enforced by an unrestrained right to use the weapon of impeachment; that parliament should have the right to debate and criticize the king's speeches; and that placemen should be excluded from the House of Commons. They insisted on the sanctity of parliamentary privilege and tradition; and they were among the earliest exponents of a reformed franchise; but, after the

[1] *Character of a Protestant Jesuit* in *Bodley, Ashmole,* G. 12.
[2] Locke, *Of Civil Government,* ii, ch. xix.

Revolution, when they became strongly entrenched, this last ceased to be one of their distinctive doctrines. Consistently with the fiction of the king's absolute innocence, they would have taken from him two of his personal responsibilities—the right to choose his consort and the right to direct his foreign policy. Lastly, the contract theory as enunciated in the Bill of Rights and expounded by Locke gave a semi-philosophic element to whiggery; and so, by the time of the Revolution, this party might make some claim to both enlightenment and political morality.

It is easy, however, to read too much into the distinction of whig and tory as it was known during the Exclusion controversy. Provincialism still counted for much in English life;[1] parties were less clearly defined than personalities; politics were local rather than national, and a man might vote at the dictation of his landlord or militia officer; or the politics of a borough might reflect not a conflict of principle, but a contest among the neighbouring gentry, or even a feud between different trades. The strategy of the polling-booth was subtle, but it was not always the strategy of men fighting for a great cause.[2] Nevertheless, in the years 1678–81, there was one dominant influence which, for the time, made politics national. This was fear. It was the panic fear engendered by the Popish Plot which compelled Englishmen to take sides, and to concern themselves actively with matters of state hitherto beyond their ken; hence it was the simple choice of exclusion or a popish successor that crystallized amorphous masses of prejudice, instinct, and misgiving into the clear-cut forms of political party. The audacity of Titus Oates and the driving force of Shaftesbury set a pace which opponents could not follow; nor for many years afterwards could the tories boast a set of political doctrines comparable with those professed by the whigs.

To this extent the whigs might claim to be the party of progress, but this word was rarely used in the seventeenth century, and its connotation is distinctively modern. Both parties appealed to the past. The whigs were the heirs not only of the Puritan revolution, but of the accumulated labours of those scholars, jurists, and antiquaries who, earlier in the century, had

---

[1] For a good account of this see K. Feiling, *History of the Tory Party*, 14–18.
[2] For this see *supra*, 474–8.

discerned in the mists of remotest medievalism the majestic lines of a constitution wherein common law and civil right were supreme. It is true that these researchers committed (in perfect good faith) many mistakes of interpretation, and that the monument which they dedicated to the achievements of the past was little more than a record of their own aspirations; but nevertheless, since no tory was learned enough to expose misconceptions about the *Mirror of Justices*, or the *Statutum de tallagio non concedendo*, or Alfred's common-law judges, the whigs were left in undisturbed possession of their magnificent pedigree. On their side the tories could point to precedent even more hoary, because from the Old Testament they deduced a doctrine of divine and indefeasible hereditary right, whereby disobedience was counted for sin, and criticism for blasphemy. To the tory, therefore, government was both absolute and paternal, its unvarying principles expounded in the careers of biblical potentates and in the pages of Filmer's *Patriarcha*.[1] The unqualified submission entailed by these principles was not only a Christian duty, but was something which satisfied that natural instinct whereby men subordinate their wills to some great external force or personality, and at least this instinct is less artificial than the hypothesis of the social contract on which whig philosophy came to be based. But here, for a time, religion had to give way to philosophy; for it was an age of research into the forces of nature, and inevitably therefore the Old Testament lost some of its authority as a guide to statecraft; nor could divine right be satisfactorily adjusted to the newer creeds which rejected revelation for reason. In consequence, the title-deeds of toryism were called in question. That the creed survived at all may have been due to the warm blood of human sentiment with which it was permeated; it was with this that Bolingbroke, Burke, and Disraeli afterwards restored and recreated the party.

Such was the state of parties in January 1681 when the danger threatening the monarchy and the succession by the dissolution of parliament may have roused Charles from the lethargy

---

[1] Sir Robert Filmer died in 1653 and his manuscript of the *Patriarcha* was printed by the tories in 1680, and a second edition in 1685. It was considered by many as the classic English exposition of the theory of divine hereditary right. For this see J. N. Figgis, *The theory of the divine right of kings*.

into which he had fallen a few months before.[1] Now that
he was rid of both Halifax and Sunderland, he was less likely
to be deterred by the one or cheated by the other; and in
Hyde and Jenkins he had subordinates who, if not eminent,
were at least faithful and serviceable. He had survived a plot
in which his consort and brother were accused of the design of
murdering him; his natural son, Monmouth, was a tool in the
hands of experienced rebels; his nephew, the prince of Orange,
was displaying a public and occasionally tactless interest in
English affairs;[2] his House of Commons was demanding exclusion, and his Lords rigid limitations of the power of his successor;
everywhere there were rumours of the appeal to force and civil
war. It was not surprising, therefore, that Charles turned again
to France, as he was pressed to do by the duke of York, who
sent John Churchill from Edinburgh with the advice that
Charles should enter into such an engagement with Louis as
would enable him to dispense with parliament, and thereafter
engage in 'resolute counsels'. Only Hyde and the duke were in
the secret of the verbal treaty of March 1681, whereby Charles
undertook to free himself from the slender shackles of the
Anglo-Spanish treaty of June 1680, and take measures to counteract commitments to parliament that might be inconsistent with
the obligations which he was assuming by the treaty. Louis,
in return, promised to preserve European peace, and to pay
Charles two million crowns for the first year, and 500,000 crowns
for each of the succeeding years.[3] These were generous terms;
as in the secret treaty of Dover, the conditions imposed on
Charles were vague, and Louis appears to have desired not so
much English neutrality,[4] as the maintenance of friendly rela-

---

[1] Baschet, 147, Nov. 1/11, 1680.

[2] The evidence for this is in the Diary of Henry Sidney (ed. R. W. Blencowe),
passim. There is reason to believe that William, in spite of his friendly
correspondence with James, approved of the exclusion project. This is
asserted for a fact by lord Guilford, Add. MS. 32520, ff. 204–6. The Italian
envoy Rizzini states that, during his visit to England in the autumn of 1681,
William was reproved by Charles for encouraging the efforts to supplant
James. (Campana de Cavalli, Les derniers Stuarts, i. 378.)

[3] Baschet, 148, Feb. 3/13, 1681; March 4/14, March 7/17, and March
24/April 3.

[4] Supra, 600–1. 'Quant aux stipulations réciproques je vous ai déjà dit qu'il

tions with the Stuarts and the eventual succession of James. It is significant that Hyde referred to the subsidy as a gratuitous payment.[1]

According to Barrillon, Hyde had advised the dissolution of the fourth parliament, and now recommended that the fifth should be summoned to Oxford,[2] where the Commons, free from the influence of the London mob, might prove more conciliatory than their predecessors. From the point of view of the Court, therefore, the Oxford Parliament was a gamble, and from the point of view of Charles (already practically assured of the subsidy) it was little more than a comedy. But it was taken very seriously by the whigs, and a whole party organization was exercised at the elections by Shaftesbury,[3] whose efforts nevertheless failed to maintain the whig majority of the previous parliament.[4] The alternatives were exclusion or limitations. The latter, known as 'the expedient', had been formulated by Halifax, possibly at the suggestion of Littleton;[5] it had the approval of the king,[6] and contained these provisions: (1) banishment of the duke during his lifetime; (2) on the death of Charles, the princess of Orange was to be regent, and, failing her or her issue, the princess Anne; (3) if the duke of York had a son educated a Protestant, then the princess should have the regency only during the child's minority; (4) the regent was to nominate members of the privy council with parliamentary approval; and (5) the regent was to govern in the name of James, but it was to be a capital offence for any one to take up arms on behalf of James.[7] These conditions were less stringent than the limitations previously proposed, and their acceptance would have destroyed the party of Shaftesbury and Monmouth; they show how far Charles was prepared to go in order to secure peace.

n'était pas nécessaire de rien signer et je suis bien persuadé que le roi d'Angleterre étant dans une alliance secrète avec moi, il ne fera rien contre mon intérêt.' Louis XIV to Barrillon, March 4/14 in *Aff. Étr. (Angleterre)*, f. 227. This statement should be compared with Louis's earlier statement that he could not rely on Charles's promises, *supra*, 601.

[1] *Baschet*, 148, March 24/April 3.   [2] Ibid. 148, Jan. 27/Feb. 6.
[3] For this see E. Lipson, *Elections to the Exclusion Parliament* in *E.H.R.* xxviii.
[4] *Baschet*, 148, Feb. 10/20.   [5] *Halifax*, i. 286.
[6] Hyde to the prince of Orange, March 29, 1681, in *Prinsterer*, v. 490.
[7] *Add. MS.* 38847, f. 83.

The alternative to this was Shaftesbury's plan, that is, exclusion, together with (1) a recognition of the right of the people to have annual parliaments 'for the despatch of their important affairs', and (2) restoration of the liberty enjoyed until the last forty years of being free from guards and mercenary soldiers.[1]

The arrangements testified to the great things expected of this, Charles's last parliament. Lord Oxford's regiment was placed on the road from London to be ready for emergencies, and many members came armed. Elaborate provisions were made by the vice-chancellor of the university. All the younger students were required to go down, but their time of absence was to be counted for degrees; accommodation was procured for the court in Christ Church, Merton, and Corpus Christi; and all other available places were to be at the disposal of parliament. Each college housed those legislators who were old members, as had been done when parliament met at Oxford during the Great Plague. Convocation House was assigned for the deliberations of the Commons; the Geometry School (now occupied by the Bodleian) for the Lords. The king's arrival on Monday, March 14, was marked by a demonstration, people in the streets shouting into the royal coach: 'Let the King live and the Devil hang the roundheads'; there was such 'flinging about' and throwing of hats that several limbs were broken, and tables of reception were set out in the streets at which all who passed were forced to drink a health to Charles on their knees.[2] On Tuesday Charles was hailed in a speech by the Public Orator, and from the vice-chancellor he received one more bible for his collection.

Proceedings commenced on Monday, March 21, when the king in a speech, probably penned by Halifax, adjured the Commons not to lay such weight on any one expedient against popery as to determine that all others were ineffectual; without the safety and dignity of monarchy, he said, neither religion nor property was safe; he would therefore be willing to receive favourably any expedient for preserving the administration in Protestant hands, in the event of a popish successor coming to

[1] These were drawn up as instructions by the electorates for their representatives. B. Martyn and Dr. Kipps, *Life of the first earl of Shaftesbury*, ed. E. Wingrave Cooke, ii. 268.   [2] *Wood*, ii. 525 sqq.

the throne.[1] But this, the last formal exposition of the older prerogative, was made to an assembly the majority of which had already made up its mind. The Commons began by resolving to print their votes and proceedings; they then debated the miscarriage of the Bill to repeal the Elizabethan statute[2] which had passed both Houses in the preceding parliament. It was next resolved to impeach Fitzharris of high treason. Edward Fitzharris was one of the Irish informers employed by the Court against the whigs; and the Commons were convinced that, in an impeachment managed by themselves, some damaging disclosures would be made. Secretary Jenkins refused to carry this impeachment to the Lords, but after an angry debate he was obliged to comply.[3]

Not till Saturday, March 26, did the Commons debate the vital point—exclusion or a regency. Historical precedents were quoted in favour of the latter; but against these it was argued that the person of the king could not be divided from his power, and that, moreover, regency was never heard of except where the prince was a minor or a lunatic, when it had generally proved to be an unfortunate device. Sir Francis Winnington pointed out the inconsistency of making a man king and denying him the exercise of sovereignty; sir T. Meres reminded the House that their business was religion, and that something must be done for the people, to quieten their fears of popery.[4] The sense of the House was definitely against a regency, and it was then resolved to bring in the Bill excluding James and all popish successors from inheriting the imperial crowns of England and Ireland.[5] At this point a message was received from the Lords that they refused to accept the impeachment of Fitzharris, on the ground that they were not required to proceed on any one not a member of their own body. A minority in the Lords, led by Shaftesbury, had protested against this refusal, for the reason that an impeachment is at the suit of the people, and that there-

---

[1] *L.J.* xiii. 745–6.
[2] For this see *supra*, 457. The Elizabethan statute was 35 Eliz., cap. i; the Bill of repeal was sent up to the Lords on Nov. 26, 1680. *C.J.* ix. 664. It passed the Lords, but was not tendered to His Majesty for his assent. *C.J.* ix. 708.　　　　　　　　　　　　[3] *Parl. Hist.* iv. 1314.
[4] Ibid. iv. 1326–8.　　　　　　　　[5] *C.J.* ix. 711, March 26.

fore the Lords ought to entertain it;[1] but meanwhile, intimation of the Lords' decision produced consternation in the Lower House, which contrasted this denial with the Lords' willingness to take up the cause of Skinner in his original plea against the East India Company. Once more the Commons had to admit that they were in the dark. 'There is something in this more than ordinary,' said sir Robert Howard; to Maynard, it seemed that the action of the Lords had made them no parliament; sir T. Player interpreted the Lords' conduct as confirmation of the plot to murder the king. The Commons at last brought a momentous day to a close by resolving that it is the undoubted right of the Commons to impeach before the Lords any peer or commoner for treason, or any other crime; and that the Lords' denial of this principle in the case of Fitzharris was a violation of the constitution of parliaments and an obstruction to the further discovery of the Plot. They resolved also that for any inferior court to proceed against Fitzharris was a breach of the privilege of parliament.[2]

On the same day as these resolutions were passed in the Convocation House a remarkable scene occurred in the Geometry School, where the king was present while the Lords were taking their places. By the aid of the marquis of Worcester, Shaftesbury passed to Charles a paper whereon was the proposal that, in order to guarantee the Protestant succession, the duke of Monmouth should at once be declared successor. There then followed a conversation between the two men, overheard by some of the peers, including Monmouth. Charles objected that the proposal was contrary to law and justice; Shaftesbury replied: 'If you are restrained only by law and justice, rely on us and leave us to act. We will make laws which will give legality to a measure so necessary for the quiet of the nation.' It was a tempting offer, and was made on behalf of a son whom Charles loved against the interests of a brother whom he disliked. But the bait was refused:

'Let there be no delusion,' said the king; 'I will not yield, nor will I be bullied. Men usually become more timid as they become older; it is the opposite with me, and for what may remain of my life I am determined that nothing will tarnish my reputation. I have law

---

[1] *L.J.* xiii. 755, March 26, 1678.   [2] *C.J.* ix. 711.

and reason and all right-thinking men on my side; I have the Church'—(here Charles pointed to the bishops)—'and nothing will ever separate us.'

In these words was the doom of Shaftesbury's cause.[1]

Charles may have derived a certain amount of amusement from the proceedings of his last parliament. On March 22, the day after its session commenced, he had definitely concluded his verbal treaty with Barrillon; and as the Commons were resolved on exclusion, it remained only to dissolve parliament. On Monday, March 28, the Commons read their Exclusion Bill, against which Jenkins repeated his old arguments, with the explicit addition: 'We ought to pay obedience to our governors, whether good or bad, be they ever so faulty or criminal.'[2] His speech passed without notice; his motion for rejection of the Bill did not even find a seconder, and his doctrines sounded out of place in the midst of allusions to *lex terrae* and *judicium parium suorum*. It was while Magna Carta was being cited in support of their impeachment of Fitzharris that the Commons were startled to hear the knocking of Black Rod on the door; this time they were not prorogued, but dissolved. 'It is His Majesty's royal pleasure and will that this parliament be dissolved; and this parliament is dissolved,' such was the formula in which the chancellor announced the sequence of cause and effect. Round them were tennis courts and college gardens on which the Commons might have reunited themselves by an oath more solemn than any which they had yet sworn; but they dispersed: some to London, others to the country, and many to the horse-races at Burford.

---

[1] *Baschet*, 148, March 28/April 7. The dispatch in full is printed in Christie's *Shaftesbury*, ii. cxvi–cxvii.
[2] *Parl. Hist.* iv. 1338.

XVII

THE STUART REVENGE, 1681–5

CHARLES, who had so long parried checkmate, could now deal leisurely with his pieces, and could select from a variety of alternatives the best method of attack on the disordered forces of Shaftesbury and the whigs. He could secure the support of the church by harrying Dissenters; he could win over the nation by persecuting Papists; he might release Danby from the Tower and restore the policy of Anglicanism and economy, or leave his ex-minister in custody and practise these virtues with the help of Hyde, Seymour, and Jenkins. Or he might choose to be guided by Halifax, and complete the discomfiture of the exclusionists by conciliating the Dissenters and the moderate whigs. A more daring plan was to be guided by the Duke of York and secure obedience and uniformity by exile and the gibbet. Of two things Charles was assured—the subservience of the judicial bench and a popular reaction in favour of the crown.[1]

Foreign affairs demanded immediate attention; for Louis was now provoking European opinion by his enforcement of pretensions on neighbours unable to retaliate. In the midst of Louis's *réunions* Charles had to maintain some degree of consistency between his public alliance with Spain and his secret agreement with France; for his subsidized 'neutrality' had now to withstand the scrutiny not of his parliament, but of his nephew. William realized that he had shown his hand too clearly in his dealings with the exclusionists; but he had sufficient confidence in his influence to think that he might yet obtain active English support against France. Accordingly, the old expedient of a personal visit was revived and, with the consent of Charles, he came to England late in July 1681, and at Windsor had a long interview with the king in the presence of Halifax (again restored to favour), with Hyde and the two secretaries, Jenkins and Conway. At this conclave the prince urged the intervention of England in order to save Flanders; he talked of the advisability

---

[1] For example, a large number of London apprentices offered to serve the king wherever he pleased and at their own expense. *Baschet*, 149, Aug. 11/21, 1681.

of summoning parliament, and hinted that if Charles preserved
an ambiguous attitude, the States General might send their ships
into the Thames in order to unite with the English people in the
demand that Charles should come into line with the Dutch. The
allusion was not a tactful one; but the king, who preserved his
patience, contented himself with reminding the prince that the
recall of parliament involved the revival of exclusion or limitation projects. Of these things William expressed his disapproval;
and when asked to suggest an alternative, he requested permission to confer with his friends in London. There he consulted
with lord Russell and other exclusionists, and his acceptance of
an invitation to attend a public dinner given by the lord mayor
and aldermen caused Charles to recall him to Windsor.[1]

But William did not go away empty-handed, for he added
to the number of his English correspondents, and restored his
amicable relations with Halifax; moreover, he had obtained some
promises from a king for whom it was now second nature to make
apparent concessions in order to gain time. Charles, it is true,
would not actively assist his Spanish ally until France declared
war; but he had promised William that, in the event of Flanders
being invaded, he would summon a parliament and break with
France; he promised also to join with the Dutch in a remonstrance against the aggressions of Louis.[2] In the verbal treaty the
French king had undertaken in a general way that he would not
disturb European peace; but when, in September, he took over
Strasburg and Casale, it was apparent that he did not interpret
this condition strictly, and it seemed inevitable that the English
king would have to implement his public promises. So one more
anti-French alliance was formed; this was the compact between
William and Charles XI of Sweden, whereby both united to
maintain the terms of the treaty of Nimeguen. If his promises
meant anything, Charles must join this league and summon parliament; he would thereby have the honour of heading a great
'peace' confederation, with the additional advantage that his
foreign policy would provide a remedy for internal troubles. To
this demand Charles replied that English interests did not extend
so far as those included in the treaty of Nimeguen; that the

[1] *Baschet*, 149, July 25/Aug. 4, 1681, and *Halifax*, i. 307–8.
[2] *Halifax*, i. 309.

German princes, far more than England, were concerned in that treaty, and that only when they, with the Emperor and Denmark, were included in the league would he join it. But, that this might not sound too uncompromising, it was coupled with a renewal of the promise to summon parliament if French troops invaded Flanders. This was the reply handed to the Dutch ambassador on November 8; it had previously been submitted to Barrillon, who received a verbal assurance that the promises contained therein would not be fulfilled. As the existence of the secret treaty was unknown to Halifax, the prince of Orange, the Dutch agents, and even the duchess of Portsmouth, all of these were deceived by Charles's response.[1]

Within a few weeks Charles's 'neutrality' was subjected to an even greater strain. In November Louis proceeded to invest Luxemburg, which he claimed as compensation for his cessions in Flanders; once more, therefore, it seemed inevitable that England must be dragged into continental politics. At Court there was talk of another parliament, and Halifax schemed measures for the conciliation of the extremists; below the surface was Ralph Montagu, soliciting more French money on the pretext that he could bribe the parliamentary leaders to acquiesce in neutrality.[2] Always polite and secretive, Barrillon listened to every one and assured them how innocuous were his master's designs. 'I am explaining how unimportant Luxemburg is,' wrote the French ambassador to Louis; 'it is not on a river, and cannot be used for the defence of the Low Countries. They will talk for a few days of Luxemburg as they did of Strasburg, and then, like the rest of Europe, they will be glad to have peace.'[3] But this proved true only in part. The French king was obviously threatening European peace, and if Charles was to hold his hand any longer, he must have an extra payment. So on November 21 Charles agreed with Barrillon to accept a supplementary sum of one million livres, in return for the promise that he would not hinder Louis's designs on Luxemburg. When, in December, the investment became a siege, Charles was so harassed by the difficulty of honouring his private promises and his public commitments that

[1] *Baschet*, 150, Sept. 29/Oct. 9, Oct. 13/23, Nov. 5/15, 1681, and *Halifax*, i. 322–3.

[2] *Baschet*, 150, Nov. 14/24.   [3] Ibid. 150, Nov. 7/17.

he begged Barrillon to extricate him: 'You know what devils my members of parliament are,' said the king; 'for God's sake get me out of this fix, or I shall have to summon parliament.'[1] The appeal was not in vain; if Charles could not get money from parliament, he could get money from the threat to summon parliament, and on this occasion he preserved reputation as well; for when, early in 1682, Louis announced that he had decided to raise the siege, this step was rightly attributed to the intervention of Charles.[2] Not until 1684, when there seemed little likelihood of parliament being summoned, did Louis eventually make himself master of Luxemburg. Meanwhile Charles, ostensibly shaping his policy under the sagacious direction of Halifax, had preserved money with honour, and his envoy in Paris could write: 'It is a most glorious figure which His Majesty makes abroad.'[3]

The king's choice of diplomatic personnel provided a further proof that he intended to retain his friendship with France and withstand the solicitation of the Dutch. In 1682 Henry Savile was succeeded in the Paris embassy by Richard Graham, lord Preston, a high tory, and a close friend of the duke of York; Henry Sydney (devoted to the interests of the prince of Orange) was recalled from The Hague and replaced by Bevil Skelton, whose French sympathies were so patent as to justify a protest from William; at the same time Bodmin was recalled from Copenhagen, Middleton from Vienna, and Charles Bertie from Germany.[4] At home, an early start had been made in the preparations for an era of non-parliamentary rule. In December 1679 the privy council had ordered retrenchments to be made in the pay of naval officers and seamen—one of the many indications that the English Navy would not be used for active intervention in European affairs; at the same time a committee was appointed to inspect the lists of justices of the peace in order to remove

---

[1] Ibid. 150, Dec. 12/22.

[2] *Add. MS.* 37980, f. 101, Chudleigh to Conway, May 2/12, 1682, and *Add. MS.* 34339, f. 86, van Beuning to Fagel, Oct. 12/22, 1682.

[3] Lord Preston to the bishop of Oxford, Dec. 31, 1681/Jan. 10, 1682, in *H.M.C. Rep.* vii, app. 278.

[4] For this see the introduction by F. A. Middlebush to *Despatches of T. Plott and T. Chudleigh, English envoys at The Hague* (in Ryks Geschiedkundige Publicatien).

unsuitable persons;[1] and three months later a circular letter was ordered to be sent to all corporations requiring them to put into force the Act of 1661 for their better regulation, and to report on how far they had achieved this object.[2] These steps were followed in December 1681 by an order-in-council requiring the justices to put into execution the laws against Papists, Dissenters, and conventicles. In this way Danby's principles of government were to be reproduced in a harsher form, with one important addition—the whole structure of local government was to be revolutionized, in order that the crown might be assured of the loyalty of justices, mayors, sheriffs, and council men. By these means the return of tory juries would be secured; and, if a parliament did have to be summoned, the reformed boroughs would be likely to return only tory burgesses. As this policy was developed, numerous loyal addresses from grand juries throughout the country confirmed Charles in the belief that he might depend on a large measure of popular support.

Against the whigs, the campaign commenced in the law courts. On April 11, 1681, Scroggs was removed from the office of lord chief justice and his post was conferred on sir Francis Pemberton, on whom the Court could rely. Two weeks later commenced the trial at the King's Bench of Fitzharris, when the grand jury returned a true Bill, after having been assured that it was fit for them to proceed in a matter which had already been the subject of impeachment by the Commons. What precisely was Fitzharris's crime may never be determined. By impeaching him, the Commons had hoped to prove the complicity of Danby and the duke of York in the Popish Plot; it is possible that he was in possession of important secrets, and the king was anxious that he should be hanged,[3] because he had been won over by the whigs with an assurance of pardon if he would reveal these secrets when impeached. His counsel included Winnington, Pollexfen, and Treby, then considered the ablest of the parliamentary advocates, who made a strenuous effort to induce the court to accept the plea that the accused could not be indicted before an inferior tribunal

---

[1] *P.C. Reg.* 68, Dec. 3, 1679. For the removals of justices see *H.M.C. Rep.* xi, app., pt. ii. 172–93. For the decline of the English Navy at this period see *supra*, i. 276, 280.

[2] *P.C. Reg.* 68, March 12, 1680. [3] *Baschet*, 148, April 4/14, 1681.

after indictment in a superior; but this plea was overruled by Pemberton, with the concurrence of Jeffreys. Not till June 9 did Fitzharris answer to the indictment, which set forth that he was the author of a libel *The True Englishman*, a pamphlet which charged Charles I with the authorship of the Irish rebellion, and Charles II with the exercise of arbitrary power; of special significance was the fact that the pamphlet cited the depositions of two kings, Richard II and Henry VI.[1] Everard, the chief witness against the prisoner, swore that Fitzharris had represented to him the advantages of adhering to the French and popish interests, and had suggested the plan of writing a seditious pamphlet in order 'to set England by the ears'. This pamphlet was then (according to Everard) to be delivered to père la Chaise in the name of the English Dissenters, and its authorship fathered on them.[2] Oates next gave evidence. He had been told by Everard that the pamphlet was to be printed and sent by the post to the most notable of the whig Lords and Commons, who were then to be 'taken up' for having it in their possession.[3] Oates had heard from Everard that the Court had a hand in the business. Other witnesses, including sheriff Cornish, sir William Waller, and lord Howard of Escrick, gave evidence pointing to Fitzharris's connexion with the Court.

Few of the witnesses called on his behalf could recollect the events alleged by Fitzharris. Secretary Conway attested that, to his knowledge, the king had employed the accused on some trifling business; the duchess of Portsmouth denied that she had received papers from him,[4] or that she had obtained by his means information of the intended impeachment against her; the money which she had given him was, she said, for charity. His witnesses having failed him, Fitzharris defended himself with the plea that his acts had been commissioned by the Court; that he had been doing paid, secret service. 'I hope what I did was with a design to serve the King in discovering what was designed against him. . . . I hope you will consider these are great persons that I have to do with; and where great state matters are at the bottom, it is hard to make them tell anything but what is for their advantage.'[5] He accused Everard of being the author of the libel.

[1] *The tryal and condemnation of Edw. Fitz-harris Esq.* (1681), 7–9.
[2] Ibid. 12–26.   [3] Ibid. 28.   [4] Ibid. 40.   [5] Ibid. 41.

The solicitor-general (Heneage Finch) and serjeant Jeffreys made short work of the defence. Finch reduced Fitzharris's argument to two heads: he was not the author of the libel, and what he did was for secret service. 'He would fain have it that you should believe the king should hire him to raise a rebellion against himself.'[1] That was precisely what the whigs suspected the Court of doing; it seemed incredible, but all the events of the last three years had been incredible, and now the jury was asked to believe that, because an incredible thing was imputed to the Court, it was therefore false. Serjeant Jeffreys followed with the conclusive argument that the prisoner was a Roman Catholic;[2] he had libelled the crown as well as Protestant witnesses; here was an Irish Papist who intended to set England by the ears and bring in the French. Then followed Pemberton's summing up. The libel was 'a piece of the art of the Jesuits'.[3] The king, it is true, had given Fitzharris money, but only for charity. It could not be believed that the king would do such things as had been laid at his door. The jury found him guilty, and he was executed at Tyburn on July 1. On the same day, and at the same place, was executed Oliver Plunket, Roman Catholic archbishop of Armagh, on charges originally brought by Oates in September 1678 to the effect that he had conspired to bring a French army to Ireland. He was the last victim of the Popish Plot, and died in the company of the first victim of the counter-attack.

The judicial campaign against the scattered forces of the whigs was soon in full swing. A joiner named Stephen College was put on his trial at the Old Bailey for seditious words and actions at Oxford during the meeting of the parliament there.[4] The Middlesex grand jury, selected by the whig sheriffs Slingsby Bethell and Henry Cornish, threw out the Bill with an *Ignoramus*. A mean device was then adopted to secure the conviction of a rash but harmless man who, with some native wit, spiced with obscenity, had made himself prominent during the Oxford parliament. It was contended that, as the acts complained of had taken place at Oxford, he should be tried there; and accordingly he was indicted at Oxford court-house on August 17, 1681, before

---

[1] *The tryal and condemnation of Edw. Fitz-harris Esq.* (1681), 44.
[2] Ibid. 46.   [3] Ibid. 48.
[4] *The arraignment, tryal and condemnation of Stephen College* (1681).

lord Norris, Francis North (lord chief justice of the common pleas), with justices Jones, Raymond, and Levinz. He was charged with having prepared arms at Oxford to wage war against the king, and with having intended to seize the king. The Oxfordshire grand jury returned a true Bill, and the trial that ensued was one of the most unfair in a period abounding in judicial murders; for College was refused both a copy of the indictment and a list of jury and counsel; he was not allowed access to his papers; and his plea that, as a freeman of the city of London, he was not impleadable outside the liberties of the city was overruled. The case against him was this: he had collected arms worth about twice the value of his estate, with the intention of seizing the king; he had armed himself with a horse, pistols, a coat of mail, a carbine, and a head-piece; 'and so, being armed cap-a-pee with that design he came hither to Oxford, and you will judge whether these be fit tools for a joiner'. Still more, he had induced others to join him, and had boasted that he would soon be a colonel; he had defamed the king in taverns and coffee-houses, and he was one of the accomplices of Fitzharris. If the matter were thoroughly inquired into, it would probably be found that he was really a papist in disguise.[1]

Dugdale, the first witness for the prosecution, deposed that College had referred to the king as one from whom nothing but arbitrary government could be expected; he had also received from the accused, for distribution, a supply of blue ribbon, on every quarter yard of which was inscribed the legend: 'no popery: no slavery'; he had also seen College carrying pistols, and he had heard him sing a song at lord Lovelace's house in which was the refrain, 'when all the bishops were changing their hats for cardinals' caps'. Dugdale admitted that the crown was paying his travelling expenses, but would not confess to any larger subsidy.[2] The informers Turberville and Haynes thereupon supported the evidence about seditious words and the hawking of blue ribbons. Oates then appeared in a role still unusual to him, namely as a witness for the defence; but unfortunately for College, the witness whose word was good enough to send nearly a score of innocent men to the scaffold did not now have sufficient credibility to save one innocent man. The Doctor

[1] Ibid. 16–17, speeches by the attorney-general.   [2] Ibid. 23.

swore (and here he may have been telling the truth) that, in talk about the College case, Turberville had said to him: 'The Protestants have deserted us, and God damn him, he would not starve.'[1]· This was a damaging innuendo against one of the witnesses for the crown; but from Oates it was valueless, and the attorney-general (sir Cresswell Levinz) sneeringly reminded Oates that he had changed sides, whereas Turberville had not. There then followed a duel between Oates and the witnesses for the prosecution; and, though College drew the attention of the court to statements made on his behalf by Oates, lord chief justice North suppressed him with the very unjudicial remark that there were three to one witnesses against him,[2] and brushed aside his defence with the significant words: 'Truth! Why, if yours or any man's word in your case should go for truth, no man that stands at the Bar could be convicted.'[3] These words aptly describe the attitude of Stuart judges in the majority of the political trials. College's ordeal had now been prolonged long beyond midnight, and feeling in the crowded court-room was tense; in vain did the accused protest that nothing of fact had been proved against him but a pair of pistols, a sword, and a horse. At three o'clock in the morning, amid a great shout, the jury announced a verdict of Guilty. He was executed on August 31, the first martyr of the whig cause.

But the Court was aiming at bigger game than the 'Protestant Joiner'; and already on July 2 Shaftesbury had been sent to the Tower on a charge of high treason. His papers were impounded; his application for bail or trial in terms of his own Habeas Corpus Act was refused on the ground that the Tower was outside the jurisdiction of the judges; likewise his offer to retire to Carolina, if released. Meanwhile 'evidence' against him was easily extracted from the Irish informers whom he had himself at one time suborned. On November 24 a special commission was issued for his trial, and he was indicted at the Old Bailey[4] of the *intention* of levying war against the king, which, in terms of the Act of 1661, constituted high treason. The grand jury of Middle-

---

[1] *The arraignment, tryall and condemnation of Stephen College* (1681), 48.
[2] Ibid. 50.   [3] Ibid. 82.
[4] *The proceedings at the Sessions House in the Old Bayly . . . against Anthony, earl of Shaftesbury* (1681).

sex (selected by the whig sheriffs) included sir Samuel Barnardiston (foreman), T. Papillon the merchant, and Michael Godfrey
(brother of sir Edmund and father of one of the first governors
of the bank of England). In his charge, Pemberton explained
how, by the Act of 1661, the treason law of Edward III had been
modified to include intention, even if no overt act followed; in
effect, therefore, words, if importing any malicious design against
the king's life or government, or any traitorous intention, were
now sufficient; and two witnesses each testifying to different or
the same words were enough. With a suggestion of menace in
his voice, Pemberton reminded the grand jury that compassion
was not their province,[1] and they must find a true Bill if there
was probable evidence for the accusation.

A hint of the careful preparation which had preceded the trial
was conveyed in the reason given by the judge in refusing the
jury's request for permission to examine the witnesses in private
—they need have no fear, he said, of betraying the king's secrets,
for the crown had carefully investigated its case, and so its witnesses were not likely to be 'raw'.[2] The indictment was then read.
It rehearsed, among other things, that, in discourse with one
Booth, Shaftesbury had intimated that, if the king refused to pass
an exclusion Bill at the Oxford parliament, he and his supporters
would use force. He had also said that the king was a man of no
faith; that he ought to be deposed like Richard II, and that he
(Shaftesbury) would not desist until he had established a commonwealth. Evidence was then given by the informers Mac-
namara, Dennis, and Haynes to the effect that the accused had
discussed the duke of Buckingham's claim to the throne, derived
from Plantagenet ancestors; he had spoken irreverently of the
king, and had talked of rebellion. Of actual rebellion the only
hint was that contained in a paper found in Shaftesbury's lodging
whereon were outlined the principles of a Protestant association,
bound by an oath against popery, mercenary armies, and the
succession of the duke of York.

Having heard these attestations, the grand jury asked if any
of the witnesses stood indicted, only to be told that this was no
concern of theirs and must be left to the petty jury, an answer
which evoked from Papillon the rejoinder that, if they could not

[1] *The proceedings . . . against Shaftesbury*, 5.   [2] Ibid. 7.

consider the credibility of the witnesses, they could not satisfy their consciences.[1] In the hope of satisfying these qualms, the witnesses swore that they gave their evidence voluntarily; and Pemberton did his best to reconcile the inconsistencies in the statements which they made; but he would not allow the jury to ask them whether they had been bribed.[2] As the case proceeded it became more clear that the Middlesex whigs would not be brow-beaten; so Pemberton was reduced to the argument that the treason laws now included a very wide range of things, while North informed them that the Protestant association imputed to Shaftesbury's authorship was not recognized by the statutes. After retiring to consider their verdict, the jurymen returned with the Bill marked *Ignoramus*, whereupon the spectators in court (many from Wapping) fell 'a hollowing and shouting', a fact which the attorney-general asked the judge to place on record.[3]

But the victory was more than discounted by an event contemporaneous with the trial of Shaftesbury—the publication of Dryden's *Absalom and Achitophel*. It was with this great political satire that the poet laureate won a national public; for, by the autumn of 1681, the Popish Plot could at last be seen in its gaunt perspective, and the nation was now rallying to the throne after the assaults of the exclusionists. The biblical background of the poem was a happy thought, since, in the turbulent history of early Israel, it was easy to find many close parallels; its personal names provided a transparent disguise, and enabled the poet to work in a medium then the best known to Englishmen. Everything conspired to draw from him his best—desire to please the king; to wipe off old scores against Buckingham; to give full expression to a mordant wit. So there were no superfluous strokes, and with a minimum of effort every thrust went home; the second lines of the couplets were not echoes of the first, but independent confirmations; a whole portrait gallery was etched in steel, every feature clear-cut from needle and acid. There are times in history when national sanity can be restored only by sarcasm. It was so in France, after the excesses of the League and the Religious Wars, when the ridicule of the *Satire Menipée* induced a measure of balance and moderation; it was so also in England

[1] *The proceedings . . . against Shaftesbury*, 33.   [2] Ibid. 36–42.
[3] Ibid. 48.

when, after three years of madness, men read *Absalom and Achito-phel* and laughed themselves out of their own follies. It was the triumph of native common sense.

In Scotland there was little relief from the trials through which the nation was passing. In July 1681 James, as royal commis-sioner, presided over a meeting of the Scottish Parliament, at which two Acts were passed, both intended to consolidate Stuart rule in the north. By the first,[1] it was enacted that the right of succession to the crown was unaffected by the religion of the heir; by the second,[2] there was imposed on all office-holders a test of such prodigious length, and such wealth of historical citation, that sworn adherence thereto might well occasion qualms in the scrupulous. This test was used as a means of removing the marquis of Argyle, son of that Argyle who had been offered as a sacrifice in 1661, an object of dislike to the executive because of his whig sympathies, and the occasion of both envy and enmity on the part of his many neighbours, anxious to share in the for-feiture of his great estates. As he was whiggish enough to offer subscription to the test 'in so far as it was consistent with itself and with the Protestant faith', there was now at hand a pretext as base as that which had cost his father his life. He had not lent his men for service in the iniquitous Highland Host; he had opposed the measures of Sharp and Rothes; as the uncrowned king of the Highlands he was an anomaly; and, worst of all, he represented the Protestant interest. His opposition to the exemp-tion of the royal family from the test stirred the easily aroused resentment of James; accordingly, on November 9, 1681, he was committed on charges of treason, perjury, and assuming the legislative power, and convicted on evidence which, as Halifax said, would not have hanged a dog in England. Sentence of death and forfeiture was pronounced on December 23; but, a few days before, the prisoner had succeeded in making his escape. After hiding for a time in London he fled to Holland, where he

---

[1] *Acts of the Parliaments of Scotland*, viii. 239.

[2] Ibid. viii. 244–5. Here the 'true Protestant religion' was defined as that enunciated by the first parliament of James VI. The oath renounced all covenants, leagues and foreign jurisdictions and had to be taken 'without equivocation'.

corresponded with the Rye House conspirators, and fell a victim at last after the failure of Monmouth's rebellion. The policy adopted towards Argyle was enforced on all suspected of disaffection. Dragoons harried the western shires in quest of covenanters, who were either shot out of hand or reserved for the mercies of the 'bluidy' Advocate, sir George Mackenzie, who boasted that he had never lost a case for the crown. He gleaned assiduously in fields from which Graham of Claverhouse had already extracted a rich harvest, and much of Scottish history was inscribed on tombstones.

During this, his second,[1] stay in Scotland (Oct. 1680–March, 1682) James had begun by a policy of conciliation, to which there was a ready response; but, as his exile became more prolonged, his vindictiveness increased, and his stay in Edinburgh seems to have accentuated a harsh element in his character. In close touch with the course of events in England, he fretted visibly at his enforced abstention from a scene where his presence would have led to civil war. His misfortunes might have elicited for him the sympathy of posterity, were it not that his conduct came to be more and more clouded by an unusual degree of obtuseness and meanness, qualities so strongly marked as to be attributable in part to the ravages of a constitutional disease on his mind and character. His obtuseness was shown by his continued faith in Sunderland; by the ingenuous confidences of his innumerable letters to the prince of Orange (all carefully preserved by their recipient);[2] by his belief in force, preferably French, against English patriots. Meanness was shown in his sustained resentment against enemies unworthy of a prince's wrath, and by his readiness to seize on some petty device for avenging himself. He swore that he would be revenged on the duchess of Portsmouth, who had played him a 'dog's trick'; he thought that the support of one of her maids, Mrs. Wall, would serve him in good stead, and he maintained negotiations with her through colonel Legge.[3]

---

[1] His first stay was from Nov. 1679 to Feb. 1680.

[2] Many of these will be found in *Prinsterer*, v. In the Record Office (*S.P. Dom.* 8/3) there is a collection of about 200, the last of which were written in June 1686.

[3] York to colonel Legge, in *Add. MS.* 18477, f. 50, Nov. 22, 1680, quoted in Campana de Cavelli, *Les derniers Stuarts*, i. 336.

Echoes from this world 'below stairs' had been heard at the trial of Fitzharris. Louis XIV was another friend with whom James was anxious to maintain stricter correspondence, and by whose help he hoped to maintain the prerogative on the basis of a standing army. He was continually urging Charles to act on bolder counsels; 'and who dare advise him to them unless I be with him to help to support him?'[1] It was indeed well for Charles that, throughout the critical period of the exclusion agitation, he was not embarrassed by his brother's presence; indeed there may be some truth in Barrillon's statement that, if the Oxford parliament had been willing to give him money and leave the prerogative intact, he would have agreed to exclusion.[2] Nor was James even consistent in his advocacy of strong measures; for at times he professed only to have reminded his brother of what he should do: 'I merely put him in mind, and pressed him to go on with what was resolved.'[3] It had been a considerable part of Charles's statesmanship *not* to go on with what had been resolved.

By the spring of 1682 England was a safer place for James, and so negotiations began for his return. He resumed communication with the duchess of Portsmouth, the price of her support being a share of the duke's Post Office revenues. This negotiation did not mature; but meanwhile James went to his brother at Newmarket, where he was well received. On returning to Leith in May 1682, in order to bring back his duchess, his ship, the *Gloucester*, was wrecked off the Yorkshire coast, with great loss of life; and contemporaries attributed to him an undue solicitude for his priests, his dogs, and his treasure while the ship was sinking. His return to England was speedily marked by changes which accentuated the reactionary character of Charles's rule. Halifax was again eclipsed; Sunderland, with the help of the duchess of Portsmouth, emerged from obscurity, and was readmitted to the privy council in August 1682, becoming again a secretary of state in January 1683. In September of that year Jeffreys was promoted lord chief justice and shortly afterwards admitted to the privy council. These men, together with Barrillon and the duchess of Portsmouth, constituted the ministry of Charles's last

[1] Ibid. i. 349.
[2] Barrillon to Louis XIV, 14/24 July 1681, ibid. i. 362.   [3] Ibid. i. 360.

years; on it was conferred at least the gilt of Anglicanism by the retention of Hyde (lord Rochester) in office.

The *Ignoramus* returned by the Middlesex grand jury precipitated the long-premeditated attack on the charters, and soon almost every franchise in the country was subjected to the scrutiny of lawyers prepared to find pretexts for their forfeiture. Most of the lords lieutenant and country gentry lent their aid to this campaign, and in the years 1682–3 compulsion and influence were freely used to procure the surrender or forfeiture of civic rights. From the correspondence which passed through the office of the secretaries of state can be deduced both the local influence of the landed gentry, and how that influence was enhanced by their active participation in measures calculated to redress the balance of power between town and country in favour of the latter. Thus, in June 1682, lord Ferrers wrote that he had prevailed with Derby to surrender its charter; he was willing, if required, to induce several Staffordshire corporations to do likewise.[1] The city of Norwich asked lord Yarmouth not to use compulsion in regard to its charter, as 900 citizens had petitioned against its surrender.[2] Reports from Cornwall and Devon showed that the gentry there were specially zealous in the king's service, and even served on petty juries;[3] Nottingham, where the duke of Newcastle was supreme, surrendered its charter, but as there was an omission to include the town lands, the process had to be repeated.[4] Poole was the subject of anathema by the gentlemen of Dorset; because, as the borough was a county, it was a nuisance to the county of Dorset, and moreover its corporation was disaffected to the government.[5] At their suggestion a *quo warranto* was issued. The privileges of the city of Oxford were examined by Dr. Fell, dean of Christ Church and vice-chancellor, who insisted that the rights of the university, especially in regard to the pernoctations of the proctors, should be safeguarded in the new charter;[6] another potentate who had to be consulted before the fresh charter was granted was lord Abingdon. The reasons why proceedings were taken against the Oxford charter were these: by its Elizabethan charter, the

[1] *Cal. S.P. Dom., 1682*, 229.   [2] Ibid. 274.   [3] Ibid. 347.
[4] Ibid. 423.   [5] *S.P. Dom., 1683/4*, bundle 436, Jan. 23, 1684.
[6] Ibid., Jan. 10, 1684.

market was to be held in Broken Heys and Gloucester Green;
but in practice the market was usually kept in the city; there were
five aldermen instead of four; three fairs were to be held yearly,
but none was kept, and the bailiffs were said to pack juries.[1]
Against Plymouth, the count was frauds on the Excise;[2] after a
visit from Jeffreys on circuit, Plymouth surrendered its charter.

Most active on behalf of the government was the duke of
Beaufort, whose influence was strongest in Wiltshire, Herefordshire, and Somerset. One of his agents gave an account of how
he dealt with the recalcitrant corporation of Leominster. The
corporation consisted of 25 council men, of whom 14 were
'fanatics' and the others loyal. One of the corporation's duties
was the annual election of a bailiff (by a majority of the 25);
and when the 14 'fanatics' were reduced to 12 by the death of
one and the imprisonment of another, the agent advised the
loyal party to absent themselves from the election, in order that
a majority could not be secured for the nominee of the 12, and
so no bailiff could be appointed. This was good enough for the
issue of a *quo warranto*, and Beaufort suggested himself as high
steward of the remodelled borough.[3] So too, lord Lindsey asked
the king's assent to his acceptance of the office of recorder of
the reformed city of Lincoln, and gave an assurance that he
would act in the interests of the Court.[4] The duke of Newcastle
secured the appointment of one of his nominees to the town-
clerkship of Nottingham, and had his dependants installed in
the corporation of Newcastle-under-Lyme.[5] As one town after
another succumbed to a *quo warranto*, the voluntary surrenders
became more frequent, most of them accompanied with that
degree of submission expected from defaulting burghers acknow-
ledging the king's mercy conveyed to them by his territorial
representatives. A typical example was that of the surrender
of its charter by Northampton and its receipt of a new one on
September 25, 1681. On that day, the mayor, aldermen, bailiffs,
and burgesses walked in their robes to the limits of the town,
where they met the earl of Peterborough, lord lieutenant of the

---

[1] *Cal. S.P. Dom., 1682*, 276.   [2] *P.C. Reg.* 70, June 29, 1683.
[3] *S.P. Dom.*, bundle 438, Oct. 8, 1684, R. Hopton to duke of Beaufort.
[4] Ibid. Oct. 28, 1684, lord Lindsey to secretary of state.
[5] Ibid. Nov. 9, 1684, duke of Newcastle to secretary of state.

county, with a great confluence of nobility and gentry, all on horseback. His lordship, having dismounted, presented the new charter, with a discourse on His Majesty's favour to the borough; while the mayor, in the name of the new corporation, received the document on his knees, 'with due reverence, joy and gratitude of mind'. Then followed a speech by the deputy-recorder, in which he stigmatized the conduct of the evil men recently in authority, and commended the wisdom of the corporation in surrendering its charter in time. 'Is there any among you have been tainted with ill principles? . . . Now there is an eye upon you which will have respect to justice as well as to mercy.'[1]

Of the whig strongholds London was by far the most important; for its overthrow, both time and persistence were necessary. Early in 1678 the city lent a sum of £150,000 for the projected war with France; in the late summer of the same year Charles asked for £200,000; and, though it was feared that this money might be used for suppressing the liberties of the subject or the privileges of the corporation, the request was, nevertheless, granted.[2] The year 1681 was a critical one for London. The two sheriffs, Pilkington and Shute, were noted whigs, and the city indicated its politics in January by petitioning the king for the summoning of a parliament, with a reference to the interruption of public justice entailed by prorogation; this petition was afterwards to figure in the indictment against the city. In June, the freemen in their common hall voted thanks to the lord mayor and common council for presenting this petition, and also accorded thanks to the outgoing sheriffs 'for their provision of faithful and able juries'.[3] These traditions were maintained by the new sheriffs, Bethell and Cornish, and the result was seen in November, when the Middlesex grand jury rejected the Bill against Shaftesbury.

The turn of the tide came in June 1682 when, at the nomination of sheriffs, the lord mayor, sir John Moore, raised his glass to Dudley North, a younger brother of lord chief justice North; who, having acquired wealth as a Turkey merchant, was now embarking on a second career as a tory politician. Since 1674 no one had challenged this method of nominating a sheriff; but

[1] *Bodley, Ashmole*, 1674, no. 79.
[2] R. R. Sharpe, *London and the kingdom*, ii. 455–7.   [3] Ibid. ii. 474.

the city companies and the livery objected to North as their sheriff, and refused to confirm his nomination. In his stead they proposed these three—Papillon the mercer, Dubois the weaver, and Box the grocer, from whom they desired their two sheriffs to be chosen. A poll was conducted by the outgoing sheriffs, Pilkington and Shute, who continued it a few days longer than was warranted by the lord mayor's order; for this offence, Moore reported them to the privy council, which promptly committed the offending sheriffs to the Tower. The king then ordered a new election, the details of which are obscure; but North and Box appear to have obtained some kind of majority through the disqualification of the votes of those whig liverymen who had not taken the oath. Box thereupon resigned in favour of Peter Rich, and shortly afterwards sir W. Pritchard was elected lord mayor; as he, with the new sheriffs, North and Rich, was a tory, this was a victory for the Court.[1] Nor did this end the discomfiture of the large whig element in the city. In the heat of the elections of 1679–81 strong words had been used, and for these full retribution was to be exacted. Pilkington was fined £100,000 in November 1682 on an action of *scandalum magnatum* for having said in public that the duke of York had burnt the city in 1666, and had come from Scotland to cut their throats. A few months after this savage sentence, he was tried, with Shute, Cornish, and Bethell, for riot at the election of sheriffs on Midsummer Day 1682, and again heavily fined. The ex-lord mayor, sir Patience Ward, had had the misfortune to give evidence on behalf of Pilkington at the first trial; for this he was indicted for perjury (May 1683), at the instigation of the duke; but, before sentence, he managed to effect his escape to Holland. Thus was England habituated to methods of justice savouring more of Edinburgh than of Westminster. Even thus, however, the city refused to surrender its charter, and accordingly a *quo warranto* was issued in January 1682.

After some preliminary arguments,[2] proceedings commenced

---

[1] Ibid. ii. 479.

[2] The arguments and pleadings will be found in *The Case of the Charter of London Stated* (1683) and *The pleadings and arguments . . . upon the Quo Warranto* (1690). See also R. R. Sharpe, *London and the Kingdom*, ii. 494–7.

in the King's Bench on February 7, 1683, when the information recited that the lord mayor, commonalty and citizens claimed, without any lawful warrant or legal grant, to exercise these privileges:

1. To be of themselves a body corporate and politic.
2. To name, elect and constitute sheriffs of London and Middlesex.
3. To hold sessions of the peace.

In the first capacity (so the indictment alleged) the common council had in 1674 passed a by-law imposing a fee of twopence per day on every horse-load of provisions brought into the public markets of the city; and from this and similar charges they had derived about £5,000 per annum to the oppression of the king's subjects. Secondly, they had presented a petition, which was 'in the nature of an appeal to the people'. To the first charge it was answered that the mayor, commonalty, and citizens were seised of the markets in fee, and had the right to levy tolls; they had imposed charges in order to rebuild the markets after the Great Fire. As regards the second charge, Treby, on behalf of the city, contended that the information had been brought against the wrong persons; it ought to have been brought against named persons who had usurped the functions of a corporation. 'The nature of a corporation', he said, 'is a capacity . . . an invisible person and capacity only, which cannot be forfeited.' At the second hearing (April 27, 1683) Pollexfen compared the importance of the case to Magna Carta itself; for not only London, but all the corporations of England were concerned. 'Consider', he said, 'what a vast part is concerned in the corporations of England.' He then cited those which are ecclesiastical or mixed, such as archbishops, deans, chapters, universities, and hospitals; secular, such as cities, towns, and boroughs, and even the very frame of government, since the Commons consist of knights, citizens, and burgesses. The members of a corporation, said Pollexfen, could be dealt with, but not the *persona ficta*, which is 'invisible, immortal, incapable of forfeiture, of treason or felony; having no soul, nor subject to imbecility or death'.

Judgement was pronounced on June 12, 1683, when the Bench declared that a corporation-aggregate might be seized;

that exacting money by pretended by-laws was an extortion, and that the acts of the common council were the acts of the corporation of London. A few days later (June 18) the lord mayor, with representative aldermen and commons, was received by the king at Windsor, where they presented an apology, which was answered by a speech from the lord keeper (North), who told them that their petition should have been presented earlier.[1] In the following September the common council refused by a narrow majority to surrender the old charter, whereupon judgement was entered against the city (Oct. 4, 1683). The corporation was remodelled, and a new charter was granted which effected a revolution in civic constitution.[2] In future, no lord mayor, sheriff, recorder, or town clerk was to be appointed without the royal approval; wherever the king disapproved of a second choice, he should himself nominate. There would therefore be no more whig sheriffs or grand juries; Shaftesbury's stronghold was now a royal demesne, and the proudest corporation in the world was at the feet of a Stuart.

The attack on the charters coincided with the stricter enforcement by the justices of the laws against Papists, Dissenters, and conventicles. Orders to this effect, issued by the privy council, were rigidly enforced in many parts of England; the prisons were again filled, notably with Quakers, and in this campaign many of the country gentry distinguished themselves by their zeal. Thus, from head-quarters at Badminton, the duke of Beaufort co-operated so successfully with his son lord Herbert as to induce the latter to express the hope that soon not a single Dissenter would be heard of in the county of Somerset.[3] An increase of emigration to the colonies at this time caused Jenkins to consider whether this might not be prohibited; another proposal for consideration was that of excommunicating the Dissenters, so that they might be unable either to vote for or be elected to parliament.[4] It was even suggested that the separate community of Walloons and Flemings in Canterbury should be expelled, the grand jury of Kent having presented them as a nuisance to the county.[5]

[1] The proceedings are described in *Bodley, Ashmole* 1674, no. 71.
[2] R. R. Sharpe, op. cit. ii. 503–5.   [3] *Cal. S.P. Dom., 1682*, 24–5.
[4] Ibid. 571, Dec. 9, 1682.   [5] Ibid., *1683*, 103.

In this campaign the government made unsparing use of informers and spies. Hitherto these had been paid by private patrons to ferret out Papists; in 1681 there was money to be had from the Treasury for swearing against prominent whigs, and now (1682–3) a good living could be made by informing against the Dissenters and the smaller fry. A judge, sir Edmund Saunders, thought that the justices might be enlisted in this system of espionage by imposing on them an obligation to reveal to the privy council all matters concerning the state that had arisen in the informations laid before them,[1] a proposal of special interest to justice Edmund Warcup, who had done much subterranean work during the Popish Plot,[2] and was now an active agent on behalf of the government. Throughout England, the informers quickly adapted themselves to the new requirements of the trade; spies prospered on a share of forfeitures and fines, and the success of the tale-bearers was estimated in financial terms; one of them, for example, when petitioning for funds, reminded the king that in the preceding six months he had convicted in London before the lord mayor 'halls, houses and preachers to the value of more than £10,000, and in Westminster to the value of £7,000'.[3] Old-established houses offered tenders for the new business on foot; for instance, the relatives of Oates; one of whom, Clement Oates, gave information to the government of what he had heard from the conversations between Tonge and Titus Oates, and claimed to have discovered the inventor of the cry: 'no popery, no slavery'.[4] More prominent was Samuel Oates, who specialized in sworn informations against his brother's patrons, including Shaftesbury. In the winter of 1682–3 he was finding evidence of a whig plot in the fact that large numbers of short blunderbusses were being made by the London gunsmiths; he was also 'smoking out' the designs of those whigs who had gone to Holland; and, as he wished to keep the business in the family, he announced that he had converted Titus from whiggery; so, if the Doctor were sent for, 'he would offer proposals which I am sure would please Your Majesty'.

[1] *Cal. S.P. Dom., 1682*, 105.

[2] His *Journal, 1676–84*, ed. K. Feiling and F. R. Needham, will be found in *E.H.R.* xl.

[3] *Cal. S.P. Dom., 1682*, 520, Oct. 1682.   [4] Ibid. 245, June 1682.

A share in the confiscated estates of Jesuits was to be the price of this information.[1]

These facts serve to illustrate the collapse of the whig cause. When Shaftesbury was discharged from bail in February 1682 he was a broken man, suffering in health, his spirit almost daunted by the sudden reversal of his party's fortunes. That party was now reduced to a mere handful of men; some eminent and principled, others furtive and dangerous. In the former category were Essex, Russell, and Algernon Sidney. Arthur Capel, earl of Essex, had proved by his tenure of the viceroyalty of Ireland[2] that he was a prudent and sympathetic administrator; his services at the Treasury had won the appreciation of Charles, and he was known to contemporaries as a man of character, industry, and taste. He had joined in the opposition to Danby, and had allied himself, first with Halifax, and then with Shaftesbury. In his political evolution he progressed from limitations to exclusion, and from Orange to Monmouth. Disappointment may have determined this part of his career; for he had hoped to become lord high treasurer. In actual conspiracy he appears to have taken no part.

William, lord Russell, was one of a house destined to play a great part in English liberalism. Opposition to Buckingham had first drawn him out of his reserve; soon he was attacking Danby and the French connexion. In 1678 he was among the parliamentary leaders courted by the French ambassador; that he was one of the dupes of Charles's foreign policy may account in part for his resentment against the Court. Like Essex, he was one of the reformed privy council of 1679; later he was known as a consistent advocate of exclusion, and, though enemies hinted that his anti-popish principles were proof of fear lest his church lands might be confiscated by a popish successor, yet this inadequately accounts for the persistent and reasoned opposition he maintained to the interest of the duke of York. He disapproved the rasher counsels of Shaftesbury; but, on the other hand, by his meetings with Ralph Montagu at Southampton House, he incurred suspicion. Equally eminent was Algernon Sidney, son of the second earl of Leicester, a republican of the type of sir Henry Vane. Though he had refused to participate

---

[1] Ibid. 236, 538, and ibid., *1683*, 18.   [2] See *supra*, 397-8.

in the trial of Charles I, he was known as a resolute opponent of monarchy; and for the greater part of Charles's reign he was engaged in study and foreign travel. Returning to England in 1677, he unsuccessfully tried to obtain election to parliament; nor did he secure the friendship of Shaftesbury, who at first regarded him as a French spy and a pensioner of Sunderland, an accusation to which some point was given by his acceptance of money from Barrillon. Of the abstract republicans he was considered the most dangerous because prepared to go to extremities with the help of France. Towards the prince of Orange his attitude was one of diffidence, because he knew that absolutism can be based as well on Protestantism as on crypto-Catholicism. Concentration on exclusion was therefore his policy, for which everything was to be sacrificed; but though, after the Oxford parliament, he discussed projects of insurrection with Russell and Essex, he does not appear to have had direct dealings with Shaftesbury or Monmouth.

The younger generation of whig peers was represented by Thomas Grey (1654–1720), styled lord Grey of Groby and later earl of Stamford. He was one of the close associates of Shaftesbury; he received a pardon for his part in the Rye House plot, and at the Revolution took up arms on behalf of Orange. He was a somewhat ineffective whig. Not dissimilar was Forde, lord Grey of Werk, first prominent as an exclusionist; then suspected of concurrence in the Rye House plot. He saved himself after the battle of Sedgemoor by turning king's evidence, and was one of those who came over with William. Older than these was William Howard, third baron Howard of Escrick, who had learned his preaching from the Anabaptists and his plotting from Cromwell's Guards. To the Restoration government he was useful because of the information he could give against his former associates among the Sectaries; during the Third Dutch War he was imprisoned for treasonable correspondence with the enemy; at the trial of lord Stafford he gave evidence against his own kinsman, and he afterwards turned informer against his associates Russell and Sidney. Another associate against whom he swore was John Hampden ('the younger'), grandson of the great Hampden, who had imbibed advanced religious and political principles during his stay in France. Hampden returned to England in 1682, and was afterwards accused of plotting an insurrection with Monmouth, Russell, Sidney, Essex, and Howard. These were afterwards known as the Council of Six.

Whatever may have been the nature of the deliberations of the so-called Council of Six, it is clear that they were all, except Howard, amateurs in the business of plotting. Unfortunately, however, some of them were suspected of association or at least communication with men of a more determined and experienced type, such as the old Cromwellian soldiers Walcot, Rumsey, and Rumbold; the last a maltster, whose house at Hoddesdon (the Rye House), on the way from London to Newmarket, was afterwards to acquire such notoriety. Equally dangerous were Aaron Smith, major Wildman, and Robert Ferguson. Smith, a shady London solicitor, had come into prominence at College's trial; he was already known as an ally of Oates, and he may have been in the pay of William of Orange. It was for his share in the defence of College that he was forced to go into hiding, and soon he was deeply engaged in plots. His skill in covering up his tracks saved him for preferment after the Revolution. John Wildman was another secretive worker who lived to secure a post from William. His seditious activities dated from the days of the New Model Army, and he still perpetuated the visionary politics of Lilburne and the Nag's Head Tavern, combining these activities with astute land speculations which had enriched him during the Commonwealth. It was because he had plotted against Cromwell that he was given control of the Post Office at the Restoration; but his propensity for opening letters caused dismissal, and thereafter he appears to have alternated periods of imprisonment with enjoyment of the favour of Buckingham and the suspicion of the government. Of ripe experience and expert knowledge, he had a simple policy—to assassinate the king and the duke of York, and give the crown to Monmouth; in consequence, like Algernon Sidney, with whom he was associated, he was considered by many whigs as too dangerous, but useful nevertheless as a consultant.

The third member of this group, Robert Ferguson, was the most extraordinary of the three, and perhaps the only one of them having any legitimate grievance against the government. Born in Aberdeenshire, he had obtained a living in Kent, from which he was ejected at the Restoration. He was imprisoned for raising money on behalf of deprived ministers, and on his release became a popular preacher of a somewhat florid type. A supporter of Monmouth, he had sense enough to perceive that the affair of the black box[1] was bad showmanship, since stronger evidence of the marriage of Monmouth's mother would be necessary; by 1681 he had become involved in deeper courses, as intermediary between Monmouth and the whigs; but, unlike .Wildman, he stopped short of insurrection. He appears to have been inspired by a measure of genuine religious zeal. He lived, not to enjoy office under William, but to plot with the Jacobites. As pamphleteer, rigorist, and headlong enthusiast he is comparable with William Prynne, and he exercised a somewhat baleful influence on the more loosely-knit men with whom he was associated.[2]

The personage on whose behalf these men were acting was James Scott or Crofts, duke of Monmouth and (after his marriage into that house) duke of Buccleuch. As a youth he was prominent in the more violent escapades of Restoration London; but a certain gracefulness of manner, coupled with a dashing exterior, made him popular with the London mob. He had first incurred the jealousy of the duke of York by his appointment in 1670 to succeed Albemarle as captain-general of the forces; he had distinguished himself under Turenne in 1672, at the siege of Meastricht in 1673, and in 1678, with a small detachment, he had held Ostend. In July 1679, when he returned to London as the clement victor of Bothwell Brig, his popularity was at its height; and, by his conjunction with Shaftesbury, Essex, and the duchess of Portsmouth, he fast became a serious problem to the executive; for as he had helped to overthrow Danby, so he made no secret that he desired the exclusion of his uncle. His Protestantism was patent to all beholders, as his legitimacy was to be revealed in the apocalyptic contents of the black box. His

---

[1] The black box was said to contain the marriage contract between Charles and Monmouth's mother, Lucy Walters. Cosin, bishop of Durham, was said to have entrusted the box to the custody of his son-in-law, sir Gilbert Gerard. For this see under Scott, James, duke of Monmouth, in *D.N.B.*

[2] For a good biography see R. Ferguson, *Robert Ferguson the Plotter*.

decline had begun with the return of James to England in September 1679, when he was deprived of his commission and obliged to leave the country; then his unauthorized return in November caused Charles to deprive him of all his civil and military offices and order him out of the kingdom, which order he disobeyed. He maintained his popularity by public worship in St. Martin's-in-the-Fields, and paid assiduous court to Nell Gwyn, the staunchest supporter of Protestantism in the inner circles of Charles's Court.

It was probably at Shaftesbury's suggestion that he began to show himself to the people in a series of progresses, beginning with Oxford and the western counties in the autumn of 1680. On his coach was painted an emblem presumed to be heraldic— a heart pierced by two arrows, surmounted by a plume of feathers, with two angels bearing up a scarf on both sides.[1] At many points on his route he was well received by the populace, amid shouts of 'No Popery, No Popery'. Thus, his entry into Chard on August 27 was preceded by 500 horsemen, and 'there was not a mute among the crowd that met him'.[2] At Exeter he was received by sir William Courtenay and a crowd shouting 'God bless the Protestant duke'. On the return journey he stayed for a few days in Oxford, where the university ignored his presence, but the city was whig in sympathy, accordingly he was entertained to dinner by the mayor and aldermen, one of the toasts being confusion to the vice-chancellor of the university[3] (Dr. Fell). He also took part at the horse-racing on Port Meadow. In March 1681 he was again in Oxford, with the parliament, and this time maintained a semi-royal state; thereafter he was the public friend and advocate of Shaftesbury and College, thereby imposing a severe strain on the patience of his indulgent father. Further indiscretions led to his deposition from the chancellorship of Cambridge early in 1682. He now talked openly of insurrection, and in the autumn of 1682 he again went on progress.

No pretender to the throne ever worked harder for a following

[1] *H.M.C. Rep.* xii, app., pt. vii. 174, *Le Fleming MSS.*
[2] *Narrative of the duke of Monmouth's late journey into the west* (1680), in *Bodley Pamph.* 149.
[3] Duke of York to princess of Orange in *Prinsterer*, v. 421, Sept. 23, 1680.

than did he. In August he was being entertained by the whig
landlords in Staffordshire, including the earl of Macclesfield;[1]
in the following month he had a great reception at the Wallasey
horse-races, where 'it wanted only a *vive le roy* to complete the
rebellion'.[2] Having won the 12-stone plate and a prize of £60
he presented the plate to the mayor's daughter, whom he
christened Henrietta. Jeffreys, who was then at Wrexham,
noted that lords Derby and Brandon were present. Nor were
these his only exploits at this northern race meeting; for he won
two foot races 'against the same gent, first stripped, and then in
his boots', whereupon the applause was so hearty that he had
to ask the spectators to give over.[3] At Liverpool he touched for
the king's evil and was made a freeman of the town; throughout
Staffordshire and Cheshire—counties said to be 'rotten with
whigs'—he was received with enthusiasm. But his movements
were being followed by a sergeant-at-arms, and at Stafford he
was taken into custody, while at the same time a warrant was
issued for Shaftesbury's arrest. Shaftesbury concealed himself
in Wapping; Monmouth was bailed out, and again the athletic
duke strove to win the populace by the fascination of his appearance and the prowess of his limbs. But his third progress
(Feb. 1683) was not a success. He chose the southern counties,
and his reception was poor. At Chichester the arrangements
for his entry were ruined by the appearance of the high sheriff
and justices with a troop of horse, at the sight of which Monmouth 'swore bloodily', but 'no other compliments passed'.[4]
Some consolation was offered by the sight of about a thousand
people at the Cross, and Monmouth insisted on attending divine
service in the cathedral, where the bishop's chaplain drew such
a close parallel between rebellion and witchcraft that the duke
left hurriedly, leaving some of his suite to curse the preacher.

The northern progress of September 1682 may have been a
feeler; at times it had the appearance of an abortive rebellion.
Throughout the autumn of 1682 there seems to have been a
number of meetings at the house of a wealthy wine merchant
named Shepherd, where schemes of insurrection or even assassination may have been discussed, but with what seriousness of

---

[1] *Cal. S.P. Dom.*, *1682*, 342.   [2] Ibid. 390, Sept. 11, 1682.
[3] Ibid. 409.   [4] Ibid., *1683*, 70, Feb. 21.

purpose it is impossible to determine. Shaftesbury and the 'Council of Six' had probably become careless, and their talk reached the ears not only of such men as Wildman and Ferguson, but of even more obscure desperadoes, such as the Irish adventurer Walcot, a free-thinking lawyer named West, and a London oil-man named Keeling, one or all of whom may have attended the deliberations. As the time for the annual pope-burning approached, the talks assumed a more serious turn; for there were negotiations by Shaftesbury with the followers of Argyle, and with Scots refugees from the battle of Bothwell Brig. What is certain is that there was no leadership, because Shaftesbury was now nearly distraught with vexation and ill health; and when, in November 1682, he heard that fresh warrants were out for his arrest, he fled to Holland, where he died on January 21, 1683. His removal and death destroyed what hope remained of a successful reaction, leaving his associates compromised by the wild inconsequences of their leader's decline, and by their rash confidences to men likely to prove traitors or informers.

Such were the preliminaries to one more mystery of the reign —the so-called Rye House Plot. On June 12, 1683, there emerged from an obscurity as murky as that which had preceded the debut of Oates the salter and oil-man Josiah Keeling, a man of anabaptist sympathies and a decaying business. Like Oates before him he had a wonderful story of an attempt to murder the king, and for some unexplained reason he took his story to George Legge, lord Dartmouth, who then held a household office at Court, and was associated in naval affairs with the duke of York. Legge sent him to the proper quarter, namely to Jenkins. Meanwhile, news of the 'plot' had leaked out; and two of the men whose names had been mentioned (Rumsey and West) appear, if Burnet is to be credited,[1] to have decided on a novel plan. This was to come in voluntarily with a 'concocted confession' which would not only save their lives, but might qualify them for employment in detective work against the numerous emissaries of Satan then flourishing in England. An alternative explanation (of which there is no proof) is that the Court prompted the 'confession' in order to implicate the whigs. The document drawn up by West[2] is comparable

[1] *Burnet*, ii. 360-1. [2] *Add. MS.* 38847, f. 83 sqq.

in its wildness and inconsistencies with the stories of Oates. In brief, it implicated many persons in one or other of two schemes —the murder of the king and a general insurrection. The object of the latter was to destroy not only the king and the duke of York, but also Halifax and Rochester; the princess Anne was then to be placed on the throne, and married to some 'honest country gentleman' in order to raise 'a Protestant brood of princes'. The former project, that of simple assassination, was to be effected either by 'lopping' the king in the playhouse, or running down his barge on the Thames, or killing him when on his way from or to Newmarket as his coach passed the moat of the Rye House, Rumbold's farm at Hoddesdon in Hertfordshire.

Charles was in the habit of visiting Newmarket regularly in April and October. It so happened that, in April 1683, he had returned from Newmarket a week earlier than usual owing to a fire. Here was the miraculous event which confirmed West as the murder of Godfrey had confirmed Oates. The king returned to Whitehall, and all the members of the Council of Six were arrested, with the exception of Monmouth. At first Essex did not seem to apprehend danger; but later he showed signs of confusion, and he must have realized that, with so many informers around him, his most innocent acts could easily be construed as treasonable. He committed suicide in the Tower on July 13, the day on which the trial of lord Russell began.

Lord Howard, once more an informer, gave evidence against Russell.[1] He said there had been talk of a rising before Shaftesbury's departure; afterwards they feared they might have gone too far. As a member of the Council of Six, Howard described the negotiations with Argyle and the Scots, evidence objected to by Russell, since it gave proof of no overt act; whereupon the court ruled that the assembling of council to raise a rebellion constituted an overt act, and that this had been proved by Rumsey, who swore that, with other persons, he went to Russell's house to find out what resolutions had been come to; by Shepherd, who swore that in October 1682 Monmouth, Ferguson, and Russell discoursed of a way to seize the Guards; and thirdly, by Howard, whose evidence, though admittedly hearsay, was

[1] *The tryals of Thomas Walcot, William Hone, William lord Russell, John Rous, and William Flagg* (1683), 42–6.

confirmed by these two preceding. Russell's defence was that he had been at Shepherd's wineshop accidentally, where he had overheard talk, but had not himself engaged in a plot. ''Tis hard', he said, 'that a man must lose his life on hear-say,' words which adequately describe the evidence on which he was convicted.[1] On July 14 he was sentenced to death with Walcot; and, though powerful family influence was exerted to procure a remission of the sentence, he was executed on July 21 in Lincoln's Inn Fields, after receiving the ministrations of both Burnet and Tillotson, in the presence of a great and silent crowd, some of whom dipped handkerchiefs in his blood.

The next victim was Algernon Sidney, whose trial began on November 21. The indictment[2] alleged that, as one of the Council of Six, he had meditated rebellion; that he had sent Aaron Smith into Scotland in order to promote sedition, and that he was the author of treasonable opinions found in papers left in his study. For the first two counts the only serious witness was again Howard, whose evidence Sidney objected to because he was his creditor, and had admitted to him that he could not procure his pardon until he had done some more jobs.[3] Extracts from Sidney's unpublished papers were read in court.[4] These contained quotations from Bracton, and statements implying that, as the king held his power from the people, he might be deposed if he violated his trust. To this evidence the accused objected that the authorship was not proved, that the papers were merely an answer to Filmer, and that in any event he was not answerable for what he wrote in his study unless he published it.[5] Thereupon Jeffreys, ever apt at quotation, recited these words: 'Curse not the king; not in thy thoughts, nor in thy bed-chamber; the birds of the air will carry it';[6] but how far this helped to substantiate the charge of high treason he did not explain. Burnet, in his evidence for the defence, said that Howard had come to him, and had sworn that there was no plot; as regards the papers, Sidney said that they had no connexion with any political design, and were written many years before. But these pleas were brushed aside by Jeffreys with the malicious innuendo: 'A man convinced of these principles

[1] Ibid. 50.
[2] *The arraignment, tryal and condemnation of Algernon Sidney Esq.* (1684), 1–8.
[3] Ibid. 30.　　　[4] Ibid. 23–6.　　　[5] Ibid. 31–3.　　　[6] Ibid. 35.

and that walks accordingly, what won't he do to accomplish his designs?'[1] The case against him, therefore, was that the principles found in papers attributed to his authorship might lead to treasonable acts if logically carried out; on this hypothesis he was found guilty, and executed on Tower Hill on December 7, 1683, the king having remitted all the sentence except the beheading. It was freely admitted at Court that though there was proof of talk about insurrection, there was no evidence of any plot to kill the king.[2]

John Hampden's trial[3] took place on February 6, 1684. The chief witness was again Howard, but his evidence was now become farcical; for his own remorse removed all conviction from his words; indeed he was alleged to have declared that Russell died an innocent man, and he was said to have confessed to a friend that he could not have a pardon until his drudgery of swearing was over. Lord chief justice Jeffreys, anxious on behalf of this witness, asked whether he had his pardon, and on being assured in the affirmative by the solicitor-general he remarked, 'Then your lordship may be covered'.[4] Evidence was then given of Hampden's 'high misdemeanour' in having agreed that a certain person should be sent to Scotland 'to incite divers persons there to come into England to consult with you, Hampden, concerning aid and assistance to be supplied from Scotland'. This hypothesis was nearly as cloudy as that which had procured the conviction of Sidney. Jeffreys, after a speech in defence of Howard and in accusation of the prisoner, directed the jury to find a verdict of guilty,[5] which was promptly done. His sentence was comparatively light—a fine of £40,000 and imprisonment until he paid it.

One more notable trial remains to be recorded of a period when history was being accelerated by judge and executioner. The duke of York brought an action against Titus Oates on the statute *De scandalis magnatum*, and the case was heard on June 18, 1684.[6] The indictment alleged that Oates had circulated false

---

[1] *The arraignment, tryal and condemnation of Algernon Sidney Esq.* (1684), 54.

[2] *Baschet*, 155, July 5/15, 1683.

[3] *The tryal and conviction of John Hambden Esq.* (1684).

[4] Ibid. 17.   [5] Ibid. 38–54.

[6] *The account of the manner of executing a writ of enquiry of damages between H.R.H. James duke of York and Titus Oates* (1684).

news and lies about the duke of York, the specific instance being
that in December 1682, in a coffee-house, 'amid divers venerable
persons' he had held up a letter and proclaimed in a loud voice:
'This letter cost me nine pence and might have been brought for
a penny; nobody is the better for it but that traitor the duke of
York.'[1] Justice Warcup gave evidence in support of the charge;
and Jeffreys (who addressed the accused with scathing emphasis
as *Mr.* Oates) demanded that he should be made an example of.[2]
The jury took the hint, and assessed the damages at £100,000
with the somewhat superfluous addition of 20s. costs; and so
Titus disappeared for a short time from public view, convicted
(so strange was the age) not as a perjurer, but as a premature
advocate of the penny post. It was indeed a melancholy fate
that had overtaken the whigs. Monmouth was in hiding; Shaftesbury had died in exile; Essex had destroyed himself; Russell and
Sidney had lost their lives, and Oates had lost his doctorate. The
Popish Plot had destroyed about a score of persons, mainly
priests or Jesuits; the Stuart revenge, on the other hand, had
removed some of the most distinguished representatives of the
English aristocracy, and was therefore the more notable as an
object-lesson. Supreme above it all was the cynical monarch,
comfortable at last; now almost domesticated by the duchess of
Portsmouth; his royal person specially protected by a Swiss
bodyguard sent over by his solicitous ally Louis XIV.[3] He was
still, it is true, being plagued by the prince of Orange, but he had
given his nephew 'a slap in the face'[4] by marrying his niece the
princess Anne to the Lutheran George of Denmark; so William
could no longer claim to be the sole exponent in the family of
virtue and Protestantism.

This marriage was acceptable to Louis, since Denmark was
among the subsidized allies of France, and it may be numbered
with the consequences of the French subsidy on English policy.
Abroad, these consequences were also demonstrated. The French
king continued his aggressions in the Spanish Netherlands, confident that he could do so without involving himself in war; while

---

[1] Ibid. 5.   [2] Ibid. 19, 21–2.
[3] *Baschet*, 155, July 14/24, 1683. It was commanded by the marquis de
Tilladet.
[4] Ibid., May 3/13. The marriage was solemnized on July 28, 1683.

on his side Charles expressed a willingness to help his Spanish ally
by arbitration; but Ronquillo, the Spanish ambassador, knew
that, as arbiter, Charles would decide in favour of Louis; so he
demanded mediation, which in his turn Louis refused to accept.
There was, therefore, an element of futility in the prolonged
negotiations whereby the Spanish and Dutch envoys strove to
induce Charles to honour his treaty with Spain and his promises
of 1681. Moreover, as the Dutch were divided, and as Amsterdam was lacking in sympathy for the policy of William, Louis
was able to proceed on his way unchecked, capturing Luxemburg
in May 1684, and foisting on the humiliated Spanish government a 'truce' of twenty years. For French ascendancy in these
years Charles must accept some of the blame; and Louis was able
to congratulate himself on the advantages secured to him by the
verbal treaty; but not for long, since he had to restore Luxemburg
with other conquests at the peace of Ryswick. He had purchased
the admittedly valueless neutrality of England, but he could not
have foreseen that the England of Charles Stuart would one day
be replaced by the England of king William, and still worse for
him by the England of queen Anne.

A period of more intense reaction followed on the discovery of
the Rye House Plot. In March 1683 Luttrell noted that the
tempers of men were now much altered from what they had been
only a year ago, 'most now seeming Tories',[1] a change nowhere
more clearly illustrated than in the fugitive literature of the
period, in which there were two main motives—hatred of whigs
and dissenters, and unbounded, indeed extravagant devotion to
the crown. In this chorus the voice of the subsidized L'Estrange
was the loudest. He had already exhausted all the similitudes
of vituperation in comparisons of 1681 with 1641; he then
exposed the Popish Plot, contending that Godfrey's death was
due to suicide; he followed up Marvell's *History of Popery* with
a *History of Knavery*, and after 1681 he produced a weekly
news-sheet, called *Heraclitus Ridens*, afterwards named *The
Observator*.[2] L'Estrange knew the importance of exaggeration in
journalism; he distorted the lines of party cleavage, but for

[1] Luttrell, *Brief narration* . . . (1857 ed.), i. 252.
[2] For a good account of L'Estrange's literary activities see G. Kitchin,
Sir Roger L'Estrange.

that reason brought them within the vision of a greater number of men.

The principles of L'Estrange were not more extreme than those advocated in the addresses which poured in from loyal grand juries. That from Kent in March 1683 condemned not only popery and fanaticism, but 'all such as pretend to moderation in execution of the laws, where the government is apparently assaulted'; from Bristol, formerly a stronghold of nonconformity, came a petition for the enforcement of the law against conventicles; Northampton sent a long list of disaffected persons, with the suggestion that they should be required to give security for keeping the peace; the jurymen of Devonshire were convinced that the Rye House Plot was attributable to nonconformist preachers; others, such as the grand jury of Southwark, blamed coffee-houses, seditious books, taverns. Other juries thought that greater control might be exercised over the talk at public places of refreshment if the keepers of these places were required to take the sacrament according to the practice of the Church of England.[1]

Charles made no secret of his intention to exact retribution for the Popish Plot.[2] So the campaign against the Dissenters was intensified, and the winter of 1683–4, one of the coldest on record, was a period of exceptional suffering for the recusants, of whom 1,300 Quakers are known to have been imprisoned throughout the greater part of the winter.[3] The year 1684 was that in which the French dragoons commenced their operations against the Huguenots; the same year saw a tentative beginning in England of the same process. But for the earnest solicitations of the justices, dragoons would have been sent into Shropshire in December 1684 in order to apply the methods of persuasion then being applied in Scotland and France;[4] and it was a striking tribute to the strength of English local government that, distorted as it had been by the remodellings, it was yet powerful enough to resist this sinister proposal. In Scotland, where there was no

[1] A large collection of these addresses will be found in *Bodley, Ashmole* 1674.
[2] *Baschet*, 149, Aug. 11/21, 1681.
[3] *S.P. Dom.* 29, bundle 436, State of the Quakers, Jan. 1684.
[4] Ibid., bundle 438, letters from Charles Holt and other Justices to Sunderland, Dec. 8 and Dec. 15, 1684.

such protection for the subject, the reign of terror was unchecked.
In December 1684 general Drummond was given a commission
to exercise military law and to hang, draw, and quarter all who
refused the king's authority. The efficacy of this measure was
seen in the fact that men condemned at two were hanged at five.[1]
These things provided a warning to any English whig who dared
to raise his head; and if he insisted on losing his head, he could
read, in the *Apology* attributed to Jack Ketch,[2] a description of
the posture most suitable at executions for ensuring 'a quicker
despatch out of this world'.

By April 1684 the royal triumph appeared to be complete.
Parliament was not again summoned, in spite of the provisions
of the Triennial Act, and the king intimated to Barrillon that he
had no thoughts of summoning parliament.[3] In the preceding
February, by the connivance of the judges, Danby was released
from the Tower, and the three surviving Catholic peers, lords
Arundel, Powis and Belasyse, were also liberated. The duke of
York resumed his effective control over the Navy,[4] and there
was talk of reconstituting him lord high admiral; moreover, when
Jenkins resigned his secretaryship, Godolphin was installed in his
place, and the likelihood of Rochester exchanging his office of
first commissioner of the Treasury for that of lord high treasurer
served to strengthen the possibility that Charles would still more
securely establish himself on the bases of reaction and sub-
serviency, with York and Barrillon as his counsellors and
Rochester and Godolphin as his tools. The completion by Louis
of his *réunion* annexations, and the return of Dartmouth in April
1684 from the evacuation of Tangier formed a fitting climax to
this policy of terrorism at home and surrender abroad.

But the reign, so full of unsolved problems, ended on a note of
interrogation. What was the purport of the ministerial changes
which caused such surprise in the summer of 1684?[5] A relative

---

[1] Fountainhall, *Chronological notes of Scottish affairs*, 48.

[2] *The apology of John Ketch Esq.* (occasioned by his bungling at the execution of lord Russell) in *Bodley Ashmole*, F. 6.

[3] *Baschet*, 157, March 9/19, 1684.

[4] On May 8/18, 1684, Louis wrote to Barrillon: 'Le roi d'Angleterre ne
pourrait prendre une résolution plus convenable au bien de ses affaires et
à sa réputation qu'est celle de rétablir le duc d'York dans toutes ses fonc-
tions.' *Aff. Étr. (Angleterre)*, 152, f. 292.   [5] For this see *Halifax*, i. 420–8.

of Halifax, Henry Thynne, was appointed to the Treasury commission; in August, Rochester, to his disgust, was 'kicked upstairs' into the office of lord president of the council; in November there was talk of sending the duke of York back to Scotland as royal commissioner; there were also rumours of a secret visit of Monmouth to England and a reconciliation with his father; there were even hints of more friendly overtures to the prince of Orange. There seemed a possibility that the moderate and humane counsels of Halifax would at last prevail, and in the *Character of a Trimmer* Halifax delineated for the benefit of Charles a philosophy of kingship wherein were incorporated all the lessons to be deduced from the shame and tragedy of these years. It seemed that an age of marvels was about to be capped by the supreme marvel of all—the repentance of a Stuart.

It is possible, however, that these things are proof not of radical change, but of vacillation or experiment. In April 1684 the verbal treaty of 1681 was at an end, and no fresh commitments were made; but that did not mean the termination of the French connexion. There had been delay and dispute in the payments of the subsidy; the money was in arrears, and some of it was still owing at Charles's death;[1] this may account in part for the omission to renew the engagement in April 1684. Of two facts the correspondence provides proof; that Charles and his brother were determined to rule as the pensionaries of France, and that Louis was willing to pay them, not only to secure acquiescence in French policy, but for a more constructive and disinterested object—to maintain a strong Stuart monarchy in England. But Charles, unlike James, had a genius for obtaining a good bargain; and it is likely that the changes of 1684 were only one more illustration of this instinct. There was a reconciliation with Monmouth, but it was short-lived, for the unfortunate duke refused to write a confession incriminating his associates; and as he would not turn informer, he was ordered to leave the Court.[2] The more friendly attitude to the prince of Orange may have sprung from the fact that in August 1684 the prince's supremacy was seriously

---

[1] The amount was 470,000 livres. See the letter of Louis to Barrillon, May 15/25, 1685, in Fox, *A history of the early part of the reign of James II*, Appendix lxxxvii.

[2] *Baschet*, 156, Nov. 26/Dec. 6 and Dec. 6/16, 1683.

threatened by the Amsterdam oligarchy, and there was a possibility of reconciliation between the States General and Louis, whereby it became the interest of Charles to support the anti-French element among the Dutch.[1] Otherwise the policy of Charles was perfectly consistent. He confessed that he had taken the side of France for the rest of his life;[2] he was secretly annoyed at William's patronage of Monmouth in Holland;[3] he declared himself resolved to dismiss Halifax from the Council;[4] he recalled Ormonde from Ireland and appointed Rochester in his place; many Catholics were released from prison, and it was freely rumoured that there was a design to create a papist army in Ireland.[5] In neither England nor Scotland was a parliament summoned, and James remained by his brother's side, relentless and vindictive, eager to clutch the sceptre which had so nearly eluded his grasp.

In October 1684 Charles and his brother inspected the troops mustered on Putney Heath, and the tory pamphleteers acclaimed this public demonstration that the crown now possessed a standing army for its preservation against whiggery and dissent.[6] Whither these things tended was a question as difficult as that occasioned in the early months of 1660, when the Rump was confronted by the veterans of Monck. But the question was not to be answered by Charles. On February 1, 1685, he had a seizure, and, after rallying, died[7] before noon on the 6th, after receiving absolution, communion, and extreme unction at the hands of a priest. Before he died he asked for the curtains to be drawn so that he might see the light of day; he besought the reconciliation of his brother and the forgiveness of his queen, and it was in this spirit of solicitude for others that Charles quitted a crowded stage whereon he had seemed as often spectator as actor.

---

[1] *Baschet*, 159, Aug. 11/21, 1684. [2] Ibid. 159, Aug. 11/21, 1684.
[3] Ibid. 159, Oct. 16/26. [4] Ibid. 159, Dec. 4/14.
[5] Ibid. 160, Dec. 29, 1684/Jan. 8, 1685.
[6] Some of the pamphlets are in *Bodley, Ashmole*, G. 15. See also *The exercise of musquet and pike as performed before H.M. and H.R.H. at Putney Heath, Oct. 1, 1684*, in *Bodley, Ashmole*, H. 23, no. 4.
[7] For the cause of the king's death see E. R. Crawfurd, *The last days of Charles II.*

XVIII

THE PLANTATIONS AND DEPENDENCIES

THREE main types of settlement have to be considered—(1) the garrison of Tangier and the dependencies in India, the latter administered by the East India Company: (2) the crown and proprietary colonies in the west, represented by Barbados, the Leeward Islands, Jamaica, New York, and New Jersey, together with Maryland, the Carolinas and Pennsylvania; and (3) the New England group, consisting of Massachusetts (with New Hampshire), New Plymouth, Connecticut, and Rhode Island.

Of English possessions in Asia and Africa the most important were those acquired by the Portuguese marriage—Tangier[1] and Bombay. Tangier, which had come into Portuguese possession in 1471, was deemed to be Spanish when Portugal lost her independence in 1580; consequently, after its acquisition by England, there was always the possibility of the revival of Spanish claims. Arrangements were speedily made for the fortification and settlement of this new possession; and in September 1661 Henry Mordaunt, earl of Peterborough, received his commission as governor. Control was vested in a committee of the Privy Council, and to the governor was delegated the power of making laws for the civil government. The port was declared free for five years to all traffic except that from the English plantations and from beyond the Cape of Good Hope.[2] As a further encouragement to commerce it was enacted that foreign merchants might freely trade in the port until six months after the outbreak of hostilities involving their native countries.[3] Tangier was valued in England because it was hoped that from this base an entry might be obtained into the rich Barbary trade of corn, hides, oils, feathers, copper, and gold. This, however, was eventually left to private enterprise.

The first problem was to provide a civil population for the new

[1] For a good account of Tangier under English rule see E. M. G. Routh, *Tangier*.

[2] Steele, i. 3369, Nov. 16, 1662.   [3] Steele, i. 3606, Jan. 13, 1675.

African outpost. Some proposed that first offenders should be sent out; others suggested a third part of the population of Scotland; the government eventually dispatched a mixed contingent containing some criminals and political offenders.[1] In order to supplement the recruits for the garrison, deceit had sometimes to be practised; men were enlisted on the understanding that they were intended for Portsmouth, when their real destination was Tangier. The total establishment was estimated to cost £70,000 per annum;[2] and when in 1663 lord Rutherford succeeded Peterborough as governor, the garrison consisted of 2,000 men. By 1678 the civilian population amounted to only 600 persons.[3] From the start, danger came from the Arabs, notably the hordes led by the crafty Ghailan, who, in pursuing his design of creating an independent kingdom in Northern Fez, was destined to prove the bane of the English garrison. Rutherford was killed in a skirmish in May 1664, and was succeeded by lord Belasyse, under whom the port developed a trade with Spain; at the same time, a great defensive mole was constructed. In the Second Dutch War the strategic value of the port was proved; for, using it as his base, sir Jeremy Smith was able to hold the Straits while the French fleet was cooped up in Toulon; it served also to support the fleet of English privateers preying on French and Dutch merchantmen in the Mediterranean. By the end of the war Tangier had received the charter of an incorporated city, having a civil court presided over by the mayor and recorder; while its commercial causes were adjudicated in a court-merchant which met daily.

But Tangier never prospered. It was isolated in a hostile territory: its garrison, barely adequate for defence, could scarcely hold its own against Arab aggressors; moreover, there was little capital circulating in the port. Because of the economies forced upon them, governors had to sacrifice the defences; the garrison was dependent on provisions sent from home, which, owing to the lack of imagination sometimes found in official victuallers, were generally more suited for a Northern winter than an African summer, consisting as they did of salt beef, pork, cheese, and

---

[1] For examples see *Cal. S.P. Dom., 1663–4*, 536, 539.

[2] E. M. G. Routh, *Tangier*, 29.

[3] *H.M.C. Rep.* xi, pt. v. 27. Dartmouth MSS.

oatmeal. Casks of meat which had outstayed their welcome else-where were sometimes thought good enough for dispatch to this Cinderella of the empire. Few 'men of credit' settled in the port, so there was little capital for trade with the Moors; and even that with Spain was carried on mainly by French merchants. It was a place of call rather than a settlement: itinerant Turks and Armenians spread out their glittering wares on the sands before the eyes of a needy populace; but even these, the most insistent of all traffickers, could do little business. There was a chance that a fruit and wine trade with England might have been established, but the difficulty was to find ships, as the port was more fre-quented by men-of-war than by merchantmen; and so merchants had often to entrust their goods to the former, at the cost of naval efficiency. Men such as Palmes Fairborne (deputy governor, 1676–8) devoted themselves to the interests of the settlement; but this self-sacrifice was outweighed by the cynical fatalism of Sun-derland, and the indifference of lord Inchiquin (governor, 1674–80). In 1680, after a siege, the fortifications were almost in ruins.

Events at home precipitated the end. Rumours that Charles intended to sell Tangier caused parliament in 1679 to draft a Bill for annexing it to the imperial crown of England,[1] so that it might not be sold to the French; but the fate of Tangier was sealed when it was made the price of Charles's consent to exclusion.[2] In the winter of 1682–3 Charles tried to sell it to France, but Louis would not have it;[3] an attempt was then made to sell it to Portu-gal, but this also failed.[4] Charles therefore decided to quit possession of a place which he could not afford to keep, and so it was evacuated in August 1683, after elaborate precautions had been taken to destroy the mole. So ended England's most un-fortunate overseas enterprise.

Bombay, 'with all rights, profits, and territories thereto belong-ing' was acquired by the crown in accordance with the eleventh clause of the marriage treaty. The wording of this clause was easily capable of dispute; for it was not clear whether the de-pendencies were included, a doubt which led to prolonged dis-pute. The Portuguese intended by the grant to facilitate English co-operation against the Dutch in the East Indies, and were

---

[1] *C.J.* ix. 625, May 20, 1679. [2] See *supra*, 603.
[3] *Baschet*, 154, Jan. 4/14, 1683. [4] Ibid. 155, April 23/May 3, 1683.

specially anxious that the religion of the Portuguese merchants should be safeguarded; while the English wished mainly to develop the commercial possibilities of the new acquisition, two points of view never quite reconciled.[1] Difficulties commenced with the arrival, in March 1662, of a fleet with 500 troops to take possession. By the English it was insisted that the dependencies were included in the grant; while the Portuguese were equally certain that only the island was referred to. More pressing was the question: where to land the troops? Oxenden, the agent at Surat, was asked for permission to land them there, but the consent of the Moghul emperor could not be obtained, and eventually the garrison was landed on the unhealthy island of Anjediva, where half of them died from disease. While these men were perishing, an acrimonious correspondence was being conducted by the two governments on the correct interpretation of the treaty, and a stage was even reached when the Portuguese offered to buy back Bombay; but they could not find the money to pay Clarendon's price of £120,000, with £109,000 for the expenses of the expedition.

Not till January 1665 did Humfrey Cooke (the 'Inofre Coque' of Portuguese orthography) take over Bombay as governor, and then only the port and island, a concession deeply resented at home. In terms of a convention not ratified by either government the Portuguese were to have free trade in the port, and the English undertook to respect the religion of Catholics, but all religious refugees and runaways were to be excluded.[2] As the dependencies were not included in this agreement, English ships were subjected to heavy duties at Thana and Karanja. But though Cooke began his governorship by concession, he soon augmented it by acquisition; for before the end of his governorship (1666) he had taken over Mahim, Sion, Dharavu, and Vadala, so that Bombay now included all the islands except Colaba and Old Woman's Island.[3] This policy was followed by his successor sir Gervase Lucas.

So far, Bombay had brought to the Stuart bridegroom not riches, but irritation and expense. In 1666 the cost of ammuni-

---

[1] See P. B. M. Malabari, *Bombay in the making*, ch. iii; also S. A. Khan, *Anglo-Portuguese negotiations relating to Bombay*.

[2] Malabari, op. cit. 98–9.　　　　　　　　　　　　[3] Ibid. 103.

tion and victuals amounted to £11,498, while the rents, including the revenue from taverns, Customs, tobacco, and coco-nuts, was only £6,490.[1] Charles's finances were too straitened to permit the retention of a possession which promised nothing but an annual deficit: accordingly, in December 1667 he granted it to the East India Company to be held in free and common socage at a rent of £10 per annum. The royal charter surrendering Bombay to the Company is dated March 27, 1668. By this, the Company acquired full dominion and jurisdiction in the port and island, thereby adding to their trading privileges the prerogative of civil and military government. The right of reversion was preserved to the crown by the terms of the grant, which specified that the laws enacted should be 'consonant to reason, and not repugnant or contrary, but as near as may be agreeable to the laws of England'. There was also a proviso for the exercise of the Roman Catholic religion by Portuguese merchants. On these terms Bombay was taken over by sir George Oxenden, the Company's representative at Surat.

The most notable of the earlier governors appointed by the Company was Gerald Aungier,[2] who first established a civil administration. He divided the inhabitants into orders and tribes, each having a representative; and by this 'Panchayat' system, as it was called, he inaugurated a measure of self-government, with the governor and council as a court of appeal. The most responsible among the English merchants were appointed justices: suits involving more than 3½ rupees were reserved for the governor and council; the nucleus of a civil service was provided by a contingent of Parbhu clerks. Disputed land titles were settled by the summoning of conventions, and, after the confirmation of land titles, the quit-rents were increased. Tolerant and enterprising, Aungier conciliated English, Italian, and Portuguese by respect for their distinctive characteristics; he encouraged traders and weavers to settle; he extended still farther the area under his governorship, until by the end of his administration the population had reached 60,000 and the revenue £9,000. The Company considered, however, that he had taken

[1] S. A. Khan, *East India trade in the seventeenth century*, 137.
[2] Malabari, op. cit., ch. iv, and *English Factories in India*, ed. sir W. Foster, 1665–7, 180 sqq.

upon himself more than was proper; so when he died (1677), the salary of his successor was fixed at £300 instead of £500, and the relative importance of Bombay declined. The victim of the Company's economies and maladministration, Bombay came most notably into public prominence in 1683, when captain Richard Keigwin, heading a revolt of the discontented garrison, overthrew the Company's civil representative and had himself elected governor. In his correspondence with Charles II he so ingratiated himself with that monarch as to obtain a full pardon.[1]

In 1687 the fortified Bombay superseded Surat as the headquarters of the western presidency.[2] By that time sir Josiah Child had become a leading spirit in the East India Company. His policy was to strengthen the coast-line in order to make trade more secure; to accord fair treatment to the natives, without binding himself by legal scruple; to follow the Dutch example of raising a revenue from natives to defray the charge of their protection; to increase the number of trading stations, and to avoid as much as possible the responsibilities and inconveniences of political domination. In the pursuit of this policy he amassed great wealth for himself and his relatives; and the political influence which he was thereby able to purchase accounts in part for the increasing jealousy and hostility with which the Company came to be regarded. After 1680 the Company had to increase its exports of broadcloth in order to conciliate public opinion; but interloping steadily increased, and by the reign of William III, when the interests of the Company became entangled with party politics, its reorganization was inevitable.

Elsewhere in India the foundations of British power were being established. The fort at Madras was strengthened in 1677 against the Marathas by sir Streynsham Masters. Defence was speedily followed by the institution of civil administration; a court of judicature and a bank were instituted, and by 1688 there existed a municipal government in Madras.[3] But with the decay of the Moghul empire the Company had to depend more and more on the guns of its ships and the enterprise of its servants. Of these servants one of the most notable was Job Charnock, appointed

---

[1] For this incident and the career of a remarkable man see R. and O. Strachey, *Keigwin's Rebellion*.   [2] *Cambridge History of India*, v. 101–2.
[3] Sir W. Hunter, *A History of British India*, ii. 233 sqq.

chief of the Bengal council in 1685. In December 1686, when the Company was at war with the Moghul, he proceeded down the Hughli with a small force to the site of the modern Calcutta, where he made a resolute stand against the land forces threatening him on every side;[1] and in the following autumn he erected a factory on the pool of Calcutta, after adventures and privations of almost epic magnitude. He was an empire-builder in the strict sense of that term. When, in 1690, the Company had to accept a contemptuous peace from Aurungzeb, Charnock returned to his ruined settlement on the Hughli and laid the foundations of one more capital in India.[2]

The East India Company had a station at Bantam in Java, from which it was hoped to develop the spice trade; but, early in 1683, the Dutch expelled the English from the fort. This was one of the events which obliged the Company to concentrate on India, and to build up political supremacy on the basis of sea power. Another event occurred which helped the Company to maintain the maritime connexions on which depended sovereignty in the east; this was the capture of St. Helena from the Dutch. The island had been taken over by the Company's ships in 1652; it was lost to the enemy during each of the later Anglo-Dutch wars; but in 1673 it was again seized (by captain Munden), and granted to the East India Company. Thereafter it was the 'sea inn' of the eastern trade. St. Helena was of special importance to English communications because the Dutch were then supreme at the Cape of Good Hope.

On the mainland of South America several attempts had been made to colonize parts of Guiana;[3] and in 1663 Charles granted to Francis, lord Willoughby all the area called Surinam. This settlement was called Willoughby Land, and contained about 4,000 persons who suffered severely from sickness. It was captured by the Dutch in the Second Dutch War, and though recaptured by admiral sir John Harman it was ceded to the Dutch by the treaty of Breda. The insalubrious Cayenne was occupied by the English for ten years (1654–64); it changed hands in the Second Anglo-Dutch War, and was eventually given up to the French. In the West Indies, the Bermudas or Somers Islands had been

---

[1] Ibid. ii. 257.   [2] P. E. Roberts, *History of British India*, 46.
[3] For this see J. A. Williamson, *English colonies in Guiana and on the Amazon*.

granted in 1615 to the earl of Southampton and others, who were incorporated into a company; in 1684 the company's rights were transferred to the crown. From Bermuda were exported provisions to other colonies; among its exports to England were tobacco and cedar wood. The Bahamas were not occupied until 1670.

In the Caribbean are two groups of islands known as the Windward Islands, that is, Barbados, St. Lucia, St. Vincent, and Tobago; and the Leeward Islands, comprising Antigua, Montserrat, Nevis, and St. Christopher. Officially, the ownership of the Caribbean islands was taken over by the king after the Restoration; but actually something of the old proprietary right survived in the terms of the patent of Francis, lord Willoughby, who was appointed governor-in-chief of all the Caribees. He ruled with the assistance of a council and island representatives, and the planters' right to their estate was confirmed by their agreement to pay the four-and-a-half per cent. export duty. Of strategic importance, the Leeward Islands had had to bear the brunt of French attacks during the Second Anglo-Dutch War, the English being driven from Antigua and Montserrat, as well as from their portion of St. Christopher (St. Kitts), while Nevis was preserved for England only at great cost. But in May 1667 the French fleet was decisively defeated in Nevis roads. Antigua and Montserrat had been recaptured a few months earlier, and the English parts of St. Kitts were restored by the treaty of Breda. The administration of these islands had therefore to face the question of obtaining locally a contribution to the cost of defence. It was proposed to start a fund for this purpose, but this was refused in 1682 by a general assembly representing each of the island legislatures; this body also refused to grant a perpetual revenue to the crown, and the planters declined to pay for the maintenance of an agent in England.[1] These refusals implied a challenge not successfully contested by the governments of either Charles II or James II.

Of the Windward group, by far the most important was Barbados,[2] an island having a population reckoned in 1668 at about 20,000 planters and whites, and 40,000 negroes, its trade

[1] C. S. S. Higham, *The Development of the Leeward Islands*, 230 sqq.
[2] For a good account see V. T. Harlow, *Barbados*.

carried on by 10,000 tons of shipping.[1] With its militia of 6,000 men it was the best fortified of the islands, and its 100,000 acres were worth from £10 to £20 an acre. At first tobacco was the staple crop; but this was superseded by sugar, the production of which necessitated a large supply of black labour; this was provided by the Royal African Company, which, after its reconstitution in 1672, was able to dispose of negroes at £16 per head.[2] This increase in the proportion of the African element helped to accentuate the problems of population in Barbados, where unusual conditions prevailed; for land was concentrated in the hands of the large proprietors,[3] and few servants who had served their indentures could hope to acquire a holding; moreover, it had been the practice of Cromwell to ship felons and desperate characters to the island.[4] Another problem was that of overproduction. Sugar, assessed in the Book of Rates (1660) at 30s. per hundred pounds, steadily fell in price owing to gluts and competition from French and Portuguese sugar colonies; by 1685 the price[5] had sunk to 20s. By that time England had lost the European market in refined sugar, but continued to maintain her re-export trade in raw sugar, which, as it needed more shipping than refined, was given preferential treatment when additional duties were imposed in 1685. This policy was at the expense of the refiners in the West Indies, notably Barbados; and caused such discontent that there was at times a danger of the island going over to the French.[6]

The largest and most important of the English West Indian possessions was Jamaica, having an area of over 4,000 square miles. Captured from Spain in 1655 by Penn and Venables, it was the 'pet' colony of the Restoration, for its climate favoured the production of those sub-tropical products most in demand, namely, sugar, coffee, ginger, pepper, and cinchona bark; moreover, it abounded in cattle and horses. Jamaica conformed most closely to the current conception of the ideal plantation; because

---

[1] *Cal. S.P. Amer.*, *1661–8*, 586–7. Report of lord Willoughby, July 9, 1668. See also ibid. 207, Report of sir T. Modyford, May 10, 1664.

[2] Higham, op. cit. 150–4.

[3] In 1667 they were said to be only 760 in number. *Cal. S.P. Amer.*, *1661–8*, 529.   [4] Harlow, op. cit. 117.   [5] Higham, op. cit. 192.

[6] *Cal. S.P. Dom.*, *1676–7*, 464. Notes by Williamson of information about Barbados.

its size favoured both commercial development and effective control; it offered a good market for English manufactured goods; it absorbed many of the negroes sent out by the African Company, and it exported those commodities in demand for home consumption and for re-export to the Continent. Special encouragement was given by the home government. In 1663 its exports were freed from Customs dues for five years,[1] and settlers there were given thirty acres, on condition that they served in arms and reserved one-twentieth of mineral rights to the crown.[2] This special favour was justified by results, for the history of the island under the later Stuarts was one of almost uninterrupted progress. In 1670 the population consisted of about 15,000 persons occupying 209,000 acres; there were about 57 sugar refineries, 49 indigo works, and 47 cocoa walks.[3] The revenue from quit-rents and duties on wine was then £1,870, and the expenses of government, including salaries of governor, deputy governor, major-general, and chief justice, together with upkeep of fortresses, amounted to £3,500. The spiritual needs of the island were seen to by five ministers, each having a salary of £100, paid by the crown.

Privateering[4] was the chief outlet for planters who wished to secure quicker returns on their capital. Near at hand lay some of the richest outposts of the exclusive Spanish empire; and though, in 1660, England was at peace with Spain, it was held by the council in Jamaica that the peace concerned only European waters. That the home government shared this view was seen in the instructions given to lord Windsor, who was sent to Jamaica as governor in 1661; for he was authorized to concert measures with the governor of Barbados against the Spaniards. A start was soon made, and in the following year captain Myngs took St. Iago in Cuba,[5] and early in 1663 there was a landing at Campeche[6] at the southern extremity of the gulf of Mexico. Charles was obliged to disavow these enterprises and leave this irregular warfare to the discretion of the governor; while at Madrid a succes-

[1] *Cal. Tr. Bks.*, *1660-7*, 725.   [2] *Steele*, i. 3346, Dec. 14, 1661.
[3] *Cal. S.P. Amer.*, *1669-74*, 104.
[4] For this subject see C. H. Haring, *The Buccaneers in the West Indies*.
[5] Sir C. H. Firth, *The capture of St. Iago* in *E.H.R.* xiv.
[6] Haring, op. cit. 107-8.

sion of English envoys, including Fanshawe, Sandwich, and Godolphin, were instructed to press for admission into the Spanish
empire, and in particular to secure the entry of negroes. But in
Godolphin's Anglo-Spanish treaty[1] of 1670 there was a clause
enacting that these depredations should cease. Piracy was thus
disavowed by both nations; nevertheless numerous conflicts were
occasioned by the cutting of logwood in the bay of Campeche by
Jamaican adventurers, and cargoes of this wood, though not
contraband, were generally confiscated by Spanish ships. The
English government connived at the cutting of Campeche wood;
but it was suggested that the privateers should cut it only in
unfrequented parts near the sea, and should confine themselves
to that alone.[2] Thus there existed in the years after 1670 a situation not unlike that which preceded the war of 1739 between
England and Spain.

This might be illustrated from the careers of notable pirates.
One of these was the Welshman sir Henry Morgan,[3] who, having
served his indentures in Barbados, went to Jamaica, where he
bought a ship and formed a small stock. In 1666 he was commissioned by governor Modyford to serve under captain Edward
Mansfield in an expedition against Curaçao; and on the latter's
death he became commander-in-chief of the West Indian buccaneers. In June 1668, with 10 ships and 500 men, he sacked
Porto Bello (on the isthmus of Darien), the head-quarters of
Spanish trade in central America, and destroyed the armada
sent against him, capturing 250,000 pieces of eight. In 1670 he
threatened Spanish dominion in Cuba, and was accorded a vote
of thanks by the Jamaican council;[4] this was followed by another
landing in Panama and the destruction of Spanish forts.[5] But
his actions were now disavowed, and his career at sea came to
an end. A second period of usefulness was inaugurated when,
through his favour with king Charles, he was appointed (1674)
lieutenant-governor of Jamaica and second-in-command to lord

[1] Dumont, vii, pt. i. 137–9, see supra, i. 350.

[2] Godolphin's memorandum for Arlington, May 1672, in Sloane MS. 180,
f. 71.

[3] For his career see the Transactions of the Society of Cymmrodorion, 1903–4;
also Haring, op. cit., ch. v.

[4] Cal. S.P. Amer., 1669–74, 220, May 31, 1671.

[5] Ibid., 1669–74, 190.

Vaughan,[1] in which shore occupation he distinguished himself by his piety, his interest in churches, and his zeal against pirates; but in old age he appears to have reverted to his dissolute ways,[2] and he became a serious menace to the peace of the island. He shared with colonel Blood and captain Keigwin the honour of Charles's personal esteem.

Like Jamaica, Newfoundland had a special prestige in the hierarchy of English settlements, for it had been discovered by Cabot, and its cod-fishing was of special importance to England because of the seamen who were trained in the fleets. It was thought that, if properly managed, the fisheries might have produced £50,000 per annum in Customs, and could give employment to about 10,000 sailors.[3] But these results were not achieved, because Newfoundland was not under a settled government; the French possessed the best harbours, and were trying to acquire more; there was continual hostility between the fishermen and the denizens of the island, which was regarded by Charles's government as no more than a fishery station. This was illustrated by the rules[4] for its administration which the privy council drew up in March 1671. According to these rules, Englishmen were to have freedom of fishing in any of the rivers or harbours of Newfoundland, to the complete exclusion of aliens; fishing masters were to take out men at the rate of not more than 60 for every 100 tons, and of these every fifth man must be a 'green' man, that is, an untrained seaman. Victuals for the whole season were to be taken out in each ship, the season beginning on March 1 and ending on October 1; sailors were not allowed to remain on the island during the winter. In spite of these rules a small colony of Englishmen succeeded in making a settlement, in the hope of providing for themselves by fish-curing; but their plight was a hard one, because they were frequently despoiled by the fishermen in the summer, while in the winter they had to endure the rigours of the climate. Most of their houses were really taverns. Moreover, both planter and fisherman destroyed much of the timber, for they rooted up young trees to make their stages,

[1] *Cal. S.P. Amer.*, *1669–74*, 571.
[2] Ibid., *1681–5*, 515 and 532–5.
[3] Ibid., *1661–8*, 558–9. Reasons for the settlement of Newfoundland.
[4] *P.C. Reg.* 62, March 10, 1671.

and at the end of the season the fishermen threw all their stone
ballast overboard into the shallow harbours.[1] In consequence,
the home government was insistent in its efforts to induce the
planters to go elsewhere, preferably to Barbados,[2] for the reason
that the adventurers could catch fish more cheaply than the
planters, and because the latter derived most of their products
from New England.

On the mainland Virginia was the most important crown
colony, and was occupied by Englishmen of substance, almost all
of them Anglicans, grouped not in villages as in New England,
but in plantations, most of them from 500 to 600 acres. In 1681
it was said that in the whole colony there was only one Papist
and 150 Dissenters, the latter being all Sweet Singers of Israel.[3]
The executive was vested in the Governor, assisted by a council
and an assembly of 41 burgesses. The councillors, who mono-
polized many of the best-paid offices, were nominated by the
governor; and the burgesses, who formed a close oligarchy, were
elected by the freeholders.[4] Labour was supplied by indentured
servants and by an increasing population of negroes. In temperament the Virginian planter was aristocratic, as befitted one who
directed the labour of others; his occupation afforded periods of
leisure, and his civilization reflected that of the landed classes in
England, which in some respects it surpassed. Education was
valued; the numerous Old Free Schools made illiteracy exceptional, and good teachers were recruited from the clergy.[5] The
machinery of English local government was preserved intact;
justice was administered 'according to the laws of England so
far as we are able to understand them'; matters of fact were tried
by juries, and included among the fundamental ordinances of
the state were Magna Carta, the Petition of Right, and the writ
of Habeas Corpus. In at least one respect there was an improvement on English custom, for penalties were more carefully
graduated to the offence, and corporal punishment was more

[1] *Cal. S.P. Amer.*, *1669–74*, 148–9.
[2] Ibid., *1675–6*, 226–7. Order in Council of May 5, 1676.
[3] Ibid., *1681–5*, 145.
[4] For this see P. A. Bruce, *Institutional History of Virginia in the seventeenth
century*, one of the most valuable contributions to the history of America.
[5] Bruce, op. cit., i. 331 sqq.

frequent than hanging; moreover, deeds of conveyance were enrolled in a public record office.

The charge of administration was raised by private levies in each parish for the minister, courts of justice, and payment of burgesses' wages; the sums so raised were not accounted for publicly. There was also the public levy, raised from time to time by the Assembly sitting in Jamestown; this was generally paid in tobacco, and was responsible for the production of much 'trash' tobacco.[1] Another serious difficulty in the management of the colony's revenues was that the general levies might be engrossed by particular persons, and applied to one fort at the expense of another; indeed it was the weakness of the colony's defences against the Indians that constituted the planters' greatest grievance. Another source of difficulty was the over-production of tobacco, which, coupled with the shortage of shipping, frequently caused acute economic distress. But in the midst of these things the House of Burgesses showed a zeal for constitutionalism as great as that of the English House of Commons. Thus in November 1683 they spent a day in wrangling with the Council over the swearing in of the Clerk of Assembly, and the appointment of joint committees. The Council gave way in the matter of the Clerk; the Burgesses then sent up their list of committees, which the Governor (lord Howard of Effingham) rejected, with a rebuke; whereupon the Council sent up an address to the effect that, as the Council had yielded over the Clerk, 'it might as well yield over the joint committees'. The governor then suggested the Stuart expedient of adjournment; but the Burgesses quoted precedents in support of their claim to nominate committees, and the matter was eventually settled by a conference between the two Houses.[2] The spirit of Westminster was abroad in the empire.

Hints of an even more ardent spirit had already been revealed in the rebellion known as Bacon's Rebellion. This arose mainly from the failure of the governor, sir William Berkeley, to listen to urgent requests[3] for protection against the repeated Indian raids. A crisis came with the invasion of the Susquehanna Indians in

[1] *Cal. S.P. Amer., 1681–5*, 154–5.
[2] Ibid., *1681–5*, 548–9, Nov. 20, 1683. Journal of the Assembly.
[3] Ibid., *1675–6*, 437–8.

May 1676. Meeting with no response from the governor, the
men of Charles City County organized themselves into a volun-
teer force under the command of a remarkable and hot-headed
man Nathaniel Bacon, member of a younger branch of the great
chancellor's family. Bacon and his men were ordered by Berkeley to disband; when they refused, they became technically
rebels, and during the summer months of 1676 the governor,
then approaching a vindictive and calculating dotage, was pitted
against the supporters of the popular leader. He won time by
acquiescing in the demand for a new assembly on an enlarged
franchise. Meanwhile Bacon formed an expeditionary force of
500 men, and, when Berkeley summoned the Militia against
him, civil war followed. It was in the midst of this (August 3)
that Bacon issued a manifesto, called a Declaration of the People
of Virginia, signed by him as 'general by consent of the people',
and containing an indictment of the government under these
heads: taxes on pretext of public works were diverted to favour-
ites; fortifications and trade were neglected; the governor's
friends were appointed to judgeships; the governor had made the
beaver trade a monopoly, and was protecting the Indians against
His Majesty's subjects.[1] One of Bacon's avowed objects was the
extirpation of the Indians.[2] The death of the leader in October
practically ended a movement which, had it been successful,
might have led to a more popular constitution in Virginia, and
even to a readjustment of relations with the mother country; it
was finally stamped out by ruthless executions. Commissioners
were sent out from England for its investigation, and as they
reported unfavourably on the conduct of Berkeley, he was sent
home in disgrace.

The justification for Bacon's rebellion lay in the bad government of the Virginian oligarchy, a government which left many
isolated planters defenceless against raids. In succeeding years
the colony fared ill at the hands of some of its governors, notably
lord Culpeper, whose object in coming to America was to retrieve
his fortunes, an object in which he succeeded at the expense of

[1] Ibid., 1675-6, 448.
[2] A good account of Vir_ nia nd the American plantations in this period
will be found in C. M. A d) s C onial Self-Government, and in E. Channing,
A History of the United St es, i

the colony. Otherwise he proved himself a good administrator, and was one of the first to suggest that the King in Council should formulate some uniform scheme of home defence or mutual assistance for the western plantations.[1] Poverty and thriftlessness appear to have caused a general irritability, which Culpeper's successor, lord Howard of Effingham (who succeeded in 1684), did something to intensify by his tactless handling of the Assembly; and not till after the Revolution, which was eagerly welcomed in Virginia, was the prosperity of the colony restored.

The association of Maryland with the Baltimore proprietors dated from their first charter of 1632. Protestants of all sects were encouraged to settle in order to counteract the original Roman Catholic element, a policy which made the position of the Roman Catholic proprietor lord Baltimore one of some difficulty. His almost feudal supremacy was restored at the Restoration; thereafter Maryland was a typical proprietary colony, its prosperity hampered to some extent by discord between the proprietor and his Puritan subjects, who contrived to extract a somewhat precarious subsistence from small, isolated farms and scattered tobacco plantations. As the colony had little shipping, its inhabitants suffered even more than did Virginia from gluts. In 1676 the population was about 20,000, and St. Mary's, then a small port of not more than about 30 houses,[2] was the seat of the Assembly of Burgesses, which held its session of six weeks once a year. These men were 'good ordinary householders, doing more by conscience than by syllogisms'.[3] Conflict between the officials of the Customs and of the proprietary increased with the more strict application of the Navigation laws, and a crisis was very nearly precipitated in 1684 when an English official was murdered by the deputy governor. This act almost caused the forfeiture of the proprietor's charter.[4]

Many of the Puritan settlers of Maryland lived in conditions of almost patriarchal simplicity and detachment. The Susquehanna divided the colony by a broad belt of deep water, thus

---

[1] *Cal. S.P. Amer., 1681–5*, 156. Culpeper to the Lords of Trade and Plantations, Dec. 12, 1681.

[2] Ibid., *1675–6*, 226.

[3] G. Alsop, *Character of the province of Maryland*, in *Narratives of Maryland*, ed. C. C. Hill, 351.   [4] *Cal. S.P. Amer., 1681–5*, vi.

helping to intensify the isolation of the homesteads, where there existed men and women who were perpetuating the traditions of an older and simpler England. They were thus described by an observer:

The Christian natives, especially those of the masculine sex, are generally conveniently confident, reservedly subtle, quick and apprehending, but slow in resolving; and when they spy profit sailing towards them with the wings of a prosperous gale, there they become much familiar. The women are extreme bashful at the first view, but after a continuance of time hath brought them acquainted, they become discreetly familiar and are much more talkative than men. One great part of the inhabitants are zealous, great pretenders to holiness; and where anything appears that carries on the frontispiece of its effigies the stamp of religion, tho' fundamentally never so imperfect, they are suddenly taken with it . . . and are very apt to be catch't. Quakerism is the only opinion that bears the bell away. The Anabaptists have little to say here; the Adamite, Ranter and Fifth Monarchy Man Maryland cannot digest within her liberal stomach.[1]

Maryland was therefore exceptional among the Puritan colonies in these respects: there was no clash of creeds; the fanatical sects were in a minority, and the Protestantism of the colony was tempered by the catholicism of its ruler and proprietor. In regard also to labour the colony was fortunate, for after four years' service the servant might become a freeman with 50 acres of land, a kit of tools, and three suits of clothes.[2]

Very different were the conditions in the Carolinas. The earliest grant of land in Carolina was that of 1629 to sir R. Heath; the first charter to lords proprietors was that dated March 24, 1663. Notable among the proprietors were two men, closely associated with the Usurpation—col. John Colleton, a man of great influence in Barbados, and Anthony Ashley Cooper. For some time both men had had in view the unoccupied lands in Carolina; and when the discontented elements in Barbados talked of another settlement, Colleton suggested an application for these lands. With Clarendon, Craven, Albemarle, Carteret, lord John Berkeley, and sir William Berkeley (governor of

[1] G. Alsop in *Maryland Narratives*, 352 sqq.
[2] Ibid. 358.

Virginia), Colleton, and Shaftesbury constituted the original eight proprietors, each of them contributing £25 capital. By their first charter they were granted the land on the continent between the 36th and the 31st parallel, the patentees to hold the land in free and common socage at a nominal rent, with power to make laws in conjunction with the freemen; they were also given the unusual right of conceding liberty of conscience to the settlers. The intention of this clause may have been to encourage settlers from Barbados, who, by their charter of 1652, were already endowed with this privilege.

There was no immediate response, for by 1672 only about 450 persons had settled in the province;[1] by which time it was thought that indigo, öil, silk, and tobacco might be produced, and, while sugar and cotton could be grown, the winter frosts were considered likely to prove fatal. The meagre population was hampered by shortage of provisions; only in constitutional experiment was there super-abundance. The first set of constitutions, dated 1669, was intended to encourage the settlement of 'ingenious and industrious persons' by the advantages of liberty of conscience, popular choice of governor and assembly, one hundred acres of land for each male, fifty for a female, and one thousand acres for a rent of ten shillings. This scheme owes much to the inspiration of Shaftesbury, and of Locke, who was secretary to the proprietors. It provided for a territorial aristocracy, the eldest called a palatine; the territory was divided into counties, each having eight seigniories, eight baronies, and twenty-four colonies of 12,000 acres; the seigniories pertaining to the proprietors, the baronies to the subordinate nobility, and the colonies to the commonalty. The subordinate nobility was divided into landgraves and caciques according to the number of their baronies. Executive and judicial power was vested in the eight proprietors sitting in their palatine court; they had the prerogative of summoning parliaments, pardoning offences, and vetoing the acts of parliament. The Church of England was to be established by law when occasion permitted, and meanwhile any body of at least seven members was accorded the rights of a church. Persons not members of a church were ostracized but not persecuted. There was no attempt to mitigate slavery. A lack

[1] *Cal. S.P. Amer., 1669–74*, 319.

of elasticity in the original scheme of 1669 led to changes in 1670 and 1682.[1]

As the experiment proceeded, the proprietors showed a zeal and forethought rare in such enterprises. The new-comers were enjoined to raise an adequate supply of provisions; they secured the remission for seven years of Customs duties on wine and silk exported to England; reservations were made for Quakers and Huguenots, and the town of Charlestown was built on a definite plan. With each fresh contingent of settlers the aristocratic owners showed an almost Gilbertian willingness to alter the 'fundamentals' in their favour; but they found some difficulty in soothing the susceptibilities of a party of Scots who 'doubted whether we have sufficiently provided against the oppression of the people by their administrators'.[2] 'We have no other aim', wrote Ashley in 1671, 'in the framing of our laws but to make every one as safe and happy as the state of human affairs is capable of.'[3] The laws were to be the 'equalest' that a state could have; terms which attracted many Protestants from England in the years 1679–1688, so that the population of the colony increased to about 3,000.

But the settlement did not at first answer the hopes of its founders. The proprietors were speedily in debt, and as their holdings depreciated in value, an inferior type of both proprietor and settler succeeded.[4] North Carolina became the refuge of Virginian renegades and the sink of America; a form of slave-trade was developed by capturing Indians and selling them back again; Acts were passed in the legislature prohibiting suits for debt at the instance of foreigners; and, by procuring an Act prohibiting the sale of arms to the Indians, illicit dealers were able to secure a monopoly of this trade. In the most idealist of all constitutions men boasted how for a bowl of punch they could secure the election of whomsoever they would for parliament,[5] and even the most salutary of legislation was often merely a cover for the activities of the organized law-breaker. Unfortunately,

---

[1] For a good account of this subject see J. A. Doyle, *The English in America. Virginia, Maryland, and the Carolinas*, 447–51.

[2] *Cal. S.P. Amer., 1681–5*, 338, Nov. 1682.

[3] Quoted in C. M. Andrews, *Colonial Self-Government*, 141–2.

[4] Ibid. 148. [5] *Cal. S.P. Amer., 1685–9*, xxii.

the political realists in England and the enemies of Shaftesbury could point to the Carolinas as a sinister comment on idealist experiment.

Next in date after the first settlement of Carolina was the occupation of New York. The Dutch colony, wedged among English possessions, was always in a precarious position; these were added to by the energetic but high-handed conduct of the governor Peter Stuyvesant. Meanwhile, complaints against the Dutch were more eagerly listened to at home, and in July 1663 a committee of the English Council for Plantations was ordered to report on the practicability of an attack on the New Netherlands. After inquiries of the English inhabitants on Long Island the committee in January 1664 reported favourably on the project of driving the Dutch from North America.[1] Action was speedily taken. Having obtained a royal grant (February 1664) and a charter (March 12), James, duke of York, commissioned captain Richard Nicholls to be governor of the new province, and allotted that portion of it between Hudson and Delaware to sir George Carteret, treasurer of the Navy, and John, first baron Berkeley of Stratton, brother of sir William Berkeley of Virginia. In the original patent granted to the duke were included lands not actually occupied by the Dutch, such as Long Island and Nantucket. The town of New Amsterdam fell an easy conquest to a small English fleet on August 26, 1664, and was renamed New York.

Except for the provisions that the laws enacted in the colony must be conformable to the laws of England, and that appeals were allowed to the King in Council, the patent conferred absolute power on the ducal proprietor. The administration of his first governor, Nicholls, was marked by moderation and prudence. He encouraged the Dutch population to remain, on the assurance of liberty of conscience and of all the rights of English subjects; while at the same time he reorganized the settlement on English lines and set himself to increase population and trade. As Ashley showed his distinctive political views in the constitution of Carolina, so the duke of York showed his in framing the polity of his American acquisition; for he prohibited the summoning of a representative assembly, and insisted that the

[1] C. M. Andrews, op. cit. 77–8.

city of New York should be governed as a municipal corporation. Accordingly, mayor and aldermen were appointed by the governor; they were empowered to make only by-laws, and to try only cases involving forty shillings or less. In effect, therefore, Nicholls had to do much of his own legislation.[1] This curtailment of initiative was resented by both English and Dutch, and caused increasing difficulty under Nicholls' successor Francis Lovelace, in whose absence the city surrendered to a Dutch fleet in 1673; but, after little more than a year New York was restored to the duke's authority. Under its third governor, major Edmund Andros, an attempt was made to introduce some unity into this cosmopolitan community of English and French, Dutch and German, Protestant and Catholic, and to wrest from Connecticut that part assigned to the duke in the original grant. Though he did not succeed in this last design, Andros nevertheless ruled with as much benevolence as could be included in the narrow limits assigned him by his master.

Their exclusion from legislative functions was keenly resented by many of the towns, notably by those on Long Island, and as the demand for some share in law-making became more insistent, it was coupled with a threat of refusal to pay Customs dues, or to provide money for the upkeep of forts. It was this threat to the revenue that eventually obliged the duke to yield to the demand for a representative assembly; and when in 1682 Thomas Dongan was sent out as governor, the duke empowered him to summon a general assembly of freeholders to co-operate with the governor and council in the raising of revenue and the making of laws.[2] This assembly met in October 1683 and formulated the achievements of English constitutionalism in a Charter of Franchises and Liberties, wherein were rehearsed select fundamentals from Magna Carta, the Confirmatio Cartarum and the Petition of Right.[3] As duke, James confirmed the charter; but afterwards,

[1] The code which he drew up contained rules copied from the codes of Newhaven and Massachusetts; it also made allowance for Dutch custom. It allowed toleration. For an account of this see A. E. McKinley, *Transition from Dutch to English rule in New York* in *Amer. H. R.* vi. 693–724. The code was promulgated in Nov. 1667, *Cal. S.P. Amer., 1661–8*, 515.

[2] C. M. Andrews, op. cit. 94–5.

[3] It will be found in *Colonial Laws of New York*, i. 111–16. Cf. also E. Channing, *History of the United States*, ii. 297–8.

as king, he countermanded it, and so Dongan had to rule and
tax with the concurrence only of his council. By his gifts of
diplomacy and conciliation Dongan continued the work of
Andros, and proved himself one of the ablest colonial administrators of the time. Peace with the Indians, defence against the
French, development of communications, and increase of population and trade were the concrete results of government by the
nominees of the duke of York.

The territory between Hudson and Delaware, granted by the
duke to Berkeley and Carteret, was named New Jersey, because
it was regarded as compensation to Carteret for loss of his office
of governor of Jersey. The form of government adopted by the
proprietors was defined in the Concessions of February 1665,
whereby liberty of conscience and rights of property were
guaranteed. A governor and council were to legislate with 12
representatives of the freemen.[1] There were already in existence
a number of Swedish and Dutch settlements in the province, and
in 1665 a contingent of men from Jersey arrived, with Philip
Carteret (the first governor), a kinsman of sir George. These new
arrivals were joined by a number of Puritan immigrants from
New England; and, as the proportion of the latter increased,
there was imposed on the colony a spirit of theocracy and civic
independence inconsistent with the temper of the proprietors
and the executive. A Quaker element was added in 1674 when
Berkeley sold out his share of the lease to Edward Byllynge, a
friend and co-religionary of George Fox; but the duke of York's
unwillingness to recognize this transfer delayed the establishment
of a Quaker colony in West New Jersey. Difficulty was also
caused by the duke's attempt to resume possession of New Jersey
(in spite of the lease) and to vest its control in the governor of
New York; but eventually East New Jersey (after the resignation
of Philip Carteret in 1682) and West New Jersey (after Byllynge
obtained his grant from the duke in 1680) became predominantly
Quaker colonies. These changes hindered the pursuit of a con-

---

[1] The original documents for the history of New Jersey will be found in
Archives of the state of New Jersey (1631–1776), ed. W. A. Whitehead, 1880–
1903. A general history of the colony is that by S. Smith. There are good
accounts in E. Channing, *History of the United States*, and C. M. Andrews,
Colonial Self-Government.

sistent policy; and accordingly the Jerseys may be cited as examples of proprietary colonies wherein economic progress was impeded to some extent by the successive bargaining of their owners.

One of these Quaker proprietaries has given his name to the colony of Pennsylvania, which was founded in 1680–2 in order to provide a refuge not only for English Quakers, but for the scattered communities of Friends to be found throughout English North America. Like Ashley, William Penn wished to implant in the virgin soil of the west the seeds ripened from the fruit of political and religious experience in the east. He had acquired his first experience of colonization in the Jerseys; but there he did not have the full personal scope requisite for the realization of his schemes. His influence with the duke of York, and the fact of his being a substantial creditor of the king's, enabled him to secure by charter (dated March 4, 1681) a grant of territory west of the Delaware river, to which was given the name of Pennsylvania. This was supplemented by the addition of New Castle and territory on the right bank of the Delaware in 1682. To Penn, as proprietor, was accorded the right to make laws with the consent of the freemen, and to appoint magistrates. The veto of the crown and the right of appeal to it were safeguarded; and it is notable that by his charter Penn was obliged to observe the Navigation Laws.

The founder's appeal for settlers was answered by Quakers from England, Ireland, Wales, Germany, and Holland. Under the first deputy-governor, William Markham, lands were allotted on a definite scale. These for the most part proved to be very fertile. Philadelphia also was founded, and several industries, including shipping, were established. Penn's ideal was liberty with obedience; but his constitution as formulated in 1682 did not differ materially from that of the other American colonies, consisting of the recognized hierarchy of governor, council, and assembly, except that both council and assembly were elective, and the governor was dependent on his council. More noteworthy were the laws, especially the code known as the Great Law, wherein, on the basis of English jurisprudence, Penn superimposed his distinctive doctrines. This code provided for liberty of conscience, and limited capital punishment to murder and treason. So far as legislation could do so, the Great Law was intended to foster a very high standard of morals; the same exalted ideals were to be found in the character of the relations which Penn strove to maintain with the Indians. With this auspicious start, the development of the colony was rapid, due in part to the fact that Penn himself supervised its early growth. Progress was, however, impeded by racial and religious disputes, by controversies between council and assembly such as were bound to arise in a constitution where the governor had no independent power, and, lastly, by the personal misfortunes of William Penn.[1]

The common concerns of the New England confederation (Massachusetts, Plymouth, Connecticut, and New Haven) were managed by an assembly of two commissioners from each colony; each of the four states preserving its jurisdiction intact. For long, this confederation had acted as an independent power; for example, in their relations with the Dutch in the New Netherlands; but after the Dutch province came under English rule as New York, the cohesion of the New England federation weakened, and eventually came to an end, leaving Massachusetts pre-eminent, as she had formerly been domineering. Massachusetts was a cause of special disquiet to the statesmen of the Restoration. The colony had passed severe laws against the Quakers—these were tacitly approved at home—but, on the other hand, Anglicans were practically ostracized, and two regicides, Whalley and Goffe, were harboured. So it was resolved to deal with the four New England states; and in April 1664 commissioners were sent out in order to devise measures for settling the peace and security of the confederation. They were well received, except in Massachusetts; where only with difficulty could the General Court be induced to use His Majesty's name in their forms of justice. Indeed the coming of the commission was regarded as a breach of the colony's privileges.[2]

[1] For early accounts of Pennsylvania see *Narratives of early Pennsylvania, Delaware and New Jersey, 1630–1708*, ed. A. C. Myers. (*Original Narrative series*.) The Pennsylvania documents were published in the series *Pennsylvania archives* . . . (Philadelphia, 1852–1907). There are good accounts in E. Channing, op. cit., and C. M. Andrews, op. cit. See also F. R. Jones, *Colonization of the Middle States and Maryland*.

[2] For a good account see P. L. Kaye, *Colonial administration under Clarendon*,

Nevertheless, the charter of Massachusetts was confirmed, and its comparative independence left practically unchallenged, mainly because the home government was anxious most of all to knit the plantations in the scheme of the Navigation Acts, and was not at first prepared to press questions of principle in an area so remote. In effect, therefore, by acquiescence in the separatism of the New England federation, the colonial policy of Charles II confirmed principles of government reminiscent more of 1649 than of 1660, and so gave unwitting sanction to a breach between the static fundamentals of New England on the one hand, and the evolutionary politics of England on the other, a breach widened to impassable breadth when, in the eighteenth century, this rigid constitutionalism of the colonists was pitted against a doctrine of parliamentary sovereignty. Meanwhile, however, judicious presents of masts deflected the attention of Whitehall from too close inspection of the implications underlying the potential separatism of the New England colonies.

The history of these colonies throughout the reign of Charles II was predominantly one of prosperity. Trade was good, notably that in provisions and manufactured goods with the other plantations;[1] in the towns, there were ironworks and in the ports shipbuilding; there was abundant supply of timber, from which were made window frames and ready-made houses, for export to a good market in the West Indies. In all, Massachusetts, Plymouth, and Connecticut had 200 sail of ships; they could muster about 50,000 able-bodied men;[2] their merchants were mostly rich, usually thrifty, and always intent on fresh ventures for their capital. In spite of the Navigation Acts the New England shippers built up a considerable connexion with other colonies and a direct trade with Europe;[3] indeed they were the Dutchmen of the empire, deriving no great advantage from their

76–124. The report of one of the commissioners, col. Cartwright, is in Clar. MS. 83, f. 335; it is printed in *New York Historical Society Collections*, xxxiii, 1869.

[1] For an account of their industries see Randolph's report, Oct. 12, 1676, in *Cal. S.P. Amer., 1675–6*, 463–8.

[2] *Cal. S.P. Amer., 1669–74*, 232.

[3] J. A. Williamson in *Cambridge History of the British Empire*, i. 258. For evasions of the Navigation Acts by New England ships see professor C. M. Andrews, ibid. i. 277–9.

soil or climate, but ever ready with equipment and transport for handling the produce of others. With this development of wealth and population there followed extension into the interior, and consequent war with the Indians; while at times Indian reprisals caused a threat of famine, and both the beaver and fishing trades were imperilled. There soon followed assaults from another quarter. The 'peevish' humour of Massachusetts was well known at home, where an opportunity was awaited for an attack on its charter. This came in 1676, after the conclusion of prolonged hostilities with the Indians, who had pillaged Rhode Island; and in June of that year Edward Randolph, as government commissioner, commenced in Boston his inquiry into the laws of the colony, with a view to bringing it more directly under the control of the crown.

After a year of investigation he formulated his accusations. Massachusetts, he contended, was violating the Navigation Acts; the colonists had harboured regicides; they coined their own money; they put Quakers and others to death because of their religion; they imposed an oath of fidelity to their government; they oppressed their neighbours in boundary disputes. They had no right to the land which they called their own, and were usurpers; worst of all, they really constituted an independent commonwealth, for appeals to England were denied, and the oath of allegiance was not taken. Moreover, their laws were arbitrary and objectionable; for example, galloping in Boston streets was punished by a fine of 3s. 4d.; and such diversions as bowling, dancing in ordinaries, playing cards for money, and celebrating Christmas, were all penalized.[1] So the colony was ordered to send commissioners to England to answer these charges; but there was so much delay in sending them, and they were given such restricted powers, that the Lords of Trade had to threaten Massachusetts with a *quo warranto*. Randolph meanwhile remained in the colony as crown collector and surveyor, thereby increasing the resentment of the colonists.[2]

[1] The charges will be found in *Cal. S.P. Amer., 1677–80*, 129–31, and 133–4, July 1677.
[2] One of the best modern accounts is that in J. T. Adams, *The Founding of New England* (1930), chapters xiii–xv. Professor Adams shows the influence of the Puritan clergy on the public opinion of New England.

In June 1683 articles of high misdemeanour against the governor and company of Massachusetts were formulated, and a writ of *quo warranto* was issued. But expiry of this writ caused the government to proceed by a *scire facias*, and in October 1684 Chancery adjudged the charter of Massachusetts to be forfeited. At the same time it was decided to annul the charters of Connecticut and Rhode Island, so that these colonies could be merged with Massachusetts, New York, and the Jerseys in a new plantation of New England, directly under the control of the crown. Of this new dominion col. Percy Kirke was selected the first governor; but the death of Charles necessitated another appointment, as Kirke was needed at home; accordingly in May 1686 sir Edmund Andros was appointed governor of this transformed New England. Not till late in 1687 did Andros succeed in adding Connecticut to his dominions, a province which evaded the surrender of its charter by hiding it in an oak tree.[1] The task imposed on the new governor was impossible of fulfilment; for even with the utmost powers of conciliation he could not have done anything to compensate the colonies for their loss of representative assemblies; nor could he have dispelled the rumours of anti-Protestant activities which floated across the Atlantic from the land of James II and father Petre. Accordingly, the Revolution of 1688–9 was repeated almost concurrently in Massachusetts. In April 1689 the Bostoners seized the castle, and imprisoned both Andros and Randolph. A declaration, followed by a Convention, established the Revolution settlement in New England; and Boston, as much as London, might claim the honour of having vindicated against the Stuarts the principles of constitutionalism.

A comparison of the accusations against Andros with those against James II shows how susceptible were the New Englanders to the weight of any man's yoke. Most of the counts against the governor were untrue: of those that were substantiated, the chief were (1) that his carriage to the New Englanders was insolent, and (2) that, to the annoyance of the members of the Old South Church, Boston, he used the building for episcopal services when it was not otherwise being used.[2] 'England', wrote Cotton

---

[1] Andrews, op. cit. 271.
[2] *The Andros Tracts* (Prince Society, 1868), i. xxv.

Mather, 'made and saw a happy revolution. And New England upon (and almost before) the advice of it, made as just and fair an one in conformity to it.'[1] The words in parenthesis are significant. An English traveller in Massachusetts at this time recorded some impressions which provide interesting comment on these events. Of the inhabitants he[2] wrote: 'They are generally very backward in their payments, great censors of other men's manners, but extremely careless of their own. As to their religion, I cannot perfectly distinguish it, but it is such that nothing keeps 'em friends but the fear of exposing one another's knavery. As for the rabble, their religion lies in cheating all they deal with. . . . You must read 'em like Hebrew backwards; for they seldom speak and mean the same thing, but like watermen look one way and row another. Amongst all this dross there runs here and there a vein of pure gold.'

Some New England characteristics may be deduced from the titles of the books most in demand, and from the sermons preached at the executions of malefactors. An inventory[3] of a Boston bookseller's estate included the following assortment, typical of that union of the spiritual with the practical so eloquent of seventeenth-century Puritanism:

> Love's Art of Surveying.
> Christ's Tears for Jerusalem's Unbelief.
> Norwood's System of Navigation.
> Shour of Earthquakes.
> Mr. Doolittle's Funeral Sermon.
> Mr. Doolittle's Call.
> History of the Plot.
> Vernon's Compting House.
> Violations of Property.
> Sion in Distress.
> Stub's Conscience Best Friend.
> Bride's Longing for her Bridegroom's Second Coming.

Men brought up on such literature were not likely to be distinguished for the quality of compromise. Then there were the executions. Felons had sometimes to face three sermons before

---

[1] *The Andros Tracts*, ii. 25.

[2] *John Dunton's Letters from New England* (Prince Society, 1867), 67, March 25, 1686.   [3] Ibid., Appendix B.

they were dispatched; and in one preached by Cotton Mather on March 25, 1686, the victim was addressed in these words: 'The sharp axe of civil justice will speedily cut you down. Oh for a little good fruit before the blow'—an invitation responded to by 'the dying bloody sinner' in a speech against Sabbath-breaking. There is abundant evidence that the New Englanders were reincarnating a rule of the Saints such as Englishmen, by the end of Charles's reign, had long outlived.

Of this, one instance may suffice. In 1666 appeared the famous poem *The Day of Doom* by William Wigglesworth, in which was graphically described a contest of wits between the supreme judge on one side and accused persons urging divers pleas in arrest of judgement on the other. Calvinist predestinarianism and the forensic possibilities of common law were the inspirations of this effusion; as witness the reply to the fore-doomed who contended that, knowing their hopeless plight, they had adopted the line of least resistance:

> Christ readily made this reply:
> I damn you not because
> You are rejected, or not elected,
> But you have broke my laws.
> It is but vain, your wits to strain
> The end and means to sever,
> Men fondly seek to dash or break
> What God hath linked together.

Equally ineffective was the defence put forward by children who had died in sin. Hence, the heaven depicted by Wigglesworth was not a new Jerusalem, but a new Westminster Hall set up in Geneva; and so, while England was discarding these preconceptions of an earlier age, there survived in the west, in their pristine vigour, those scruples and convictions which were destined to trouble the more effete world of George III and lord North.

In conclusion, it may be noted that the colonial administrators of this period knew little of the pride of empire, for they thought of colonies mainly from a utilitarian point of view. This attitude is seen in the methods employed for peopling the plantations. The East India Company, as a highly organized trading and administrative body, was able to recruit a select personnel;[1] but these were not permanent settlers. The population of Tangier was far from selective, as it consisted mainly of the garrison.[2] Of those who went voluntarily to the western plantations many were disbanded soldiers, fugitive rebels, religious recusants, and persons ruined in the Civil Wars. Felons were frequently exported, and might mingle freely with men who had left home not because of crime, but because of high principle; there were also children and orphans, some stolen away, others sent out on indentures. In a sense all the American colonies, other than New England, were penal settlements; though colonies such as Virginia protested vigorously against the policy of sending out 'Newgateers'.[3] There were also Scottish, Irish, and Continental elements. The Irish preponderated in Montserrat; in Barbados they were sometimes considered troublesome, and a preference was expressed for Scottish settlers;[4] elsewhere, notably in New York and New Jersey, there were Dutch and Swedes, and in Newfoundland there were French. Older colonies, such as Massachusetts, Bermuda, and Barbados had surplus men who became frontiers-men elsewhere in the empire;[5] moreover, a steady increase of negro population, notably in the sub-tropical colonies, served to increase the amount of superabundant white labour, and to make urgent the problem of military defence.[6]

This absence of a 'sentiment' of empire is perhaps sufficient to explain why no attempt was made to apply any general administrative policy to the haphazard collection of possessions which were being quietly accumulated. Scarcely any two colonies had the same title-deeds, so there was great diversity in their constitutional rights. Fundamental questions of principle were raised, and the committees of privy council applied themselves with zeal to the study of local circumstances influencing each settlement, but they could not enforce any general principles of

[1] *Supra*, i. 224.   [2] *Supra*, 504.

[3] The governor and council succeeded in prohibiting this. *Cal. S.P. Amer.*, *1669–74*, July 17, 1671.

[4] e.g. in Virginia, ibid., *1661–8*, 429–30; in Barbados, ibid. 486; in Jamaica, ibid., *1669–74*, 96.

[5] J. A. Williamson in *Cambridge History of the British Empire*: the Colonies after the Restoration, 249.

[6] *Cambridge History of the British Empire*, i. 266–7.

colonial administration on the heterogeneous possessions which then constituted the Empire.

In two spheres—the legislative and the fiscal relationship between crown and possession—imperial problems were raised and left unsettled. In regard to the first (the legislative connexion) the history of Jamaica is of particular interest. The island differed from other crown colonies because (it was held) the inhabitants had no privileges granted them by letters patent, and the king had found Jamaica 'an acquisition to England' at his accession.[1] On their side, the Jamaicans demanded that the revenue raised by them should be applied in accordance with the directions of the native legislature, and not at the crown's discretion; they therefore objected to a change introduced in 1677 whereby their laws were to be enacted not, as hitherto, 'by the Governor, Council, and representative of the Commons', but 'by the King's Most Excellent Majesty, by and with the consent of the General Assembly'.[2] Throughout this dispute, the Lords of Trade attempted to reduce Jamaica to the status of Ireland as administered by Poyning's Law, supporting their contention with the curious reason that the legislature of Jamaica could not be subject to more accidents than Ireland; to which it was properly replied that the distance of Jamaica from England destroyed the force of the analogy.[3] This was no mere dispute over words; because the colonial legislators feared that the new style of enactment deprived them of deliberative power. So they refused to pass a revenue act; and the crown had eventually to yield, leaving in suspense the question whether the crown had deprived itself of the right to modify the constitution of the island.[4]

This was not unconnected with the question whether the laws of England applied to the colonies. In practice, many of the colonial legislatures embodied fundamental principles of English common law in their legislation; nowhere else indeed were these principles held in deeper veneration. For the proprietary

[1] *Cal. S.P. Amer.*, *1677–80*, 461.

[2] Charles Howard, earl of Carlisle, was instructed to use the new style when he went out as Governor in 1677. *Cal. S.P. Amer.*, *1677–80*, 367–9.

[3] Ibid., *1677–80*, 445.

[4] Ibid., *1677–80*, 622, Oct. 22, 1680. For a full account of this struggle see A. M. Whitson, *Constitutional Development of Jamaica*, 1660–1729, ch. iv.

possessions it was generally a condition of the grant that the laws sanctioned by the proprietor should be in accordance with English jurisprudence. This matter had some constitutional importance; since if English laws were valid in the overseas possessions, then colonists might feel secure in the safeguards which these laws implied; otherwise, if the crown could determine what was law and what was not, then these safeguards might have to be sacrificed. At home, there was not always a clear determination on this subject; for example, the law courts did not know whether the laws of England applied to Barbados or not.[1] But, so far as the later Stuarts had any definite colonial policy, it was to bring the colonies into closer dependence on the crown; inevitably, therefore, in the years when the English borough franchises were being destroyed, a similar process was applied to those plantations which hitherto had maintained some independence. This was the fate of the New England states. After these had lost their charters in 1684, Halifax eloquently pleaded in Council that English laws should be applied to Englishmen in the colonies;[2] but he was overruled, and the remodelled New England confederacy was entrusted to a governor and council, responsible solely to the king, and required to administer a code of laws drawn up by the crown. One characteristic reason was adduced in defence of this policy, namely, that by their subjection the New Englanders would be able to supply 'well-seasoned men' for the reduction of any rebellious colony.[3] Fortunately, the Stuarts did not have to try this experiment.

There was similar dubiety in the fiscal relationship. The colonist had to pay a Customs duty of five per cent. on his exports to England, according to their valuation in the Book of Rates; half of this amount was refunded on enumerated goods re-exported to the Continent.[4] Then followed the Act of 1673 imposing special plantation duties;[5] this was primarily a preventive, not a fiscal measure, but it had some legal importance,

[1] Daws v. sir P. Pindar, in *Modern Reports*, ii. 45.

[2] *Halifax*, i. 428.

[3] Randolph to Jenkins April 30, 1681, ibid. 1681–5, 34–6. For a good account of the working of the new constitution under Andros see J. T. Adams, *The Founding of New England*, 398–430.

[4] For this subject generally see G. L. Beer, *The Old Colonial System*, i, ch. iii.   [5] 25 Car. II, cap. vii. See *supra*, i. 239.

because it was the earliest direct tax (other than Customs dues) on colonial produce not initiated by colonial legislatures. In addition to these levies, the colonies were mostly bound by their charters to make payments, some nominal, such as Indian arrows, or sheaves of corn; some more substantial, such as a fifth part of the precious metals found in the soil; but neither of these sources could be considered to provide a substantial or regular revenue. With these exceptions, the proprietary and New England colonies enjoyed a large measure of fiscal autonomy.

It was otherwise in the crown colonies, where there were governors and judges appointed by the crown; there were also forts, and in some cases regiments of English soldiers to be maintained. The general policy of the home government was to raise locally such a revenue, preferably on a permanent basis, as would defray these charges, and make these possessions self-supporting; while the colonial legislatures on their side objected in principle to a permanent revenue, and insisted on such strict clauses of appropriation as to imply complete suspicion of the crown. In this respect, there was a wide repercussion of the financial mismanagement at home; and the suspicion engendered by Charles's extravagance was reflected in the unwillingness of Jamaica, Virginia, and Barbados to surrender control of the revenues which they voted; in consequence, the salaries of officials and the requirements of military defence were often seriously jeopardized. There was an additional complication in Barbados and the Leeward Islands (St. Kitts, Montserrat, Nevis, and Antigua), all of which voted in 1663–4 an export duty of four-and-a-half per cent. From the start there was confusion about this payment. The crown, which had just succeeded to the proprietary rights under the old Carlisle patent, regarded this grant as a return for the confirmation of defective land-titles, and assigned a portion of it to the new Governor, Francis lord Willoughby, in composition for his inherited proprietary rights; while another portion was allocated for payments to creditors of the deceased James Hay, first earl of Carlisle, a Stuart favourite, to whom the West Indian islands not occupied by Spain had been granted by charter in 1627.[1] In effect, therefore, the revenue granted by these possessions was to be used for the liquidation of proprietary claims; but

[1] G. L. Beer, op. cit. i. 171.

the yield did not prove sufficient for this purpose, and the men who paid the tax contended that it should be devoted to the expenses of civil and military administration. This led to much strife and misunderstanding; even more, the defences suffered, and so French and Dutch were able to play havoc in the Leeward Islands during the Second Dutch War. Eventually, the crown had to repudiate the claims of the Carlisle creditors, and apply this revenue to the needs of these islands.[1]

In Jamaica and Virginia the crown, as original owner of the soil, was entitled to quit-rents, which provided a permanent source of revenue. But this was insufficient to meet the costs of administration and defence; so attempts were made to secure additional and equally permanent grants, the proceeds to be applied to the needs of these possessions. The Jamaicans insisted on limiting this extra revenue to periods of two years, in order to ensure the summoning of their legislature; and on one occasion they used the expedient of 'tacking'[2] in order to ensure the passage of Bills. It was only by threat and wheedling that governor Lynch succeeded in 1683 in persuading the island Assembly to vote a revenue for twenty-one years from spirits and licences of taverns, a vote free from the objectionable 'tacking', and in return the crown surrendered the quit-rents.[3] Until 1679, the salary of the governor of Virginia was paid by a local export duty of two shillings on every hogshead of tobacco; but in 1680 the Virginian assembly consolidated this with a poll tax (on immigrants) into a permanent revenue. In return for this, the home government had to acquiesce in the statutes of Virginia which discriminated against English shipping.[4] But elsewhere it was not possible to enforce the maxim that the crown colonies should pay their way. No independent revenue could be obtained from the Bermudas; and for long the quit-rents of New York were insufficient for the salaries of officials. The net result was that, before 1689, the crown derived no financial advantage from the colonies; and was called upon to give satisfactory assurance that what money the colonists raised locally was applied

---

[1] G. L. Beer, 172–95.

[2] *Cal. S.P. Amer., 1681–5,* 137, Nov. 6, 1681. The Lords of Trade objected to the 'tacking', ibid. 315.

[3] G. L. Beer, op. cit. i. 219.   [4] Ibid. i. 205–6.

solely to colonial needs. When it is added that there was another source of irritation, namely the friction caused by the enforcement of the Navigation Acts, it will be seen that imperial progress in this period did not settle administrative problems, but helped to accumulate them.

XIX
A RECORD OF ACHIEVEMENT

I. SOME ASPECTS OF TRADITIONAL ENGLISH CULTURE

So far as it is possible to describe in one phrase the intellectual character of a generation, the phrase 'sustained curiosity' might be used of the England lying behind the religion and politics of the reign of Charles II. It is true that the spirit of inquiry is the inspiration of every age that can boast any real intellectual achievement; but this is specially true of the later seventeenth century, because, though Bacon and Descartes had already acclimatized scientific scepticism in European thought, it was not till after 1660 that Englishmen definitely applied the new principles, and sought for truth in experiment and research rather than in theological debate. This curiosity was balanced and tempered by a vindication of the native common sense. It is the purpose of this concluding chapter to illustrate some aspects of traditional culture as known to the universities, the schools, and the press; and against this background to set the achievements of those who helped to make this an age of more than usual intellectual progress.

The old grammar schools, one of the glories of Medieval and Tudor England, had trained such men as Cromwell (Huntingdon Grammar School), John Hampden (Lord Williams's School, Thame), John Milton (St. Paul's), and John Selden (Chichester Grammar School); later in the century Newton received some of his early education at Grantham Grammar School, Somers at Worcester Cathedral School, while Locke, like Dryden, was a product of Westminster. But nevertheless these schools show evidence of the decline which overtook many educational foundations in the course of the seventeenth century. Various reasons for this may be suggested. The temper of Restoration England was not favourable to the ideals of frugality and industry embodied in these establishments; there were few great benefactors, and there were many critics, ranging from the statesmen who thought that too many boys were taken from the plough to pore over books, to recluses like Hobbes, who argued that the devotion of these schools to ancient history and classical studies tended to promote republicanism. Other reasons were that, as Dissenters were now debarred by Statute from teaching, the grammar schools lost the services of men pre-eminently fitted for this vocation: still more, there were numerous rival establishments.

But perhaps the main reason why the performance of the older schools compared unfavourably with that of their rivals was that in many cases the first were strictly bound by their original charters, and so did not have the opportunity for initiative or experiment enjoyed by the second. Thus, the curricula of the grammar school showed little deviation from Greek and Latin grammar, a somewhat narrow range of classical authors, with sometimes Hebrew and declamations or themes on abstract or religious topics. Such an education would now be considered narrow, but it was narrow not so much in its choice of material as in its methods and objects; for the classics were studied not as the foundation of the humanities, but mainly as illustrations of rules of syntax, or for the attainment of proficiency in prose and verse composition. This tradition is not extinct, but at least there is a tendency in modern times to value the Latin and Greek languages not altogether as ends in themselves, but as keys to great store-houses of wisdom and inspiration. To-day many men in retirement read or profess to read the classics for intellectual enjoyment; this was rare in the seventeenth century for any but the professed scholars, though sir William Temple was an exception. Intellectual curiosity was as likely to be repressed as encouraged by the education of the endowed school, and in this respect the university was sometimes a continuation of the same routine.

What it meant to be bound by medieval statutes may be illustrated from Winchester College. Our oldest public school was founded by Wykeham as a boarding grammar school for seventy poor scholars and clerks who, after a thorough training in accidence, were to be sent to New College, there to be trained for all the professional posts that might be filled by an educated clergy. The founder's experience of how easily the intentions of a pious donor might be evaded caused him to draw up most elaborate and carefully planned statutes for both foundations;

x

but even his ingenuity proved no match for that of the generations who had to apply these rules, with the result that the
letter of the laws was scrupulously regarded, while their spirit
was often ignored. Thus, it was the duty of the senior foundation,
New College, to see to it that the sister college carried out the
regulations, for which purpose there was an annual scrutiny or
examination conducted by the warden of New College and two
fellows. For convenience, this was sometimes held half-way
between Winchester and Oxford, at the Bear Inn in Newbury;
more often it was held at Winchester. At these scrutinies, elections were made to the Oxford College; the scrutineers also
required answers to questions concerning the discipline and
studies of Winchester; and it was open to all foundationers
of the school to bring complaints against any of their fellows or
even against the warden himself. On these occasions, therefore,
two great dignitaries faced each other, the one prepared to
hear accusations by schoolboys against the other, with resort
to the Visitor, the bishop of Winchester, as the umpire. It was
medieval and democratic; but it may also have encouraged
the practice of tale-bearing, which was not then viewed with
disfavour.

Among the interrogatories levelled at heads of the Winchester
authorities in the scrutiny of 1680 were these:[1] (1) Are there
always two bursars at the receipt of money? (the innuendo
was patent), (2) do the schoolmaster and the usher teach dili-
gently? (3) do the fellows reside regularly in the College? (4) is
Chapel regularly attended by all? (5) are commons served regularly in Hall, and subtracted from those who do not attend?
(6) are 'estraneous' persons entertained at College expense?
(7) does any fellow, scholar, or servant keep sporting dogs or
hawks? (the statutes had limited the founder's charity to the
poor), (8) is every one present at the anniversary *obit* for the
founder's soul and at the four annual commemorations? (9) is
the spare cash locked up in the chest appointed for that purpose
by the Founder? (10) are the statutes read three times a year
before the whole society in chapel and is a copy kept in the ante-
chapel for reference? (11) does every fellow read the statutes
privately once a year 'with due attention'? and lastly (12) do

[1] MS. in New College muniments.

the warden and fellows convert to their own use any more of the College estates than that which the statutes allow them?

These questions often evoked accusations of the most personal character; after investigation penalties might be imposed on the delinquents. Scholars who acquired the key of the beer-cellar were punished; a boy who stole money from a school-mate's strong box was expelled; another who made no progress in his studies, and of whom it was said that by no possibility could he make progress, was warned of impending expulsion. This annual inspection descended to the minutest details. Defaulters from chapel were reprimanded; the scholars had to be dressed in that quality of cloth prescribed by the Founder; the bursars had to see to it that the dormitories were supplied with suitable locks; the beer had to be brewed in a proper manner and with good utensils; the choristers had to sing, and the organist was ordered to teach them, in spite of his statement that they were incapable of singing; Latin was to be spoken; the servants were to be respectful, and townsmen were to be kept out of the cellar. No one was spared in this chapter of faults. On one of these occasions the warden of Winchester had to answer certain serious allegations. It was alleged that, at the brewing of beer, he drew off for his own use a large quantity of 'the first brewing, whereby the rest was weaker'; he had neglected to enforce the statute requiring the wearing of furred gowns in chapel, and he rarely dined in Hall. To the first accusation he replied that it was the custom; to the second he made no reply, and to the third he answered that he had married, and had a family. By the time this last confession was elicited there was a display of temper on both sides, moderated somewhat by the use of the sober Latin tongue. He in turn then accused the chaplains of carrying victuals outside the College, contrary to the statutes; to which the chaplains replied that they had a licence for living in the country.

As the observance of these statutes was enforced by a solemn oath, their violation, even in minute respects, was technically perjury; in consequence the very strictness of the rules, however necessary they may have been for a medieval community, was often a pretext for their evasion wherever some defence or exception, however subtle, could be adduced. Such regulations were therefore little better than millstones round the neck of educational progress, and in the seventeenth century they could have provided little more than a training in casuistry. An exceptional example has, it is true, been quoted; exceptional in the sense that then as now Wykeham's foundation was held in special esteem, and moreover it was the model on which the statutes of other schools, including Eton, were based. What was true of Winchester was true of those older institutions which were still attempting to carry out strictly the intentions of their founders; and it is a great tribute to the original spirit of these foundations that, at a later date, they were able quickly to adapt themselves to new conditions, and to rival or surpass establishments which had never known the dead hand of completely obsolete restrictions. But our greatest schools had to wait many years for this change; and the fact remains that in the reign of Charles they were on the whole educationally unproductive.

Nevertheless, there were not lacking schemes of educational reform. The writings of the Bohemian educational reformer Comenius were made known in England by Samuel Hartlib, a prolific writer on pedagogy, husbandry, land surveying, and silk culture; an encyclopaedist, whose enthusiasm for knowledge and its wide diffusion was not without influence on educated society of the Restoration. Later in the reign, a scheme of reform was propounded by Aubrey.[1] He deplored the enormous time and labour spent on grammar and accidence; rather than such slavery, he would prefer that only English and Mathematics should be taught. The home education of the rich he condemned; because young men of position were flattered by servants and dependants, and so, when they entered into the world, they were likely to give offence; nor did he approve of the fashionable academies, which turned out the 'chevalier', or, in plain English, the trooper. Instead of these expedients he proposed that the rich should be educated on more national lines. He would accommodate his ideal school in 'a fair house, with a little park', presided over by a provost, who would be a layman, well travelled, of good birth, and unmarried. He and his staff would have to remain celibate, as their daughters might prove a distraction to the select pupils of this model academy. In

[1] In *Bodley, Aubrey MS.* A. 10.

Grammar he would have three 'informators', none of them English, but all of them Swiss or Scottish; 'men of presence, bonne mine and address', 'not little contemptible rattons'. There were to be teachers of Mathematics, Rhetoric, and Logic; in Rhetoric he included oratory and translations; in Logic, the rudiments of civil law and ethics. Of somewhat less importance were the Penman and the French Dancing Master, who might be non-residents; the cooks were to be French or Swiss, and the porter was not to be an old man, but a 'lusty young fellow', able to speak Latin, and also, if possible, French or German. Mingled with the pupils there were to be ten or twelve Swiss, Dutch, or Scottish boys, fluent Latin speakers, and therefore likely to encourage the young gentlemen to use that language. Even the scullions were to use Latin.

Aubrey's scheme reflects the dissatisfaction with which many enlightened Englishmen regarded the educational methods of their day, and errs on the side of attributing too much importance to foreign models. Moreover, he reveals one pronounced characteristic of the educational practice of that time—the use of Latin as a language in which colloquial proficiency was an end in itself. At the universities, conditions were somewhat better; but even there the incubus of formal routine weighed heavily on grown men. During the Commonwealth their reform had played an important part in Puritan propaganda, and there was a proposal for the establishment of a new university at Durham; but the Restoration effectively quashed these schemes, and for two centuries thereafter the two universities were little more than annexes to the state church. In the later seventeenth century there were, it is true, a number of university and college benefactors, such as Clarendon, Ashmole, Williamson, and Jenkins; there were great vice-chancellors such as Dr. Fell; at Cambridge there were men of international reputation, such as Newton; but nevertheless the fact remains that neither Oxford nor Cambridge was contributing to the intellectual life of the nation in a measure proportionate to the endowments and opportunities enjoyed by them; and both were outstripped by the Royal Society, to which Oxford was at first somewhat antagonistic.[1]

[1] Evelyn (Diary, July 9, 1669) records that at the Oxford Encaenia the

Both universities could boast a distinguished list of alumni, including Newton, Barrow, Wren, Halley, Evelyn, Locke, and Pepys; nevertheless, an educational institution must be judged not from the brilliant or exceptional, but from the more numerous and average of its products. Such men were trained in methods still semi-scholastic, and were encouraged by public disputation to draw readily from a narrow range of classical texts for arguments on one side or another of a set theme. Exhibition of this dialectic subtlety had already been condemned by Eachard.[1] The lectures of professors played little part in the life of the undergraduate, who, until the twentieth century, was dependent for tuition almost solely on the resident tutors and fellows assigned him by the college. Thus, at Queen's College, Oxford, one of the Fleming family read with his tutor in Sanderson's *Logic* once or twice a week; on Saturday, he made Latin verses, and in his spare hours he read Florus and Sallust. His tutor, when writing to the pupil's father, said that the boy lacked courage, 'but I hope that disputing in Hall will put some briskness into him'.[2] At Queen's, if one may judge from the Fleming correspondence, the level of tuition was comparatively high, and the tutors were solicitous of their charges' interests; moreover the college profited by the benefactions of sir Joseph Williamson, who provided scholarships for travel in France and Germany,[3] an unusually early recognition of the value of training in modern studies. To Williamson also Queen's owed the establishment of a lectureship in Anglo-Saxon.[4] Another college associated with modern subjects was University College, which numbered a high proportion of scientists among its alumni.[5] At Cambridge, Newton and Barrow were building up the great scientific reputation of the University, and Caius College was ably maintaining its fame in medicine.

But these were exceptional; for elsewhere studies tended to be of the traditional character. Witness the evolution of an

---

Public Orator indulged in 'some malicious and indecent reflections on the Royal Society as underminers of the University'.

[1] See *supra*, i. 99.
[2] *H.M.C. Rep.* xii, app., pt. vii. 148, Sept. 28, 1678; *Fleming Correspondence.*
[3] Ibid. 146.   [4] Ibid. 163, Nov. 1679.
[5] For this see E. J. Bowen, *The study of science in University College, Oxford.*

Oxford professor of Greek. William Taswell graduated bachelor of arts from Christ Church in 1674, and thereupon obtained £4 per annum as a moderator at disputations, then the equivalent of an examination fee. This, with the same sum for tuition and a studentship (i.e. fellowship) of Christ Church, enabled him to remain at Oxford, where he was first employed by Dr. Fell, the Dean of his college, in the somewhat superfluous task of turning Lidyat's Chronological Canons into Latin verse. From this he proceeded to the more useful work of collating the Greek Testament, Livy, and Quintilian with manuscripts in order to prepare new editions. The Dean then offered him advancement—either the post of schoolmaster at £50 per annum, or a tutorship to two noblemen's sons near Oxford, but Taswell preferred his poverty and his studies, so he declined the offer and pawned some of his books. In 1677 he was able to muster £10 for his mastership of arts; but he lost the support of his patron because he voted against Fell's nominee for the public oratorship; three years later, however, he was restored to the favour of the great man, and received six young pupils from him. He was now so well established as a tutor that he bought books and clothes, a gold watch, a silver-hilted sword, a collection of cups, and a supply of bows and arrows; in which state of affluence he was appointed professor of Greek at Christ Church, and he then took holy orders. He recorded one complaint against the Church of England, namely, that on the many days of abstinence prescribed by the Church, his college provided no supper, so he was obliged to dine out on these occasions.[1]

Like Winchester College, the sister foundation in Oxford was labouring under its ancient statutes, and had to suffer also the incubus of Founder's Kin fellows. One of the families from which generations of such fellows was drawn was the great Oxfordshire family of Fiennes, and the measure of their right to places on the foundation may be gauged from a casual reference by Celia Fiennes, who, when she visited New College in the summer of 1695, referred to it as the college 'which belongs to the Fiennes's'.[2] These family rights led to innumerable disputes about precedence; and the social distinctions thus introduced helped to

[1] *The autobiography of William Taswell, D.D.* in Camden Miscellany, ii (1853). [2] Celia Fiennes, *Through England on a side-saddle*, 28.

prevent New College from playing that part for which it was fitted by its traditions and endowments. To govern such a close but divided corporation was no easy task; it called forth all the ingenuity and firmness of which warden Woodward was capable. As he had to keep strict watch in his progresses lest manorial rights might fall into desuetude, so in College he had to see that the statutes were observed, that due precedence and ceremony were regulated, and that his own privileges were vindicated against the menace from junior fellows infected with the 'distemperature' of the times. So he began his tenure of office in a characteristic way. From old members he obtained answers to long lists of questions relating to the practice of the College before the anarchy of the Commonwealth; and, with the authority of recorded precedent on his side, he was able to hold his own against the truculent and the disobedient. The place of the Founder's Kin in chapel; the standard of hospitality expected from him; the regulation of 'sleeping days'[1] in the long vacation; his power to appoint and to eject the chaplains, and his right to the 'fee buck' from Whaddon Chase (without the participation of his colleagues)—all these vexed questions were settled once and for all. Even the 'lopp and topp' of the trees in the College garden came within the scope of this inquisition; it must henceforth go to the kitchen, and was not to be used for the fires of fellows in their chambers. None of the ancient rights of his office was allowed to slip away.[2]

As he asserted himself against his colleagues, so he strove to maintain discipline among the junior members of the society; and it may be recalled that many of the fellows were included in this category, as some were little more than schoolboys. Thus, in 1663, there was the case of the fellow who broke two of the statutes. His first offence was that of staying out of college when he was 'gated', that is, confined to its bounds; the second was more complicated: he had taken out bread and beer in his own name and had supplied them to other persons. This was the medieval sin of 'manutention'. Family influence and the inter-

---

[1] Sleeping days may have been those days when attendance at morning chapel was not required.

[2] Miscellaneous memoranda of warden Woodward in New College muniments.

vention of the Visitor were both invoked by the delinquent, who was one of the law fellows; but Woodward, with the consent of the thirteen seniors, sent him down for a period. Against this sentence the offender appealed in the following letter:

Gentlemen. To resist your authoritie or to stand on terms of defiance is not my present purpose; onely to lett you understand what my sense is of my present condition; and if a favourable audience can be granted to mee, which I cannot question from such, who in a special manner live on mercy [a home thrust]. My plea is that for the first breach of the statute, wherein I was ignorantly apprehended, being the Statute of Manutention; my thoughts are with all submission to your judgement, that upon the strictest enquiry I may find some mercy; my threepenny charity being bestowed in no contemptuous manner, or to encourage offenders against your power. Consider, I beseech you the score on which they requested it, and for which I gave it, to entertaine a stranger, the main end which our Founder commends to us, hospitalitie. . . . Then the frequencie, though I accuse none, of such examples made me presume on doing what I did. . . . But such is the extravagancie of youth that I did transgresse my bounds limited, and cannot excuse the times yee object against mee of going abroad, for which I am heartily sorry, and offer myself to be punisht in any sort, unless by my utter ruine, which expulsion will bee.

But withall not to derogate from your power, pray lay it to your hearts whether I am guiltie of perjury in not perfectly submitting to an injunction which the Statutes never dreamt of: it being in one rubrick absolutely decided totidem verbis: Sint manutentores pro prima vice privati a dimensis per quindenam: pro secunda, per mensem: pro tertia per duos menses: pro quarto, penitus removeantur a Collegio, and if any other rubrick proceeds more vigorously against mee, yet according to Justinian: in dubiis quod minus est prejudiciale eligendum est. . . . Now, Gentlemen, I humblie cast myself at your feet, beseeching you, as able interpreters of the Statutes as ever I believe yett were, to consider whether some milder course may not be taken to preserve you blameless and mee in my place; if not, I am your undone servant.

Thus Woodward had to contend with the lawyers of the College as well as with the lawyers of the Village.

The ingenuity fostered by school and college discipline was not wasted in the larger and more public life of the university;

and spare moments snatched from *studia severiora* might well be spent in the collection of votes or the management of elections; or the chancellor might visit the university, bringing with him a train of persons of quality, on whom degrees by creation were conferred; accordingly, by a well-timed dedication or influence exerted in the right quarter, one might be presented with such persons of quality, and so not only receive a degree free of charge and without examination, but also an introduction into that larger life which surged round the two universities.[1] Many things therefore helped to train some of the qualities requisite for success in the service of church or state. At its lowest, the university system encouraged the informer with money, and the assurance of secrecy;[2] more often it turned out products guaranteed to be invariably fluent and dexterous. This intellectual agility was to be found not only in those studies now designated Arts subjects, but also in the scientific pursuits; and so, while at the Royal Society men were discussing the conclusions to be drawn from ascertained and recorded facts, at the Sheldonian Theatre in Oxford bachelors were debating whether medical practice should be altered because of recent anatomical discoveries; whether contraries might be cured by contraries, and even whether love could be induced by philtres.[3] These may have been vital questions in the fifteenth century, but not in the seventeenth, when real scientific progress was rapid. More useful, perhaps, or at least more elegant were the university prize compositions on such themes as these: Did Duns Scotus write better Latin than Cicero? Is expectation better than fulfilment? Should young men travel abroad? There was a breath from the outside world when in 1680 it was debated: *an tabernae cofficenses sunt permittendae?*[4]

The intellectual agility thus engendered at the universities

---

[1] On the occasion of Ormonde's visit to Oxford in 1677 Dr. Fell warned the duke against this practice. *Carte MS.* 36, f. 374.

[2] For example, the printed announcement issued by the vice-chancellor of Oxford in April 1681 offering a reward of 40s. and a promise of secrecy to informers revealing the names of undergraduates who had recently broken windows. *Bodley, Wood* 276 A, no. 374.

[3] For these Quaestiones debated at Oxford in this reign see *Bodley, Fol.* θ 659.

[4] *Bodley, Wood* 276 A, no. 394.

may be traced also in a new conception of education which came to displace the more pedantic equipment of earlier times. As the capital became more populous, as foreign affairs engaged the attention of intelligent Englishmen, and as the influence of French civilization asserted itself, much of the old insularity disappeared in exchange for a measure of cosmopolitanism, a keen sense of proportion, and a conception of education as a means to a social end, an ideal enunciated by Henry Peacham,[1] who prescribed a method whereby one's 'style' might pass for current, namely: 'Imitate the best authors as well in Oratory as in History . . . with much conference with those that can speak well'. This object was made more easy of attainment by the fact that the education of the middle and upper classes was then more uniform; it was based on the Classics and on the same range of classical texts; consequently, with an apt quotation one could win the plaudits of one's associates, as later one might use it with effect in the House of Commons. But this was only the basis for the polish to be acquired by continual contact with the right kind of society. 'The proprieties and delicacies of English are known to few,' wrote Dryden:[2] ''tis impossible even for a good wit to understand and practice them without the help of a liberal education, long reading and digesting of those few good authors we have among us; the knowledge of men and manners; the freedom and habitude of conversation with the best company of both sexes; and, in short, without wearing off the rust he has acquired while laying in a stock of learning.'

A similar change can be traced, though more insensibly, in the evolution of English prose style. Compare any pamphlet of Prynne or Milton with an essay by Dryden or Addison, and at once there will be noted a complete change in the use of the paragraph; for the earlier writers compress so many facts and opinions into the paragraph that it rarely has any unity of its own, and its dividing lines might often be altered without either improving or spoiling the sequence; whereas the later writers use this division for an essential purpose—for the exposition or completion of one idea, or the comparison of two ideas. This latter method of subdivision promotes easier and quicker

[1] *The Compleat Gentleman*, ch. vi (1661 ed.; first published in 1613).
[2] Preface to *Sylvae* (1685) in *Essays of J. Dryden*, ed. W. P. Ker, i. 253.

reading; because the eye becomes trained to deduce from a few lines something of the essential argument of a whole section; by this method also an exposition may be spun out longer, or greater degrees of differentiation may be introduced. This change may be due to the fact that, with a steady increase in the size of the reading public, authors were beginning to think more of their readers' convenience; they may have been saying less than their predecessors, but they were saying it more clearly, and in such a way that their meaning could be discerned more quickly. At the same time, increasing resort was made to that large class of secondary words derived from Latin either directly or through the French—a change the causes of which were probably as much historical as literary, since Englishmen were now coming into contact with each other in ways necessitating more highly-developed means of expression; for many were entering parliament, aware of the increased consequence attached to expression of opinion in the legislature; others were serving on committees, where their views might be modified or adjusted in confidential discussion; or resort to a coffee-house might bring with it the revelation that there are generally two sides to a question; and so, with the increased volume of the written and spoken word, there dawned on publicists and politicians a clearer realization of the value of circumlocution or reservation in all statements likely to incur public scrutiny.

This process had not gone very far in the reign of Charles, though its beginnings can be detected in the diplomatic and political correspondence, and in the parliamentary oratory. It was fortunate perhaps that, as the language became more pellucid, it became more innocuous; for no democracy can work until it has for its service a sufficiently large stock of non-committal terms, and the England of Charles's reign was at least formulating some of the principles on which democratic government was afterwards based. One consequence of this linguistic development was a deepening of the contrast between the language of the humble and that of the polite; the one remaining a sterling, uninflated currency, surviving mostly in local dialects; while the other was minted in such high denominations that its users were all rich, and gradations of poverty and wealth tended to disappear. Dryden found that in this respect we had been anticipated by the Japanese, who, according to his information, made use of certain words in familiar discourse, while reserving others for studied compositions:

The men of quality have a language quite different from the vulgar. When they write of a sublime subject (for example, religion or affairs of state) they serve themselves of particular terms.[1]

A similar instinct for the non-committal may be traced in the expressed views of men regarding the conduct of life; and in this respect it is noteworthy that we have no native equivalent for the French *savoir faire*, the only phrase to describe those social aptitudes which were now being more closely studied by the heirs of Saxon bluntness and simplicity. In its most ingenuous form this can be seen in the twenty maxims[2] drawn up for his son by 'an eminent lawyer' in 1682. Among his precepts were these: acquire some knowledge of physic, divinity, and law at the university, so that your conversation may be more agreeable, though your knowledge need only be superficial; do not study anything unless there is profit to be had by it; never lend money on the public faith, because common debts like common lands are the most neglected; do not marry a celebrated beauty, because your house will become as frequented as a confectioner's shop; when travelling, see to it that the irreligion of foreign parts does not cause you to neglect divine duties, and remember that God heard Daniel in Babylon; show honour to new families, whatever your opinion of them; avoid writing about the faults of great persons, as your correspondence may be intercepted; and, lastly, always avoid disputes about religion. Lord Chesterfield himself could not have been more sagacious.

The above illustrations from English education and language have been cited to support the contention that, though English civilization was becoming more sophisticated, more self-conscious, and more assimilative of foreign influence, a national distinctiveness was nevertheless preserved. Among the foreign influences was that of the Court. In exile, Charles had acquired a taste for French music and French drama; as king, he exercised some influence in both these spheres. Thus he helped to

---

[1] Dryden, *Life of St. Francis Xavier*, in *Works*, ed. Scott, xvi, bk. v.
[2] They will be found in *Bodley, Ashmole* G. 12.

create the demand for a new, secularized type of church music, consisting mainly of solo and dialogue, with instrumental accompaniment—a type sometimes florid and theatrical, and not altogether in accord with English taste. Our church music of the Restoration was therefore a somewhat isolated or at least self-contained product, deriving little from older English tradition, and leaving no successor in its wake; but on the other hand its venturesomeness may have helped to stimulate the genius of Purcell, who composed many of his best pieces for church or theatre. But in spite of the very definite French influence to which he was subjected, Purcell preserved characteristics of a distinctively English kind; amid his mannerisms and crudities he maintained a vigorous individuality, which has come to be more generally appreciated by his countrymen in recent years, through the publicity given to his compositions by the Purcell Society. In music as in everything else the king loved experiment; and it was by experiment with new forms that Purcell helped to transmute the old devotional music of the church into the more organized secular music of modern times.[1]

The value of the king's influence on the English drama is more debatable.[2] He was fond of the theatre; his players were part of his retinue, and at least he helped to make the actor a person of more public consequence. The technique of the stage was developed in his reign: scenery was used; important parts were played by actresses; great nobles such as Buckingham, Newcastle, and Rochester emulated the king by their patronage, and the stage became the most fashionable diversion of the Court and of all pretending to social distinction. Nearly all the literary men of the day wrote plays, which were seldom acted for more than a week, with the result that quality was generally sacrificed to quantity. The French influence was seen in the use of rhyme and in the popularity of the heroic play, in which was depicted a world infinitely remote from the actualities of the present; where the characters were mostly stereotyped exponents of the

[1] For a good general account of music in the reign of Charles II see *The Oxford History of Music*, vol. iii, *The Seventeenth Century*, ch. vii, by sir C. H. Parry.

[2] For good accounts of Restoration Drama see the standard books by Allardyce Nicoll and B. Dobrée, *Restoration Tragedy* and *Restoration Comedy*.

grand virtues and the grand manner, always liable to break forth into wearisome tirade, and sometimes defying everybody, including, on at least one occasion, God himself.[1] In such a world there could be little differentiation of character, so the author constantly interposed his own sentiments, and contented himself with putting these into the mouths of his puppets. The drama of the Elizabethans was often tawdry and obscene, but it was spontaneous; that of the Restoration contained hardly an echo of the great events which were being enacted beyond Whitehall. Against its turgidity and bathos Buckingham's *Rehearsal* was a witty and effective protest, a protest which showed incidentally that Englishmen had now acquired a keener appreciation of sarcasm as a literary weapon.

Almost as popular as the heroic play was the comedy of manners. Here there was more scope, but nothing was achieved comparable to the masterpieces of Molière, for this literary form was not completely adapted to the English genius. Saint-Évremond once defined the ideals as the Englishman who can talk and the Frenchman who can think; the Restoration dramatists seldom succeeded in providing either thought or wit. The accusation of obscenity cannot be levelled by the present age against any of its predecessors; but, with more justice, much of the dramatic output of the Restoration may be indicted of tediousness, for even the courtiers became tired of it; and, in 1682, so diminished was the popularity of the stage, that the duke of York's company had to combine with that of the king.[2] Thereafter, the theatre was displaced in importance by the pamphlet and the newspaper. Thus in drama as in music the taste of Charles was partly responsible for a diversion from the main stream of English tradition, a diversion which was not pure loss, as witnessed by the names of Dryden, Otway, and Purcell.

In one respect, however, the French influence proved a real blessing. This was in the development of literary criticism; and, more especially, in the expression of that criticism by means of the 'causerie' or short essay, in which literary analysis is effected

[1] Dryden's *Maximin*.
[2] For a very interesting account of this decline see A. Beljame, *Le public et les hommes de lettres en Angleterre, 1660–1744.*

with moderation and grace. In this the French excelled; but Dryden, who had French models to help him, showed how it could be done almost equally well in English. The essays which he prefixed to many of his compositions are models of clarity and condensation.[1] They are of more than literary interest; for they reflect a subtle change, due perhaps to the greater influence of women in Restoration England, or possibly even to the personal example of Charles himself. It was an entirely different method of expressing disagreement. Hitherto, literary polemic had been handled mainly by scholars, shut up in their studies; it was therefore generally vituperative, and often vindictive; now, in the hands of Dryden, it reflected not the vitiated atmosphere of the study, but a more polite world where there was always a suggestion of femininity, enlivened by the *bons mots* of a king whose humour never failed him. It was not that Dryden had any close personal connexion with the Court, but rather that he interpreted a new attitude of mind popularized by the king and by French influence. In this more rare atmosphere criticism might be both courteous and effective, for the devotee of literature was no longer a pedant but a man of the world; and the 'mob of gentlemen that write with ease' had at least commenced life as gentlemen. Many took their cue from the king, who preferred unhorsing an opponent with a lance to annihilating him with a culverin; hence, at a time when the nation was passing through one of the most sensitive and receptive periods of its history, his personal influence may have counted for much:

Whence is it that our conversation is so much more refined? I must freely and without flattery ascribe it to the Court; and in it particularly to the King, whose example gives a law to it. His own misfortunes and the nation's afforded him an opportunity which is rarely allowed to sovereign princes, I mean of travelling and being conversant with the most polished courts of Europe; and thereby of cultivating a spirit which was formed by nature to receive the impressions of a gallant and generous education. At his return he found a nation lost as much in barbarism as in rebellion; and as the excellency of his nature forgave the one, so the excellence of his manners reformed the other. The desire of imitating so great a pattern first awakened

---

[1] See the edition of these essays by W. P. Ker, with a valuable introduction showing the French influence.

the dull and heavy spirits of the English from their natural reserved-
ness; loosened them from the stiff forms of conversation, and made
them easy and pliant to each other in discourse. Thus, insensibly our
way of living became more free; and the fire of the English wit,
which was before stifled under a constrained, melancholy way of
breeding, began first to display its force, by mixing the solidity of
our nation with the air and gaiety of our neighbours.[1]

Dryden possibly exaggerated the value of royal[2] and French
influence; but of the fact of that influence there can be no doubt.
It eventually gave us the age of Pope and Chesterfield for that
of Bunyan and Milton. Who is to decide between them?

Wider than the influence of university, school, or court was
that of the popular press.[3] There was first the newspaper. At
the close of the Commonwealth two publications of a government news-book were in circulation—the *Mercurius Politicus*,
published on Thursdays, and the *Public Intelligencer*, on Mondays,
both compiled by Marchamont Needham; but in December
1659 a rival journal the *Parliamentary Intelligencer* was brought
out by Henry Muddiman, one of the professional journalists of
his age. This newspaper had a definite object—to popularize
the demand for a free parliament; and when this object was
achieved, Muddiman succeeded in acquiring a more official
status for his papers. For some years he had a monopoly of
supplying printed and written news to the public, in return for
which monopoly he conveyed intelligence to the government.
As the press came to be more effectively controlled by the
Licensing Act and by the supervision of the secretaries of state,
Muddiman was displaced in importance by Roger L'Estrange,
who combined the two roles of government agent or spy and
editor of a semi-official weekly paper named *The Intelligencer*; but
Muddiman was left as the most important of the news-letter-
writers, who sent their weekly summaries at regular intervals to

[1] Dryden, *Defence of the Epilogue*, in *Essays*, ed. W. P. Ker, i. 176.

[2] A useful corrective to Dryden's estimate is provided by Halifax's
Character of Charles II, in *Halifax*, ii. 343–60. Halifax thought that Charles
told his good stories too often, and that the frank manner of expression
acquired abroad was not always in accord with English taste.

[3] For the history of the press in England see H. R. Fox Bourne, *English
Newspapers*; J. B. Williams, *A history of English journalism to the foundation of
the Gazette*; S. Morison, *The English Newspaper* (1932).

clients on payment of a fee, generally £5 per annum. In November 1665, when court and parliament were at Oxford, Arlington secured the publication of the bi-weekly *Oxford Gazette*, an infringement of L'Estrange's monopoly which was made possible by the special privileges of the University Press. This journal was afterwards printed in London, and was known as the *London Gazette*; but at first it was not fully official because (owing to disagreements between the two principal secretaries of state) rival papers were licensed. The Great Fire destroyed these competitors; so in this fortuitous way the *London Gazette* came to be a semi-official organ. The meeting of the Oxford Parliament in 1681 provided another occasion for journalistic activity; but this was short-lived. In the last four years of the reign L'Estrange pilloried Whigs and Dissenters in *Heraclitus Ridens* and *The Observator*: newspapers which, though frequently parodied, did not have to face the sustained competition of rival journals.

The newspapers were small, closely-printed sheets, containing a few items of foreign and domestic intelligence, together with announcements of horses stolen and strayed, and advertisements of quack medicines. There was a certain amount of specialization; for in 1675 appeared *The City Mercury or Advertisements Concerning Trade*, a journal intended for the needs of merchants and the commercial world. In this were trade announcements: such as ships offered for sale, houses and shops to be let, offers from purchasers of life annuities, and the time-tables of stage-coaches. It does not appear to have been long-lived.[1]

While the newspaper provided for those who wished to be abreast of the times, there was a great increase in that literature whose object was merely to provide diversion. As this was not written for a critical public, and was intended to attract purchasers from those who do not usually spend money on books, its productions were not likely to be found in the studies of the learned, nor among the well-bound folios of the rich; they were circulated 'below stairs', and found a resting-place behind the pots and pans in the kitchen. In this way a reading public grew up. Accounts of murders, fires, and disasters, in rhyme or prose, with or without the help of the woodcut, satisfied in some

[1] Copies will be found in *Bodley, Nicholl's Newspapers*, i.

measure the human demand for accounts of the marvellous. These are evidences not that crime and misfortune were more than usually common, but that thousands of humdrum existences were varied by resort to that half-real world in which the literary artist worked. Thus there were ghost stories, such as that of the haunted house in Cherry-Tree Alley, near Bunhill Fields, where the apparition took the form sometimes of a man, sometimes of a dog, and manifested itself by pulling the clothes from people in bed. The owner of the house intimated that he proposed to ask a divine to 'lay' the ghost.[1] Another early example of this kind of literature was the story of the hackney coachman who picked up a curious passenger in Fleet Street. Some uncanny influence at once permeated the vehicle; the horses became restive; and when the fare dismounted, he turned first into a bear, and then 'of a sudden vanished away in a terrible flash of fire with great sparks, as if a flambeau had been dashed against the wall'.[2] This was in 1684. But if there were few ghost stories, there were many that bordered on the miraculous, a favourite theme being that of the man or woman who slept for unusually long periods. Thus there was the Dutchman, a patient in St. Bartholomew's Hospital, who slept regularly for five days and nights every August. Nor was this all, for on these occasions he had dreams which came true; and at the same time his mother had identical dreams. On one occasion, the dream was about two fellow patients in the hospital; the one he saw 'hurried to a dismal, dark carstle' (sic), while the other was taken away 'to a place of bliss'. Sure enough, these two men died while the sleeper was dreaming about them. A woodcut showing the Dutchman in bed added to the novelty of this story.[3]

A new and more vivid world was coming more prominently into existence, peopled by men who were heightened above the ordinary human dimensions; for whom glory, disaster, and death were as things of ordinary routine. It was as unreal as that of the heroic drama, but it made a much stronger and wider appeal. This world of imagination was not so densely peopled as its counterpart of to-day, when there are so many devices for bridging the gulf between fact and fancy, but in Charles's

---

[1] In *Bodley, Ashmole* G. 12, no. 214. [2] Ibid., no. 213.
[3] *The sleepy man awak'd . . .* in *Bodley*, 2702 e. 1.

England its existence was being noted as a new phenomenon. 'It is nothing', said an observer, 'to kill a man this week, and with ink instead of *aqua vitae* to bring him alive the next; to drown two admirals in a week, and to buoy them up again the next, so that many of these pamphlets may be better termed The Weekly Bills of Truth's Mortality.'[1] The student of this literature cannot but notice the great increase in its popularity after 1679, an increase sometimes attributed to the lapsing of the Licensing Act in that year; but this cannot be the sole cause, because the executive still retained some power of censorship, and exercised it by proclamation;[2] moreover the pamphlets here in question were not of a character likely to offend the licensing rules. It is equally probable that the Popish Plot stimulated the vogue for the miraculous; and so, at a time when there was real difficulty in distinguishing the natural from the supernatural, when the extraordinary was not the exception but the rule, it is not surprising that the purveyor of the wonderful came into his own; indeed, for perhaps the first time in English literature, the lie became a legitimate motive, and to tell it well became one of the recognized objectives of art. Not for some time was this accomplished with real skill, but meanwhile there were some creditable attempts.

Some of these attempts are not without interest in the history of that literary form which came to displace the epic, the lyric, the elegy, and the funeral oration, namely the novel. Many critics find the seventeenth-century prototypes of the novel in long, rimed romances, such as Davenant's *Gondibert* (1651), or in the comparatively short stories of Aphra Behn, or even in the wearisome narratives of madame de Scudéry; but it is possible that humbler ancestors had a share in the development of this literary type. It is at least likely that some of the more obscure romancers of the Restoration period were seeking for expedients intended to create the illusion of verisimilitude. The poorest device was to say that, if the reader doubted the truth of the events narrated, he could obtain confirmation by interviewing the inhabitants of a particular place; or, if even that were not enough, by inspecting the remains of the villains of the piece on

[1] *The Tears of the Press* (1681), in *Bodley, Ashmole* 730.
[2] *Steele*, i. 3699. See *supra*, 515.

a specified place of hanging.[1] A slight improvement on this was to say that the qualities of the hero or heroine would sufficiently appear in the sequel about to follow, a subterfuge adopted in a historical novel entitled: *The English Princess or the Duchess Queen: a relation of English and French Adventures, a Novel*[2] (1678). This title was certainly an attractive one; but after being lured into a record of cosmopolitan adventures, the reader was asked to accept this unconvincing description of the heroine, queen Margaret of Scotland: 'as to her body, nothing was wanting that might render it perfect; her complexion was fair, and the round of her face inclined near to a perfect oval'. These descriptions of female beauty or virtue are still notorious stumbling-blocks for the male novelist.

It was in the romances of roguery that the lie was told well; indeed, the tramp is a progenitor of the novel, as the burglar of the detective story. These rogue stories had begun as translations of Spanish picaresque novels; but in the later part of the seventeenth century original narratives were being produced, and there was at least one extensive cycle relating to the exploits of a single great rogue. This was the German Princess, alias Mary Carleton, alias Jenny Voss, whose real name was Mary Moders. She was born in humble circumstances at Canterbury in 1634 and had a local reputation as a cheat. Her marriage to John Carleton, who pretended to be a lord, brought her a wider circle of acquaintance and opportunity, which she utilized to the fullest advantage, as may be seen in the numerous accounts of her exploits.[3] After being tried for bigamy, she went on the stage in a play depicting her own career;[4] she then returned to thieving, and is said to have emulated the exploits of colonel Blood by stealing the more picturesque valuables, such as the lord

---

[1] These were the tests suggested in a story about a witch and her two sons who murdered a Mr. Harrison, who came to life again and was transported to Turkey. The inhabitants of Camden and the remains on the gibbets on Broadway Hill would provide confirmation. (*Bodley, Wood* 401, no. cxci.)

[2] In *Bodley*, 8 R. 72 Art.

[3] For instance, F. Kirkman, *The Counterfeit Lady Unveiled* (1673), in *Bodley, Wood* 267. See also E. Bernbaum, *The Mary Carleton Narratives* (1914). See also the account in the *D.N.B.*, *s.v.* Mary Carleton.

[4] *The German Princess.* It was seen by Pepys on April 15, 1664.

chancellor's mace.[1] She was executed at Tyburn in 1673. It was said by one of her biographers that when young she was addicted to pleasure, loved fine clothes, delighted in reading books, especially love stories, and sometimes imagined herself a princess.[2]

In at least one of the rogue stories can be detected that attention to minute detail afterwards so brilliantly exemplified in the work of Defoe; in this way an apparent irrelevancy is only one of many units making a concerted work of art. Examples abound in *The English Rogue*, by R. Head (1680). Thus, in his boyhood, the hero of this romance killed a turkey and was extremely proud of his exploit. This youthful pride might have been emphasized by a free use of adjectives; but Head makes it convincing by recording a trivial incident—the boy stuck some of the turkey's feathers in his cap, and, through constantly looking at these proofs of his prowess dangling before his eyes, he became squint-eyed. So, too, his mother was always admiring his beauty. More conventional writers would have tried to describe the boy's charms; but Head merely records the fact that, at table, the mother so doted on her son 'that she forgot to eat'. These are small things, but they show the beginnings of a new aim in English literary art—the presentation of falsehood in such a manner that it seems as natural as the truth.

The Popish Plot may also be held responsible for an increased interest in national history, an interest accentuated by hatred of France as personified in Louis XIV. Hitherto men had read history in sombre folios or long chronicles; for the learned, there were the researches of Selden, Coke, and Spelman; but now, for perhaps the first time, it was possible to read at least some of it in the short biography, such as that of Mary, Queen of Scots,[3] a book specially written for those who doubted the truth of the Plot. There were also published historical comparisons of parliaments, such as those of 1680–1 with those of 1640–1;[4] and there were reprints of old books, such as Doleman's *Conferences about the next succession to the throne of England*,[5] or Birkenhead's

---

[1] *The German Princess Revived, or the London Jilt*, 1684, in *Bodley, Ashmole* F. 5.
[2] F. Kirkman, *The Counterfeit Lady Unveiled*, 9.
[3] *History of the life of Mary, Queen of Scots*, 1681, in *Bodley, Ashmole* F. 6.
[4] *Multum in Parvo*, by Theophilus Rationalis, in *Bodley, Pamph.* 146.
[5] Printed by the Whigs in 1679 in support of the exclusionist cause.

sarcastic *Assembly Man*. More important than these was a new venture—a short, general history of England, from the 'beginnings'. This was H. Cressey's *The Plain Englishman's Historian* (1679), a compendium of only 140 pages: 'a brief epitome of English History', which traced national origins to heroic sources; for it began with the landing (2855 B.C.) of Brutus on our shores. Most famous of all was Gilbert Burnet's *History of the Reformation in England* (commenced in 1679), a work which received such a welcome as to earn for its author the congratulations of both Houses of Parliament. Condemned though he is by modern experts, Burnet was nevertheless our first popular historian.

Almost as wide in their appeal were those books which popularized scientific theories about the origin of the universe, the constitution of matter, and the nature of the human body. Then as now there was some distinction between those researchers who were patiently contributing to the sum of knowledge, and those who, possessed of the gift of exposition, were familiarizing the layman with what was already known. A good example of this latter class was Thomas Burnet, master of the Charterhouse, whose *Sacred Theory of the Earth* (1684) was dedicated to Charles, and was much appreciated by that monarch. In this book the early history of the globe was described. The world was nearly 6,000 years old, and had been produced from a liquid chaos; its surface was at first perfectly smooth— no rocks, no mountains, no seasons; the air was calm and serene, and natural conditions produced a golden age amid 'the first innocency of Nature'. This perfect state was ended when the world fell into an abyss, where it suffered the Deluge, or forty days' rain, which created mountains and valleys through erosion; this fact alone, noted the author, was sufficient to disprove Aristotle's doctrine of the permanence of the earth's form. An entirely new world emerged from the Deluge; for the crust of the old earth had fallen into the abyss of waters, everywhere there were changes and irregularities, such as storms, rains, and seasons; into this new world only about eight people survived. Everything pointed to the view that the world would eventually be destroyed by fire. This would prove to be a mixed fatality: that is, a divine judgement supported by natural causes. Among the natural causes were the sulphureous quality of the soil, and the hollow construction of the ground; moreover, Scripture tells us that the Fire will start at the seat of anti-Christ, obviously in Rome, and the country round about, where the earth contains much sulphur and there are fiery mountains and caves. Rome will therefore be swallowed in a lake of fire. But there are men who incur an even greater measure of divine wrath than the papists: these are the infidels and atheists, who will be the first to perish. However antiquated Burnet's views may appear, it should be recalled that scientific geology did not begin until the nineteenth century, and moreover, Burnet handled his great theme with a dignity of expression which at least stimulated respect for the mighty forces at work in the universe.

Both popularizer and researcher recognized the need of harmonizing the new discoveries with truth as already revealed in the Scriptures; in this sense, there was no antithesis between the two, and the greatest scientists of the period, such as Newton and Boyle, were men of profoundly religious character. But at least this spread of scientific knowledge, even where crude or inaccurate, may have helped to break down a barrier which had been immeasurably strengthened by the Reformation and its consequences—the barrier of dogmatism. Before the human mind could be set in order, much heavy lumber had therefore to be removed. This was the theme of a notable book published in 1661: *The Vanity of Dogmatizing*, by Joseph Glanvill, a book which showed what a tiny fraction of our experience can be explained or accounted for in a completely satisfactory way. The human body was itself, he contended, a mass of unexplained problems;[1] the motion of a wheel round its centre was inexplicable on currently accepted hypotheses;[2] sensation and memory were not completely accounted for; we live in a world of mysteries of which we perceive only an infinitesimal part. Aristotle's teaching, he thought, was completely inadequate for the new world of nature being unravelled before men's eyes; moreover the Stagyrite's philosophy had been responsible for no new invention, and was impious.[3] Because of the mutual 'dependence and concatenation' of causes we cannot know one thing without

---

[1] *Vanity of Dogmatizing*, ch. v.   [2] Ibid., ch. vi.
[3] Ibid., ch. xix.

knowing all.[1] Dogmatizing is therefore the effect of ignorance, the disturber of the world, and the consequence of a narrowness of spirit. This plea for philosophic doubt was perhaps premature; it was enunciated in an age when most men were still thinking in definite, theological terms; but it aptly embodied that constructive scepticism which Bacon and Descartes had already applied to the preconceptions of their times.

This mingling of tradition with free inquiry is to be found in much of the philosophy and science of the later seventeenth century. It may be illustrated from chemistry. Here the ancient Greek and Arab traditions had been modified in the sixteenth century by Paracelsus, and later by van Helmont of Brussels; their views were further developed by Sylvius (Francis Dubois), who was born at Amsterdam in 1614. Briefly, Sylvius correlated all diseases with chemical properties, everything being referred to acids and alkalis; diseases were therefore divided into two main classes, according as they were due to the acidity of one of these substances. The bile is one of the main factors producing such acridities, according as it is influenced by food, air, and emotion; thus fevers are caused by acid acridity of the pancreatic juice. In England these doctrines were developed by the physician Thomas Willis (1621–75), who is also known in the history of medicine for his important researches into diabetes. Willis adopted the three primary chemical qualities of Paracelsus, namely salt, sulphur, and mercury. Salt is the cause of fixity in bodies, and is the residue left after burning; mercury is the spirit which volatilizes their constituent parts, and is isolated by distillation; sulphur causes colour and combustibility, and thus unites the spirit to the salt. On this basis he expounded a whole theory of medicine. He held that, in the process of digestion, an acid ferment is produced in the stomach; together with the sulphur of the food, this forms the chyle. The chyle enters into fermentation in the heart; in other words, the salt and sulphur are set on fire. This combustion produces the vital flame, which permeates all life; it creates also the vital spirits in the brain by a process of distillation. Fevers are attributable to an effervescence of the blood; spasms and convulsions are caused by explosions of salt and sulphur; gout

[1] Ibid., ch. xxii.

is due to the coagulation of the blood; scurvy is caused by the blood becoming 'vapid'.[1]

Such were the main principles of the Iatrochemists, so called because they referred all medical phenomena to chemical processes. For the student of science, these doctrines show an attempt to utilize, in the healing art, the chemical researches into the properties of metals which Paracelsus had inaugurated in the preceding century; and they directed attention to one of the most fruitful fields of modern research—the chemical composition of the blood. For the student of history they have this interest, that they illustrate the vast importance of chemistry in the speculative inquiries of the seventeenth century, and the influence of that science in spheres where it no longer has a monopoly; indeed, it can be demonstrated that much of the thought of the later seventeenth century was coloured by chemical similes and doctrines. Thus, human character like the human body was determined mainly by chemical composition. The 'humours' illustrated the balance of components in this composite entity, the preponderance of any one of the four elements producing certain distinctive idiosyncrasies, so clearly defined that they might be deduced from the complexion, the hair, or the eyes.[2] A humour was defined[3] as 'a moist and running body into which the food in the liver is converted'. It might be of different kinds—sanguine, phlegmatic, choleric, or melancholic, and an excess of one might produce disturbance amounting to a disease, such as Melancholy, the fashionable complaint of the century; while the ideal character was based on a perfect balance of all four elements. Chemistry was an essential element in the inquiry of the time, not, as is sometimes supposed, because Charles dabbled in laboratory experiments, but because its principles and nomenclature underlay so much of seventeenth-century thought.

[1] T. Thomson, *History of Chemistry* (2nd ed.), 184–201; W. C. Dampier-Whetham, *A History of Science*, 124–8. See also C. Singer, *A short history of Medicine* and *Studies in the history and method of Science*, and E. J. Holmyard, *Makers of Chemistry*.

[2] A good account of the humours and their importance in literature will be found in Dr. Percy Simpson's introduction to his edition of Jonson's *Every Man in his Humour* (1919).

[3] W. Vaughan, *Directions for Health* (1633), 127.

Increasing resort to mineral wells helped to spread this popular interest in chemistry; indeed, one of our earliest text-books of chemistry is a guide-book to the spa at Bath,[1] and for long men were induced to think of health and sickness in metallurgical terms. Metals were classified in a hierarchy which put gold at the top, because the most solid, the most heavy, and completely devoid of impurities, as was proved by the fact that it lost nothing in heating; silver came next; most impure of all was iron; intermediate were the 'half metals', such as bismuth, or tin glass, and antimony; there were also the minerals some-times classified as 'spirits', such as mercury, sulphur arsenic, and cadmium. All these had their medicinal qualities. Sulphur provided a valuable fumigant, and could be taken internally in rhubarb as a purge by the choleric man; but for the same pur-pose the melancholic man would resort to senna or polypody. Nitre appears to have been grouped with elements like sulphur; it was of great value for its supposed qualities, and was used in juleps. Public health was thought to be influenced and even determined by the purity of the nitre available; and Boyle believed that the supplies of saltpetre could be classified in this way, that from the East Indies being the purest.[2] Scurvy was attributed to impure nitre,[3] plague to its exhalations in the air.[4] Some writers resolved the whole question of health into sulphur and nitre: 'Nitro-sulphurous spirits or salts are, as it were, the soul of the world, and the authors and carriers of all produc-tions and generations'.[5] With these explanations at hand, few diseases were attributed to occupation or nutrition, with the possible exception of rickets, then coming to attract the atten-tion of the physician because of its wide prevalence. This disease was said to be due to 'a soft and debauched way of living',[6] probably the reverse of the truth. Another substance to which great importance was attached was tartar. This might be adventitious or innate; the former being one of the by-

[1] E. Jorden, *Discourse of natural bathes* (1631).

[2] Boyle, *Works* (ed. 1772), i. 327. Boyle concluded that the differences in nitre were due to differences in the soil from which it was dug.

[3] G. Castle, *The Chemical Galenist* (1667), 41.

[4] N. Hodges, *Loimologia*, 32. See also *supra*, i. 292-3.

[5] G. Castle, op. cit. 61.

[6] Ibid. 44.

products of digestion, which usually found a lodging in the joints, where it produced gout.[1]

So long as Chemistry and Medicine were thus interlocked, the progress of each was impeded; phenomena had to be interpreted to comport with the doctrine of the four 'elements' and the three 'primaries'; nor, until Boyle defined it, was the conception of a chemical element understood. There were other instances of this interlocking. Many of the seventeenth-century thinkers were mathematicians, or had had a mathematical training; the importance of Harvey's discovery, coupled with the influence of Descartes, helped to create a school which linked medicine with mathematics or even hydraulics. From this point of view, physiology was a branch of mechanics. Contemporary, therefore, with the Iatrochemists, there were the Iatrophysicists; the first thinking in terms mainly of minerals and acids, the second in terms of pressure and suction. To these may be added a third school, the Galenists, who claimed to follow the older traditions of the Greek and Arabic doctors.[2] While it is true that modern research favours this use by one science of the discoveries of another, yet this stage cannot be reached until each of the great branches of science is thought worthy of independent investigation. It was perhaps the most important intellectual achievement of Charles's reign that medicine, surgery, chemistry, physics, and astronomy all came to be regarded as great sciences, each having its distinctive aims and methods; and even more, that in all these subjects the authority of tradition was finally set aside in favour of independent investigation and experiment. If for this only, the period of the Restoration was one of the most important in the history of human thought.

2. THE ROYAL SOCIETY: SCIENTIFIC RESEARCH

Towards this achievement the universities at first contributed little; it is to the Royal Society that we owe the differentiation of the sciences and the encouragement of research. The Royal Society had its origin in the meetings of certain philosophers and inquirers which can be traced as far back as 1645; these

[1] H. Nollius, *Hermetical Physick* (1655 trans.), 294 sqq.
[2] A. H. Buck, *The Growth of Medicine*, 419–20.

men, detached from the troubles around them, were an informal group, called the Invisible College, a name which may have emphasized their dissociation from the religious and political parties of the time. After 1648 they held gatherings at Oxford, where their members included Dr. Wilkins, warden of Wadham College; Dr. Ralph Bathurst, afterwards president of Trinity College, Oxford; Seth Ward, afterwards bishop of Salisbury, and Dr. Petty. For a time Oxford was the centre of the new experimental philosophy, because in the university city were held the meetings of the Invisible College; Dr. Willis presided over an experimental club, which met at an apothecary's shop (Tillyard's in the High Street); and next door but one in the same street Boyle had a laboratory, into which he introduced the first teacher of practical chemistry in England—Peter Sthael, a native of Prussia.[1] These activities were outside the supervision of the University; but in 1683 Oxford acquired a laboratory of its own—the Ashmolean (now the 'old' Ashmolean), a benefaction of the antiquary Elias Ashmole, and Chemistry was there taught by the indefatigable Dr. Plot.[2]

With the Restoration, the Invisible College resumed its meetings at Gresham's College, when it numbered fifty-five; and, after a lecture given on November 28, 1660 by Christopher Wren, it was proposed to found a college for 'physico-mathematical learning', the members to pay a subscription of 1s. per week.[3] For nearly two years the society existed on this basis; but, by charter of July 15, 1662, it was incorporated as the Royal Society, and received a mace from Charles II. Its first president was lord Brouncker, who was succeeded fourteen years later by sir Joseph Williamson, and in 1680 by Boyle. In 1682 the members had so increased in number that it was necessary to discriminate carefully among the candidates for admission; this was possibly owing to the prestige bestowed on the Society by the king, who was himself interested in experiments, and enjoyed the conversation of ingenious men. Many eminent workers contributed to the success and prestige of the Society. Thus Dr. Jonathan

---

[1] R. T. Gunther, *Early Science in Oxford*, i. 9–22. For a good, short history of the Royal Society in this period see H. B. Wheatley, *Early history of the Royal Society*. See also E. J. Bowen, *The study of science in University College, Oxford*.

[2] For this see Gunther, op. cit. i. 43 sqq.   [3] Wheatley, op. cit. 7.

Goddard made telescopes, which were more useful and less expensive than his 'drops'[1]; and in Robert Hooke the Society had not only a curator of experiments and (afterwards) an enterprising secretary, but a noted mathematician, architect, optician, and physicist; one of the most ingenious and prolific researchers of his day, who, while he anticipated many discoveries, did not have the sustained power requisite for bringing them to maturity. Among its fellows were to be found practically all the men of note in the reign of Charles II; for these included Newton, Boyle, Dryden, Petty, Evelyn, Sandwich, Barrow, Buckingham, and Pepys.

The scope of the Society's inquiries may be gathered from the names of the committees and their purposes. Among these were the mathematical, the astronomical and optical, the chemical, the agricultural, and those for correspondence and the history of trade. The communications were classified into the following, among other categories: mechanics and trade; journals of the weather; statics and hydraulics; architecture, ship-building, geography, navigation, voyages, and travels; pharmacy and chemistry; monsters and longevity; grammar, chronology, history, and antiquities. These attest the diversity of the Society's interests,[2] and serve to show that the Royal Society was not a scientific institution in the narrow sense of the term, but a body for the encouragement, collection, and classification of knowledge on almost every conceivable subject. By its agency also were conducted extensive inquiries which would now be the subject of royal commissions. Such an inquiry was that into English agriculture.[3] In this way the whole character of philosophic speculation (in the wider sense of the term) was completely changed. Hitherto the investigator had worked as a solitary student; he had been taught to despise the methods of the 'sooty empiric', and to place his faith in books; he published his results in Latin, and would have resented most strenuously the criticism that he had strayed from accepted authority. Now he was encouraged to go into his workshop or laboratory or the outside world in order to use his powers of observation; his

[1] See *supra*, i. 331.
[2] See A. H. Church, *Royal Society Archives: Classified Papers* (1907).
[3] See *supra*, i. 60–1.

results were communicated in English to a body of men with whom he could discuss their relevance or import; and he was induced to think, not that men were at the end of their knowledge of nature, but at the beginning. Similar forces were at work in the scientific Academies of France and Italy.

Nor were these things confined to a small and select circle; for in 1665 began to appear the *Philosophical Transactions*, printed for the Royal Society and edited by its first secretary, Henry Oldenburg. This was intended to give publicity to the 'undertakings, studies and labours of the Ingenious in many considerable parts of the world'. Its first number was prefaced by a statement of the importance of communicating scientific knowledge through the press. There then followed an account of improved optic glasses made in Rome; there was a communication by Hooke intimating that, with a 12-foot telescope, he had seen a spot in one of the belts of Jupiter; to this was added an account of a book in the press—Boyle's *Experimental History of Cold*; there was also a description of a 'very odd, monstrous calf' born at Lymington in Hampshire; and finally there was a short article on the new 'American whale fishing about the Bermudas'. Subsequent numbers maintained this variety of topic, and so provided reading of interest to every man of intelligence. The mercury mines of Friuli; a method of producing wind by falling water; revelations by the microscope of minute bodies on the edges of razors, on blighted leaves, on the beard of the wild oat, on sponges, hair, the scales of a sole, the sting of a bee, the feathers of a peacock, the feet of flies, and the teeth of sharks; a baroscope for measuring minute variations in the pressure of the air; a hygroscope for discerning the watery steam in the air (these were Hooke's inventions); Mr. Wing's Almanac giving the times of high water at London Bridge; a new way of curing diseases by transfusion of blood; the process of tin-mining in Cornwall; and the making of mulberry wine in Devonshire—these are only a minute number of the subjects on which writers conveyed information derived from their experience and investigation. Such things may well appear commonplace or jejune to a surfeited or over-educated world; but in their original freshness they must have opened up new worlds to men circumscribed by the older traditions.

Of actual intellectual achievement, many examples might be cited from the careers of scientific men in the reign of Charles. It may suffice to record a few of the results obtained in medicine, surgery, chemistry, and physics; for which purpose the names of Sydenham, Wiseman, Boyle, and Newton may be selected. The last two were members of the Royal Society; the first two were not.

Thomas Sydenham (1624–89) came of an old Dorsetshire family, and varied his studies at Oxford with service in the Civil Wars (on the parliamentary side). Having obtained a medical degree and a fellowship of All Souls he began to study medicine with such facilities as the university then afforded, these consisting mainly of the specimens which the enterprising Petty provided for the dissecting-room. Further military service and studies at Montpelier delayed his establishment in practice; nor, until 1663, did he obtain the licentiate of the College of Physicians. Thereafter he built up a good practice in London. He suffered much from ill health, and his personal experience of gout enabled him to write an important account of that ailment. By contemporaries he was held in high esteem, because of his zeal and ability as a physician, and from a certain nobility and modesty of character, but otherwise he was not numbered among the notable men of his time. Two treatises, *Methodus curandi febres* and *Observationes Medicae*, brought him into European notice.

Sydenham's importance in the history of the healing art lies in the fact that he was the first to illustrate accurate clinical observation of disease. That observation could be trained, and that it must be trained in order to achieve scientific results, was the principle which he taught and acted upon; that it is a truism to-day does not detract from the importance of its earlier enunciations in medical history. He defined this principle in four axioms: (1) all diseases must be reduced to certain definite species, as the botanists have done for plants; (2) 'every philosophical hypothesis that has inveigled the writer's mind should be set aside', and the clear and natural phenomena of the disease, no matter how small they may appear, should be recorded; (3) in describing a disease it is necessary to distinguish between the 'peculiar and perpetual phenomena' and those that are accidental and adventitious; (4) the seasons of the year are to be observed, because some diseases follow the seasons as do birds and plants. In these axioms[1] was Sydenham's challenge to the traditional practice as derived from Galen; even more, he showed how these new methods might be applied. Accordingly he recorded his observations of plague, ague, cholera, and fevers as he had witnessed them in different years; and from these observations he made his recommendations for treatment. He did not believe in bleeding as a universal panacea, and considered that idiosyncrasy and habit should be considered before this was resorted to. He succeeded in a fairly accurate diagnosis of measles—accurate enough to distinguish it from small-pox; and he noted also the liability of measles to result in bronchial complications—peripneumonia was the name which he gave to the broncho-pneumonia which frequently supervenes. His treatment of this ailment did not differ greatly from that of modern physicians—namely warmth, light diet, and a linctus for the cough.[2]

Sydenham was by no means the first English physician to use his powers of observation; for Francis Glisson (1597–1677), who was professor of Physic at Cambridge, adopted the same method for the study of morbid conditions, and embodied his investigations in a standard treatise on rickets (1650). But it was Sydenham who first advocated and applied these new principles of clinical medicine to the whole range of the healing art, thus systematizing and illustrating what others were applying to particular diseases or special branches of the subject. In Surgery there was also an important advance, exemplified in the work of Richard Wiseman (?1622–76). Like Sydenham he had seen much military service (on the royalist side), which proved of great value to him, since it enabled him to study his subject at first hand. When he was about fifteen he was apprenticed to a surgeon; in 1652 he was made free of the Barber-Surgeons, and in 1672 he was sworn sergeant-surgeon to the king. He had a considerable practice, in the course of which he did much to differentiate his profession from that of barber and bone-setter on the one hand and physician on the other; indeed he helped

---

[1] These will be found in the author's preface to *The whole works of* . . . *Dr. Sydenham* (8th ed. 1722). [2] Ibid. 131-4.

to make surgery a scientific subject. Before it could be differentiated, there were required a nomenclature and a set of definitions; in this respect the work of Wiseman was to prove of permanent importance. Here is his definition of a wound; it is a model of concision and clarity:

A wound is a solution of continuity in any part of the body suddenly made, by anything that cuts or tears, with a division of the skin.[1]

Wiseman coupled this scientific spirit with devotion to a sentiment; for as a royalist he believed in the efficacy of the royal touch for Scrofula, or the King's Evil, and he described those cases which he thought specially amenable to treatment from this source.[2] Moreover, he had considerable power of literary expression, and his volume of *Chirurgical Treatises* is one of the most remarkable 'case books' in the history of medicine; so clearly written as to win the commendation of Dr. Johnson, and so easily understandable as to provide the lay reader with much information about the practice of both medicine and surgery in the later seventeenth century. He used the knife only when absolutely necessary; he was quick to detect every circumstance that might help better diagnosis or promote speedier cure. Thus he noted the effect of air on his patients; that of Hampstead he thought particularly good; he recorded also the case of a patient who improved in Knightsbridge and relapsed in Holborn.[3] He believed moreover in the value of exercise, and the benefits to be derived from adapting diet to bodily habit. Many of the cases which he attended were not surgical at all, and he frequently prescribed the powerful drugs then in vogue; but, in the midst of his work as a general practitioner specializing in fractures and wounds, he helped to lay the foundations of the great traditions of British surgery, to be built upon in the next century by Hunter, and entirely remodelled in the nineteenth by Lister.

Like Wiseman, Robert Boyle knew the need for scientific definition and nomenclature. Chemists, still labouring under the four Aristotelian categories of matter, could not distinguish

---

[1] R. Wiseman, *Eight Chirurgical Treatises* (4th ed. 1705), 322.

[2] He recommended for royal treatment those cases where the tumours were about the neck, and also where the lips or eyes were affected. Ibid. 241.

[3] Ibid. 370.

between element and compound; until there was such a distinction, little progress could be looked for in chemistry. It was Boyle who supplied the definition of an element:

I mean by elements . . . certain primitive and simple, or perfectly unmingled bodies; which, not being made of any other bodies, or of one another, are the ingredients of which all those called perfectly mixed bodies are immediately compounded, and into which they are ultimately resolved.[1]

The author of this definition was one of the most distinguished and creative men of his age. The Hon. Robert Boyle (1627-91) was a son of the first earl of Cork. After a short stay at Eton (in the provostship of sir Henry Wotton) he travelled in Italy; and like many of his contemporaries he devoted himself to study and research while the great Civil Wars were being fought out. One of the Invisible College, he was induced by Petty to interest himself in dissection; but from his earliest days chemistry was his favourite subject. By means of an air-pump, invented by Hooke, he demonstrated the compressibility and weight of the air; while by his experiments in hydrostatics he succeeded in elucidating the laws of fluid equilibrium. He was in touch with most of the learned men of his time, including Newton, Locke, Evelyn, and Sydenham; and his busy life, passed in indifferent health, was marked by intense piety, and even fervour. He had the modesty of genius.

The achievements of Boyle in the many fields which he investigated have not yet been adequately valued;[2] but from his published writings the non-scientific reader may gauge something of the general importance of these achievements. His best-known work *The Sceptical Chymist* was published in 1661 and is in dialogue form; one of the speakers, Themistius, being an exponent of the older traditions, while Carneades, that is Boyle, shows how unsound are many of his assumptions. The hypotheses of the four 'elements' fire, air, earth, and water are shown to break down as a universal description of matter; nor is there even any evidence that any one of these is simpler than the substances of which they form a component; so, too, with the three

[1] Boyle, *The Sceptical Chymist.*

[2] A step in this direction has been made by Dr. Fulton's *Bibliography of the Writings of Robert Boyle* (1932).

'primaries' salt,[1] sulphur, and mercury. In this way it was possible for Carneades to define the real nature of an element, a conception of such vast importance for scientific investigation that its import could not at first be realized. It was too early for any isolation or enumeration of the elements; but once the significance of Boyle's distinction was realized, the process could not be long delayed.

His miscellaneous writings touch on many questions of moment. He impugned Hobbes's disparagement[2] of experiments; the philosopher of Malmesbury may be noted as perhaps the last exponent of the view that truth is evolved in the mind, and must never be sought for in the crucible. Failures in chemical experiments were thought by Boyle to be due to the practice of adulterating drugs;[3] generally, therefore, the materials available were 'sophisticated'. Throughout his writings he pleaded for a recognition of the need for practical as distinct from theoretical chemistry; characteristically, he was obliged to support this with the argument that, by such experiments, 'some meliorations' of mineral and metallic bodies might be effected.[4] His plea would have had little weight had it not been continually reinforced by illustration; invariably his conclusions were supported by very full and clear records of practical demonstration, and in the course of these he came upon many lines of investigation which have not been fully worked out until comparatively recent times. This is true of his inquiries into the nature of phosphorus and phosphorescent substances (then known as the 'noctiluca'); the illumination from these might, he thought, be used in places, such as the gun-rooms of ships, where candle-light might cause an explosion;[5] it is true also of his suggestion that a freezing mixture might be made with saltpetre as one of its ingredients.[6] He knew the importance of saltpetre (i.e. potash) in vegetable life; and, after researching into soils and seeds, he threw out a hint that fertility might be vastly increased by the use of chemical fertilizers.[7] He was fully aware of the importance

---

[1] In the sense defined *supra*, 717.

[2] *An examen of Mr. T. Hobbes his Dialogue* in *Works of the Hon. Robert Boyle* (6 vols. 1772), i. 186.

[3] *Two essays concerning the unsuccessfulness of experiments* in *Works*, i. 218 sqq.

[4] *Works*, i. 359. [5] Ibid. iv. 384. [6] Ibid. ii. 632. [7] Ibid. iii. 404.

of crystalline form as a guide to chemical structure. These are only a few instances to show how Boyle had entered very far into the domain of modern chemistry.

His writings have a range of speculation paralleled only by those of Descartes, Pascal, and Newton. As he cleared chemistry of dangerous preconceptions, so he removed from metaphysics the hypothesis of substantial forms. The substantial forms were supposed to be entities or inseparable qualities of matter, quite distinct from its physical or chemical qualities; thus both steam and ice tended to return to their substantial form—that is, water; and so, on this assumption, there was generated in matter some force which preserved and restored its identity. The doctrine had been of great service to the theologians. Boyle had little difficulty in showing that extraneous causes such as heat or solution were in themselves sufficient to account for those predeterminable qualities of matter. This does not mean that he adopted a materialist interpretation where his predecessors had invoked a spiritual cause; for, while the Epicureans held that the universe of atoms was not made by a deity, and the Cartesians that matter, having had its original impetus from God, needed no further influence from that source, Boyle rejected both theories; holding that neither explanation was sufficient to show how matter was brought 'into so orderly and well-continued a fabric as this world'. There was divine creation and divine energizing of the orderly creation in which men lived.[1] Hence the possibility of miracles.[2]

It was in this mingling of the experimental with the speculative that Boyle was greatest. Side by side with accounts of practical investigations there are in his writings disquisitions of a general and often lofty nature, in which he shows how the religious spirit is quickened and deepened by exploration of the forces of nature. Thus in his *Discourse about the final causes of natural things*[3] he instances the membrane covering the eye of the frog as evidence of design; for, as the frog is amphibious, living among sedges and prickly things, it must have a strong protection over the eye. 'God declares his intentions particularly in the making of his creatures'; if these declare the divine purpose, still more is that purpose revealed by sun, moon, and stars.

[1] Ibid. iii. 38–48.   [2] Ibid. iv. 201.   [3] Ibid. v. 392.

But this consideration of final causes must not be an excuse for neglect to study any of the infinite intermediaries interposed before that end. Observation of natural phenomena, he claimed, was in itself an incitement to devotion: 'they who would deter men from the scrutiny of nature tend to deprive God of much of the glory due to him'.[1] Thus Boyle placed the justification for scientific study on very high ground. He taught and exemplified a conception of religion very much higher than any expounded in the formularies of his time; and he allied it to speculative inquiries which opened up new fields in scientific research. Added to this, his character and birth gave to his words a weight and influence which would have been less had his origin been obscure, or his personal reputation dubious. Boyle made the man of science eligible in good society;[2] no longer could he be dismissed as a quack or dabbler in alembics; no longer were culture and intelligence deemed incompatible with test-tubes and crucibles.

While Boyle did much to explode obsolete hypotheses, his work cannot be estimated except in reference to the revival of the atomist theory which Gassendi initiated. This revival helped to discredit the Aristotelian system; indeed it was the Latin poet Lucretius, not the Stagyrite, who was to prove the inspiration of real scientific achievement. Boyle as an atomist was a direct continuator of Gassendi and Galileo; and as an exponent of this *philosophia corpuscularis* he held that everything was reducible to 'one catholick or universal matter'. The corpuscle constituting this matter had magnitude, shape, motion or rest, and was indivisible and indestructible. What Boyle interpreted in chemical terms Newton interpreted in mathematical and physical; in this way was perfected one of the most remarkable achievements of human thought.

Sir Isaac Newton (1642–1727) was the greatest product of the new scientific movement; but while his achievements can be linked with those of contemporaries and predecessors, his genius and the range of his investigations had a universality which elevate him above the eras and periods recognized by the

[1] *The usefulness of natural philosophy*, ibid. ii. 15.
[2] According to an (alleged) Irish epitaph, Boyle was the 'father of Chemistry and the son of the earl of Cork'.

historical student. Moreover he was not a popularizer, and it needed all the persuasions of his friend Halley to induce him to consent to the publication of his *Principia* (1687); hence an accurate statement of his theories and discoveries can be expressed only in mathematical or physical terms. But, on the other hand, no student of English civilization under the later Stuarts can afford to ignore Newton on the ground that he is of exclusively scientific interest; for it was through his influence that whole branches of scientific investigation were transformed, and the outlook of educated man entirely altered.

Early in his career Newton approached the problem of gravitation, and in 1666 the fall of an apple in his orchard is said to have suggested to him the idea of a force which varied in proportion to the square of the distance. Earlier thinkers such as Descartes had supposed the existence in space of a primary substance or ether which accounted for those qualities of matter not directly attributable to extension; but to Newton it seemed that the fall of the apple illustrated a force which could be determined empirically. For the time, however, the problem had to be set aside, because of one serious difficulty, namely, that while the sun and planets could be treated as masses, each concentrated at mathematical points (owing to the disproportion between their size and their distance apart), this (seemingly) approximate method was inapplicable to the earth and the apple, because of their small distance apart in proportion to the size of the earth. Meanwhile several important advances were made which ultimately made it possible for Newton to solve the problem. The French physicist Picart obtained a more accurate measurement of the radius of the earth; and the Dutch scientist Huygens established the relation between the length of a pendulum and its time of vibration; and, most important of all, in investigating the movement of a mass describing a circular path, he determined the acceleration of the force impelling such a moving mass to the centre in terms of the velocity of the mass and the radius of its path. In 1685 Newton, prompted by Halley, returned to the problem of 1666, and he now made the vital discovery that, where there is gravitational pull, the mass of the gravitating sphere may be assumed to be concentrated at its centre. The result was a general law of gravitation, namely that its force varied directly in proportion to the product of masses and inversely to the square of their distance apart; a discovery which enabled him to link the phenomena of astronomy with the fall of bodies to the surface of the earth. Observation of the motion of the moon in its orbit enabled him to confirm this empirical law; and in this way he made it possible to determine the movements of the whole solar system. There were many immediate results of great consequence. Thus the tides could now be explained in terms of the inertia of water and the gravitational attractions of sun and moon;[1] hitherto many inquirers had attributed them to chemical causes.[2]

Accurate statement of Newton's discoveries in mathematics, optics, astronomy, and physics is for the scientist; here it may be permissible to note one general result of his influence. He definitely severed science from metaphysics in the sense that he made clear the scope and purpose of each. Scientific knowledge in its incomplete and empiric form could never, he held, be metaphysics, which is concerned only with real and final causes. These he did not try to determine, and he stated his law of gravitation not as the cause of gravitation, but as a formula by which its phenomena might be measured. Nevertheless, he believed that a complete knowledge of the universe would show it to be not a mechanism, as Descartes had supposed, but a providential arrangement;[3] not something originally set going and left to its own devices, but a coherent unit continually directed by some unseen and intelligent force. To him, therefore, the world was both geometrical and theological; religion and science were thus not antagonists, but were ultimately explicable each in terms of the other. This conception was bound to prove a potent influence in intellectual development. By thinking of gravity in universal, not terrestrial, terms Newton extended infinitely the horizons of men's minds, and linked the fall of a

[1] For a good account of the stages by which Newton evolved his law of gravitation see W. C. Dampier-Whetham, *A History of Science*, ch. iv.

[2] e.g. J. Philpot, *Brief discourse of that grand mystery of nature, the flux and reflux of the sea* (1673), where tides are attributed to a 'vitriolated, volatile or ammoniack salt'.

[3] A. J. Snow, *Matter and gravity in Newton's physical philosophy*, 81.

stone with the movements of the planets in a system more awe-inspiring than anything ever conceived by prophet or philosopher. Both the infinite and the infinitesimal were thus acclimatized in thought, the twin conceptions best fitted to inspire a more reverent approach to the problems of knowledge.

3. SOME ILLUSTRATIONS OF RESTORATION THOUGHT AND ACHIEVEMENT

Restoration England abounded in great and interesting men; few ages of history were so prolific of genius and ability. This can be evidenced by even the scantiest of selections. There was sir Christopher Wren, not only a scientist of real eminence but the architect of a restored capital; Halley, the continuator of Galileo, one of the first of astronomers among the last of astrologers; Purcell, whose music is at last coming into its own; prince Rupert, who, having achieved fame in the field, proved himself one of the most dashing of Charles's admirals, as well as an inventor, a patron of exploration, and an artist—a medley of activities eminently characteristic of his age. Or tribute might be paid to Clarendon as a historian; or to Burnet, who started a new school of autobiography by making the indiscretion a literary motive; or to Prynne, who by his researches in the Tower inaugurated the professions of archivist and scientific historian. Modern specialization makes such kaleidoscopic brilliance impossible or difficult of achievement; but in Charles's England the world was nearly three centuries younger, and the nation had the vigour and confidence of adolescence. At least a fraction of the total intellectual achievement of the Restoration may be deduced from its evidence of three things: curiosity, revolt, and good sense. The first may be illustrated from Petty, Evelyn, and Pepys; the second from Bunyan and Hobbes; and the third from Locke and Halifax.

Few careers[1] can have been more diversified than that of sir William Petty (1623-87). Born at Romsey in Hampshire, he showed a keen, boyish interest in everything mechanical; he

[1] See the account by *Aubrey*, ii. 139 sqq. For a good modern biography see that by lord Edmond Fitzmaurice. See also *The Petty Papers*, ed. marquis of Lansdowne, 2 vols., 1927, and *The Petty-Southwell Correspondence*, ed. marquis of Lansdowne, 1927.

loved to watch artificers at work, and he learnt many of the secrets of their trade. He served in boyhood at sea; but defective eyesight ended his career as a sailor, and for a time he studied abroad, notably at Caen, Amsterdam, and Paris. In 1649 he took a degree at Oxford and was one of the Invisible College. For a time he taught anatomy at the university, supplying his own specimens, which were brought by water from Reading and preserved by a special process of his own; and as the professor of Physic disliked dissecting, Petty's teaching found ready appreciation, so that he was 'beloved by all the ingeniose'. He soon found more lucrative employment; for in 1652 he was appointed physician-general to the Army in Ireland, and later he was commissioned to carry out the land-surveying requisite for the Cromwellian scheme of Irish resettlement, a task for which he was well qualified by his mathematical knowledge; and his 'Down' survey is one of the first attempts at surveying on a scientific scale. From this he derived advantage as well as reputation; indeed he was said to have acquired an estate in every province of Ireland. After the Restoration he devoted himself to the study of navigation, and was one of the men in whose conversation the king delighted. His double-bottomed ship performed at least one successful trip across St. George's Channel, but it does not seem to have done all that was expected of it, and was afterwards wrecked. One of the original fellows of the Royal Society, he abounded in novel ideas, the most notable being his belief in the value of statistics as the sound basis of efficient government. He wanted to be Registrar General of England, but as that office was not yet in existence he had to content himself with the posts of judge of admiralty in Ireland and a commissionership of the Treasury. As economist, he exposed the fallacies of those who limited wealth to the precious metals; he showed the vital importance of population in economic speculation; and he constantly reiterated the advantages of profiting by the Dutch example of free, unfettered commerce, encouraged by a state which did not throw all its energies into the crushing of religious dissent, or the enforcement of prerogative rights.

Judged by the reports of contemporaries Petty must have been a singularly attractive man; unusually well-informed, and

yet anxious to learn; possessed of a dynamic force which communicated some of its energy to those with whom he came into
contact. Nor was his demeanour always of that seriousness
which one would expect in the patriarch of political economy,
for he was known as a good mimic; he could preach in various
styles; and once, when challenged to a duel by sir Alan Brodrick,
he proposed weapons suitable to his short-sightedness, namely
a dark cellar and hatchets. At the Royal Society he aptly
suggested that the general annual meeting should be held not
on St. Andrew's Day but on St. Thomas's Day, because the
saint who insisted on personal verification was indeed the right
patron for that society. Humour, enterprise, sociability, and
an extremely broad and enlightened view of the good that
might come from the collection and co-ordination of information and its proper use by the state—these were the qualities
which made Petty distinctive in an age of remarkable men.
'There is no darkness but ignorance' might have been his motto.
It is characteristic that, like Hobbes, he did not read much,
because he knew the dangers that may come from too ardent
pursuit of learning for its own sake; and he typified many of the
best qualities of the 'practical' Englishman, with a touch of
genius to set off his more matter-of-fact qualities.

John Evelyn (1620–1706) was the son of a landowner and was
born at Wotton in Surrey. As a young man he travelled in
France and Italy, as well as in England, in the course of which
travels he developed a keen appreciation of art and architecture; his *Diary* also shows some appreciation of landscape, and
he may have been susceptible to the environment of his Surrey
home. Travel, with reading and gardening, was his main occupation in the time of troubles; but he was not a solitary, for he
was in frequent communication with Wilkins and Boyle, and
he was one of the first fellows of the Royal Society. During the
Second Dutch War he did good work as a commissioner for the
sick and wounded; he remained at his post in the Plague; in
1671 he was appointed a member of the Council of Plantations;
and for a time, in the reign of James, he was one of the commissioners of the privy seal. He twice declined the honour of
presidency of the Royal Society. His numerous writings cover
a great range of subject, including 'sculpture' (i.e. engraving),

gardening, silviculture, navigation and trade, numismatics, and the problem of London smoke. His *Diary* is a classic, of great value not only as a record of incidents, but for its revelation of a singularly graceful and thoughtful character, free from the pettiness and self-seeking so common among his contemporaries.

The dissoluteness of Restoration England helps to place the qualities of Evelyn in sharper relief. He had many of the attributes characteristic of the best type of Englishman—loyalty to the throne, devotion to his family, a high sense of duty, moderation in speech, and regularity of conduct. These were not the virtues which brought men success or fame in the reign of Charles; nor would they have been remarked by posterity had they not been coupled with a rich humanity, which enabled him to participate fully in all the best movements of his time. He is remembered for no single achievement, but his personality was a refining influence in a society where there was a temptation to relax every restraint; and in a minor key he voiced that intelligent curiosity which inspired the highest intellectual achievements of his time. He set a high standard, for he was an embodiment of the qualities which constitute the gentleman, and he proved that landed wealth was not incompatible with public spirit, refined taste, and a fair measure of learning.

His thirst for information was shared by Samuel Pepys, whose *Diary* is a serious rival to the plays of Shakespeare, and about whose activities there is a considerable literature which shows no sign of diminishing. His personal habits, his butterfly amours, his early risings and late to-beds, his childlike glee at the signs of his steady rise in life—all these have entered into our literary currency, though Pepys probably never intended that they should. Perhaps the secret of his charm is that he could take such genuine pleasure in small things. 'All the morning in my cellar ordering some alterations therein, being much pleased with my new door into the back yard'[1]—had he been a man of introspection he would not have had this interest in the door into his back yard. So too his delight when he was first addressed as Esquire; hence also the energy which he put into the cause of his further advancement; indeed, he rose several times at four in the morning to learn the multiplication table.[2]

[1] *Pepys*, Jan. 31, 1662.　　　　　　　[2] Ibid., March 25, 1660.

Indirectly, he once gave the explanation of his own charm; for, after spending some time in the company of a major Waters, 'a most amorous, melancholy gentleman, under a despair in love', he noted that for this reason he found the major poor company.[1] Pepys is always good company, because though he was continually falling in love he never allowed these episodes to destroy his buoyancy; and like a cork he quivered with every ripple from the sea of life.

The involuntary revelation in his Diary that he was human has helped to obscure the fact that Pepys was a great administrator, possibly the greatest in the history of the British Navy. Where previously there had been indifference and ignorance, he stimulated zeal and the spirit of inquiry; and he was a pioneer in naval research, collecting vast materials now distributed in great libraries.[2] Curiosity was the mainspring of his herculean labours, as this enabled him to master the most profound technicalities, and was accompanied by an unfailing optimism; a curiosity for which nothing was too small—it might be the nautical history lurking behind the street-names of London, or the arrangement of his books, or the nature of the timber used by Noah in the building of the Ark—all these things provided welcome material for his omnivorous mind. A landsman by nature, he yet learnt more of things nautical than any sailor of his day, and he devoted that learning to the service of the Navy. In few men were the habitudes and passions of life so completely co-ordinated as in him; for he was able to return from the distractions of the park or the bargaining of the yards to the work of preparing a parliamentary report, or the devising of new official forms; with equal facility he could lose his heart to a woman and find his soul in a ledger. Living in an England ignorant of maritime affairs and often indifferent to them, having a landsman for a patron saint, and a proverb 'the sea and the gallows refuse nobody', he helped to inspire in his countrymen both a greater interest in ships and the sea, and some measure of pride in English sailors.

The greatest of diarists, Pepys was also the greatest of civil

[1] Ibid., July 9 and 11, 1662.
[2] In the British Museum, the Bodleian, and the Pepysian Library in Magdalene College, Cambridge.

servants. Eminence in this latter profession requires a sense of responsibility and a capacity for enforcing that sense on subordinates in a manner which shall be effective without being offensive. It is in the wording of the official rebuke that this quality calls for exercise, and here Pepys was breaking fresh ground, as may be seen in this letter[1] written on behalf of the Navy Board to negligent dockyard officials:

Gentlemen,

In answer to yours wherein we find you making complaint that the displeasure of this Board in the particular therein mentioned had been occasioned by our not being acquainted with what you had lately wrote on the same to Mr. Hayter, we cannot but take notice thereof as too obvious an instance of the perfunctoriness with which we find the service of His Majesty generally attended to by the officers of the yards; and assure you that we are in no little measure troubled to find such a proof thereof in reference to yourselves; who, had you considered our letter of the 14th. of December last with a regard anyway suitable to what you ought to pay to all that comes to you from this Board, you could not have overlooked the first three lines of our said letter, but found reason then, as we doubt not you will do now to be ashamed of your own negligence rather than judge us backward to do you the right due to you in that particular. . . . Therefore let not your want of considering your instructions longer occasion any prejudice to His Majesty by your not performing them.

We are,

Navy Office,   Your Very Loveing Friends,
22nd Jan. 1669.   Brouncker, Mennes, Pepys.

The structure of the first sentence could be improved, and the valedictory subscription might have been written by scribes of an earlier school; but in its restrained phrasing and pontifical detachment this letter has all the dignity and authority of Whitehall.

Had they known each other, Pepys would have found Bunyan 'very odd', and Bunyan would have assigned Pepys high office in the administration of the city of Carnal Policy. *The Pilgrim's Progress* was published in 1678, and its success proved both immediate and continuous. Its author has been the subject of praise and patronage because he, a tinker and former repro-

---

[1] *Add. MS.* 9307, f. 86.

bate, wrote the greatest allegory in the English language. But he was not of the gipsy race, for he was descended from a long line of English small-holders; he had a settled habitation; and the sins which he had to live down do not appear to have been more serious than profanity and sabbath-breaking. Itineracy he did not regard as a sin, nor imprisonment a shame. He cannot be definitely grouped with any one sect; indeed he rose above the distinctions of creeds, and directed his appeal not to one church but to all men. He spent many years in prison when he might have obtained liberty by undertaking to give over his mission; and he announced his message to an England wherein every fibre seemed to be relaxed.

The language of compromise is smooth and facile; that of rebellion is hard-grained and piercing. Unencumbered with book-learning, and burning with the fires of a conviction more enduring than that of Luther or St. Augustine, Bunyan permeated every sentence with a vigour such as no amount of training could have achieved. Compared with that of his contemporaries, his style is like some strange survival from a more primitive and elemental life. Everywhere men were learning to write agreeably, to see both sides of a question, to think in terms of their readers' likes and dislikes, and to keep going, in the cadence of the paragraph, the stately procession of the innocuous or the evasive; whereas, for Bunyan, each word had a sterling individuality. Hence with a few deft touches he can bring a man to life. Witness how the jury in Vanity Fair springs into animation:

And first among them Mr. Blind Man, the foreman said: I see clearly that this man is a heretic. Then said Mr. No Good: Away with such a fellow from the earth. Ay, said Mr. Malice, for I hate the looks of him. Then said Mr. Love Lust: I could never endure him. Nor I, said Mr. Live Loose, for he would always be condemning my way. Hang him, hang him, said Mr. Heady. A sorry scrub, said Mr. High Mind. My heart riseth against him, said Mr. Enmity. He is a rogue, said Mr. Liar. Hanging is too good for him, said Mr. Cruelty. Let us despatch him out of the way, said Mr. Hate Light. Then said Mr. Implacable: Might I have all the world given me, I could not be reconciled to him; therefore let us forthwith bring him in guilty of death. And so they did.

Bunyan devoted himself to a campaign not against sin, but against complacency. Any moralist can discredit the first; it was the tinker of Elstow who routed the second. By prayer and patience, the pilgrim might escape Giant Despair; but Mr. By Ends, whose principles were both harmless and profitable, was a far more elusive enemy. In the course of Christian's pilgrimage a climax was reached when Mr. By Ends, having failed in his onslaught on the hero's convictions, was joined by a powerful band of auxiliaries; these being Mr. Hold-the-World, Mr. Money-Love, and Mr. Save-All, old schoolfellows of Mr. By Ends, all having been educated at the academy kept by Mr. Gripe-Man, a schoolmaster in Love-Gain, a market-town in the county of Coveting. The pupils had been so well taught the art of getting 'either by violence, cozenage, flattery, lying or by putting on a guise of religion' that each of them could have kept school himself; and so, when they joined forces, they could make out an impregnable case for associating religion with profit. Did not Abraham and Solomon grow rich in religion? Did not Job say that a good man shall lay up gold as dust? Surely piety was justified by its material results; nor could anything be more reasonable than to be both virtuous and successful. With this proposition the attack on Christian was renewed, and old Mr. Hold-the-World (as the most moderate in demeanour) was put up to propound the question. The reply of Christian was devastating: 'Even a babe could answer ten thousand such questions.' The man who takes up religion for the world will throw it away for the world; the Scriptures ring with judgements meted out to the formalists and the hypocrites; the Pharisees, Judas Iscariot, and Simon the Sorcerer are the eternal prototypes of Mr. By Ends' principles and Mr. Gripe-Man's pedagogy. There could be no resisting the torrent which flowed from Christian's lips; for it caused Mr. By Ends and his company to stagger and fall behind.

Thus did Bunyan weave a halo round the uncompromising and the uncomfortable; and he raised a tribunal more solemn than any by which he was himself judged—that of human conscience. He set spiritual values against the petty objects for which humanity strives, and he practised as well as preached a doctrine in which these values had supreme and solitary force. That his book should still be read wherever the English language is used is a tribute not only to his supreme literary gift, but to the finer things in that rule of the Saints which was terminated by the coming of Charles Stuart.

Another great rebel was Thomas Hobbes of Malmesbury (1588–1679), who, after desultory study at Oxford, was for twenty years tutor and secretary to the Cavendish family. During the Commonwealth he spent some years in France, and gave mathematical lectures to Charles II, with whom he shared a lively intelligence and from whom he received a small pension. He knew most of the learned men of his day and had acute controversies with many of them, notably in matters mathematical. He preserved his faculties to a ripe old age, and was fortunate in that he was allowed to die a natural death; for on at least one occasion the Commons proposed to burn the *Leviathan* and the bishops proposed to burn its author. In appearance he was tall, erect, and bright-eyed; at times he dallied with hirsute adornments, but he deprecated a full beard, as implying philosophic professionalism.[1] The amateur status was thus preserved, and his life in the country afforded long periods of meditation without books; indeed he believed that if he had read as much as his contemporaries, he would have been as ignorant as they.

His books, notably the *Leviathan* (1651), puzzled and deceived some readers, who found in his readiness of scriptural quotation and apotheosis of absolute power what appeared to be no more than the divine right theory in another guise; on the other hand, most of those who fathomed his meaning regarded his books as works of darkness, and at least one sinner was obliged publicly to recant his blasphemy, debauchery, and Hobbism.[2] Clarendon wrote a book[3] specially intended to undeceive those who regarded the *Leviathan* as a legitimate defence of monarchy. Hobbes often wrote in a somewhat oblique way, partly because it was safer, and partly because his peculiar literary style was well adapted to the veiling of original and daring thought in words

[1] *Aubrey*, i. 339–40.
[2] *Recantation of Daniel Scargil in Great St. Mary's, Cambridge, 1669*, in *Bodley, Wood*, 608.
[3] *A brief view and survey of the dangerous and pernicious errors to church and state in Mr. Hobbes's Leviathan* (1676).

apparently innocuous. His 'starcht, mathematical method' does not always lend itself to easy interpretation; but his English is always terse and virile.

Hobbes did many things by contraries, and a clue to the meaning of his *Leviathan* may be obtained by starting at the end. His last chapter: 'Of the benefit proceeding from darkness and to whom it accrueth' is apparently an exposure of the practices of the Roman Catholic Church; but closer inspection reveals the fact that he is attacking the whole of religious professionalism, under whatever name it may be practised. His argument is that, on the basis of revelation, the clergy have established a cult, having its distinctive language, its supernatural invocations, its terrifying threats, its demonology, and 'frivolous distinctions, barbarous terms and obscure language' (these taught in the Universities)—in fine, a complete paraphernalia of weapons for cheating the laity and dividing their allegiance. The benefit accruing to the clergy from this darkness consists of money, power, and reputation. Almost the last sentence makes it clear that he was not thinking only of popery; 'for it is not the Roman clergy only that pretends the kingdom of God to be of this world'. Here is Hobbes's starting-point. It was not merely that he was agnostic or anti-clerical; for he himself had no grievance against any particular religion, and he frequently attended the services of the Anglican church, because he liked its order and ritual. His position was fundamental. He believed that, by means of clerical obscurantism, the whole of contemporary thought had been tinged with conceptions which destroyed the possibility of clear and exact analysis; nor, until the state assumed all the secular powers and privileges of the church, would such exact thought be possible of exercise.

His purpose was therefore primarily an intellectual one—to destroy not a doctrine but a whole attitude of mind. Reading backwards in his book, the implications of this are illustrated. In his forty-sixth chapter he treats of 'darkness from vain philosophy and fabulous tradition'. Prominent in these categories is the hoary doctrine of substantial forms; with these 'separated essences', argues Hobbes, the theologians have been able to play many tricks; for, as they juggle with the bread and wine, so they give out that 'faith, wisdom and other virtues are

sometimes poured into a man, sometimes blown into him'.
Some would think that no great harm results; but Hobbes
believed that thereby was set up a rival power to the state.
'Who will endeavour to obey the laws, if he expect obedience
to be poured or blown into him? Or who will not obey a priest
that can make God, rather than his sovereign, nay than God
himself? Or who that is in fear of ghosts will not bear great
respect to those that can make the holy water that drives them
from him?' Probably few of Hobbes's readers read so far as
this chapter. Some may have stopped at chapter xxxviii, where
Hell is stated to be determined not 'by any note of situation,
but only by the company'; those who persevered as far as
chapter xxvii would have read some disturbing things about
miracles, and this statement: 'a private man has always the
liberty, because thought is free, to believe or not believe in his
heart those acts that have been given out for miracles'; or this:
'the first rainbow that was seen in the world was a miracle,
because the first, and consequently strange'. These passages
might have been written by Voltaire; but Voltaire had an easier
and less dangerous task. There was a hint of his real meaning
in chapter xxxii, where he speaks of the 'captivity of our understanding'; by this, he understands not a submission of the intellectual faculty, but a submission of the will to a power which
has no right to demand such obedience. This obedience, he
thought, was stimulated by a whole host of accessories—by
an anthropomorphic conception of the deity, by revelations in
dreams, and by prophets. He would accept a prophet only if he
preached the established religion and performed a real miracle.

These daring heresies were skilfully concealed in a heavy
undergrowth of scriptural quotation, and the wolf which entered
among the lambs was thickly covered with wool. He devoured
many of the choicest specimens in the flock. Man in the state
of nature had already been badly mauled by the Jesuits; but by
the time Hobbes had finished with him his bones seemed those
of a non-gregarious animal. The social contract had been
fattened up by the Huguenots, and was regarded as an exhibition specimen, having a record of awards and prizes which
completely discredited his one-time rival of the absolutist breed;
there remained only an empty fleece when the wolf had finished;

for the contract was shown to bind only the subject, not the sovereign. There was the celebrated *Jus Naturale*, or natural inborn right, a pedigree creature, for which international triumphs were prophesied, though some thought it too good for this world; but after a little skirmishing (with words) this also was dispatched; for the *Jus Naturale* was proved to be Natural Right, that is Natural Liberty, that is Natural Licence, that is Anarchy, and so fit only for the state of savagery. Then followed a whole batch of *Leges Naturales*, each the embodiment of some virtue, such as justice, complaisance, and pardon; these were destroyed one after another; for it was demonstrated that they had their force not from any innate or supernatural power, but simply from the fact that they had the backing of the state. There remained only Liberty and Law. But even they succumbed. For Liberty had no separate existence, being merely what was left over after the decrees of the sovereign had been subtracted from the total of human activity; while Law, so far from being the emanation of reason, or discussion, or morality, was merely what the sovereign commanded. Not a single ideal was left.

Probably few who read those chapters of the *Leviathan* realized what a holocaust was taking place. If there was a cherished social or political aspiration, that was enough to invite attention from Hobbes; his aim was to undermine a whole fabric of thought, but he burrowed so deeply that few realized what he was doing. In place of the old structure torn by rival allegiances he substituted one which was completely enveloped by the secular power. The sovereign had taken upon himself the person of the state; all acts and opinions had their sanction in him; he was the incarnation of the secular spirit, enforcing opinions deemed necessary not for the salvation of the soul but for the safety of the state; himself the clearly defined source of authority, and the unlimited extent of his power the guarantee of peace. So expressed, Hobbes's opinions might seem to have merely academic import; but the date (1651) of his book should be recalled. It was a time when it might well have seemed that the whole principle of secular government was at stake. The king of England had recently been executed, and a 'purged' House of Commons was assuming executive functions; France was plunged in the wars of the Fronde; elsewhere there was revolt and disaffection; and in the background was the Roman Catholic Church, the one united political force, towering above innumerable and quarrelling Protestant sects. An acute observer might well have quailed at the prospect; and at least the remedies of Hobbes were not half-measures.

These remedies appeared to surrender every human sentiment in politics, to disparage everything hitherto accepted as good, and to exclude the possibility of progress. In place of the natural instincts which make men social and therefore political, Hobbes appeared to erect a mechanical and crushing despotism, a Moloch on whose altars were sacrificed all that men had hitherto held true or sacred. In this work of destruction Hobbes was doing in the seventeenth century what Calvin had done in the sixteenth century, and what Lenin was to do in the twentieth; the work of all three was primarily intellectual, and had the limitations inherent in all systems which ignore human nature. It is therefore not surprising that English political theory has derived more from Locke than from Hobbes; more from the traditionalism of Burke and the optimism of Bentham than from the cast-iron theorems of those who reduce politics to an exact science; for representative English thinkers have started from Aristotle's assumption that man is a social and political animal, and have rejected theories which force men into some preconceived conception of the state.

In mentality therefore the philosopher of Malmesbury was un-English; but his theories were to find their most complete vindication in Restoration England; and if he was not the inspiration of later Stuart absolutism, he was its prophet. Charles was restored without conditions; he was protected against seditious talk by a special treason act; he was given absolute control over all the armed forces; his judges often considered themselves merely the mouthpieces of the royal will; he was empowered by statute to remodel corporations, and so was enabled to destroy those 'worms' which, according to Hobbes, consumed the entrails of the body politic. Each of these things had been advocated as a principle in the *Leviathan*. Still more, the Test Act of 1673 and the Act of 1678 imposed a state religion, for a political purpose and by secular penalties; with this cement

Charles established an impregnable power, whereas James transferred his foundations to the shifting sands of compromise and toleration. Hobbes's ideal was peace for the subject and liberty of thought for the philosopher; these things have been secured not by weak but by strong government; not by a division of power but by its concentration and monopoly in one clearly defined source. In this respect later political philosophy on the Continent has endorsed some of Hobbes's fundamentals, and the progress of intellectual freedom has often coincided with an approximation to the conception of the strong secular state dominating the erastian church. But the anti-idealist elements in his thought have been intensified by the epigrammatic cynicism of Treitschke, as they have recently been developed by some of the exponents of Bolshevism; in the latter case the seventeenth-century doctrines have been wrenched out of their setting, and what was only implicit in Hobbes has been preached as dogmatic principle. It is a curious irony that the philosopher who prided himself most of all on the security and rigidity of his ideal state should be hailed as an apostle by exponents of subversion and experiment.

In contrast with these two extremists, Bunyan and Hobbes, were those who, like Locke and Halifax, vindicated the characteristic English quality of good sense. As a thinker, John Locke (1632–1704) is almost the complete counterpart of Hobbes; for he did not specially pride himself on freedom from inconsistency; he did not try to reduce his doctrines to the inevitability of a Euclidean proposition; and, above all, he wrote plain English, seldom disguising his meaning in metaphor, sarcasm, or innuendo. He therefore had none of that recondite charm which makes Hobbes beloved of connoisseurs; in its place he had that clarity and high seriousness which seldom fail to carry conviction. It is true that his published works belong to a period after Charles's reign, as Hobbes's *Leviathan* to a period before it; but both philosophers have this interesting link with the reign, that, while the Restoration period witnessed the application of some of Hobbes's most characteristic doctrines, the same period created that public opinion which made possible of realization many of the ideals professed by Locke. The one pushed to extremes the results obtainable from the older mechanical method of reasoning; the other restored human nature to its place in the state, and propounded a system which, though liable to logical objection, was nevertheless eminently practicable and reasonable.

The events of his earlier years helped to accentuate the balance which was so distinctive of Locke's maturity. His schooling at Westminster was under strict Puritan auspices; but later he made friends among the Royalists, and became one of the Oxford pioneers who afterwards formed the Royal Society; so too, though he welcomed the Restoration for its return to political normality, he deplored the religious and political excesses by which it was followed; and, as early as 1667, in a manuscript essay on toleration, he expounded his view that while there should be an established church, outside its frontiers there should be a toleration of independent opinion, with the exception of Catholicism and Atheism, which he thought dangerous to the state. At Oxford he had obtained an introduction to mathematical and oriental studies; but his mind was bent on less academical pursuits, and this may account for his choice of medicine as a career. His medical services brought him into contact with Shaftesbury in 1668, and the two were closely associated, first in the constitution-making for Carolina (the first draft, dated June 1669, is in Locke's handwriting), and, later, in the administration of the reconstructed council of trade, of which Shaftesbury was president, and Locke secretary (1673). To the end Locke remained faithful to his patron; but he was the friend of Shaftesbury the idealist, not Shaftesbury the plotter, a fact which did not prevent his expulsion from Christ Church in 1684, in consequence of an order from Sunderland. Meanwhile he had completed his education by travel in France and Holland, and the fruits of his meditation were to be reaped after the Revolution, notably in his *Essay on Toleration* (1689), the *Two Treatises of Government* (1690), and his *Essay concerning humane understanding* (1690).

The *Essay on Toleration* raised the subject from the level of theological polemic, and placed it on almost universal grounds. In general, he contended that toleration was due to all who are themselves tolerant; conversely, the state should expel only those whose principles incite either to persecution or to subversion.

In this way he gave an abstract setting to the latitudinarian doctrines of the whigs. To the same party he did a signal service by his *Treatises of Government*. Primarily written as a confutation of Filmer, the *Treatises* disposed of two things: first, the sovereignty which divine right genealogists traced back to Adam; and, secondly, the social contract as distorted by Hobbes, whereby men were supposed to have surrendered their powers to an irresponsible abstraction. He started from the assumption that man had once been in a state of nature, but he wisely avoided any attempt to describe that state; for he claimed that it was merely a non-politic condition, similar to that which prevails between two independent states not bound by treaties or agreements. The beginnings of the body politic were, he held, to be found in common consent, every one putting himself under an obligation to submit to the determination of the majority; and, in order to promote that preservation of property, which he claimed to be the main object of the state, there were required an established and known law, an impartial judge, and a power to give execution to the sentences of the judge.

On this stock Locke grafted those tender scions of whig doctrine which even in Charles's reign had given promise of a rich maturity. Still using the old categories, he declared that, once men have established themselves in a body politic, the first and fundamental natural law impels them to establish a legislative power. This is not only the supreme power, but 'sacred and unalterable in the hands where the community have once placed it'; nor does it rule by extemporary decrees, but by 'promulgated standing laws, and known, authorised judges'. Hence a clear distinction between the legislative and the executive; the latter responsible to the former, and the former responsible to the people. But as the world is in a constant state of flux, that part of the legislative which consists of elected representatives must, in course of time, be reformed or altered so as to correspond with changes in the distribution of population. Prerogative he defined not as something outside or above the laws, but as a power in the hands of the Prince to provide for those exceptional cases which cannot be left to the determination of the laws.

Other writers have constructed the ideal state and fitted man into it; Locke, on the other hand, built his edifice on the foundation of experience, and adjusted the categories and preconceptions of an earlier philosophy to accord with the results of that experience. Metaphysically his conclusions may have been untenable; but humanly and historically they were sound. Another factor may have helped to give his views wider currency, namely that he was neither a lawyer nor a stylist. Earlier in the century the cause of constitutionalism had been fought by men such as Coke, Selden, and Spelman, all of them learned or erudite rather than intellectual; but Locke expounded the same cause not from statutes or law books, but from general considerations of expediency and reasonableness. Moreover, his exposition gained wide acceptance not by brilliant but by moderate expression; not once is the reader perturbed by a deviation from the course of lucid and consecutive reasoning; there are neither lapses nor epigrams in the writings of Locke. He could therefore be understood by a very wide class of reader; and it was characteristic that, after their visits to England, both Montesquieu and Voltaire returned to France enthusiastic disciples of that cause for which Shaftesbury fought and his secretary wrote.

Another empirical thinker was George Savile, marquess of Halifax (1633–95), whose counsels are filled with a mellow wisdom and personal detachment reminiscent more of the repose of eighteenth-century classicism than of the acerbities and strivings of his age. At times his statesmanship was somewhat ineffective; for generally he preferred retreat to failure, nor would he have died for a lost cause. His natural gifts, his wealth, and his social status all help to account for his pre-eminence; but he had none of the austere consistency of Clarendon, nor the creative force of Shaftesbury. Yet in his career and writings will be found a measure and balance by which the excesses of his contemporaries may be revealed as excesses. To Clarendon he might have applied these words: 'to know when to leave things alone is a high pitch of good sense'; to Shaftesbury and the political idealists: 'the best definition of the best government is that it hath no inconveniencies but such as are supportable; but inconveniencies there must be'; to the religious zealots: 'singularity may be good sense at home, but it must not go much abroad'; to the divine-right clergy: 'experience maketh more prophets than revelation'; to the learned professions: 'the clergy and the lawyers, like the free-masons, may be supposed to take an oath not to tell the secret'.[1] Halifax sounded no clarion-call to action, but his tuning-fork served to discredit the slightest violation of harmony.

This quality pervades his writings, and gives them a unity of spirit and direction. It can be seen in his *Character of a Trimmer*, where he showed that mistakes, like everything else, have their periods, 'and many times the nearest way to cure is not to oppose them, but stay till they are trussed with their own weight';[2] in his *Letter to a Dissenter*, where he counselled patience until 'the next probable revolution';[3] in his *Advice to a Daughter*, where, after hinting tactfully at the inequality of the sexes, he gave this counsel: 'let your method be a steady course of good life that may run like a smooth stream'.[4] It was a simile which had already been used by Denham:

> O could I flow like thee, and make thy stream
> My great example as it is my theme,
> Though deep yet clear, though gentle yet not dull,
> Strong without rage, without o'erflowing full.[5]

There was the same shrewd discrimination in his character-sketches; his picture of Charles II is by far the most faithful of contemporary portraits. 'His wit was better suited to his condition before he was restored than afterwards. The wit of a gentleman and that of a crowned head ought to be two different things'.[6] 'That some of his ministers seemed to have a superiority did not spring from his resignation to them, but to his ease. He chose rather to be eclipsed than to be troubled.'[7] There was the same discernment in his appreciation of a very different character—that of Gilbert Burnet. He saw that Burnet's faults as a historian rose mainly from the warmth of his heart and the

---

[1] These are taken from the miscellaneous thoughts and reflections of Halifax in *Halifax*, ii. 505–27. [2] Ibid. ii. 337.

[3] Ibid. ii. 377. This should not be taken as a prophecy of the Revolution of 1688.

[4] Ibid. ii. 392. [5] Denham, *Cooper's Hill*.

[6] *Halifax*, ii. 355. [7] Ibid. ii. 351.

depth of his humanity. 'Dull men do not miss one blot he makes; and being beholden to their barrenness for their discretion, they fall on the errors which arise out of his abundance.'[1] What Halifax said of the critics of Burnet may be applied to many of the critics of Macaulay.

By rights Halifax ought to have been a cynic. 'God hath made mankind so weak that it must be deceived. The several sorts of religion in the world are so many spiritual monopolies';[2] 'Anybody that is fool enough will be safe in the world, and anybody that can be knave enough will be rich in it.'[3] These remarks might have been made by Hobbes or La Rochefoucauld. But it was seldom that he indulged this humour. He had a strong sense of patriotism. For him good sense meant a penetrative quality, a power to see ourselves and others in perspective, an instinct for perceiving the sham and the false, where others find truth and virtue. But in a world where there are as many opinions as human beings, he thought that private conviction might often have to yield to peace and decorum; that good sense should give way to common sense. He expounded this ideal in these words:

Little words and motions of respect and civility do often recommend men more to the company than the knowledge of all the liberal sciences; but the truth is, all good sense hath something of the clown in it, and therefore though it is not to be suppressed, it must be softened so as to comply with that great beast the world, which is too strong for any man, though never so much in the right, to go to cuffs with.[4]

Here was defined that high social accomplishment whereby a man can so express his personal opinions that he retains both his individuality and his friends. It is an ideal not easy of achievement, but it was at least made possible by that good nature which Clarendon had already noted as a national characteristic, a virtue which, surviving Plague, Fire, and Plot, provided a basis for the training of those qualities which enable

[1] Ibid. ii. 531. Here Halifax was thinking mainly of Burnet's *History of the Reformation.*

[2] Ibid. ii. 502.   [3] Ibid. ii. 523.

[4] Halifax to Henry Savile, March 29, 1680, in *Savile Correspondence* (Camd. Soc.), 150.

men to co-operate harmoniously in the life of the well-ordered state.

Thus the reign of Charles II, which ended the experiments of Puritan idealists and led insensibly to the rule of expediency and practical politics, was a period of discovery and achievement, neither so spectacular as the Elizabethan age nor so incontestably pre-eminent as the era of Chatham and Pitt, but a period nevertheless wherein were tested and brought to maturity many of the greatest qualities of the English race.

BIBLIOGRAPHICAL NOTE

The contractions here used are those set forth at the beginning of Vol. I of this book with these additions:

Bulletin of the Institute of Historical Research.   *Bull. Inst. H. R.*
Cambridge Historical Journal.   *Camb. Hist. J.*
Economic History Review.   *Econ. Hist. Rev.*

THE standard bibliography is Professor G. Davies's *Bibliography of British History 1603–1714* (1928), which must now be supplemented by the bibliographies in *English Historical Documents*, viii, 1660–1714, edited by Professor A. Browning. For Scottish history, H. M. Paton's *The Scottish Records* (1933) should be used, and reference may be made to a select bibliography in *Econ. Hist. Rev.* iii (1931). For Ireland, there are lists in *Irish Historical Studies*, a journal which began to appear in 1938, and includes both Eire and Ulster within its scope; for Wales, there is the *Bibliography* by R. T. Jenkins and W. Rees (1931). The annual *Writings on American History* began to be published in 1906; and the *Writings on British History*, which A. T. Milne has been editing for the Royal Historical Society, begins at 1934.

In practice, every researcher has to build up his own bibliography. He will be greatly helped by the monumental *Catalogue of Printed Books* in the British Museum, of which the first volume appeared in 1931, and the fiftieth (to *Denz*) in 1954. For miscellaneous and manuscript sources he should consult, as a general guide, the *Bulletin of the Institute of Historical Research*, with its supplements, because these contain not only important articles by scholars, but summaries of theses, *corrigenda* to the *D.N.B.*, and notes regarding the migration of manuscripts, a topic which is also dealt with in *Archives*, the journal published twice yearly since 1949 by the British Records Association. This journal also gives information about facilities for access to manuscripts and guidance for the preservation of documents. In this connexion it may be noted that, in the last generation, there has been great development in the organization and efficiency of county archives, so that today there can be few counties in England where provision has not been made for the custody and classification of muniments, as well as arrangements for accessibility thereto by students. This development may well have great influence on the direction of historical studies in the near future, since the amount of local material easily available is so vast. As well as this, there are now more journals devoted in whole or in part to historical studies. The *Huntington Library Bulletin* has been issued since 1938 as a *Quarterly;* the *Journal of the National Library of Wales* first appeared in 1939; the *Historical Journal of the University of Birmingham* dates from 1947–8. A welcome revival is that of the *Scottish Historical Review*, which made its reappearance in 1947.

Of the sources which have been made available in print since 1933 the most important are the *Calendars of Domestic State Papers* from 1 July 1683 to 5 February 1685 (3 vols., 1934, 1938, and 1938 respectively: Her Majesty's Stationery Office); the third volume has an introduction by F. Bickley. These documents have special interest as authentic evidence of the characteristics of non-parliamentary Stuart rule, and help to prepare the way for the sequel in James's reign. Generally, their contents convey the impression that the ruthless suppression of the Rye House Plot and the relentless search for more victims created an atmosphere of tension not unlike that which has been experienced by some continental countries in this century. The prisons were filled with Dissenters and Quakers; many conspirators were in hiding, or had fled abroad, hoping to make plans for their return; innumerable informers, some for money, some as the price of their lives, were retailing stories in which it is almost impossible to disentangle the true from the false; and the reappearance of old Oliverians gave some point to talk of revolution. The loud hysteria of the Popish Plot was followed by the silence and furtive whispering which greeted the Stuart revenge. Most significant of all was the concerted and wholesale attack on the corporations, which was intended not only to give the crown complete control over the local administration but to ensure the return to parliament of burgesses who would be completely subservient, whenever it was deemed necessary to summon parliament. It was natural that the full implications of all this should be revealed in Scotland, where, because of the comparative backwardness of political institutions, a totalitarian régime could more easily be established. On 14 June 1684 the Secret Committee of the Scottish Privy Council was ordered to raise the Highland clans 'for preventing and suppressing commotions' in Fife and in the south-west; those suspected of complicity in the late 'commotions' were to be examined 'by torture and other effectual means' (*Calendar*, May 1684–Feb. 1685, p. 55).

Of the volumes more recently published by the Historical Manuscripts Commission, two are of special interest for this period: the supplementary *Report of MSS. of Montagu Bertie, twelfth earl of Lindsey,* at Uffington House, Stamford, 1660–1702, edited by C. G. O. Bridgeman and J. C. Walker, 1942; and *MSS. of R. R. Hastings* at Ashby de la Zouch, 1947. Of these the first is miscellaneous, including private, semi-official, and official documents. Some relate to Treasury business; some to the contracts of the Navy Board; some to Danby's imprisonment in the Tower and the efforts to obtain his release. There is an account of Charles Bertie's mission to Denmark in 1671, when he was instructed to adjust differences about saluting the flag. On p. 155 there is a memorandum on the coal trade; on p. 162 an account of the operations in the Mint. The second of the above sources is of some interest for its notes on speeches and proceedings in the House of Lords, 1670–95, some in the handwriting of the seventh earl of Huntingdon. These new publications add to the great mass of original material already available for this period. A selection from original material will be found, in convenient form, in Professor Browning's *English Historical Documents*, viii, 1660–1714 (1953), with valuable introductions, bibliographies, and appendixes. This book is of great service for the study and teaching of the period.

Of general books covering the reign of Charles the most comprehensive is *The Later Stuarts*, by Sir George Clark, which first appeared in 1934, in the Oxford History of England. This may be supplemented by books dealing generally with certain aspects of the subject, such as Professor Mark Thomson's *A Constitutional History of England 1642–1801* (1938) and Sir D. L. Keir's *The Constitutional History of Modern Britain 1485–1937* (4th ed. 1950). Among the more specialized books and contributions to learned journals the following may be enumerated:

(*a*) Crown and Parliament. Two important diaries of members of the Commons are now available in good editions, namely, that of John Milward, 1666–8, edited by Caroline Robbins (1938), and that of Sir Edward Dering, 1670–3, edited by B. D. Henning (New Haven, 1940). Miss Robbins has contributed an account of the Oxford session of the Long Parliament in October 1665 to *Bull. Inst. H. R.* xxi (1948). Mr. E. S. de Beer has analysed the membership of the Court party in the Commons 1670–8 in *Bull. Inst. H. R.* xi (1934); and a general account of parties and party organization in Charles's reign is that by A. Browning, in *Trans. R. H. Soc.*, 4th series, xxx (1948). Division lists are rarely come by for this period, but one for the Exclusion Bill has been communicated to *Bull. Inst. H. R.* xxiii (1950) by Professor Browning and Miss Doreen Milne. All these contributions have done much to elucidate the complicated history of Charles's Long Parliament. Reference should also be made to G. Davies, *The Elections of Richard Cromwell's Parliament, 1658–9*, in *E.H.R.* lxiii (1948), as evidence of the strength of Royalists and Presbyterians on the eve of the Restoration. In *Camb. Hist. J.*, vii (1941), will be found a general account of the Whig theory of the constitution by Mr. B. Behrens.

Of books relating to the crown there are few serious studies. In the *Huntington Library Bulletin*, x (1946–7), Professor Davies has subjected the concluding lines of Dryden's *Absalom and Achitophel* to careful examination in order to link the poem with the king. An episode in Charles's diplomacy is handled by Mr. K. H. D. Haley in his *William of Orange and the English Opposition 1672–4*, a study based mainly on the Dutch archives. Less directly, the king has come into his own again in Mr. Peter Laslett's scholarly and sympathetic edition of the *Patriarcha* and other works of sir Robert Filmer (1949). M. A. Thomson's *The Secretaries of State 1681–1782* (1932) is a worthy successor to the brilliant study by Miss F. M. G. Evans (Mrs. Higham) on the same subject for the period 1558 to 1680 (1923). Miss Doris M. Gill has contributed an informative account of the Treasury in the years 1660 to 1714 to *E.H.R.* xlvi (1931); and in her study of the relations of the Treasury with the Excise and Customs commissioners in *Camb. Hist. J.* iv (1932) she shows the increased control exercised by this body over subordinates.

(*b*) Finance, Commerce, and Trade. Although Professor E. Hughes's *Studies in Administration and Finance 1558–1825* (1934) is concerned mainly with the Salt Tax, it may be regarded as possibly the first serious attempt to study the Stuart fiscal system. It may be supplemented by the same writer's *The English Stamp Duties 1664–1764*, in *E.H.R.* lvi (1941). In vol. li (1936) of the same journal there is an analysis of the Hearth Tax by Miss L. M. Marshall which shows how this levy combined most of the evils of the Stuart system. The banker-goldsmith Edward Backwell is studied by Miss D. K. Clark in *Econ. Hist. Rev.* ix (1938); and the same writer has contributed 'A Restoration Banking House' to *Essays . . . in honour of Wilbur Cortez Abbott* (Cambridge, Mass., 1941). Although concerned mainly with a later century, W. R. Ward's *English Land Tax in the Eighteenth Century* (1953) contains much of interest for the earlier period. For commerce and shipping generally reference should be made to L. A. Harper, *The English Navigation Laws* (New York, 1939); and to Miss V. Barbour's *Capitalism in Amsterdam in the Seventeenth Century* (Johns Hopkins Press, 1950). Trading relations with Spain are the subject of Miss J. O. MacLachlan's *Trade and Peace with Old Spain 1667–1750* (1940); those with France are examined by Miss M. Priestley in her *Anglo-French Trade and the Unfavourable Balance Controversy*, in *Econ. Hist. Rev.*, 2nd series, iv, no. 1 (1952), where she shows that the unfavourable balance was much less than was commonly supposed. The part played by merchants in Mediterranean ports is illustrated by H. Koenigsberger (for Naples and Sicily) in *E.H.R.* lxii (1947) and A. G. Ambrose (for Aleppo) in *Econ. Hist. Rev.* iii (1931–2). Of general importance for our overseas trade are Miss L. S. Sutherland's *The Law Merchant in England in the XVIIth and XVIIIth Centuries*, in *Trans. R. H. Soc.*, 4th series, xvii (1934), and Sir George Clark's *The Barbary Corsairs in the Seventeenth Century*, in *Camb. Hist. J.* viii (1944).

For English industry in this period reference should be made to the very full and informative *The Rise of the British Coal Industry 1550–1700* (2 vols. 1932), by Professor J. U. Nef. But objection may be taken by some readers to the phrase 'Industrial Revolution', when applied to this period; moreover, it is by no means certain that increasing resort to coal implied increasing industrialization, because much of the coal was used for domestic purposes; while, in the metal industries, coal had by no means displaced wood.

(c) Local Government and Social Life. Two valuable bibliographies for this subject are *Local History Handlist . . . ,* published in 1947 by the Historical Association; and F. G. Emmison and Irvine Gray, *County Records* (1948). Studies of borough corporations are well represented by Philip Styles, *The Corporation of Bewdley under the later Stuarts*, in *University of Birmingham Historical Journal*, i, 1947–8. In vol. iii of the same journal Mr. Styles, in his *Census of a Warwickshire Village* (Fenny Compton), has made an interesting contribution to the subject of rural population. Newark in the period 1549–1688 is the subject treated by Mr. C. G. Parsloe in *Trans. R. H. Soc.*, 4th series, xxii (1940); a county, *Dorset* (1952), is the subject of Mr. R. Douch, a book which contains much guidance for the local historian. Wage assessments in Herefordshire after 1666 provide the subject of Mr. R. K. Kelsall in *E.H.R.* lvii (1942). Some important work has been done on the history of London. Its population in the later seventeenth century is studied by P. E. Jones and A. V. Judges in *Econ. Hist. Rev.* vi (1935–6); and two pieces of research are of great interest for this period: T. F. Reddaway, *The Rebuilding of London after the Great Fire* (1940), and N. G. Brett James, *The Growth of Stuart London* (1935). In his *Studies in Stuart Wales* (1952) Mr. A. H. Dodd has described the revival of the Welsh gentry after 1660.

Much information about local turbulence and the means for its suppression will be found in Max Beloff's *Public Order and Popular Disturbances 1660–1714* (1938); R. B. Schlatter's *The Social Ideas of Religious Leaders 1660–1688* (1940) connects social conditions with contemporary religious opinion. Additional evidence about social and economic conditions will be found in *The Journeys of Celia Fiennes*, ed. C. Morris (1947). *Life in a Noble Household 1641–1700* (1937) by Miss Gladys Scott Thomson is based on the papers of the duke of Bedford. Miss Joan Parkes's *Travel in England in the Seventeenth Century* (1925) may now be supplemented by the volumes of T. S. Willan, *River Navigation* (1936) and *The Coasting Trade* (1938), which both cover the period 1600–1750. H. C. Darby, *The Draining of the Fens* (1940), is of capital importance for the study of land and agriculture in the period.

(*d*) Scotland, Ireland, and the Plantations. In his *Religious Life in Seventeenth-century Scotland* (1937) Professor G. D. Henderson has greatly added to our knowledge of social and intellectual conditions in Scotland. *Scottish Population Statistics*, edited by J. G. Kyd for the Scottish History Society (3rd series, xliv, 1952), relates mainly to the eighteenth century, but contains some information about the later seventeenth; the same is true of K. H. Connell, *Population in Ireland 1750–1845*, and J. C. Beckett's *Protestant Dissent in Ireland 1687–1780*. More directly concerned with our period is E. Maclysaght's *Irish Life in the Seventeenth Century* (1950). The older books by W. E. H. Lecky and J. A. Froude are by no means so obsolete as is commonly supposed.

For the Plantations generally, two of the most important sources are *Proceedings and Debates of the British Parliaments respecting North America*, ed. L. F. Stock, 3 vols. (Washington, 1924–30), which incidentally serves as a partial index to the voluminous *Journals* of the Lords and Commons; and E. Donnan, *Documents illustrative of the History of the Slave Trade to America* (3 vols., Washington, 1930–2). For the slave trade, A. B. Keith's *West Africa* (1933) should also be used. For Newfoundland, there is R. G. Lounsbury, *The British Fishery at Newfoundland 1634–1763* (New Haven, 1934); for the Hudson's Bay Company, the *Minutes* for 1679–1684, edited by E. E. Rich, appeared in 1946. A selection from a wide range of sources will be found in K. E. Knorr, *British Colonial Theories 1570–1850* (1944). In 1933 appeared A. P. Newton's *The European Nations in the West Indies, 1493–1688*.

(*e*) Biographies and Miscellaneous. For biographies, the *D.N.B.* should be consulted, supplemented by the *corrigenda* in the *Bull. Inst.*

H.R.; also *The Complete Peerage*, edited by G. E. Cokayne, an invaluable source, now in process of completion. The standard life of Shaftesbury is that by Miss L. F. Brown (New York, 1933); of Pepys, that of Sir Arthur Bryant, 3 vols. (1947–9). Mr. C. H. Hartmann has contributed two biographies: *Charles II and Madame* (1934) and *Clifford of the Cabal 1630–73* (1937). A scholarly account of a great ecclesiastic is C. E. Whiting's *Nathaniel Lord Crewe, Bishop of Durham 1674–1721* (1940). M. Ashley's *John Wildman, Plotter and Postmaster* (1947), is of value for its account of early republicanism in England. Colonel B. Fergusson's *Rupert of the Rhine* (1952) provides a short, well-balanced biography. Although concerned mainly with events before 1660, Mr. B. H. G. Wormald's *Clarendon: Politics, History and Religion, 1640–1660* is of interest for the understanding of Clarendon.

Of miscellaneous sources, there may be cited J. Walker, *Censorship of the Press during the Reign of Charles II*, in *History*, xxxv (1950); and in the same journal Miss D. Ross, *Class Privilege in XVIIth-century England* (xxviii, 1943). D. C. Coleman's *Naval Dockyards under the later Stuarts*, in *Econ. Hist. Rev.*, 2nd series, no. 2 (1953), is a good account of a neglected subject, and provides a useful list of the tonnage of H.M. ships completed each year 1660–88. Another important contribution to this subject is *The Tangier Papers of Samuel Pepys*, edited by E. Chappell for the Navy Records Society (1935). *The Diary of Robert Hooke 1672–80* has been edited by H. W. Robinson and W. Adams (1935); another, more extensive Diary, that of John Evelyn, was edited in six volumes by E. S. de Beer (1955).

Among the more important contributions to this subject within the last few years may be mentioned: G. Davies, *The Restoration of Charles II 1658–1660* (1955), a faithful record of events from the death of Cromwell to the accession of Charles; J. L. Cope, *Joseph Glanvill, Anglican Apologist* (Washington University Studies, St. Louis, U.S.A. 1956), of great interest for the conflict of religious and scientific thought; Miss Jane Lang, *Rebuilding of St. Paul's after the Great Fire of London* (1956), shows the part played by Wren and his associates. K. G. Davies, *The Royal African Company* (1957) is an important contribution to the study of company organization and of the slave trade; Sir Godfrey Fisher's *Barbary Legend: War, Trade and Piracy in North Africa, 1415–1830* (1957) dispels many misconceptions on the subject; S. B. Baxter's *The Development of the Treasury 1660–1702* (1957) explains how the Treasury attained 'maturity' in this period; G. R. Cragg, *Puritanism in the Period of the Great Persecution 1660–1688* (1957) shows the increasing severity with which the Puritans were treated after 1681; R. Schlatter (ed.), *Richard Baxter and Puritan*

Politics (1957) illustrates the political opinions of Baxter by extracts from his writings.

Notable biographies for this period include: J. Summerson, *Sir Christopher Wren* (1954), a well-balanced study; M. Cranston, *John Locke* (1957), the standard biography; and J. P. Kenyon, *Robert Spencer, Earl of Sunderland, 1641–1701* (1958), an important study of an enigmatic statesman who influenced the policy of three reigns.

INDEX

Denmark, relations of England with, i. 183, 289–90, 350. See also *Bergen*.
Deportment, i. 117.
Derby, ii. 634.
Derbyshire, i. 39, 79–80.
Derwentdale Plot (1663), i. 209.
Desborough, John, major-general, i. 2, 5.
D'Estrées, vice-admiral, i. 357, 349–60, 372, 374–6.
Devon, i. 37, 46, 61.
Digby, George, second earl of Bristol, i. 205–6, 382.
Dispensing Power, see *Suspending and Dispensing Power* and *Indulgence, Declaration of*.
Dissenters, in the towns, i. 207; the main sects, 214–18; Danby and, ii. 529–60; parliamentary resolution regarding, 606; increased severity against, after 1681, 624, 639, 641, 653. See also *Breda, Declaration of, Church of England, Clarendon Code, Indulgence, Declaration of, Savoy Conference, Test Act, Uniformity, Act of*.
Don, river, i. 40.
Dongan, Thomas, governor of New York, ii. 677.
Dorset, i. 61.
Douglas, William, third duke of Hamilton, ii. 414–15, 418.
Dover, i. 51, 234–5, ii. 426.
Dover, secret treaty of (1670), i. 342–6.
Dover, bogus treaty of (1670), i. 346–8.
Downing, sir George, i. 246, 247, 249, 283, 355, ii. 443–4.
Drama, Restoration, ii. 706–7.
Draperies, New, i. 45, 81.
Droitwich, ii. 474.
Drumclog, skirmish of (1679), ii. 417.
Dryden, John, i. 372, ii. 630–1, 703, 708.
Dugdale, Stephen, informer, ii. 604, 627.
Dunkirk, sale of, i. 204–5.
Duquesne, Abraham, French admiral, i. 357.
Durham, i. 46–7, 78.
Dutch, the, their mercantile advantages, i. 222; their ships, 233; their determination to retain North Sea fisheries, 246; their mercantile marine, 265; their use of 'stink pots', 267; their diplomatic isolation in 1672, 371–2; their allies in 1673, 377; their rivalry with England not determined by war, 387–8; their sympathizers in England, ii. 526; proposed alliance with (1675), 536; treaties with Eng-

land (1677–8), 548–9. See also *Commerce, Charles II, Louis XIV, Navigation Acts, Navy, War*.

East India Company, see *India*.
Écu, the French, value of, i. 186, n. 3.
Education in England, ii. 692–9, 703–5.
Edward the Confessor, cult of, i. 9.
Elections, disputed, ii. 462.
Elections, general, i. 30, ii. 585–6. See also *Bribery* and *Reform, parliamentary*.
Elections, Abingdon (1679), ii. 476–7; Aldborough (1673), ii. 477–8; Bedfordshire (1679), ii. 479; Buckingham (1679), ii. 479; Norfolk (1675), ii. 474–6.
Eliot, sir John, i. 353.
Elizabeth, queen, cult of, i. 145, 146, ii. 595, 598, 609.
Ellis, sir William, ii. 432.
Enclosures, and open fields, i. 57–9, 86–7, 90.
Engagers, the Scottish, i. 175.
England, agriculture, see under separate heading; cloth-making, i. 81–2; coffee-houses, i. 100–2; commerce, see under separate heading; cotton industry, i. 82–3; counties, i. 41–7; culture, development of, ii. 707–9; drama, ii. 706–7; deportment, literature of, i. 115–17; economic products, i. 65–77; education, ii. 692–703; estate management, i. 63–4; games, i. 104–7; gardens, i. 62–3; geological structure, i. 35–6; health, public, see under separate heading; health-resorts, i. 107–8; kingship, i. 139–41; labour, conditions of, i. 83–5; land, development of, i. 55–65; lawyers, i. 130–3; literature, popular, ii. 710–15; merchants and tradesmen, i. 126–30, ii. 426; mining and metal-working, i. 77–81; music, ii. 705–6; neutrality, advantages from, i. 387–8, ii. 538–9; newspapers, ii. 709; office holding, i. 113–15; orchards, i. 62; parishes, ii. 490–4; parsons, i. 133–6; paupers, i. 120–4; peers, i. 136–9; ports, i. 50–1; prisoners and prisons, i. 118–20; provinces, life in, i. 48; rainfall, i. 35; rivers, i. 39–41; roads, i. 103–4; schools, ii. 692–6; science, ii. 715–33; sermons, i. 98–100; society, classes of, i. 118–41; speculation, i. 110–13; stage-coaches, i. 102–3; town and country, contrast of, i. 52–5; towns, provincial, i. 48–51; universities, ii. 697–703; vagabonds, i. 124–6; wealth,